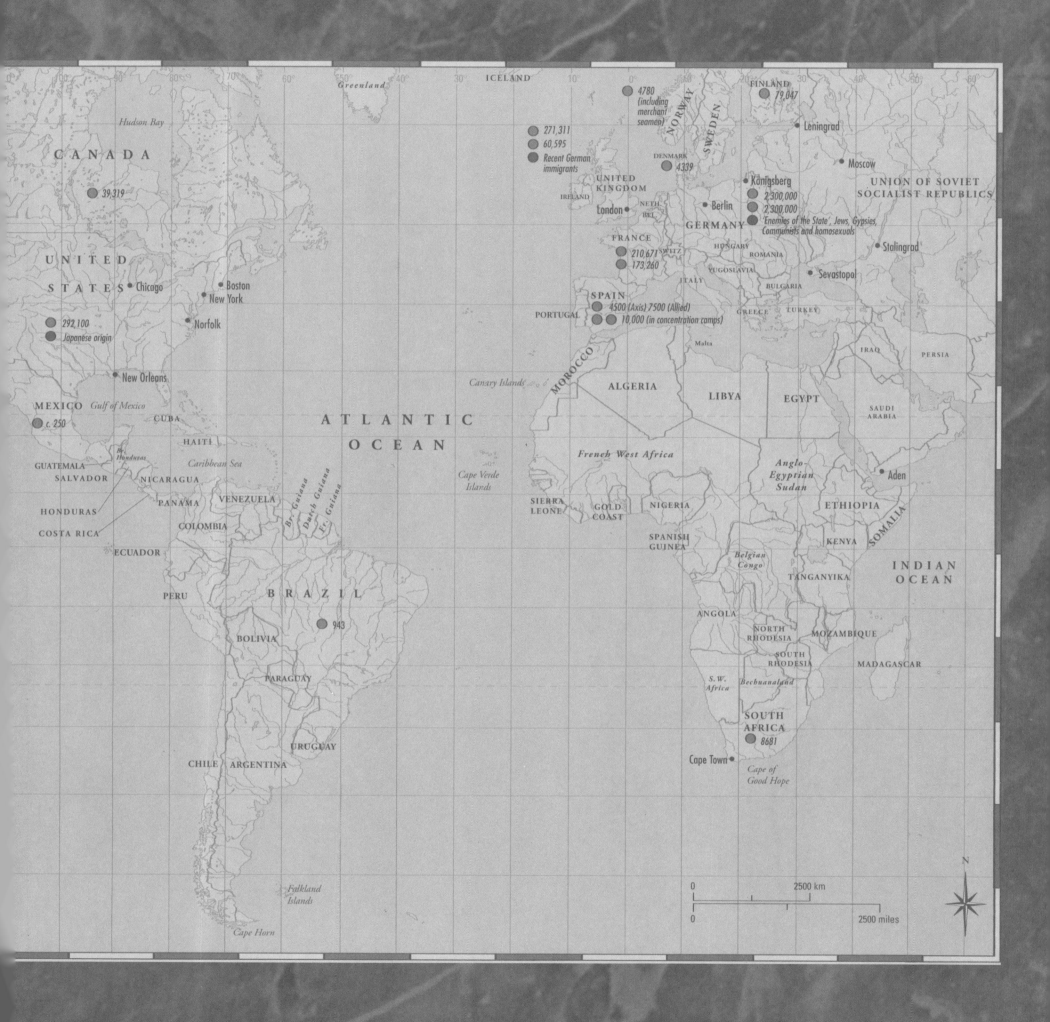

CANADA

Hudson Bay

39,319

UNITED

STATES   • Chicago   • Boston
                            New York

292,100   • Norfolk
Japanese origin

MEXICO Gulf of Mexico
c. 250   CUBA
        • New Orleans
                HAITI
GUATEMALA Br.
SALVADOR Honduras Caribbean Sea
        NICARAGUA
HONDURAS   PANAMA VENEZUELA
COSTA RICA   COLOMBIA
        ECUADOR

PERU   BRAZIL   943

BOLIVIA

PARAGUAY

URUGUAY

CHILE ARGENTINA

Greenland

ICELAND

4780
(including
merchant
seamen)

271,311
60,595
Recent German
immigrants

DENMARK 4339

IRELAND   NETH.

London   BEL.

FRANCE   SWITZ.
210,671
173,260

SPAIN
4500 (Axis) 7500 (Allied)
PORTUGAL   10,000 (in concentration camps)

Canary Islands

MOROCCO   ALGERIA

ATLANTIC
OCEAN

Cape Verde
Islands

French West Africa

SIERRA   GOLD
LEONE   COAST   NIGERIA

SPANISH
GUINEA   Belgian
        Congo

ANGOLA   NORTH
        RHODESIA
        SOUTH
        RHODESIA
S.W.   Bechuanaland
Africa

SOUTH
AFRICA
8681

Cape Town •   Cape of
            Good Hope

NORWAY   SWEDEN   FINLAND
                79,047

                    • Leningrad

                    • Moscow

Königsberg   UNION OF SOVIET
2,300,000   SOCIALIST REPUBLICS
2,300,000
'Enemies of the State', Jews, Gypsies,
Communists and homosexuals

Berlin   • Stalingrad

GERMANY
    HUNGARY
        ROMANIA
    YUGOSLAVIA
ITALY   BULGARIA   • Sevastopol

        GREECE TURKEY

Malta   IRAQ   PERSIA

LIBYA   EGYPT
                SAUDI
                ARABIA

        Anglo-
        Egyptian   • Aden
        Sudan

            ETHIOPIA

            KENYA SOMALIA

        TANGANYIKA   INDIAN
                OCEAN

        MOZAMBIQUE

            MADAGASCAR

UNITED
KINGDOM

Falkland
Islands

Cape Horn

0   2500 km

0   2500 miles

N

THE MILITARY
ATLAS
OF WORLD WAR II

CHRIS BISHOP

CHARTWELL
BOOKS, INC.

This edition published in 2013 by
Chartwell Books, Inc.
A division of Book Sales, Inc.
276 Fifth Avenue Suite 206
New York, New York 10001
USA

ISBN: 978-0-7858-3037-5

Project Editor: Michael Spilling
Design: Zoë Mellors

Printed in China

ARTWORK CREDITS

All photographs courtesy TRH Pictures.

All map artworks © Amber Books Ltd.

CONTENTS

Symbol Guide

XXXXX Army Group	XX Army Division	X Brigade
XXXX Army	Airborne	III Regiment
XXX Corps	Armoured	II Company
II Artillery	II Antitank	II Mechanized Infantry
II Engineer	II Communication	Naval

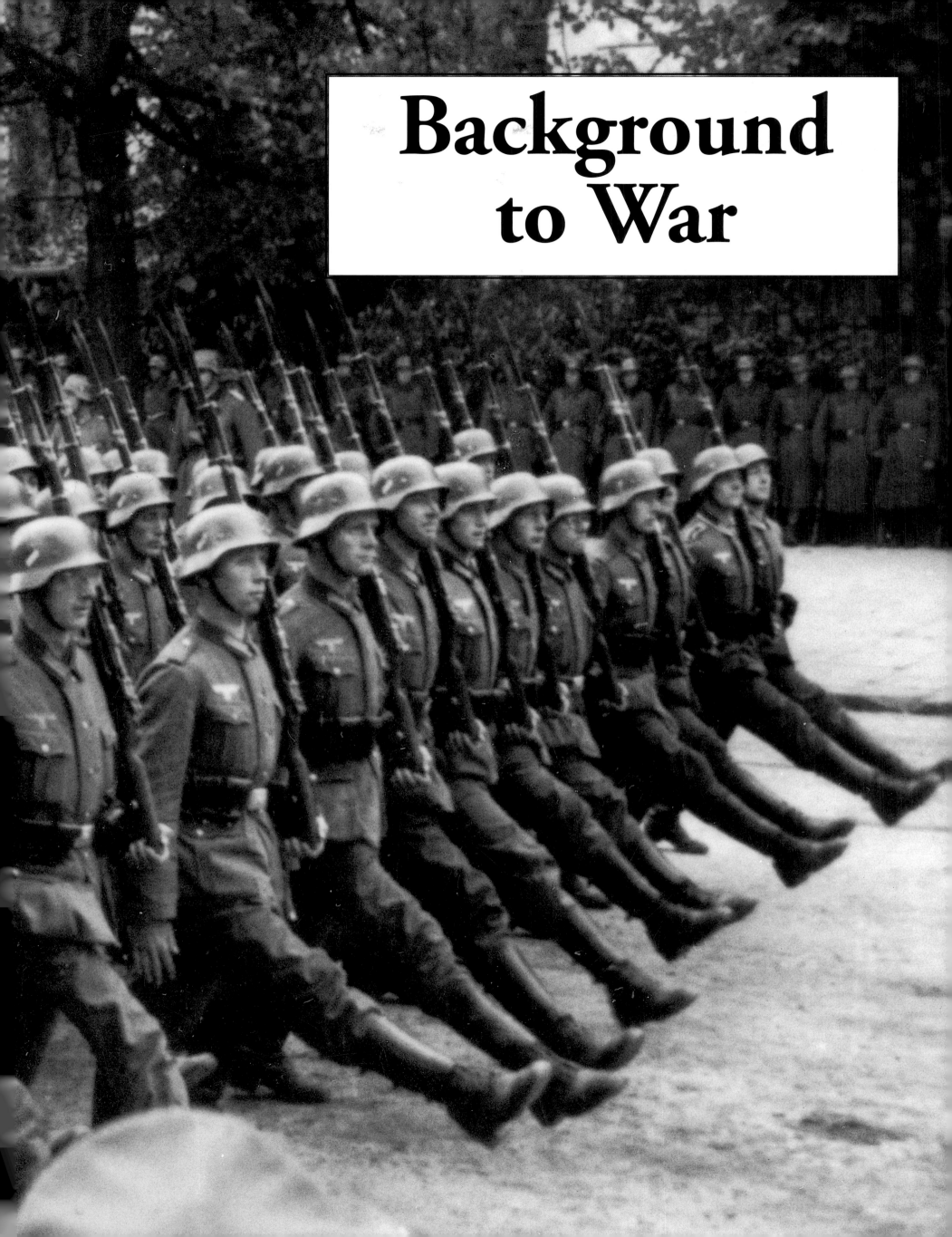

Background
to War

Europe 1914–18

The roots of World War II can be found in the shape of Europe at the end of the nineteenth century and in the redrawing of Europe's borders at the end of World War I. At the turn of the century, Europe was dominated by the great imperial powers. Britain and France had worldwide interests, while Central Europe was dominated by the economic power of the German Empire, set up under Prussian domination by Bismarck. The Austro-Hungarian Empire was a polyglot state incorporating many nationalities, languages and cultures, as was Russia, the largest of the European empires. The area of greatest tension was in the Balkans, wrested from Ottoman domination in the nineteenth century and partly controlled by Austria.

Europe 1914

Europe after the Peace Treaties 1920–21

Following the end of the Great War, the Treaty of St Germain decreed the dismemberment of the Austrian Empire, and the new states of Hungary, Czechoslovakia, Poland, and the Kingdom of Serbs, Croats, and Slovenes arose out of the remains. Finland and the Baltic States emerged from the former Russian Empire. It was the Treaty of Versailles between Germany and the Allies, however, which was to lay the seeds of future conflict in Europe.

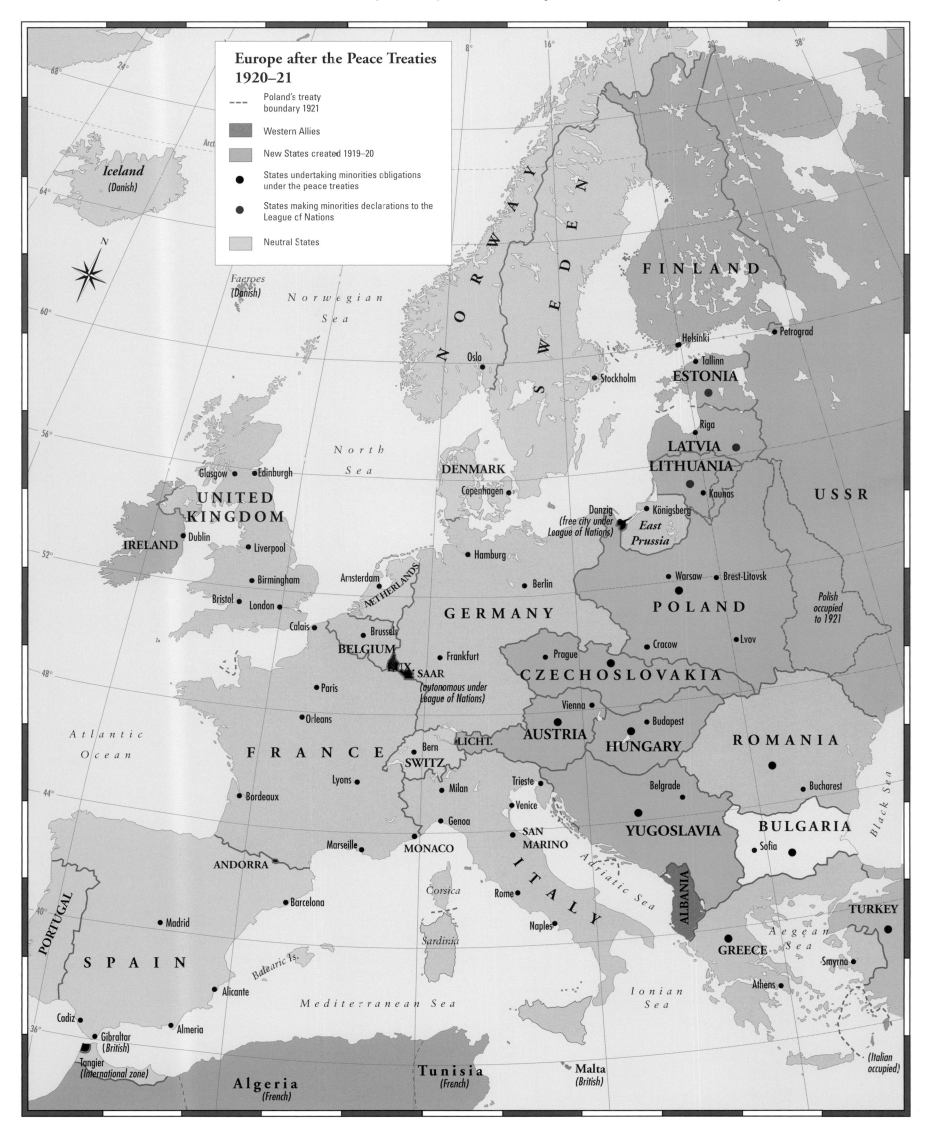

Europe after the Peace Treaties 1920–21

- - - - Poland's treaty boundary 1921

Western Allies

New States created 1919–20

● States undertaking minorities obligations under the peace treaties

● States making minorities declarations to the League of Nations

Neutral States

11

The Depression in Europe

Despite the best efforts of the victorious powers, in particular the United States, the post-war economic situation in Europe remained difficult, with the damage caused by the war presenting seemingly insoluble problems. Weakened further by the German hyperinflation of 1923, the world economy continued to struggle, with investment being hard to find and unemployment adding a further drain on any attempts to revitalize business. However, the Weimar Republic gradually put its economic house in order through the 1920s, until it was struck by a second great blow in 1929.

The Great Depression

The American stock market crash of 1929 ushered in the Great Depression around the world. Again, Germany was particularly hard hit. Much of the success of the Weimar reconstruction in the late 1920s had been funded by short-term loans from American banks, and these were called in after the crash. German industry instantly collapsed, and many companies went bankrupt. Those which survived found that export demand had vanished, and workers were laid off and businesses were shut down.

As unemployment soared, support for parties of the extreme right and left grew rapidly, and Hitler and the National Socialist German Workers' Party took full advantage of that support.

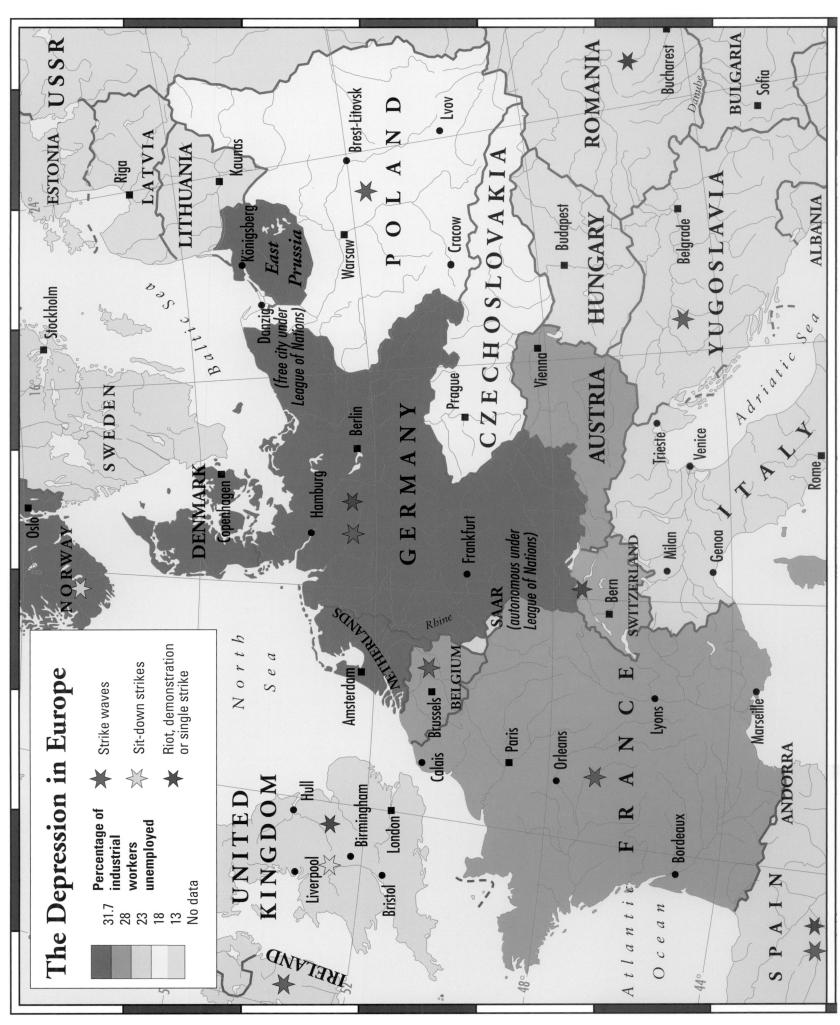

The Depression in Europe

The cost of the Great War hit most of the participants hard. Economies geared to war production found it hard to convert to peacetime needs, and millions of demobbed soldiers needed to find work, which was scarce. Germany was hit particularly hard. Key industrial areas had been lost under the Treaty of Versailles, and the crippling reparations demanded by France added a further strain to an already weak economy, leading to hyperinflation in the early 1920s.

The Depression in Europe

Percentage of industrial workers unemployed

- 31.7
- 28
- 23
- 18
- 13
- 5
- No data

★ Strike waves
☆ Sit-down strikes
✦ Riot, demonstration or single strike

Fascist States in Europe

In Europe, economic chaos caused a surge of support for political parties at both ends of the spectrum. Germany and Spain joined Italy in the fascist camp. In Eastern Europe, governments from Estonia in the north to Greece in the south installed repressive, conservative governments, equally in fear of Communist Russia to the east and the rapidly growing power of Nazi Germany to the west. Dictatorships now outnumbered democracies in Europe.

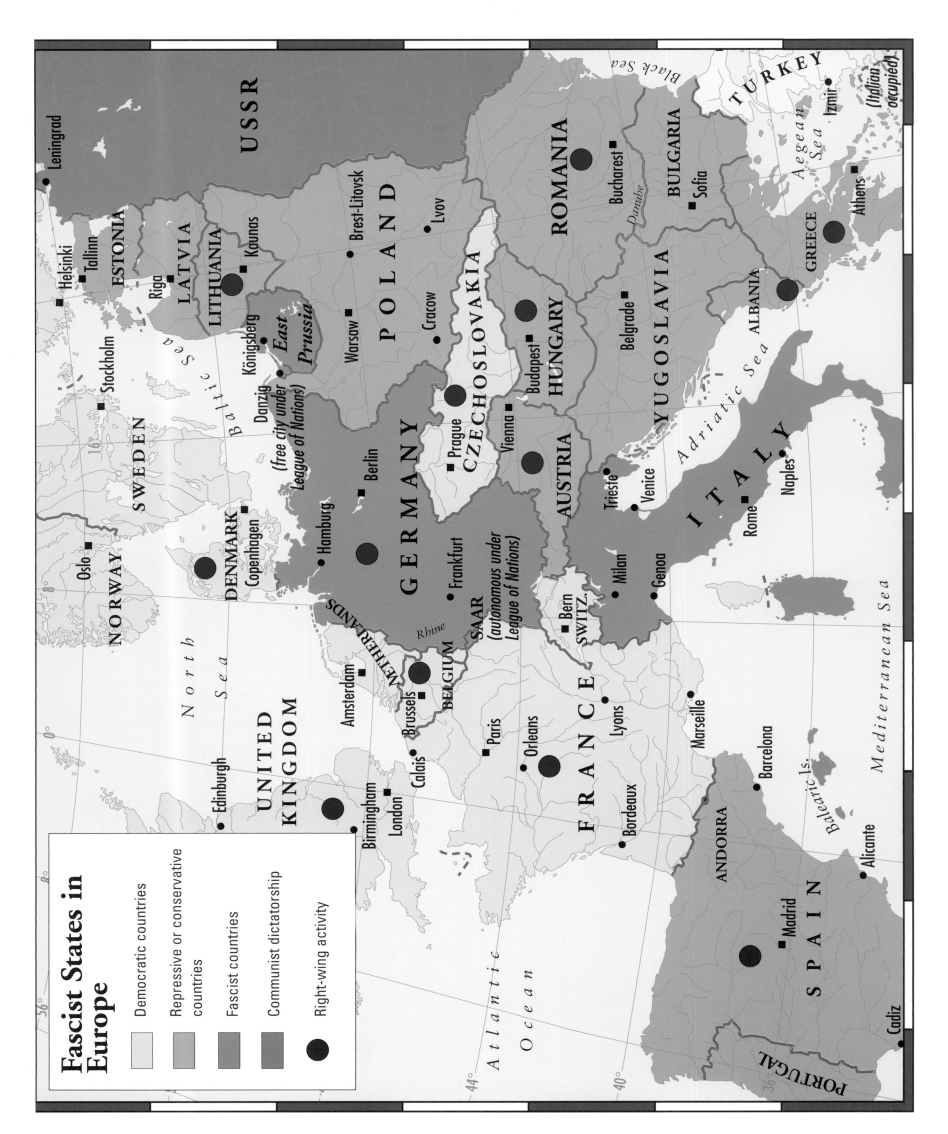

Fascist States in Europe

- Democratic countries
- Repressive or conservative countries
- Fascist countries
- Communist dictatorship
- ● Right-wing activity

Political Agreements
1934–39

The economic and political chaos which followed in the wake of the Great Depression led to a series of major foreign policy developments that would set the scene for what many saw as an inevitable conflict in Europe. Once Hitler took power in Germany in 1933, he immediately began to make good his intention to scrap the Treaty of Versailles. In 1935 he went further by announcing German rearmament, and the non-fascist countries of Europe began to take notice of the rebirth of German power.

Political Agreements
1934–35

- German-Polish non-aggression pact, 1934
- Rome protocols, March 1934
- Franco-Soviet/Soviet-Czech pact, May 1935 (also see 1936–37)

ADROIT DIPLOMATIC MOVES by Germany between 1934 and 1939 ended German isolation in Europe. The first major treaty signed by Hitler was a non-aggression pact agreed with Poland, largely as a counter to Soviet power. A premature attempt to force a union with Austria failed, however, and Austria and Hungary signed an agreement with Italy in 1934 to counter German power.

Nevertheless, Germany rapidly grew stronger and soon replaced Italy as the dominant fascist power in Europe. It was partly to counter growing German strength that France, the USSR and the Czechs made a mutual defence pact in May of 1935.

Axis pact

Mussolini was impressed with Germany's rise to prominence, and in November 1936 Italy and Germany signed the Rome-Berlin Axis. At the same time, several non-aligned countries declared themselves neutral in any future European conflict. In 1938 and 1939, German expansionism forced Britain along with France to guarantee the neutrality of Poland, Greece, Romania and Turkey.

Political Agreements
1936–37

- Axis, November 1936
- Declaration of neutrality, 1936
- Anglo-Egyptian treaty, 1936
- Franco-Soviet/Soviet-Czech pact, May 1935

Political Agreements
1938–39

- British and French guarantees for Poland, Greece, Romania and Turkey, 1939
- Copenhagen declaration of neutrality, July 1938
- Axis, May 1939

Hitler's Annexations 1935–39

Hitler's first territorial acquisitions were Germany's traditional industrial heartlands of the Saar and the Rhineland – demilitarized areas until recently occupied by the Allied powers of 1918. The Saar he regained in January 1935 by plebiscite. In March 1936, he reoccupied the Rhineland, while Britain and France did nothing but protest weakly.

ON 12 MARCH 1938 HITLER sent his troops across the Austrian border and into Vienna to a rapturous welcome. The following day he himself travelled to Vienna to declare the *Anschluss* – the indissoluble reunion of Austria and Germany in the Greater German Reich. The German General Staff used the operation as an exercise in moving large numbers of troops by road. All did not go smoothly, but valuable logistic lessons were learned in the bloodless takeover – lessons that would be put into practice in combat some 18 months later. Next, Hitler's eyes turned towards the Czechs. In Czechoslovakia, the Sudetenland, the western and northern border areas facing Germany and Austria, had a German-speaking population of three million. The area had rich mineral resources, and it also housed major munitions factories at Pilsen.

Munich Agreement

At Munich in September 1938, Britain, France, Italy and Germany agreed that the German-speaking Sudetenland should be transferred to the Reich – as the final stage of Hitler's territorial aggrandizement. Hitler had no intention of abiding by the agreement, however, and in March 1939 German troops moved forward from the Sudetenland, first to Prague and then on into the whole of Bohemia and Moravia.

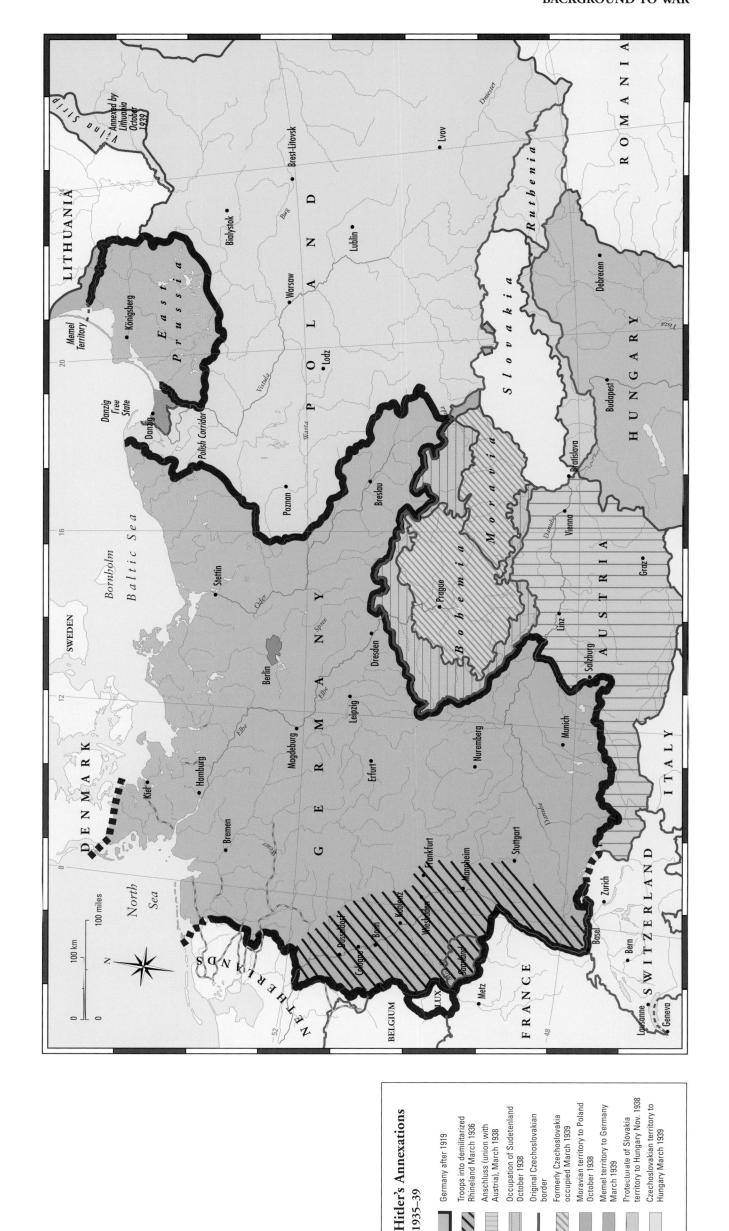

Hitler's Annexations 1935–39

Germany after 1919
Troops into demilitarized Rhineland March 1936
Anschluss (union with Austria), March 1938
Occupation of Sudetenland October 1938
Original Czechoslovakian border
Formerly Czechoslovakia occupied March 1939
Moravian territory to Poland October 1938
Memel territory to Germany March 1939
Protectorate of Slovakia territory to Hungary Nov. 1938
Czechoslovakian territory to Hungary March 1939

The European Theatre

Invasion of Poland
1–28 September 1939

The invasion of Poland saw five German armies, a total of 42 divisions, cross the border. The newly created *Panzerwaffe* was the spearhead of the German drive on Warsaw, reaching the outskirts of the city within a week. The campaign was a massive double pincer movement, the inner designed to close on the Vistula River, while the outer, faster-moving, forces were targeted on the Bug. Poland's fate was sealed when the Soviets invaded on 17 September 1939.

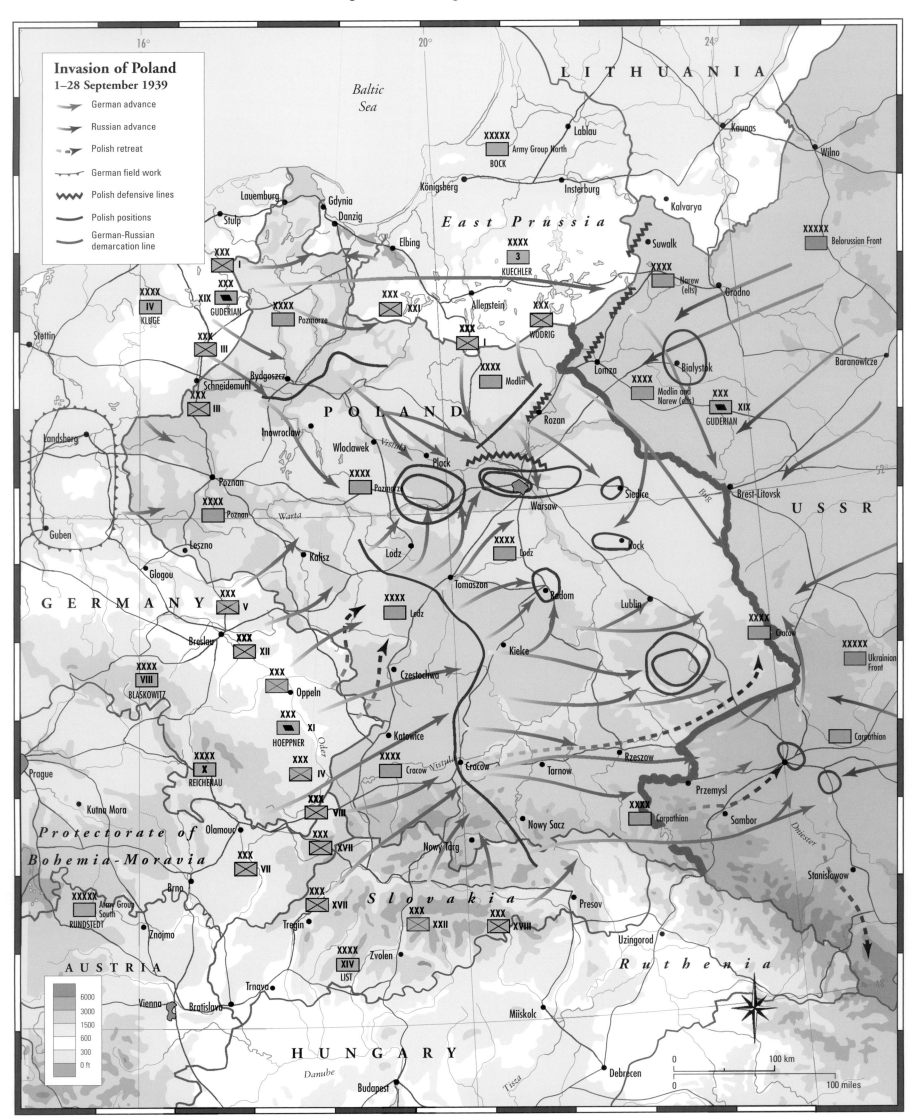

Invasion of Poland
1–28 September 1939

- → German advance
- → Russian advance
- ⇢ Polish retreat
- ⌄⌄⌄ German field work
- ∿∿∿ Polish defensive lines
- ⌒ Polish positions
- ─ German-Russian demarcation line

The Winter War November 1939–March 1940

The Winter War began when Finland, formerly a Russian province, refused Soviet demands for border adjustments. The Soviets, fearful of Hitler's future plans, wanted to consolidate their grip on the Baltic States to provide a position of strength on the northern flank of the expanding Third Reich.

O n 30 November 1939, the Red Air Force launched a surprise attack on Helsinki, followed by a full-scale invasion. Almost a million Soviet troops smashed into Finland from the east, the southeast, and from across the Gulf of Finland. Facing them were around 300,000 Finnish troops, 80 per cent of whom were reservists.

Stalin reckoned that with such overwhelming force the Red Army would occupy Finland in less than a month, but he was rudely disillusioned. The Finns proved to be ferocious fighters, and familiarity with the terrain and weather meant that they put up incredible resistance to the Soviet attack. A Russian column attacking at Petsamo in the north made brief progress before being stopped in its tracks, while the amphibious assaults in the south were all beaten back. The main Russian thrust through the Karelian isthmus was driven back with heavy losses at the Mannerheim Line.

The humiliating Soviet defeat forced the Red Army to regroup, and a further half million men were committed to the battlefront.

On 1 February 1940 two Soviet armies began battering at the Finnish defences, mounting four or five attacks each day. The Soviet high command was willing to accept any losses to achieve their aim. Eventually, on 13 February the Russians broke through at Summa, and began to roll up the Finnish defences. On 12 March the Finns were forced to sue for peace.

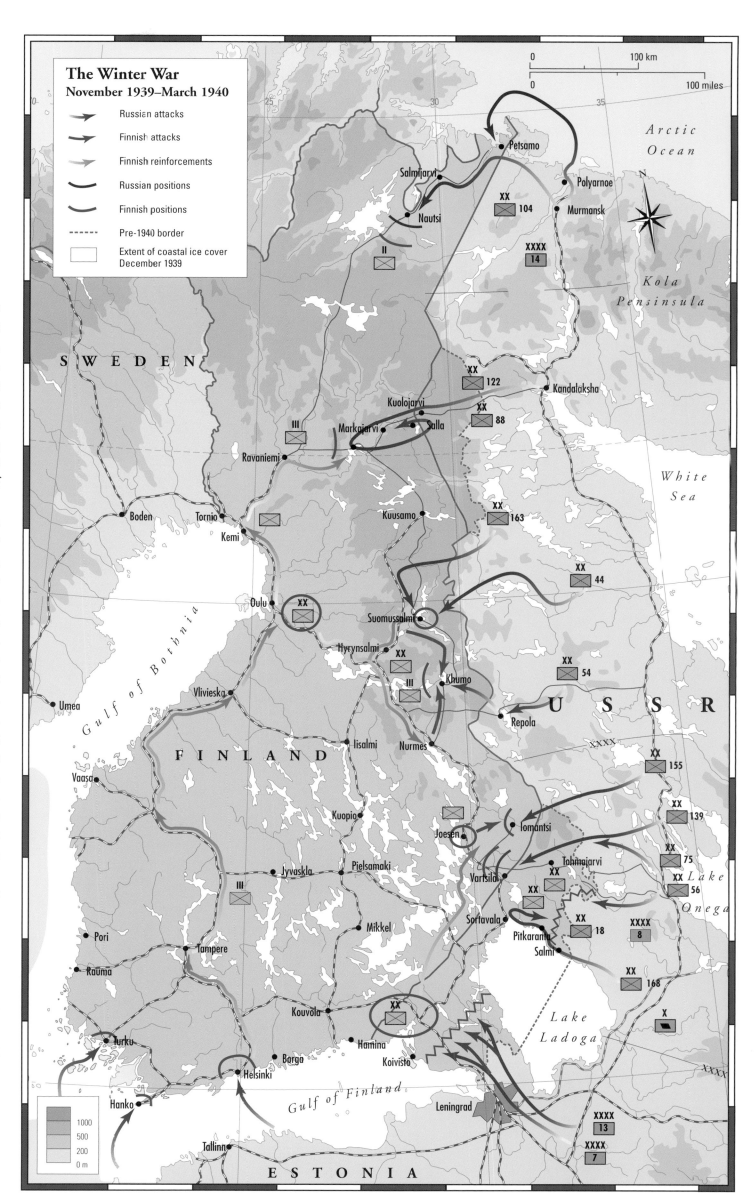

Battle of Suomussalmi
11 December 1939–
8 January 1940

While the main Soviet drive on the Mannerheim Line was being held off, other Red Army columns attempting to move through the seemingly endless forests and lakes of central Finland were run ragged by small Finnish ski units fighting a guerrilla-style war to which the Red Army had no answer, ending in a fierce battle around the village of Suomussalmi.

O N THE FACE OF IT the Red Army should have won the Battle of Suomussalmi. Two Soviet divisions outnumbered the defending Finns by four or five to one. However, the Soviet formations were too heavily equipped for the terrain, and could only operate along the narrow forest tracks. The Finnish forces were small, mobile, well led, and well coordinated. The Soviet divisions, strung out along miles of track, were too cumbersome to react to the slashing attacks of the Finnish ski troops. The terrain ensured that the Soviets could not bring their firepower to bear. The Finns, by contrast, retained their freedom of movement, avoiding any temptation to get bogged down in head-on attacks. Local commanders were allowed to exploit local opportunities, and in a series of small-unit actions they defeated the Soviets piece by piece, until there were no pieces left.

Annihilation

When the Finns took stock after 8 January 1940, they had captured, intact, 65 tanks, 437 trucks, 10 motorcycles, 1620 horses, 92 field guns, 78 anti-tank guns, 13 anti-aircraft guns, 6000 rifles, 290 machine guns, and a large quantity of precious communications equipment. They counted 27,500 Soviet dead, 43 knocked-out tanks, and 270 other destroyed vehicles. Finnish losses were 900 dead and 1770 wounded.

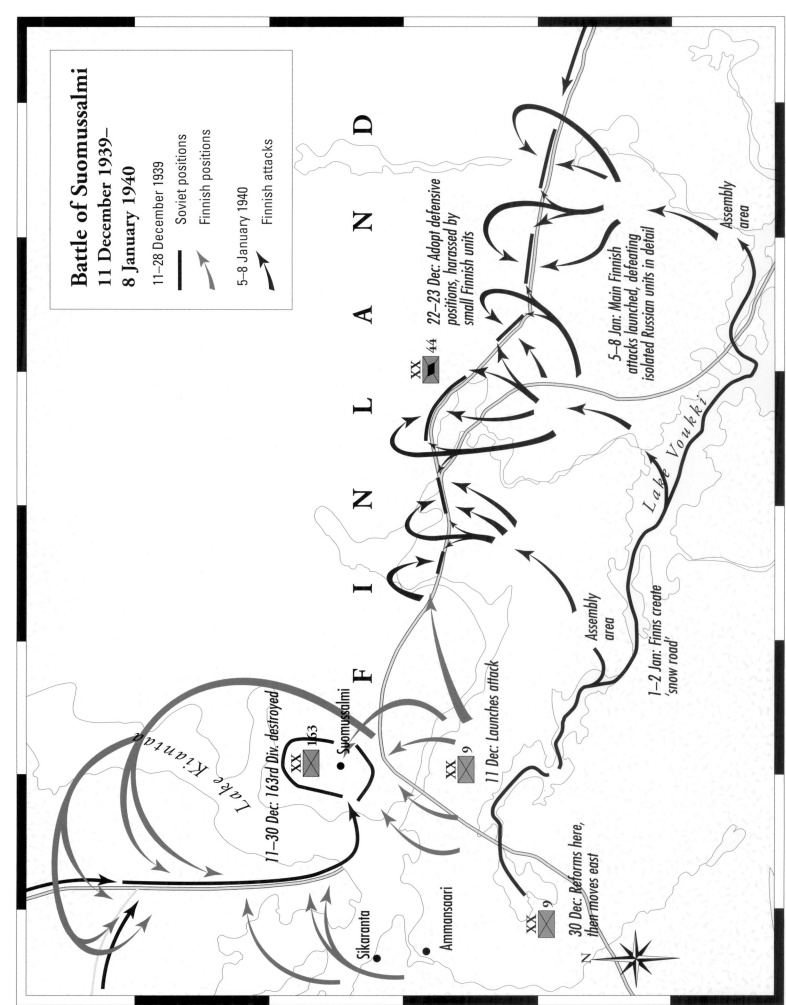

Battle of Suomussalmi
11 December 1939–
8 January 1940

11–28 December 1939
— Soviet positions
→ Finnish positions

5–8 January 1940
→ Finnish attacks

22–23 Dec: Adopt defensive positions, harassed by small Finnish units

5–8 Jan: Main Finnish attacks launched, defeating isolated Russian units in detail

1–2 Jan: Finns create 'snow road'

11–30 Dec: 163rd Div. destroyed

11 Dec: Launches attack

30 Dec: Reforms here, then moves east

Lake Kiantaa

Lake Voukki

Suomussalmi

Sikaranta

Ammansaari

Assembly area

Assembly area

163

44

9

9

FINLAND

The Phoney War
German and Allied Plans
September 1939–April 1940

The Phoney War over the winter of 1939 and 1940 saw the Allies waiting confidently for any German attack. The French felt safe behind the massive fortifications of the Maginot Line, while the British expected the Germans to attack through the Low Countries and made plans to advance into Belgium to counter a German offensive. What they did not realize was that the Germans planned to strike through the supposedly 'impassable' Ardennes.

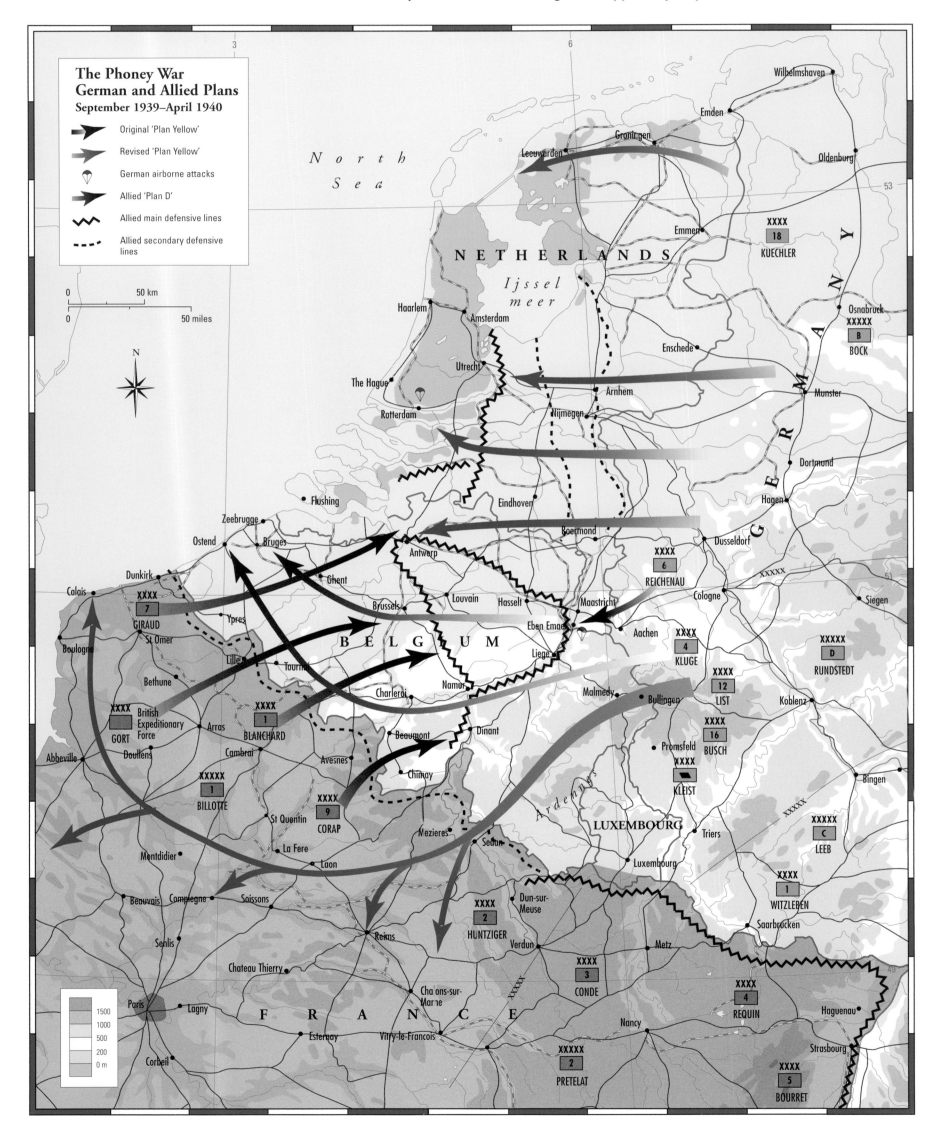

The Phoney War
German and Allied Plans
September 1939–April 1940

Original 'Plan Yellow'
Revised 'Plan Yellow'
German airborne attacks
Allied 'Plan D'
Allied main defensive lines
Allied secondary defensive lines

Denmark and Norway April–June 1940

At 05:00 on 9 April, German *Fallschirmjäger* were dropped at the unused fortress of Madneso in Denmark and then at Aalborg airport. At 06:00, a battalion of infantry which had been hidden in a merchant ship in Copenhagen harbour emerged to seize the Danish king and his government.

Two divisions of the German XXI Infantry Corps crossed the border and moved into Jutland. Totally outmatched, the Danish Army put up little resistance except in North Schleswig, and there was a brief firefight for possession of the Royal Palace in Copenhagen.

At dawn on the same day German troops were swarming ashore at Oslo, Bergen, Trondheim and even at Narvik, over 1600km (1000 miles) from the German homeland. German paratroops seized Sola airport near Stavanger and dropped later onto Fornebu airport near Oslo, while the *Kriegsmarine* ferried the army formations across the Skagerrak and Kattegat.

Allied landings and naval actions in the north around Narvik briefly reversed the tide of German success, but the British and French troops were withdrawn at the end of May after setbacks in France meant that they were more urgently needed there.

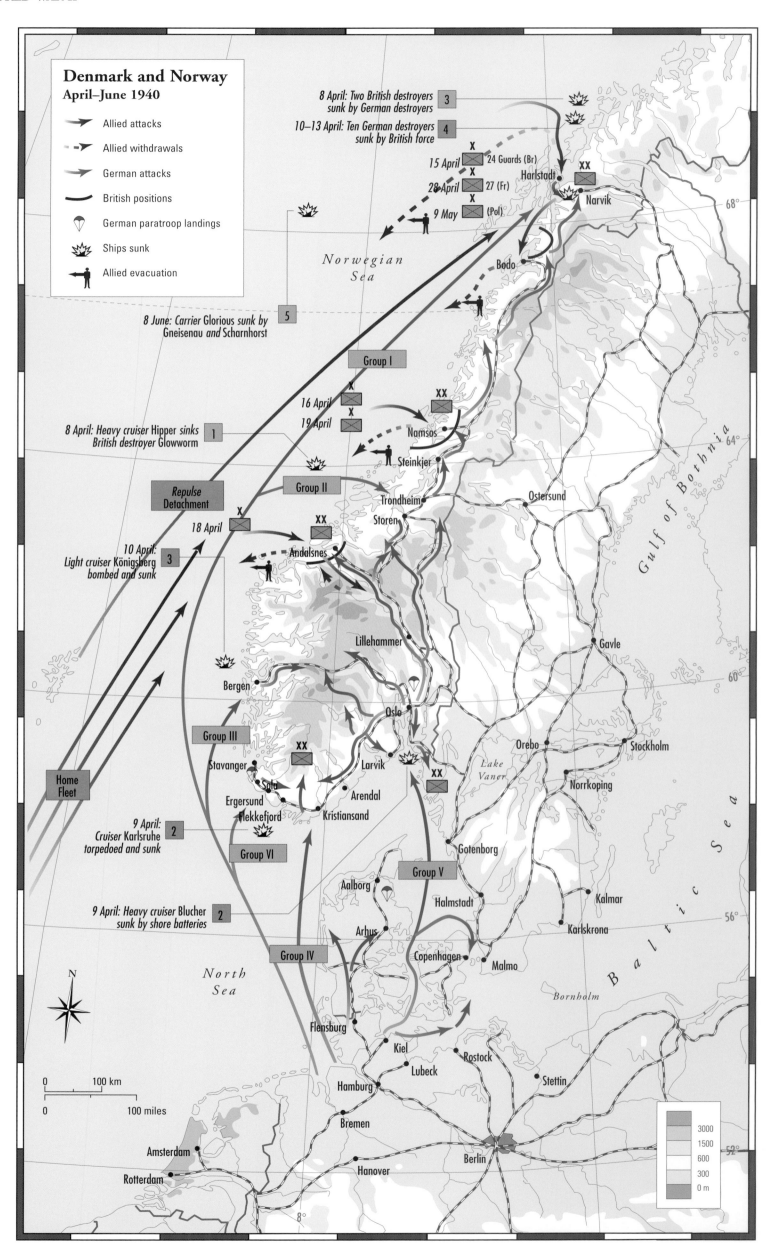

Denmark and Norway
April–June 1940

→ Allied attacks
--▶ Allied withdrawals
→ German attacks
⌒ British positions
⛉ German paratroop landings
💥 Ships sunk
↯ Allied evacuation

8 April: Two British destroyers sunk by German destroyers **3**
10–13 April: Ten German destroyers sunk by British force **4**

X 15 April ☒ 24 Guards (Br)
X
X 28 April ☒ 27 (Fr)
X 9 May ☒ (Pol)

8 June: Carrier *Glorious* sunk by *Gneisenau* and *Scharnhorst* **5**

Group I

X 16 April ☒
X 19 April ☒

8 April: Heavy cruiser *Hipper* sinks British destroyer *Glowworm* **1**

Group II

Repulse Detachment

X 18 April ☒

10 April: Light cruiser *Königsberg* bombed and sunk **3**

Group III

Home Fleet

9 April: Cruiser *Karlsruhe* torpedoed and sunk **2**

Group VI

9 April: Heavy cruiser *Blucher* sunk by shore batteries **2**

Group IV

Group V

Norwegian Sea

Harlstadt
Narvik
Bodo
Namsos
Steinkjer
Trondheim
Storen
Andalsnes
Lillehammer
Bergen
Stavanger
Sola
Ergersund
Flekkefjord
Arendal
Kristiansand
Larvik
Oslo
Ostersund
Gavle
Orebo
Stockholm
Norrkoping
Lake Vaner
Kalmar
Karlskrona
Gotenborg
Halmstad
Aalborg
Arhus
Copenhagen
Malmo
Bornholm
Flensburg
Kiel
Lubeck
Rostock
Stettin
Hamburg
Bremen
Berlin
Hanover
Amsterdam
Rotterdam

Gulf of Bothnia

Baltic Sea

North Sea

N

0 — 100 km
0 — 100 miles

68°
64°
60°
56°
52°
8°

3000
1500
600
300
0 m

Panzer strike through the Ardennes 12–14 May 1940

The German attack in the Low Countries was a massive feint designed to draw the Anglo-French field armies northwards into Belgium.

The real punch came through the Ardennes, where the 44 divisions of von Rundstedt's Army Group A planned to catch the Allies by surprise. The bulk of the French troops were in the Maginot Line, guarding against an attack across the German frontier. But the huge works did not cover the Belgian border, French planners having considered that a major attack through the Ardennes was impossible.

ENCOUNTERING LITTLE RESISTANCE from Belgian troops in the Ardennes, the panzer divisions headed down the dirt roads in alarmingly dense columns. Crashing through the 'impassable' forests and hills, brushing aside the French light cavalry unit which had been sent out to 'delay' them, the three divisions of General Guderian's Panzer Corps were across the French frontier and had reached the Meuse on each side of Sedan by the afternoon of 12 May.

On 13 May, Guderian's infantry paddled across the Meuse in rubber dinghies. At the same time, a *Luftwaffe* force of 300 twin-engine bombers and 200 Stukas pulverized the French defences. The dive bombers attacked with particular accuracy, knocking out key French gun positions. The foot soldiers were across by 3.00 p.m. Combat engineers had a ferry operational in an hour, and by 4.30 a bridge was in place and the tanks could cross to the far bank.

French counter-attacks came too little and too late. All the first-line troops had been committed to the northern flank. The Allies' strategy unravelled as the panzer divisions fanned out, racing ahead of their infantry and threatening to cut off the British and French armies in Belgium.

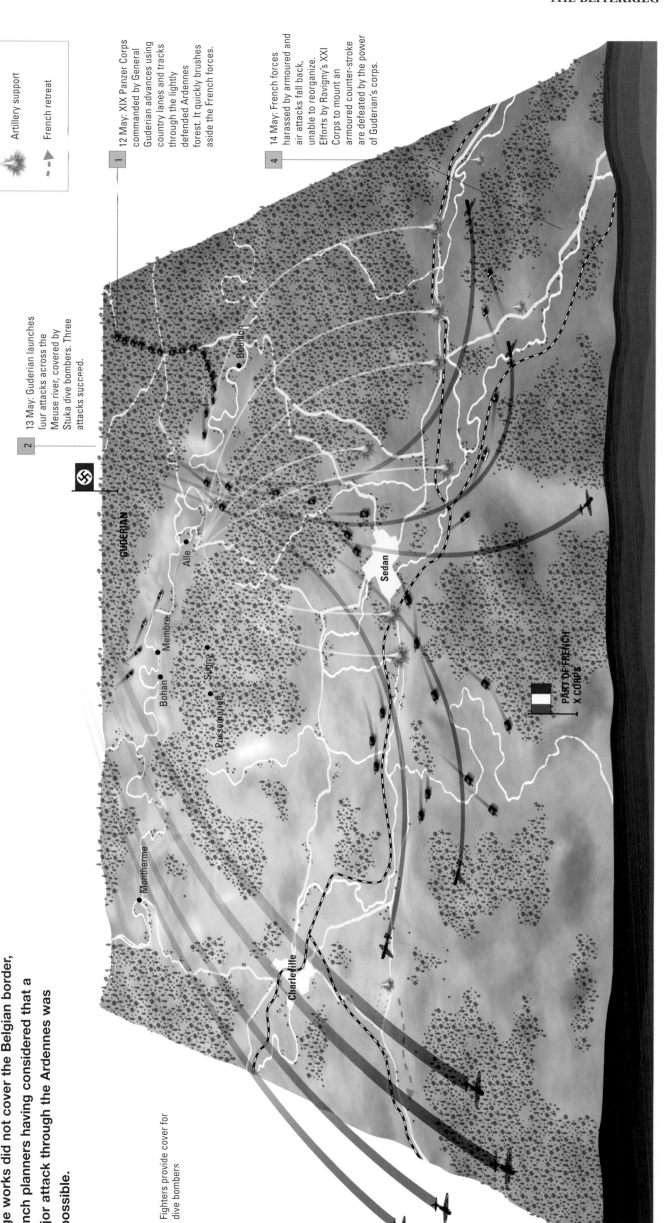

Panzer strike through the Ardennes
12–14 May 1940

- Armoured advance
- Air support
- Artillery support
- French retreat

1 12 May: XIX Panzer Corps commanded by General Guderian advances using country lanes and tracks through the lightly defended Ardennes forest. It quickly brushes aside the French forces.

2 13 May: Guderian launches four attacks across the Meuse river, covered by Stuka dive bombers. Three attacks succeed.

3 Fighters provide cover for dive bombers

4 14 May: French forces harassed by armoured and air attacks fall back, unable to reorganize. Efforts by Ravigny's XXI Corps to mount an armoured counter-stroke are defeated by the power of Guderian's corps.

GUDERIAN

Bouillon

Alle

Membre

Sedan

Bohan

Sugny

Pussemange

PART OF FRENCH X CORPS

Monthermé

Charleville

Invasion of the West
May–June 1940

Adolf Hitler hated France, and one of the principal aims of his military policy was to see the destruction of the enemy that had humiliated Germany after World War I. The massive invasion of the Low Countries was nothing more than a trap to draw the Allied armies out of position while the *Wehrmacht* prepared its killer blow through the Ardennes, penetrating deep into France and cutting off the Anglo-French armies in Belgium.

A FTER BRUSHING ASIDE the weak French resistance on the Meuse, Rundstedt's Army Group A, spearheaded by Guderian's panzer corps, broke out into the French countryside beyond. Instead of driving towards Paris, the panzers raced to the northwest, towards the Channel.

The French lacked the reserves to be able to react to the German challenge. A French tank counter-attack on 17 May, led by Colonel Charles de Gaulle, was brushed aside without difficulty by the 1st Panzer Division. A British attack near Arras was much more threatening, and was only held off when General Erwin Rommel of the 7th Panzer Division used his 8.8cm (3.465in) Flak guns in the anti-tank role.

The attacks came too late: Guderian's panzers had already reached the Channel coast on the 20th. The Allied armies were cut off.

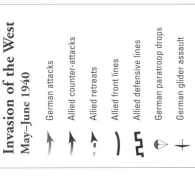

Invasion of the West
May–June 1940

- German attacks
- Allied counter-attacks
- Allied retreats
- Allied front lines
- Allied defensive lines
- German paratroop drops
- German glider assault

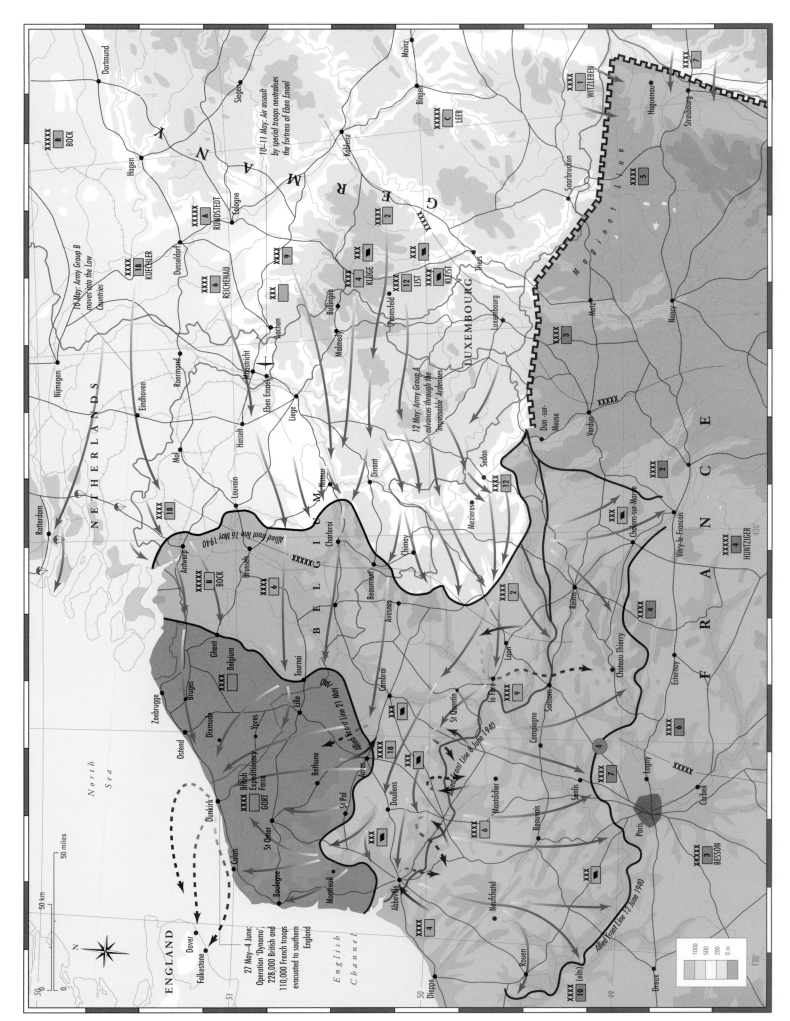

Dunkirk
Operation Dynamo
27 May–4 June 1940

Allied forces in Belgium faced annihilation as von Bock's army group pressed southwards from the Low Countries, while von Rundstedt's army group raced towards the Channel.

By the evening of 23 May, it was clear to the British commander, Lord Gort, that only a rapid retreat to the coast and evacuation to England would save even a quarter of his command. The British withdrew to the beaches on each side of Dunkirk. When the Belgian Army surrendered, it looked as though nothing could prevent a German triumph.

But then the *Führer* ordered his panzers to stop, allowing the British a breathing space. It may have been a political gesture to allow the British time to come to terms with defeat; Hitler might also have been worried about his panzers getting bogged down in the canals and marshes around Dunkirk. However, the most commonly held belief is that the order was intended to allow Hermann Goering to make good on his boast that the *Luftwaffe* could finish the job. In the event, the Germans met with stiff resistance from the Spitfires and Hurricanes of the Royal Air Force, and were consequently never able to seriously impede the evacuation.

Operation Dynamo saw some 338,000 Allied servicemen lifted safely from the beaches, small private craft being used to ferry the troops out to larger vessels waiting in deep water. Much was owed to the French troops who were fighting furiously to the south, holding back powerful German forces.

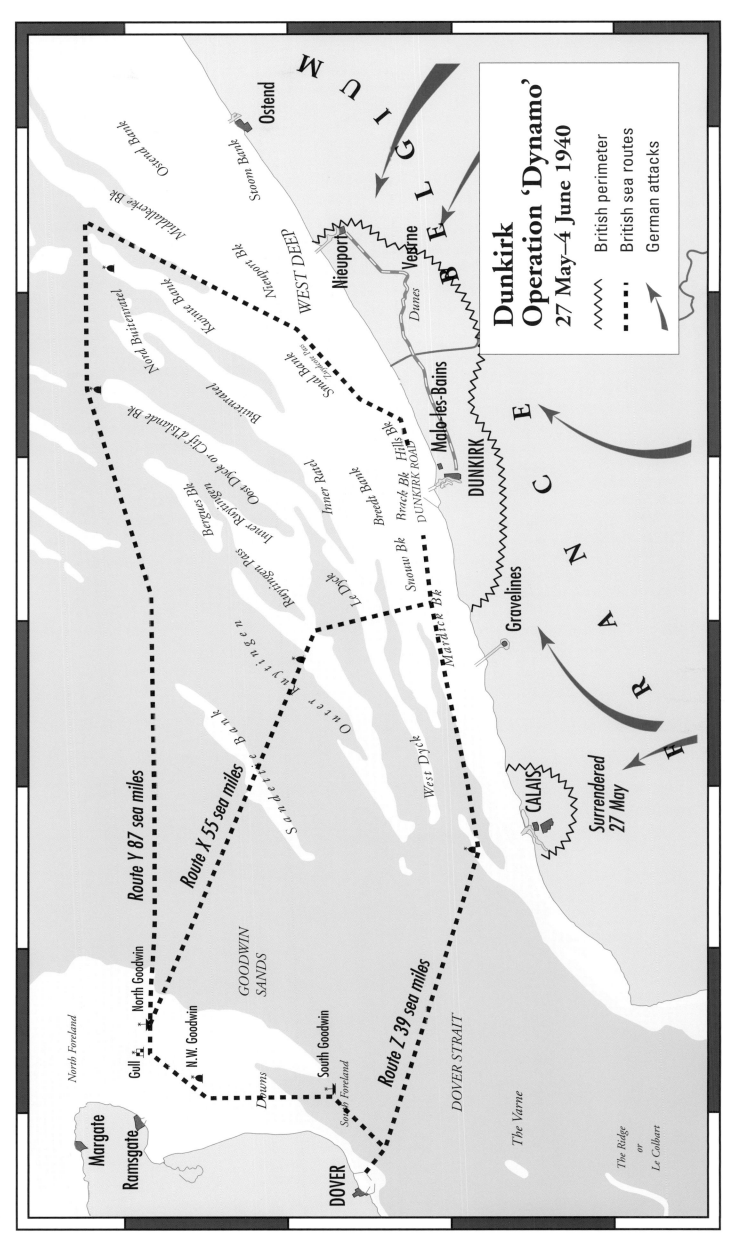

Dunkirk
Operation 'Dynamo'
27 May–4 June 1940

- British perimeter
- British sea routes
- German attacks

Ostend

BELGIUM

WEST DEEP

Nieuport
Veurne
Dunes
Malo-les-Bains
DUNKIRK
DUNKIRK ROAD
Gravelines
CALAIS
Surrendered 27 May

FRANCE

Route Y 87 sea miles
Route X 55 sea miles
Route Z 39 sea miles

GOODWIN SANDS
North Foreland
Gull
North Goodwin
N.W. Goodwin
South Goodwin
South Foreland
Downs
DOVER STRAIT
DOVER
Margate
Ramsgate

The Varne
The Ridge or Le Colbart

Ostend Bank
Stoom Bank
Middelkerke Bk
Nieuport Bank
Kleine Bank
Small Bank
Smal Bank
Zuydcote Pass
Inner Ratel
Breedt Bank
Brack Bk
Hills Bk
Snouw Bk
Le Dyck
Ruytingen Pass
Inner Ruytingen
Berques Bk
Oost Dyck or Clif d'Islande Bk
Noord Buitenratel
Buitenratel
Mardick Bk
West Dyck
Outer Ruytingen
Sandettie Bank

The Fall of France
June 1940

After a pause for reorganization, the Germans launched their assault on the rest of France on 5 June. In just three weeks, they forced the French government to sue for an armistice.

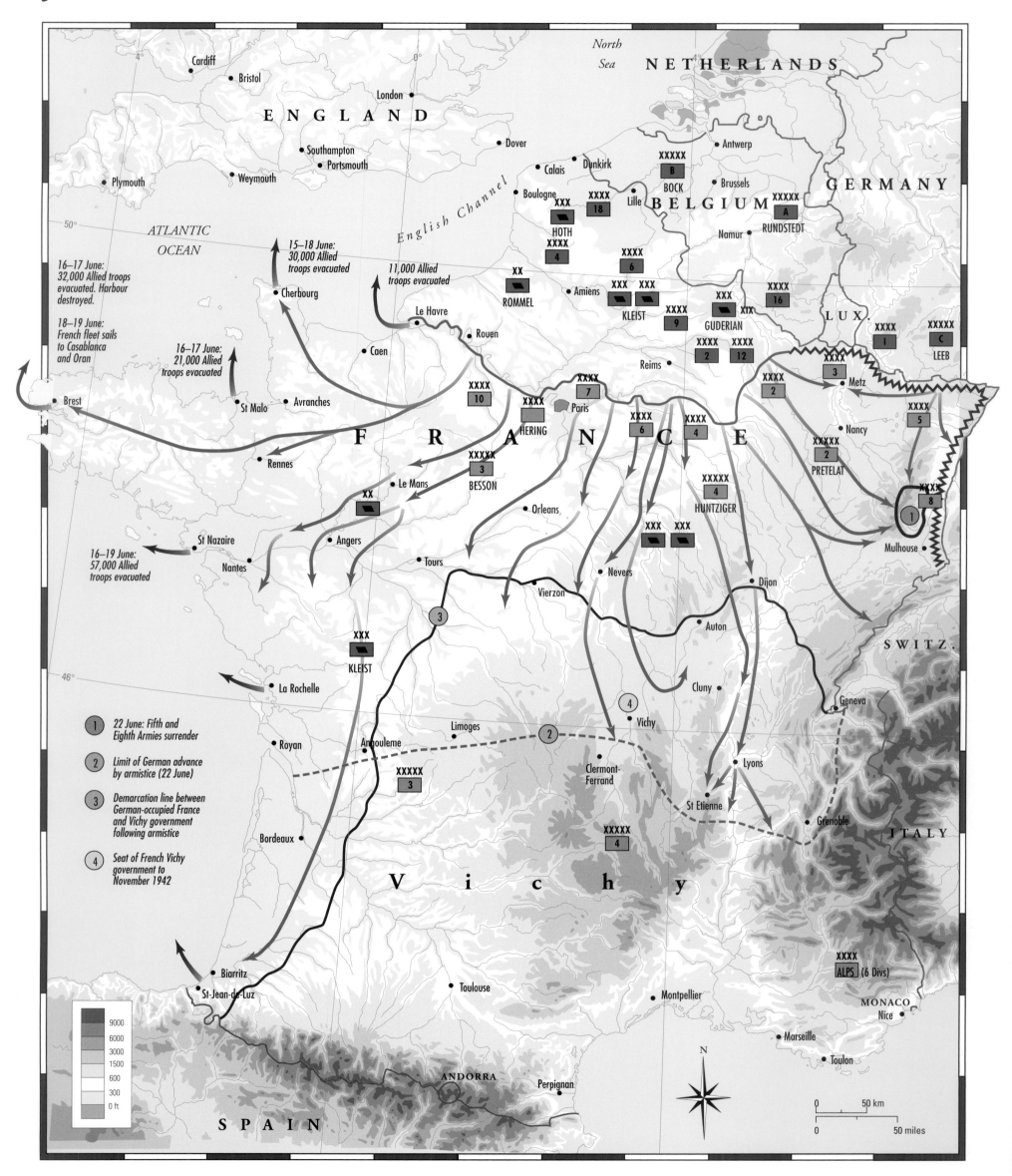

16–17 June: 32,000 Allied troops evacuated. Harbour destroyed.

18–19 June: French fleet sails to Casablanca and Oran

16–17 June: 21,000 Allied troops evacuated

15–18 June: 30,000 Allied troops evacuated

11,000 Allied troops evacuated

16–19 June: 57,000 Allied troops evacuated

1. 22 June: Fifth and Eighth Armies surrender

2. Limit of German advance by armistice (22 June)

3. Demarcation line between German-occupied France and Vichy government following armistice

4. Seat of French Vichy government to November 1942

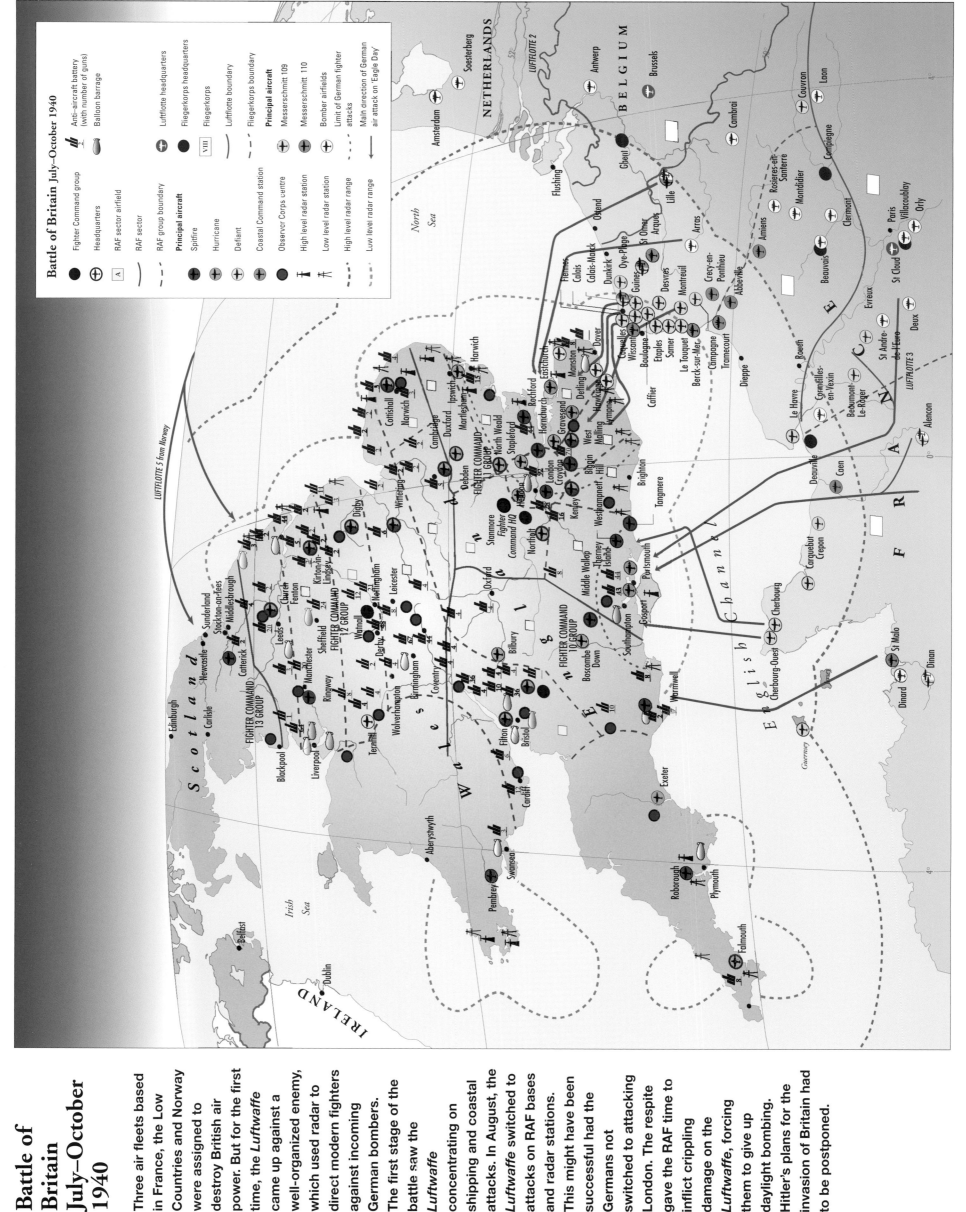

Battle of Britain July–October 1940

Three air fleets based in France, the Low Countries and Norway were assigned to destroy British air power. But for the first time, the *Luftwaffe* came up against a well-organized enemy, which used radar to direct modern fighters against incoming German bombers.

The first stage of the battle saw the *Luftwaffe* concentrating on shipping and coastal attacks. In August, the *Luftwaffe* switched to attacks on RAF bases and radar stations. This might have been successful had the Germans not switched to attacking London. The respite gave the RAF time to inflict crippling damage on the *Luftwaffe*, forcing them to give up daylight bombing. Hitler's plans for the invasion of Britain had to be postponed.

The Blitz
September 1940–May 1941

After the failure of the daylight bomber offensive, the *Luftwaffe* switched to night raids. Up to 400 bombers attacked London each night until mid-November. From January to May 1941, German bombers attacked other cities, including Coventry, Liverpool, Birmingham, Plymouth and Bristol. During the Blitz the Germans dropped 55,290 tonnes (54,420 tons) of bombs, killing 40,000 people and injuring 86,000. Two million homes were destroyed.

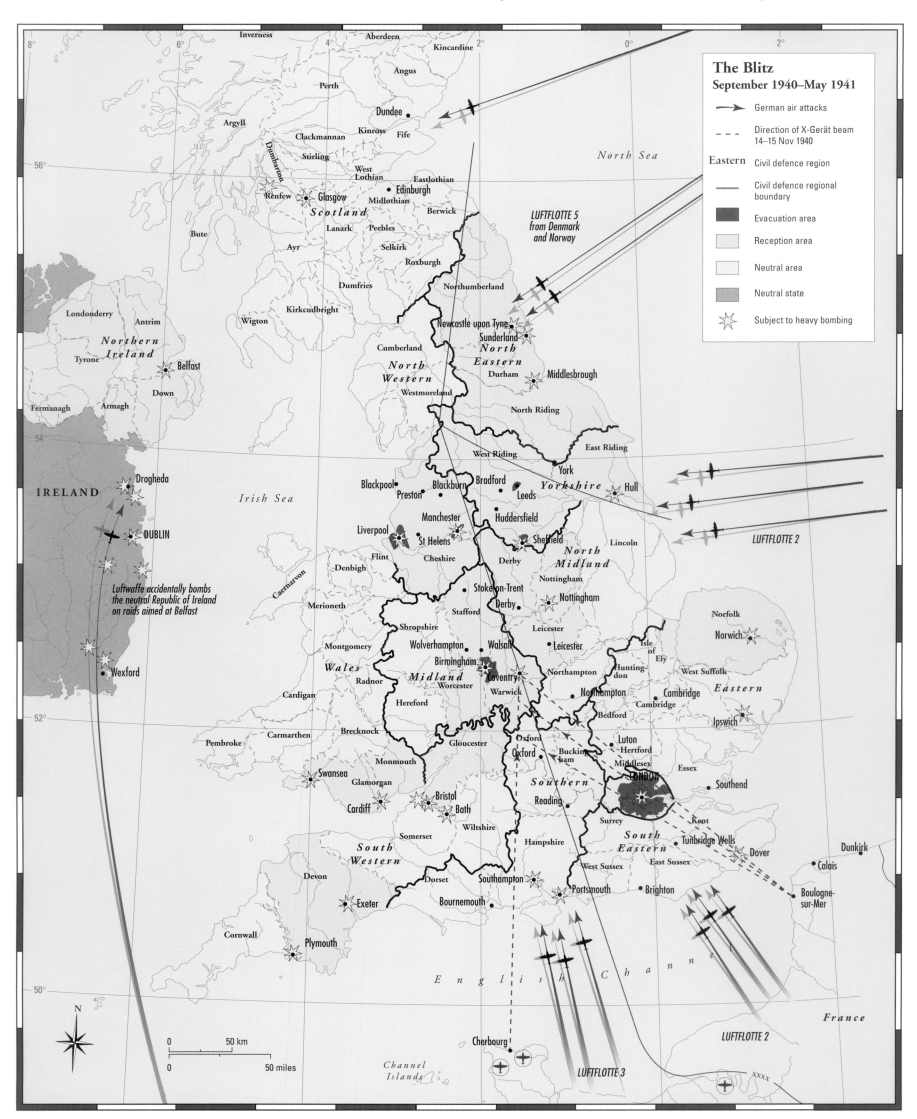

The Bombing of Europe 1939–41

The only way Britain could strike back at Germany was from the air, and the RAF mounted frequent night bombing raids over the German homeland. The attacks were initially targeted against key industrial and communications targets, but RAF crews found that accurate navigation and bombing by night was almost impossible. The poor results of the bombing came at a cost of 700 British bombers destroyed and thousands of aircrew killed or captured.

The Bombing of Europe 1939–41

● Bomber Command Headquarters

● Bomber Group Headquarters

Weight of bombs

✳ 25–1000 tonnes

✳ 1000–3000 tonnes

✳ 3000–4000 tonnes

Thousand Bomber Raid 30/31 May 1942

Hungry for success at a time when British fortunes were at a low ebb, the head of RAF Bomber Command, Arthur Harris, devised a plan known as Operation Millennium. Harris gathered a force of 1046 aircraft – virtually every serviceable bomber in the RAF – to mount the largest bombing raid ever seen up to that time, which was to be directed at Cologne.

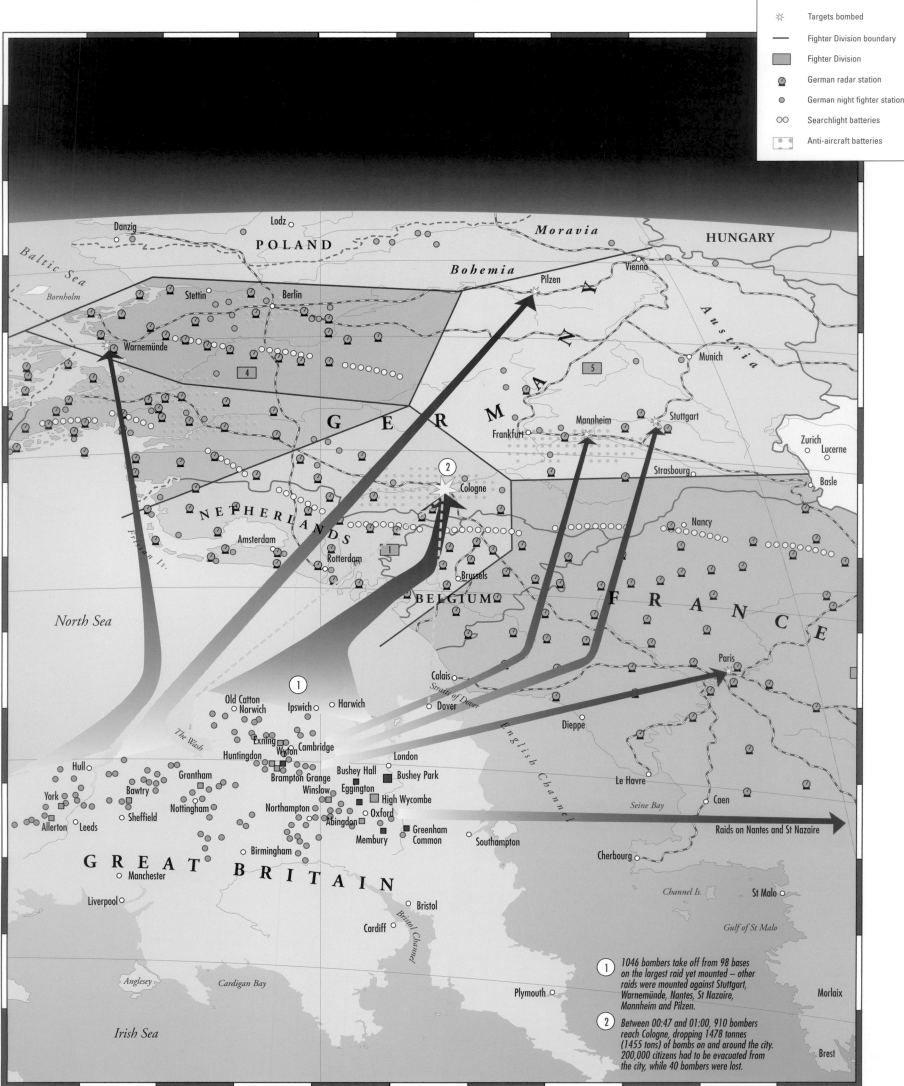

Thousand Bomber Raid
30/31 May 1942

- Main RAF night attacks
- Main Headquarters
- Group Headquarters
- Bomber Command airfields
- Targets bombed
- Fighter Division boundary
- Fighter Division
- German radar station
- German night fighter station
- Searchlight batteries
- Anti-aircraft batteries

1. 1046 bombers take off from 98 bases on the largest raid yet mounted – other raids were mounted against Stuttgart, Warnemünde, Nantes, St Nazaire, Mannheim and Pilzen.

2. Between 00:47 and 01:00, 910 bombers reach Cologne, dropping 1478 tonnes (1455 tons) of bombs on and around the city. 200,000 citizens had to be evacuated from the city, while 40 bombers were lost.

Strategic Bombing 1943

The Battle of Britain was the first major setback for Germany's armed forces. Even though the British were gravely weakened, they remained implacably opposed to Hitler and the Nazis, and would provide one of the springboards by which Germany would ultimately be defeated.

To ASSESS THE EFFECTIVENESS of the night bombing campaign, D.M. Butt of the War Cabinet Secretariat was asked to examine over 600 operational photos, comparing them with crew claims and Bomber Command assessments. The Butt Report, released in August 1941, was devastating. Many bombers were not finding the correct target – some were not even bombing the right towns. Over the vital Ruhr industrial area, which was often covered in haze, only one in ten bombers was hitting within eight kilometres (five miles) of the target. It would not be until the appointment of Air Marshal Arthur Harris to head Bomber Command in 1942 that the bomber campaign began to receive added impetus.

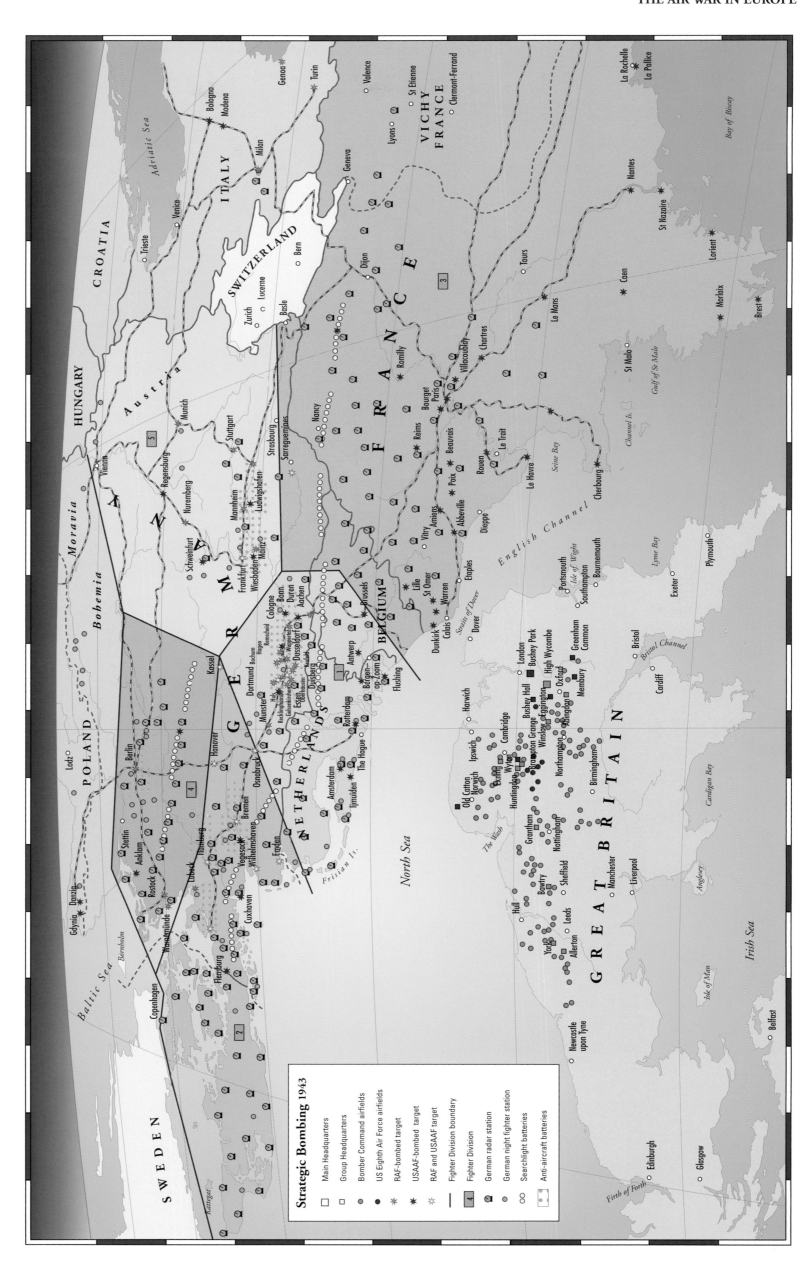

Strategic Bombing 1943

- □ Main Headquarters
- ▫ Group Headquarters
- ● Bomber Command airfields
- ● US Eighth Air Force airfields
- ✳ RAF-bombed target
- ✴ USAAF-bombed target
- ✳ RAF and USAAF target
- — Fighter Division boundary
- 4 Fighter Division
- German radar station
- German night fighter station
- ∞ Searchlight batteries
- Anti-aircraft batteries

31

Dambusters Raid
16/17 May 1943

Arthur Harris quickly revitalized RAF Bomber Command, and by 1943 he had built up a force of heavy Stirling, Halifax and Lancaster bombers. By the spring of 1943 he had been able to mount 43 heavy raids on Germany's key industrial area, the Ruhr.

IN MAY 1943 THE RAF MOUNTED a precision raid on the dams which provided the Ruhr with much of its power. Nineteen Lancasters of No. 617 Squadron, led by Wing Commander Guy Gibson and crewed by the cream of bomber command, practised delivering special 'bouncing' bombs at very low level. The bombs were designed to skip along the surface of the target lake, sinking to the bottom after hitting the dam before exploding. On the night of 16/17 May, 617 Squadron succeeded in breaching the Moehne and Eder Dams, though at considerable cost. Eight out of the 19 bombers were lost, along with their crews. The 'Dambusters Raid' was lauded as a triumph in Britain, and the bravery, skill and sacrifice of the bomber crews was unquestioned. However, the damage to the dams was not as serious as had been expected, and the Germans were able to effect repairs very quickly.

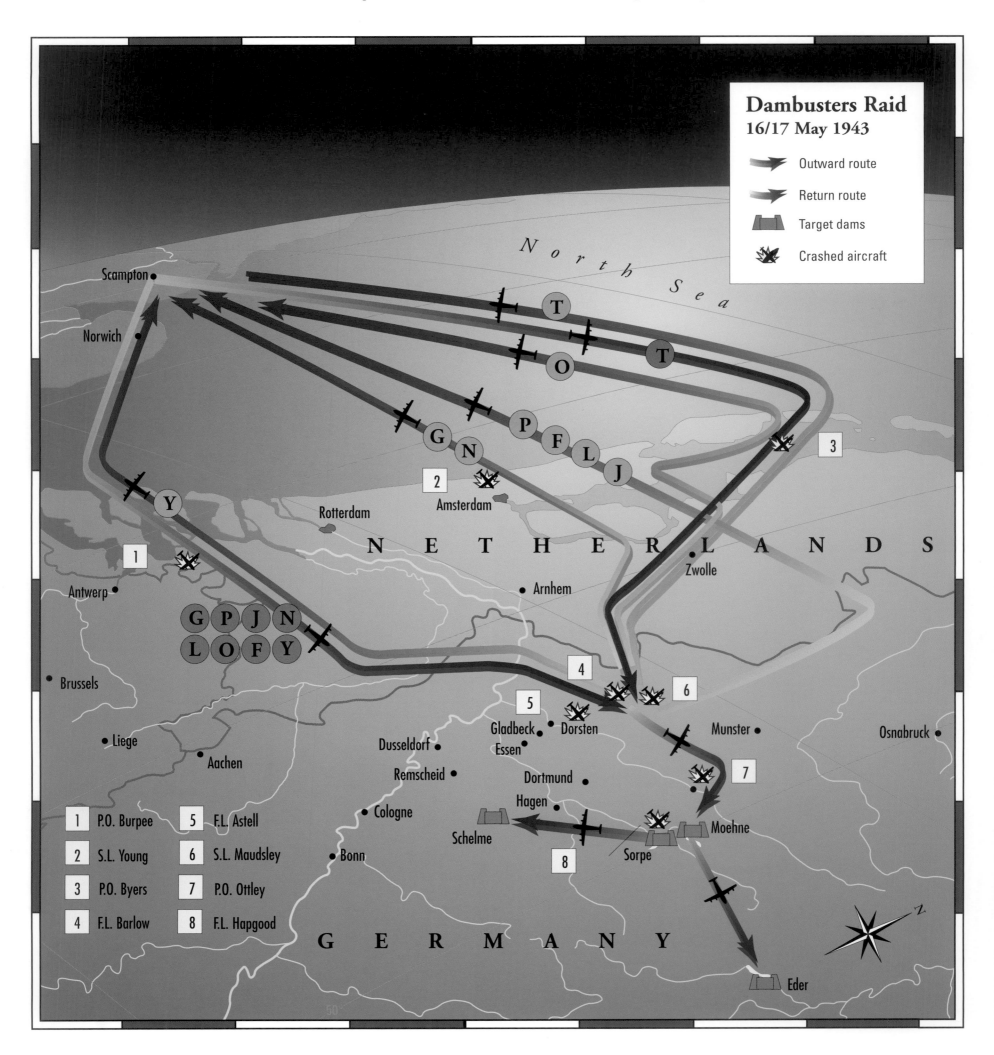

The Schweinfurt Raids 17 August 1943

By the summer of 1943, the B-17s and B-24s of the US Eighth Air Force had joined the strategic bombing campaign. The Americans concentrated on precision bombing by day, trusting to the heavy defensive armament of their bombers to see them through the German fighter and flak defences.

O N 17 AUGUST 1943 the US Eighth Air Force launched two major raids, one against German aircraft factories at Regensburg, and one against the vital ball-bearing factories at Schweinfurt. The first wave targeted at Regensburg were then to fly on to North Africa, diverting the *Luftwaffe* fighter defences from the incoming Schweinfurt raid. However, fog over Britain interfered with the timings of the American attack. The Schweinfurt raid was delayed, and some aircraft were recalled. Only 184 of the original 230 bombers pressed on into Germany, and by the time they arrived, the German fighters had had time to refuel and rearm. The tight American formations disintegrated under determined *Luftwaffe* attacks: only 380 tonnes (386 tons) of bombs were dropped on target. the 1st Combat Bomb Wing lost 36 aircraft, and 19 more returned with serious damage.

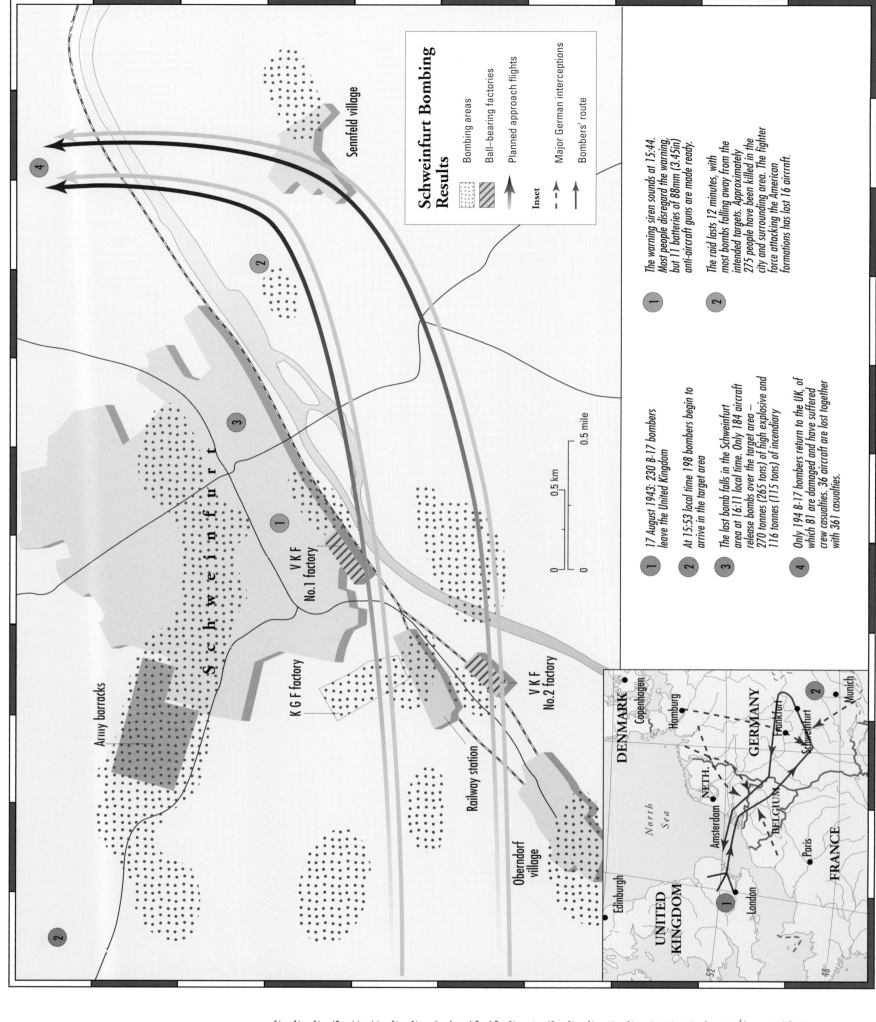

Schweinfurt Bombing Results

Legend:
- Bombing areas
- Ball-bearing factories
- Planned approach flights
- Major German interceptions
- Bombers' route

Inset:
- (dashed line) —
- (arrow) —

1 17 August 1943: 230 B-17 bombers leave the United Kingdom.

2 At 15:53 local time 198 bombers begin to arrive in the target area.

3 The last bomb falls in the Schweinfurt area at 16:11 local time. Only 184 aircraft release bombs over the target area – 270 tonnes (265 tons) of high explosive and 116 tonnes (115 tons) of incendiary.

4 Only 194 B-17 bombers return to the UK of which 81 are damaged and have suffered crew casualties. 36 aircraft are lost together with 361 casualties.

1 The warning siren sounds at 15:44. Most people disregard the warning, but 11 batteries of 88mm (3.45in) anti-aircraft guns are made ready.

2 The raid lasts 12 minutes, with most bombs falling away from the intended targets. Approximately 275 people have been killed in the city and surrounding area. The fighter force attacking the American formations has lost 16 aircraft.

Senfeld village

Schweinfurt

Army barracks

KGF factory

VKF No.1 factory

VKF No.2 factory

Railway station

Oberndorf village

0   0.5 km
0   0.5 mile

Inset map labels:
DENMARK
Copenhagen
Hamburg
GERMANY
NETH.
Amsterdam
Frankfurt
Schweinfurt
Munich
BELGIUM
North Sea
Paris
FRANCE
UNITED KINGDOM
Edinburgh
London

Battle of the Atlantic I
September 1939–May 1940

I N 1939 GERMANY'S U-BOAT SUPREMO, Admiral Karl Doenitz, had only 56 U-Boats in service, of which only 22 were ocean-going types. Initially, pickings for the U-Boat commanders were rich, as their boats sank merchantmen returning individually to the UK. Even when convoys were established, they could only be escorted through 15 degrees of longitude at either end of the transatlantic route due to a lack of suitable escorts. Even so, the U-Boats were little more than a nuisance – until the fall of France.

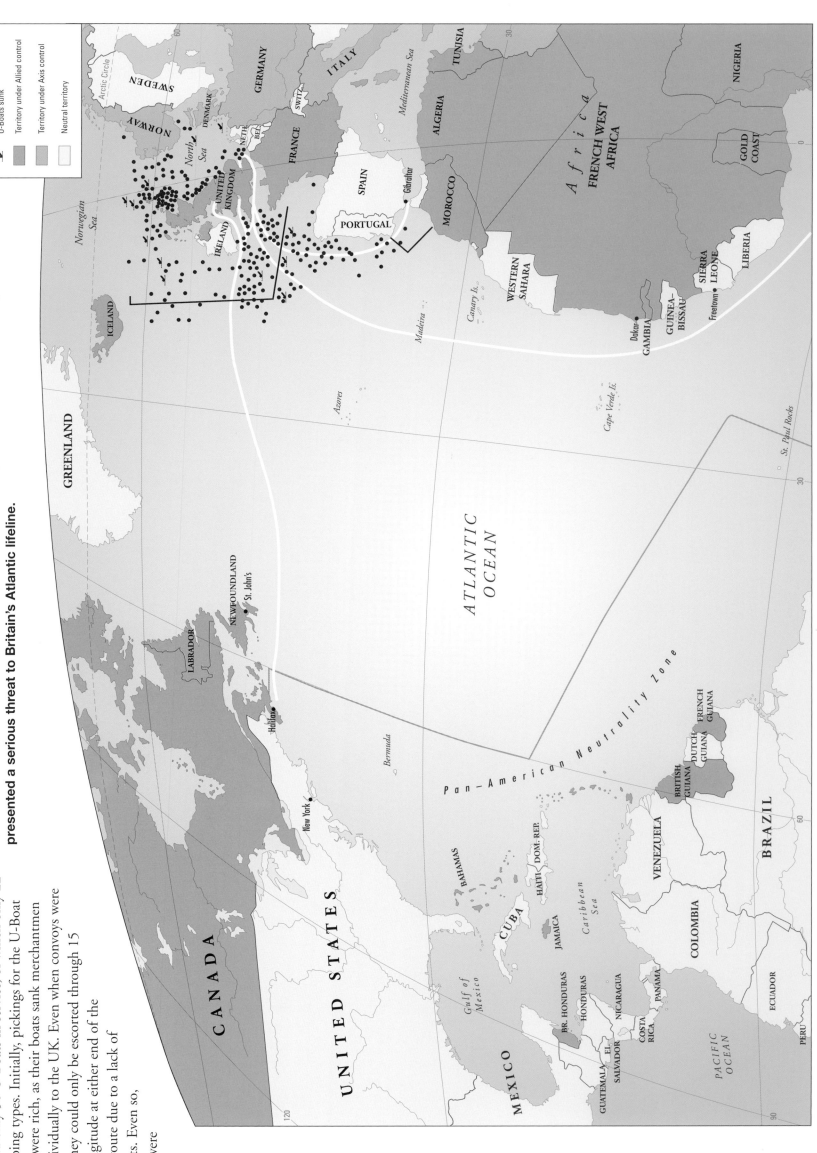

Battle of the Atlantic I
September 1939–May 1940

— Border of Pan-American Neutrality Zone (1939)
  Extent of air escort cover
— Major convoy routes
• Allied merchant ships sunk by U-Boats
• U-Boats sunk
  Territory under Allied control
  Territory under Axis control
  Neutral territory

The successful prosecution of Britain's war in Europe depended upon a steady flow of shipping reaching the United Kingdom from across the Atlantic and from the empire. The primary weapon employed by Germany in its attempts to strangle this flow was the U-Boat, though at the outbreak of war elements within the *Kriegsmarine*'s high command expected great things from surface raiders. However, although these achieved some successes, many were hunted down by the much larger Royal Navy. U-Boats, on the other hand, were much harder to find, and presented a serious threat to Britain's Atlantic lifeline.

Battle of the Atlantic II
June 1940–March 1941

T HE LESSONS OF 1917, when unrestricted U-Boat warfare had almost brought Britain to its knees, had been largely forgotten by the Royal Navy between the wars, though the British were quick to re-establish convoys in the face of the U-Boat threat. Even so, losses were heavy once the U-Boats began operating from French ports, reaching 1.6 million tonnes (1.57 million tons) between June and November 1940. The British were particularly unprepared for the German tactic of night-time surface attacks.

The capture of France and Norway in 1940 meant that Germany's U-Boats no longer had to make the long and dangerous transit up the North Sea and around the northern coasts of Britain to reach the main shipping lanes. Based in French Atlantic ports, the few boats available to the *Kriegsmarine* were able to wreak havoc in Britain's Western Approaches as well as in convoy attacks in mid-Atlantic and in attacks on British shipping off West Africa. So successful were the U-Boats that their commanders and crews were to remember this period as the 'Happy Time'.

Battle of the Atlantic II
June 1940–March 1941

- Pan-American Neutrality Zone
- Extent of air escort cover
- Extent of surface escort cover
- Major convoy routes
- Allied merchant ships sunk by U-Boats
- U-Boats sunk
- U-Boats
- Territory under Allied control
- Territory under Axis control
- Territory under Vichy government (unoccupied France)
- Neutral territory

Battle of the Atlantic III
April–December 1941

THE MAIN U-BOAT EFFORT moved from the Western Approaches out to the mid-Atlantic, beyond the range of Allied air patrols, aircraft being the biggest threat to any submarine. The introduction of Wolf Pack tactics, the use of multiple boats making coordinated attacks on a single convoy, also negated the effects of improved British convoy tactics. More long-range boats were entering service, and they found good hunting off West African coasts.

In 1941, the *Kriegsmarine* still had too few U-Boats to control the convoy routes. Improvements in British convoy tactics and the advent of a new type of escort, the corvette, made the U-Boat mission harder. The corvette was a simple design, which could be built quickly and in some numbers. Increasing Canadian strength and the decision by the United States to escort convoys out of their ports further strengthened the British position. The American decision involved the US Navy in a 'secret' shooting war, in which US escorts attacked if attacked by U-Boats. U-Boat tactics also developed, with the introduction of the 'Wolf Pack'.

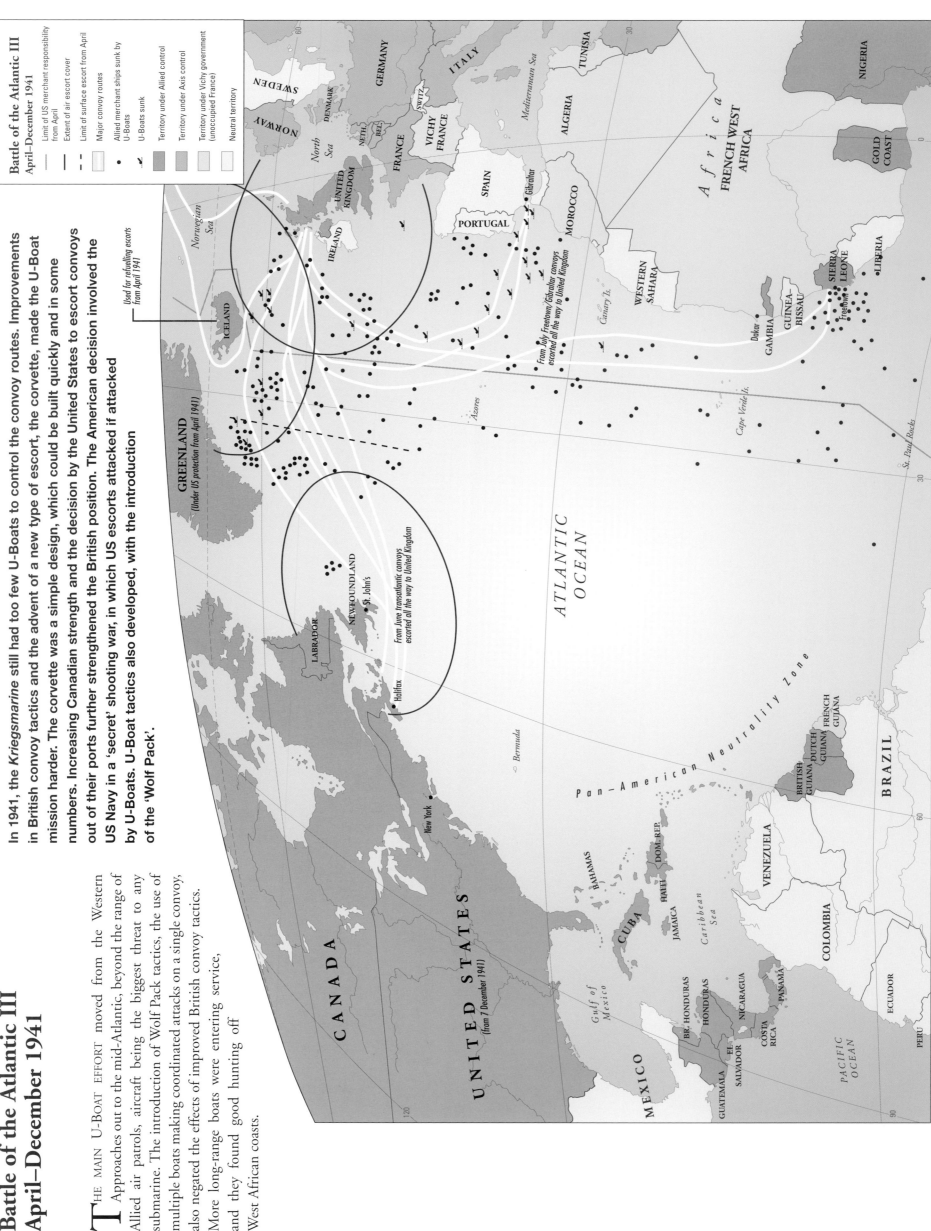

Battle of the Atlantic III
April–December 1941

— Limit of US merchant responsibility from April
— Extent of air escort cover
--- Limit of surface escort from April
— Major convoy routes
• Allied merchant ships sunk by U-Boats
• U-Boats sunk

Territory under Allied control
Territory under Allied control
Territory under Vichy government (unoccupied France)
Neutral territory

Battle of the Atlantic IV
January 1942–February 1943

IN JULY 1942 THE AMERICANS finally instituted a convoy system, so the U-Boats moved south to the Caribbean where they could strike at the vital oil supplies coming out of Maracaibo. As the US convoy system expanded to include these areas, the U-Boats prepared to move back to the shipping lanes of the North Atlantic. By now, the *Kriegsmarine* had more than 300 boats in service, and by November 1942 Allied shipping was being sunk at a rate of more than 700,000 tonnes (689,000 tons) per month.

America's entry into the war in December 1941 saw the *Kriegsmarine* extend its U-Boat operations to the American coast. The US Navy was slow to institute convoys, and the U-Boats had an easy time finding targets at night, silhouetted as they were by the bright lights of American cities. A general blackout would have cut losses, but was delayed by six months primarily due to opposition from the tourist trade! In the meantime, the U-Boats were wreaking havoc on America's coastal trade; so much so in fact that the German crews called this their second 'Happy Time'.

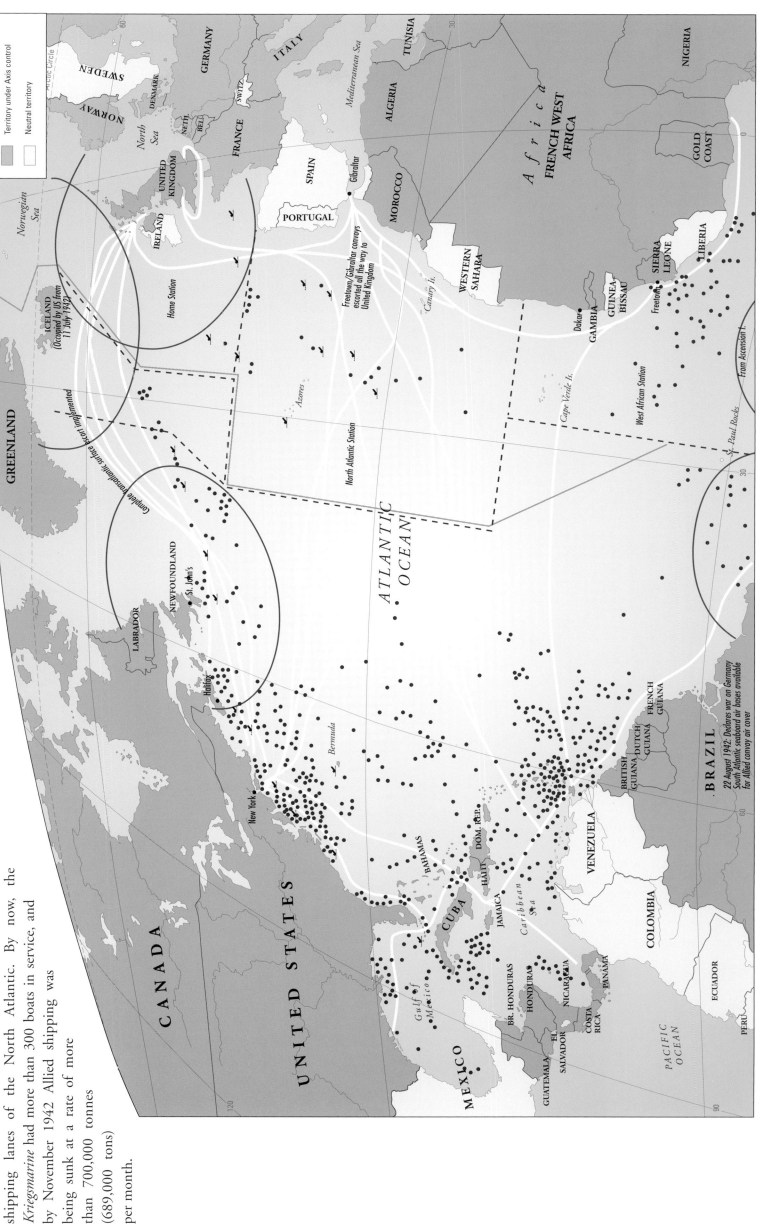

Battle of the Atlantic V
May–September 1943

Operating in mid-Atlantic again at the beginning of 1943, the U-Boats once more started sinking huge tonnages of Allied shipping. Combining in Wolf Packs of up to 50 boats, the German attackers could hit a convoy from all directions over a period of several days. In March 1943, they sank over half a million tonnes of shipping, but things were about to change. The pendulum of technological superiority was swinging decisively towards the Allies. Radar, long-range aircraft, more and better escorts, improved underwater weapons and new tactics meant that the U-Boat menace was about to be contained decisively and finally.

Between May and August 1943, 98 new U-Boats were commissioned – but 123 were lost in action. Each of those losses represented a trained crew perished or taken prisoner. By the end of 1943, the *Kriegsmarine* knew that the average U-Boat was unlikely to survive for more than three or four patrols, many being sunk by aircraft as they transited the Bay of Biscay. In 1943 the U-Boats sank 463 ships of more than 2.6 million tonnes (2.55 million tons): in 1944, though more than 400 boats were in commission, they sank only 132 ships totalling 770,000 tonnes (758,000 tons).

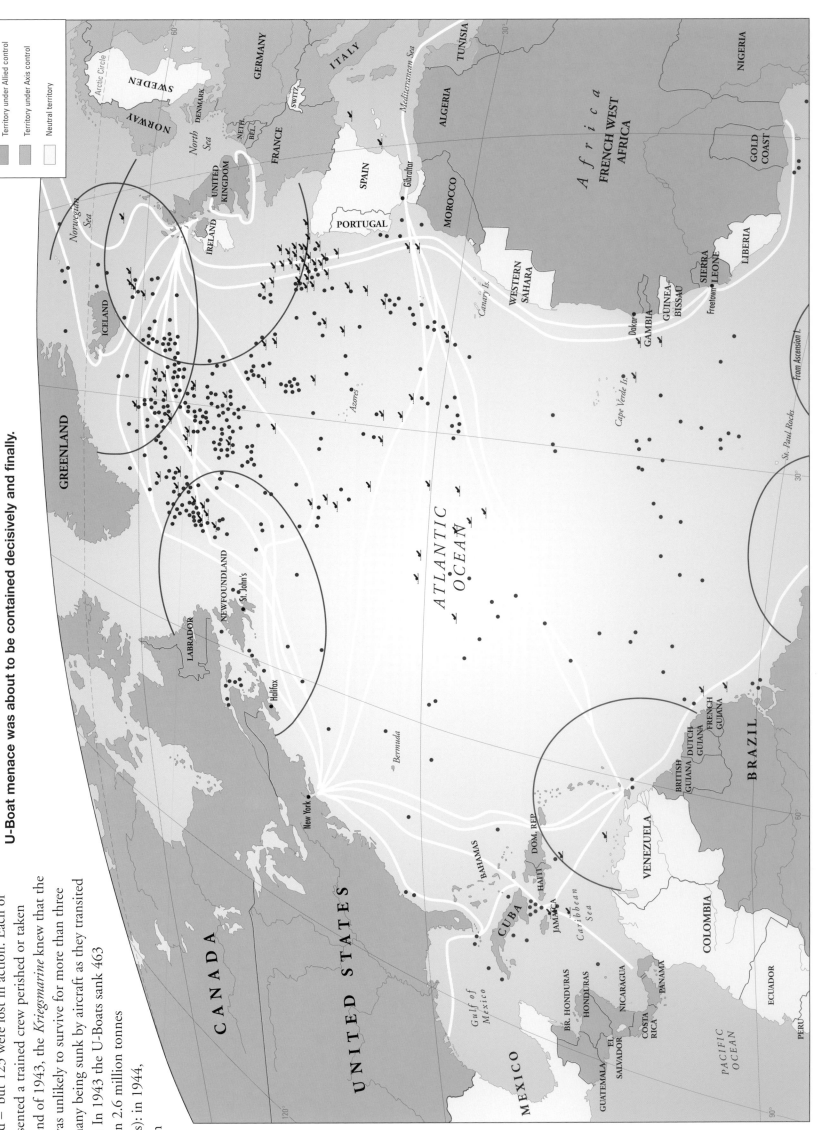

Campaign in East Africa
June 1940–November 1941

Italy entered the war in June 1940. In East Africa, where the Italians had a large if less than effective army in Ethiopia, they drove the tiny British garrison out of Somaliland. Fearing for the vital trade routes through the Red Sea, the British gathered a force of 100,000 Commonwealth and colonial troops which attacked Ethiopia and Italian Somaliland. The Italian forces, largely made up from unwilling local conscripts, were defeated in a matter of months.

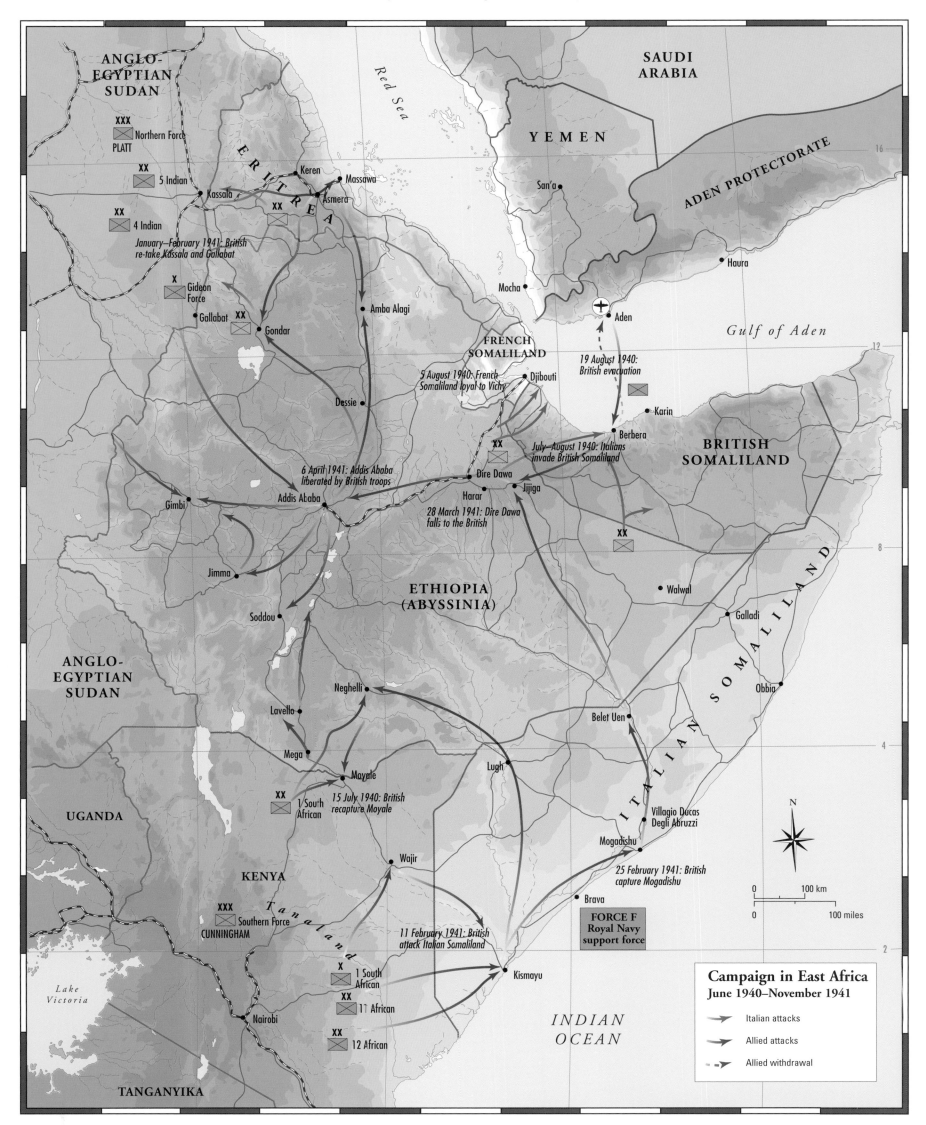

ANGLO-EGYPTIAN SUDAN

SAUDI ARABIA

Red Sea

YEMEN

ADEN PROTECTORATE

XXX Northern Force
PLATT

ERITREA

Keren
Massawa
XX 5 Indian
Kassala
Asmera

San'a

XX 4 Indian

January–February 1941: British re-take Kassala and Gallabat

X Gideon Force

Gallabat
XX Gondar

Amba Alagi

Haura

Mocha

Aden
✈

19 August 1940: British evacuation

Dessie

FRENCH SOMALILAND

5 August 1940: French Somaliland loyal to Vichy

Djibouti

Karin

Berbera

BRITISH SOMALILAND

July–August 1940: Italians invade British Somaliland

XX Dire Dawa
Harar
Jijiga

6 April 1941: Addis Ababa liberated by British troops

Gimbi
Addis Ababa

28 March 1941: Dire Dawa falls to the British

XX

Walwal

Jimma

ETHIOPIA (ABYSSINIA)

Galladi

Soddou

ANGLO-EGYPTIAN SUDAN

Obbia

Neghelli

Lavello

Belet Uen

ITALIAN SOMALILAND

Mega

Moyale

15 July 1940: British recapture Moyale

XX 1 South African

Lugh

Villagio Ducas Degli Abruzzi

Mogadishu

UGANDA

Wajir

N

25 February 1941: British capture Mogadishu

KENYA

Brava

FORCE F
Royal Navy
support force

Tanaland

XXX Southern Force
CUNNINGHAM

X 1 South African

11 February 1941: British attack Italian Somaliland

Kismayu

0   100 km
0   100 miles

Lake Victoria

XX 11 African

XX 12 African

Nairobi

INDIAN OCEAN

Campaign in East Africa
June 1940–November 1941

→ Italian attacks

→ Allied attacks

⇢ Allied withdrawal

TANGANYIKA

Gulf of Aden

Attack on Taranto
11 November 1940

The Italian Navy presented a major threat to British control of the Mediterranean. The Italian fleet included fast modern battleships, cruisers and destroyers as well as numerous older vessels which had undergone complete modernization. From their base at Taranto they could threaten British shipping lanes to the Middle East.

ONLY TIMID LEADERSHIP PREVENTED the Italian Navy from dominating the Mediterranean. Timid, however, was the last way in which the British commander, Admiral Cunningham, could be described. Operating aggressively as was his wont, he was determined to take the war to the heart of the Italian Navy by attacking its fleet base at Taranto. Cunningham's plan was made possible by the arrival in the Mediterranean of the fleet carrier HMS *Illustrious*. Probably the toughest carriers of their time, the vessels of this class could carry 45 aircraft.

On the night of 11/12 November, 1940 21 Fairey Swordfish torpedo bombers took off from the *Illustrious*. Launching their attack from a position 290km (180 miles) southeast of Taranto, the archaic biplanes attacked in two waves. Eleven were armed with torpedoes, six with bombs and four with bombs and flares. They achieved complete surprise, sinking the new battleship *Littorio* and seriously damaging the battleships *Conte di Cavour* and *Caio Duilio*. At a single blow and for the loss of just two aircraft, half of Italy's battlefleet had been put out of action. It was a blow from which the Italians never recovered.

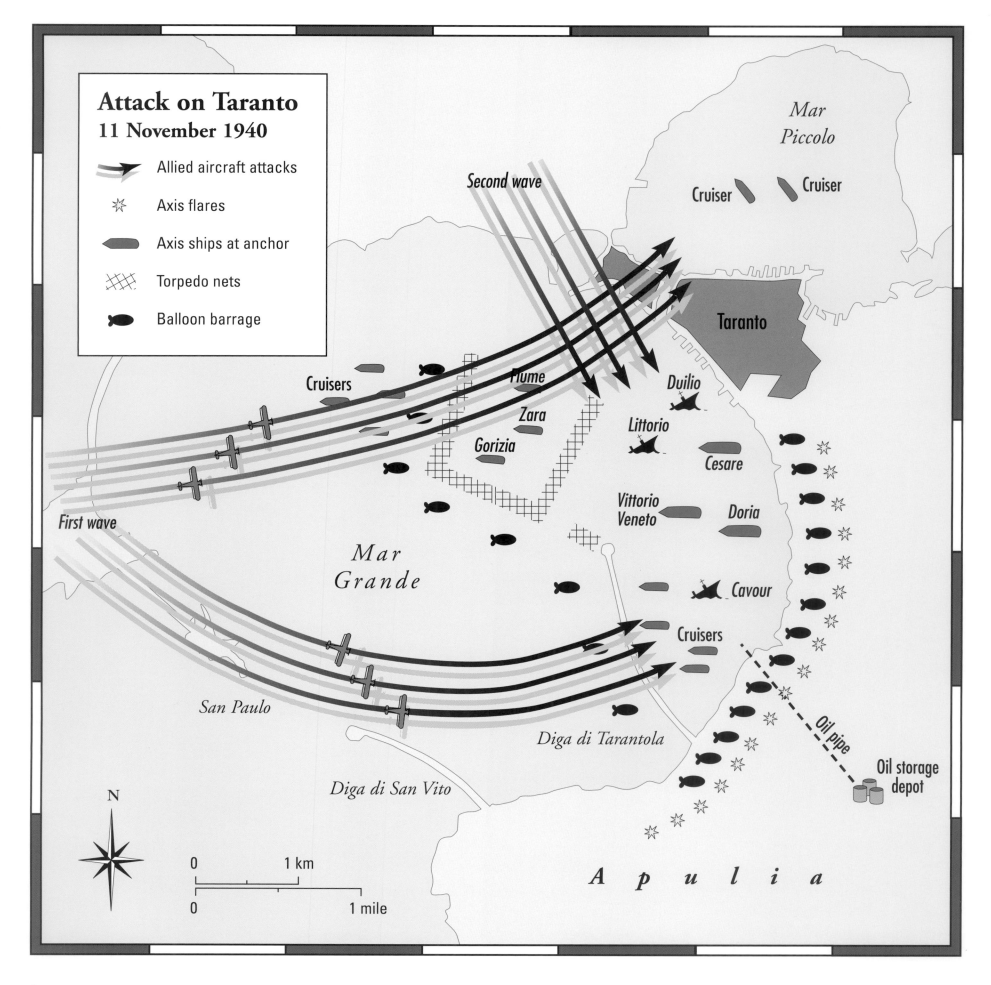

Attack on Taranto
11 November 1940

Allied aircraft attacks

Axis flares

Axis ships at anchor

Torpedo nets

Balloon barrage

Second wave

Mar Piccolo

Cruiser Cruiser

Taranto

Cruisers

Fiume

Duilio

Zara

Littorio

Gorizia

Cesare

Vittorio Veneto

Doria

First wave

Mar Grande

Cavour

Cruisers

San Paulo

Oil pipe

Diga di Tarantola

Oil storage depot

Diga di San Vito

N

0   1 km

0   1 mile

A p u l i a

Operation Compass
9 December 1940–February 1941

Although the Italian Tenth Army outnumbered the British Desert Force by six to one, its advance into Egypt was tentative and came to a halt in a series of defensive lines south of Sidi Barrani. The British launched a counter-attack on 9 December 1940. Operation Compass was intended to be a five -day raid' but it caught the Italians completely by surprise. The British Matilda infantry tanks were impervious to Italian anti-tank guns, and soon the Italians were running. Over the next two months, the British under General Richard O'Connor advanced 805km (500 miles), destroying the Italian Tenth Army and capturing 130,000 prisoners – including seven generals. They had captured Bardia, Tobruk, Derna, Barce and Benghazi and had come to rest, exhausted, at El Agheila.

When Italy declared war on the British in the summer of 1940, Mussolini confidently expected the large Italian force in Libya to overrun the relatively small British force in Egypt. At a stroke, he would seize the vital shipping route through the Suez Canal and would threaten further attacks on the vital oilfields of the Middle East. Unfortunately, his army was not up to the job.

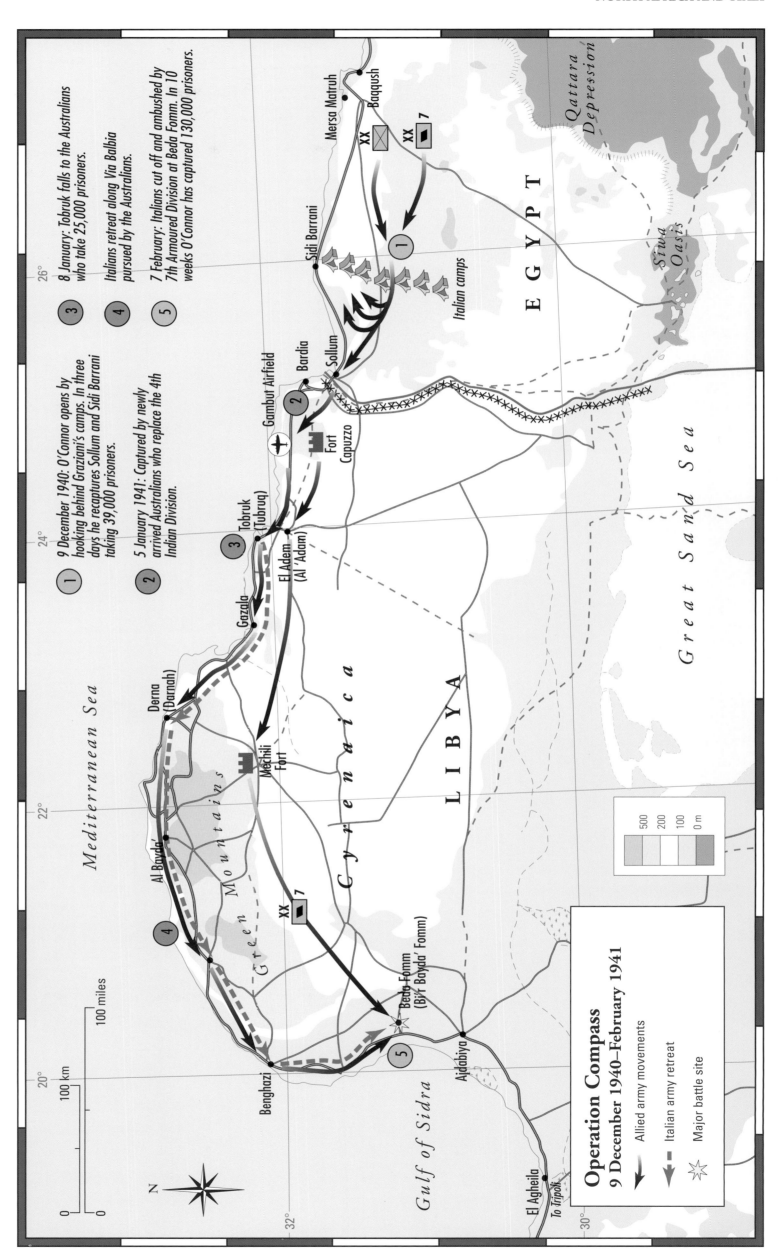

1. 9 December 1940: O'Connor opens by hooking behind Graziani's camps. In three days he recaptures Sollum and Sidi Barrani taking 39,000 prisoners.

2. 5 January 1941: Captured by newly arrived Australians who replace the 4th Indian Division.

3. 8 January: Tobruk falls to the Australians who take 25,000 prisoners.

4. Italians retreat along Via Balbia pursued by the Australians.

5. 7 February: Italians cut off and ambushed by 7th Armoured Division at Beda Fomm. In 10 weeks O'Connor has captured 130,000 prisoners.

Operation Compass
9 December 1940–February 1941

→ Allied army movements
⇢ Italian army retreat
✷ Major battle site

41

Battle of Matapan
28–29 March 1941

In March 1941, Germany was about to invade the Balkans. To block any British attempt to interfere in the region, the Germans insisted that the Italian fleet should intervene, stopping the flow of British and Commonwealth troops from North Africa to Greece. On the evening of 26 March, the Italian Navy sent the powerful battleship *Vittorio Veneto* from Naples, accompanied by three cruisers and three destroyers. They were joined at sea by other fleet units, including three Zara class heavy cruisers sailing from Taranto.

I
N A CONFUSED SERIES OF ACTIONS off the southern tip of Greece, the Italian force came under attack from British carrier-based aircraft. *Vittorio Veneto* was hit by a torpedo and slightly damaged; the heavy cruiser *Pola* was hit amidships and left dead in the water. The Italian commander, Admiral Iachino, turned for home. He sent the cruisers *Fiume, Zara* and four destroyers to *Pola's* rescue, since he thought that British cruisers might make a night attack. What he did not know was that the British battlefleet – four battleships, one aircraft carrier, and nine destroyers – was less than 120km (75 miles) away, and was approaching rapidly. It was a very dark night as the British battleships, which had located the Italian cruisers by radar, slipped to within point-blank range. Opening fire at a range of under 3500m (3828 yards), eight-gun salvos of 15in (381mm) fire ripped the unsuspecting Italian ships apart within five minutes. The unfortunate *Pola*, still drifting without power, was sunk by torpedoes four hours later.

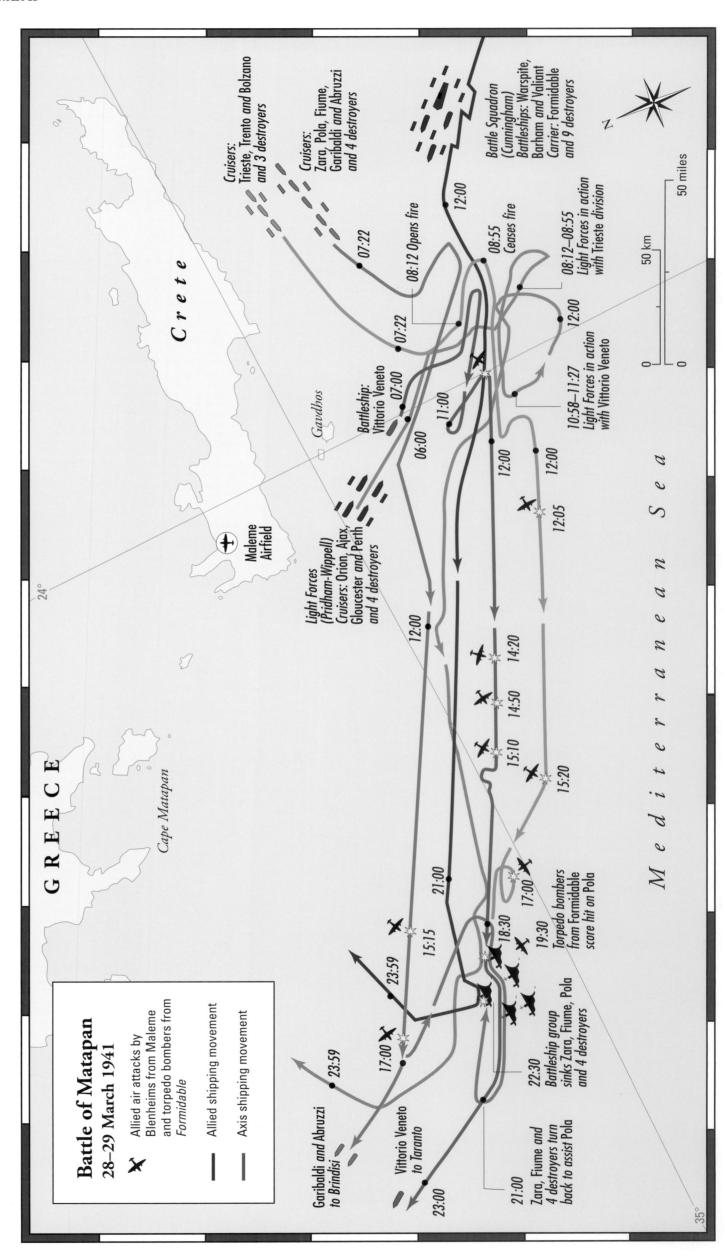

Battle of Matapan
28–29 March 1941

✈ Allied air attacks by Blenheims from Maleme and torpedo bombers from *Formidable*

— Allied shipping movement

— Axis shipping movement

GREECE

Cape Matapan

Crete

Gavdhos

⊕ Maleme Airfield

Mediterranean Sea

Cruisers: Trieste, Trento and Bolzano and 3 destroyers

Cruisers: Zara, Pola, Fiume, Garibaldi and Abruzzi and 4 destroyers

Battle Squadron (Cunningham) Battleships: Warspite, Barham and Valiant Carrier: Formidable and 9 destroyers

07:22

08:12 Opens fire

12:00

08:55 Ceases fire

07:22

08:12–08:55 Light Forces in action with Trieste division

Battleship: Vittorio Veneto

07:00

11:00

12:00

10:58–11:27 Light Forces in action with Vittorio Veneto

06:00

12:00

12:00

Light Forces (Pridham-Wippell) Cruisers: Orion, Ajax, Gloucester and Perth and 4 destroyers

12:00

14:20

14:50

12:05

15:10

15:20

21:00

17:00

18:30

19:30

Torpedo bombers from Formidable score hit on Pola

15:15

23:59

17:00

23:59

22:30 Battleship group sinks Zara, Fiume, Pola and 4 destroyers

Garibaldi and Abruzzi to Brindisi

Vittorio Veneto to Taranto

21:00 Zara, Fiume and 4 destroyers turn back to assist Pola

23:00

50 km

50 miles

24°

35°

N

The Balkans
6–23 April 1941

The *Wehrmacht* had no plans to invade the Balkans, but Italy's ill-advised attack on Greece had come unstuck, and Hitler had to send troops to help his fellow dictator. The Germans forced the Yugoslav government to allow is forces transit, but when the Yugoslav regime was overthrown by an anti-German uprising, plans for the *Wehrmacht* to pass through Yugoslavia on its way to Greece became a full-scale invasion and conquest of the country.

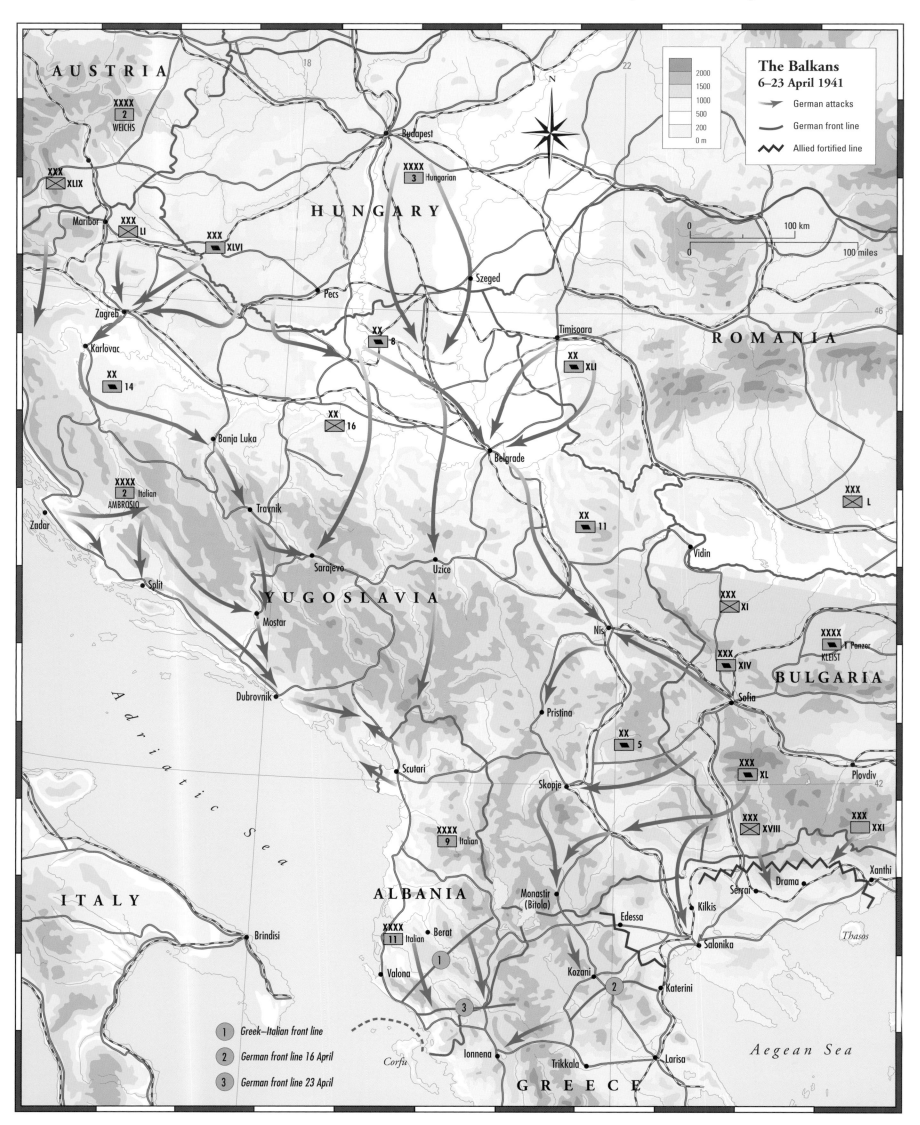

The Balkans
6–23 April 1941

2000		
1500		
1000		
500		
200		
0 m		

⟶ German attacks

⌒ German front line

〜 Allied fortified line

① Greek–Italian front line
② German front line 16 April
③ German front line 23 April

The Conquest of Greece and Crete 6–28 April 1941

After the lightning victory in Yugoslavia, the Germans moved on to Greece. They attacked the Metaxas Line from Bulgaria, while mobile troops pressed southwards through Yugoslavia. The Greeks could do nothing to stop the Germans, and their British allies were forced to evacuate what forces they could to Crete. A month later, the Germans mounted the world's first full-scale airborne assault and captured the island, suffering heavy casualties in the process.

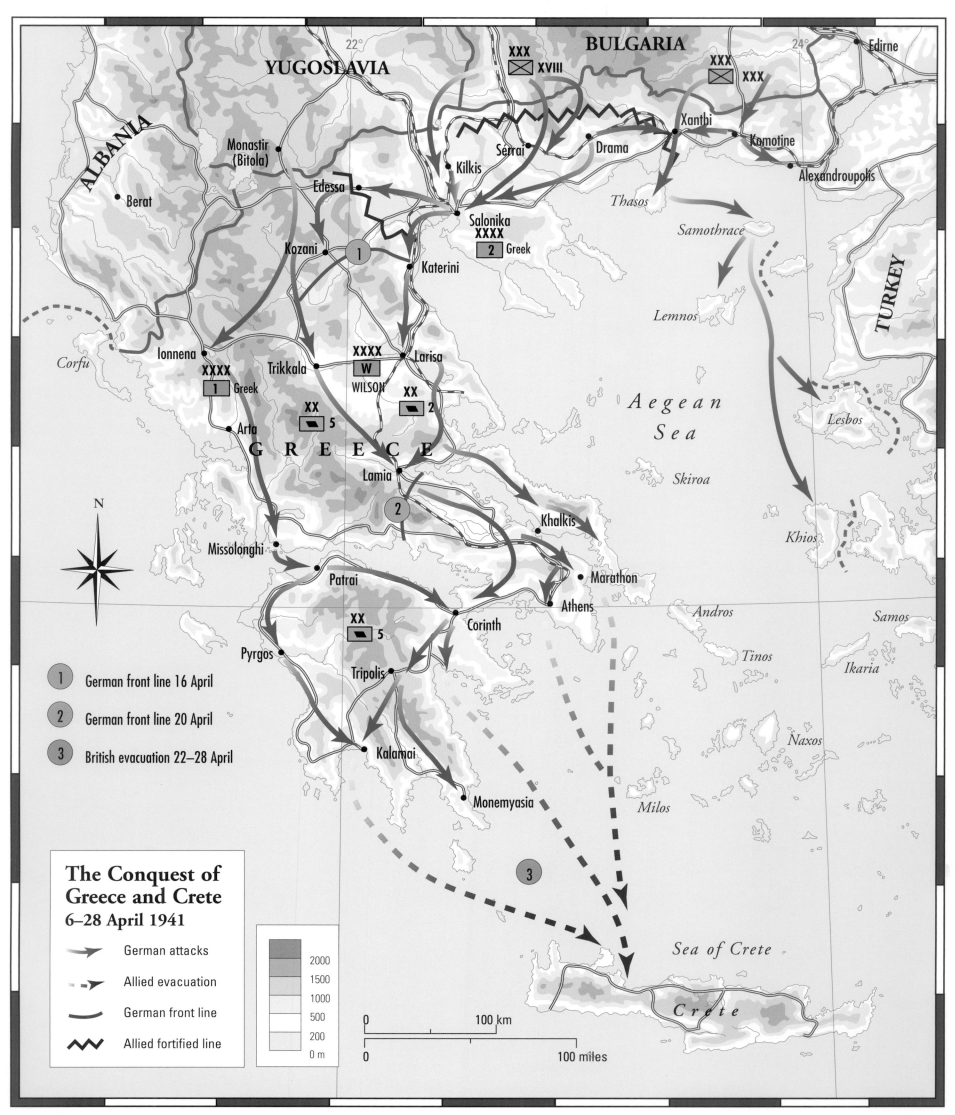

The Conquest of
Greece and Crete
6–28 April 1941

1 German front line 16 April

2 German front line 20 April

3 British evacuation 22–28 April

The Conquest of
Greece and Crete
6–28 April 1941

→ German attacks

⇢ Allied evacuation

— German front line

〰 Allied fortified line

2000
1500
1000
500
200
0 m

0   100 km

0   100 miles

Operation Sonnenblume
April 1941

The Italian disasters in North Africa again forced Hitler to send help to Mussolini's forces. Early in 1941 the *Wehrmacht* sent a force to Tunisia under the command of General Erwin Rommel. The Afrika Korps arrived when the British had been weakened after sending troops to reinforce Greece. Rommel saw this as an opportunity to launch an attack.

EAKENED BY THEIR EFFORTS OF THE PREVIOUS MONTHS, the British were in no state to resist when Rommel launched Operation Sonnenblume. Catching the Desert Force by surprise, Rommel showed how quickly he had mastered desert warfare by sending the 5th Light Division across the desert to try to cut off the British retreat. The Germans were unable to move fast enough to capture the key port of Tobruk, but they did send the Commonwealth forces into headlong retreat – in the process capturing General O'Connor. Rommel was now at the end of a long supply line, with tired troops and worn-out equipment, so he settled on the Egyptian border to prepare for a new attack.

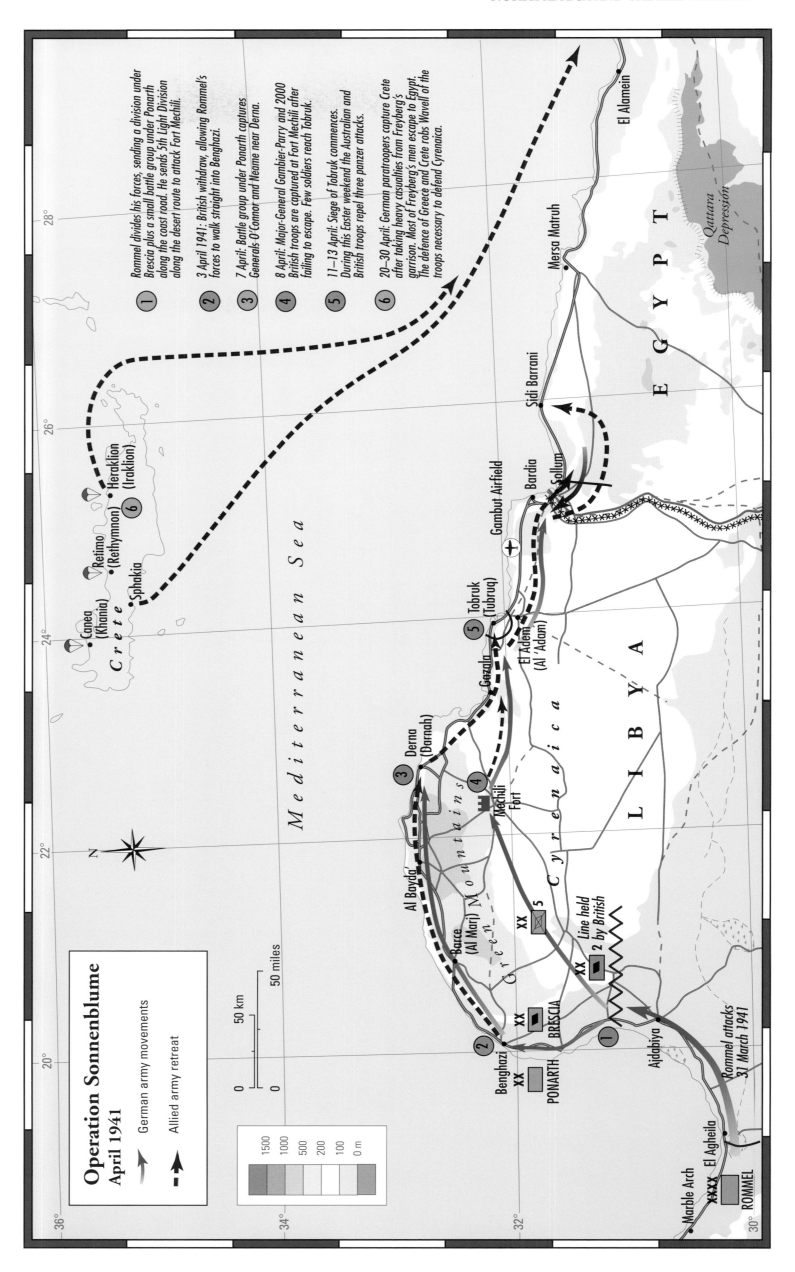

1. *Rommel divides his forces, sending a division under Brescia plus a small battle group under Ponarth along the coast road. He sends 5th Light Division along the desert route to attack Fort Mechili.*

2. *3 April 1941: British withdraw, allowing Rommel's forces to walk straight into Benghazi.*

3. *7 April: Battle group under Ponarth and Neame near Derna.*

4. *8 April: Major-General Gambier-Parry and 2000 British troops are captured at Fort Mechili after failing to escape. Few soldiers reach Tobruk.*

5. *11–13 April: Siege of Tobruk commences. During this Easter weekend the Australian and British troops repel three panzer attacks.*

6. *20–30 April: German paratroopers capture Crete after taking heavy casualties from Freyberg's garrison. Most of Freyberg's men escape to Egypt. The defence of Greece and Crete robs Wavell of the troops necessary to defend Cyrenaica.*

Operation Sonnenblume
April 1941

→ German army movements

→ Allied army retreat

50 miles

50 km

1500 1000 500 200 100 0 m

Iraq, Syria and Persia
April–September 1941

In May 1941, the Germans instigated an uprising in Iraq led by Rashid Ali, the Iraqi prime minister. The Germans provided supplies and munitions, and set up an air base at Mosul, in the north of the country. A small British relief column advanced from Palestine, and more reinforcements were sent from India. Taking the offensive, the British bombed the air base at Mosul, and a ground column advanced on Baghdad, taking the city on 30 May.

T O FURTHER ADD TO THEIR TROUBLES, the British also had to deal with the threat from 35,000 German-advised Vichy French troops in Syria. Wavell managed to scrape together another 20,000 troops who invaded Syria from Iraq and Palestine on 8 June. The British forces included Arab and Jewish units, as well as a contingent of Free French under General Georges Catroux. Damascus was captured on 21 June, and the Vichy forces surrendered on 12 July.

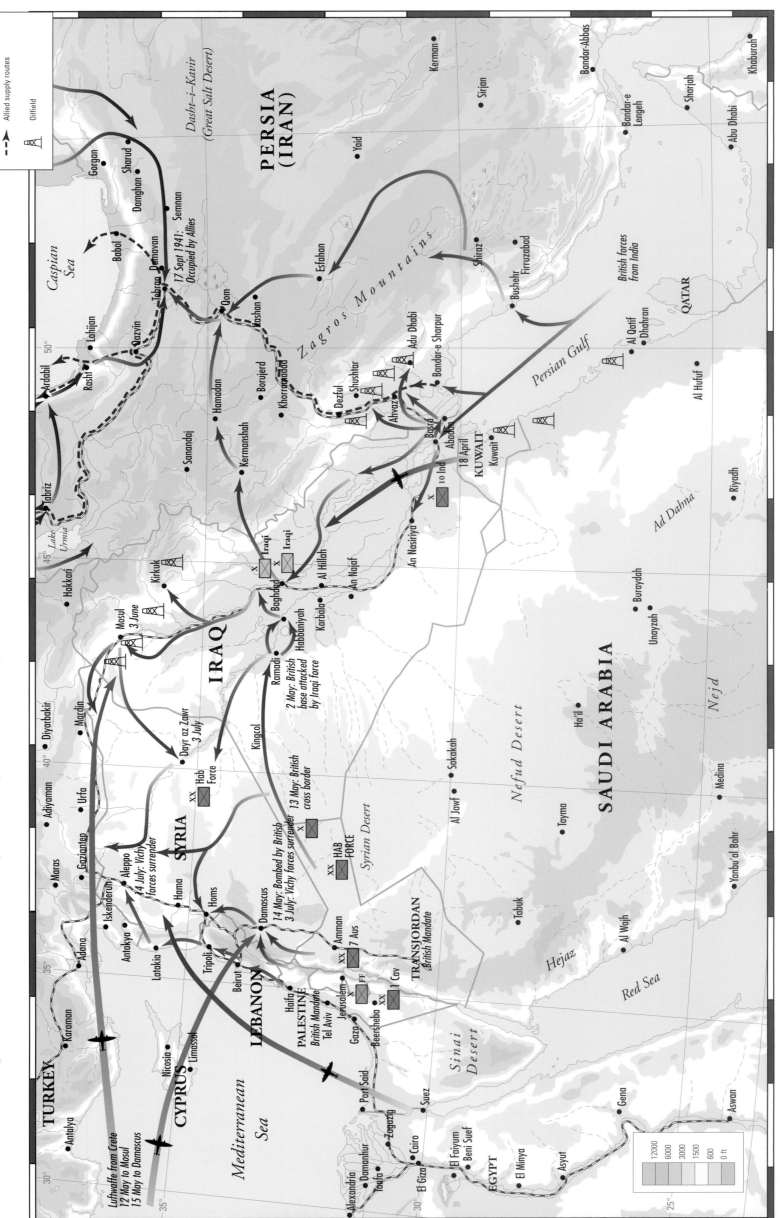

Operation Crusader
November–December 1941

On 18 November 1941, the British Eighth Army under General Alan Cunningham launched Operation Crusader. This campaign was designed to take advantage of Rommel's logistical problems. The attack was expected to force the Germans back from their positions along the Egyptian border, going on to relieve the besieged defenders of the port of Tobruk, about 140km (87 miles) further along the coast.

Wᴴɪʟᴇ Bʀɪᴛɪsʜ ɪɴꜰᴀɴᴛʀʏ ᴀᴛᴛᴀᴄᴋᴇᴅ ᴛʜᴇ ᴄᴇɴᴛʀᴇ of the German line, pinning them in place, Eighth Army tanks swept southwards around the Germans. Catching the *Afrika Korps* by surprise, the British captured Rommel's headquarters at Gambut Airfield, and pushed on to within 20km (12 miles) of Tobruk. What followed was a series of confused engagements around Bir el Gubi and Sidi Rezegh (see page 48), during which a German counter-attack almost split the British forces in two. By early December, Rommel realized that there was a real danger that his supply lines might be cut, and he had no choice but to retreat. By now he had less than 60 operational tanks, and after a brief engagement at Gazala he withdrew completely from Cyrenaica.

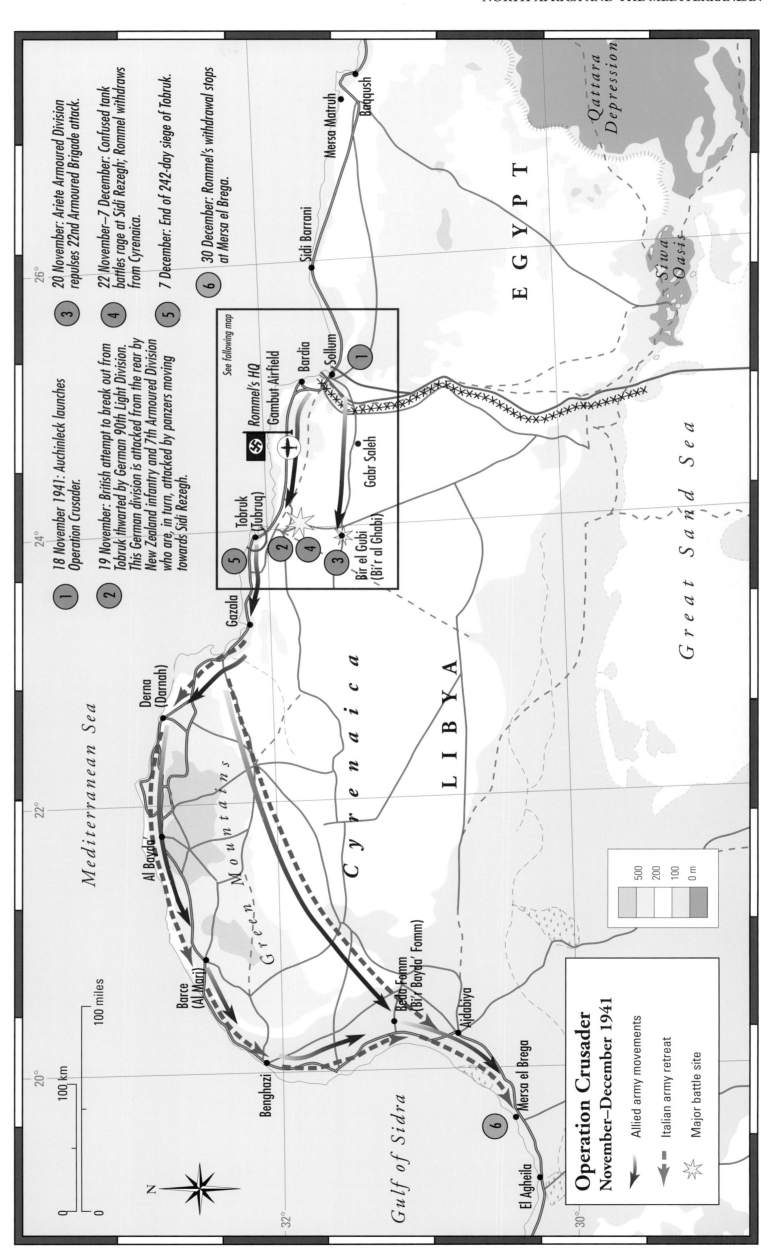

1. 18 November 1941: Auchinleck launches Operation Crusader.

2. 19 November: British attempt to break out from Tobruk thwarted by German 90th Light Division. This German division is attacked from the rear by New Zealand infantry and 7th Armoured Division who are, in turn, attacked by panzers moving towards Sidi Rezegh.

3. 20 November: Ariete Armoured Division repulses 22nd Armoured Brigade attack.

4. 22 November–7 December: Confused tank battles rage at Sidi Rezegh; Rommel withdraws from Cyrenaica.

5. 7 December: End of 242-day siege of Tobruk.

6. 30 December: Rommel's withdrawal stops at Mersa el Brega.

Operation Crusader
November–December 1941

➤ Allied army movements
⇢ Italian army retreat
✶ Major battle site

Operation Crusader – Battle of Sidi Rezegh 18 November–7 December 1941

R OMMEL PROVED HE COULD FIGHT a defensive battle when necessary at Sidi Rezegh. Using their powerful 8.8cm (3.465in) Flak guns in the anti-tank role, German troops halted the advance of the 7th Armoured Brigade. At the same time, the Italian Ariete Division was swung southwards, where it forced the 22nd Armoured Brigade to a halt. While the British waited for reinforcements, Rommel made a bid for victory by mounting a dash for Halfaya Pass, which stunned the British. Low on fuel and supplies, Rommel struck back eastwards towards Tobruk, recapturing Sidi Rezegh. The British stood firm, however, and General Auchinleck, the British commander in chief, ordered a further attack westwards to cut off Rommel's forces. As a result, Rommel, the 'Desert Fox', had to withdraw to Gazala.

The key phase of Operation Crusader was the swirling, confusing fight around the town of Sidi Rezegh. The advancing British 7th Armoured Brigade had taken the town on 20 November 1941. Further to the south, the 22nd Armoured Brigade swept round as far as Bir el Gubi, threatening to outflank the entire German position. However, poor British armoured tactics gave Rommel the chance to extract his troops.

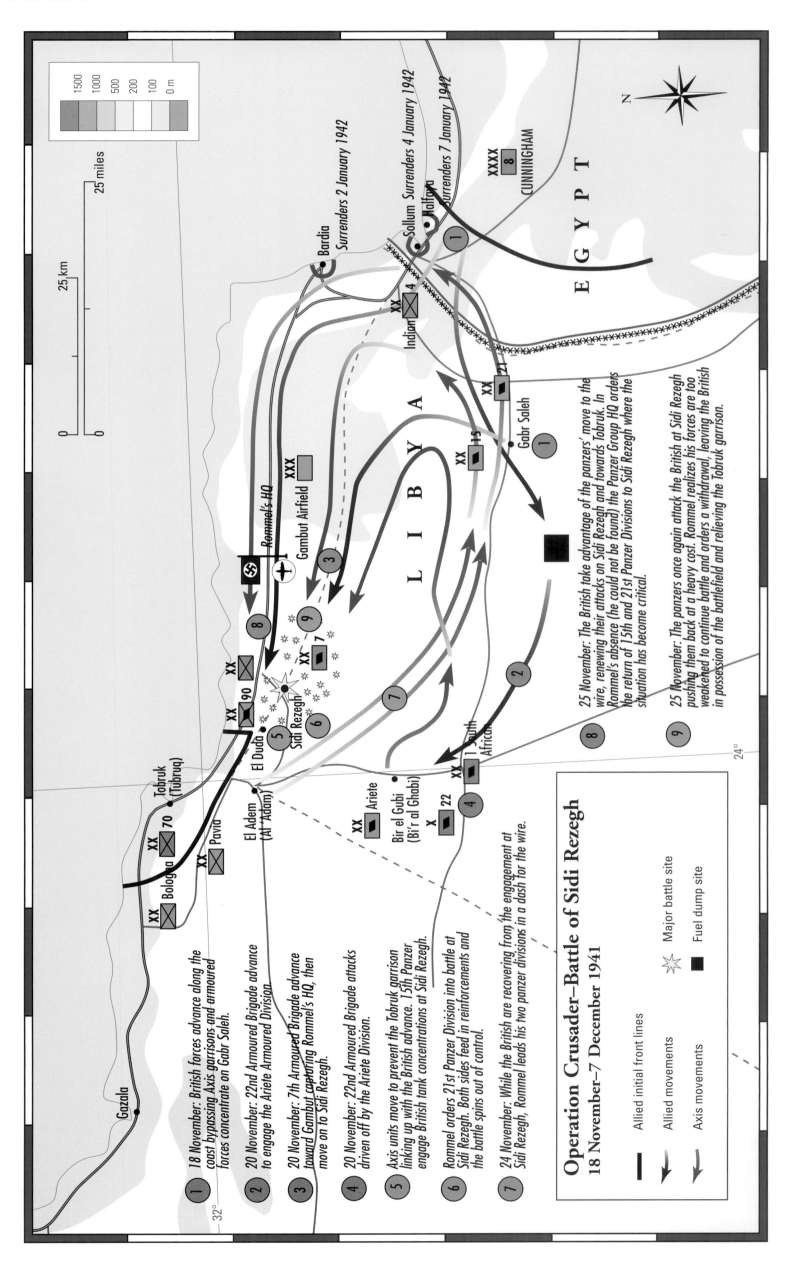

Operation Crusader–Battle of Sidi Rezegh 18 November–7 December 1941

1 18 November: British forces advance along the coast bypassing Axis garrisons and armoured forces concentrate on Gabr Saleh.

2 20 November: 22nd Armoured Brigade advance to engage the Ariete Armoured Division

3 20 November: 7th Armoured Brigade advance toward Gambut capturing Rommel's HQ, then move on to Sidi Rezegh.

4 20 November: 22nd Armoured Brigade attacks driven off by the Ariete Division.

5 Axis units move to prevent the Tobruk garrison linking up with the British advance. 15th Panzer engage British tank concentrations at Sidi Rezegh.

6 Rommel orders 21st Panzer Division into battle at Sidi Rezegh. Both sides feed in reinforcements and the battle spins out of control.

7 24 November: While the British are recovering from the engagement at Sidi Rezegh, Rommel leads his two panzer divisions in a dash for the wire.

8 25 November: The British take advantage of the panzers' move to the wire, renewing their attacks on Sidi Rezegh and towards Tobruk. In Rommel's absence (he could not be found) the Panzer Group HQ orders the return of 15th and 21st Panzer Divisions to Sidi Rezegh where the situation has become critical.

9 25 November: The panzers once again attack the British at Sidi Rezegh pushing them back at a heavy cost. Rommel realizes his forces are too weakened to continue battle and orders a withdrawal, leaving the British in possession of the battlefield and relieving the Tobruk garrison.

Allied initial front lines

Allied movements

Axis movements

☆ Major battle site

■ Fuel dump site

Rommel Returns
January 1942

Although the war in North Africa seemed to have turned against the *Afrika Korps*, Rommel realized that the British position had weakened at the end of long supply lines. On 21 January 1942, Rommel launched a new attack from his positions around El Agheila, driving the British 1st Armoured Division from its positions around Ajdabiya. The British were again retreating with Rommel in pursuit.

NEAR MSUS, ROMMEL swung his forces northeast, striking out through rough but undefended terrain to try to reach Benghazi and cut off the retreating Commonwealth forces. Though the Germans reached the coast on 28 January, the British managed to smash through the lead elements of the *Afrika Korps* and continued their retreat eastwards. Meanwhile, Rommel was forced to stop his advance while his troops were resupplied. At this point, a faction in the German high command felt that now was the time to take Malta, which had been the main base from which the Allies had been strangling the Axis logistics effort. Rommel, however, was set on continuing his advance, aimed at seizing the port of Tobruk. The British used the pause to retreat to prepared positions around Gazala.

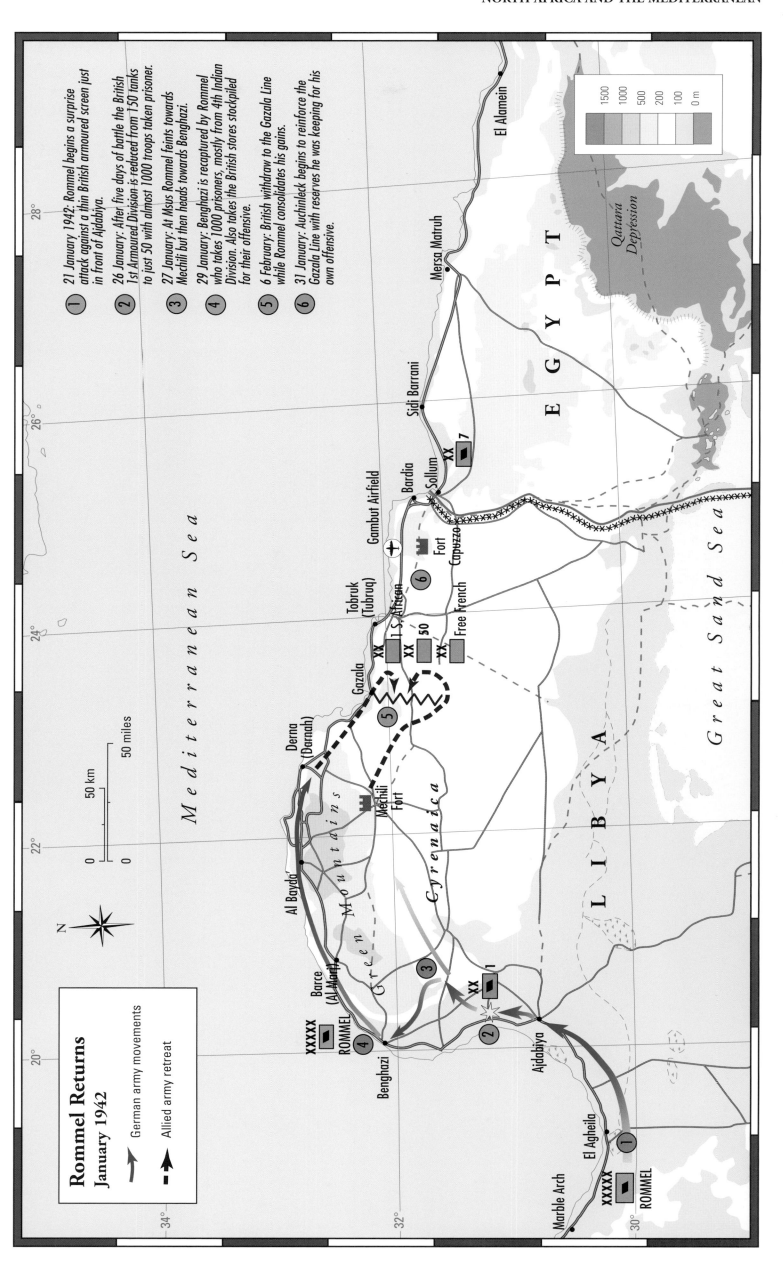

1. 21 January 1942: Rommel begins a surprise attack against a thin British armoured screen just in front of Ajdabiya.

2. 26 January: After five days of battle the British 1st Armoured Division is reduced from 150 tanks to just 50 with almost 1000 troops taken prisoner.

3. 27 January: At Msus Rommel feints towards Mechili but then heads towards Benghazi.

4. 29 January: Benghazi is recaptured by Rommel who takes 1000 prisoners, mostly from 4th Indian Division. Also takes the British stores stockpiled for their offensive.

5. 6 February: British withdraw to the Gazala Line while Rommel consolidates his gains.

6. 31 January: Auchinleck begins to reinforce the Gazala Line with reserves he was keeping for his own offensive.

Rommel Returns
January 1942

→ German army movements

▪▪▪➤ Allied army retreat

Gazala and the loss of Tobruk
May–June 1942

R OMMEL PRE-EMPTED A POSSIBLE BRITISH attack out of Gazala on 26 May 1942, by launching his own attack first. After a feint to the north, Axis mobile forces swung south around deep minefields and the tough French-held position at Bir Hacheim. After a clash near Bir el Gubi, Rommel pressed on, shrugging off a series of disorganized British assaults.

Pressing forward on 13 June, the Axis forces inflicted heavy casualties on Commonwealth troops south of El Adem, before pushing the British further east past Sidi Rezegh. With only 70 tanks left, the British continued to retreat while Rommel turned back to smash through the defences of Tobruk and take the port.

In the spring of 1942, Rommel decided that the time was ripe for *Panzerarmee Afrika* to finally take Tobruk. Seizure of the British bastion would remove a constant thorn in the side of the Axis forces, and capture of its port facilities promised to alleviate constant German and Italian supply problems, making a further attack on Egypt much more practical. However, the attack was risky as the British occupied strong defensive positions at Gazala.

1. 26 May, 16:00: Offensive starts, General Cruwell feints in the north with mainly Italian divisions.

2. 26–27 May: Rommel's real attack. His armour hooks around the Free French at Bir Hacheim.

3. 2 June: 150th Brigade falls, 3000 prisoners taken.

4. 10 June: After two weeks of siege, Koenig's Free French brigade withdraws from Bir Hacheim box.

5. 14 June: British 50th Division escapes by first heading west and then south-west breaking through Axis lines.

6. 14 June: Scots Guards and South African anti-tank gunners suffer heavy casualties delaying German advance.

7. 21 June: Rommel smashes through Tobruk perimeter and the port is captured with 35,000 prisoners taken.

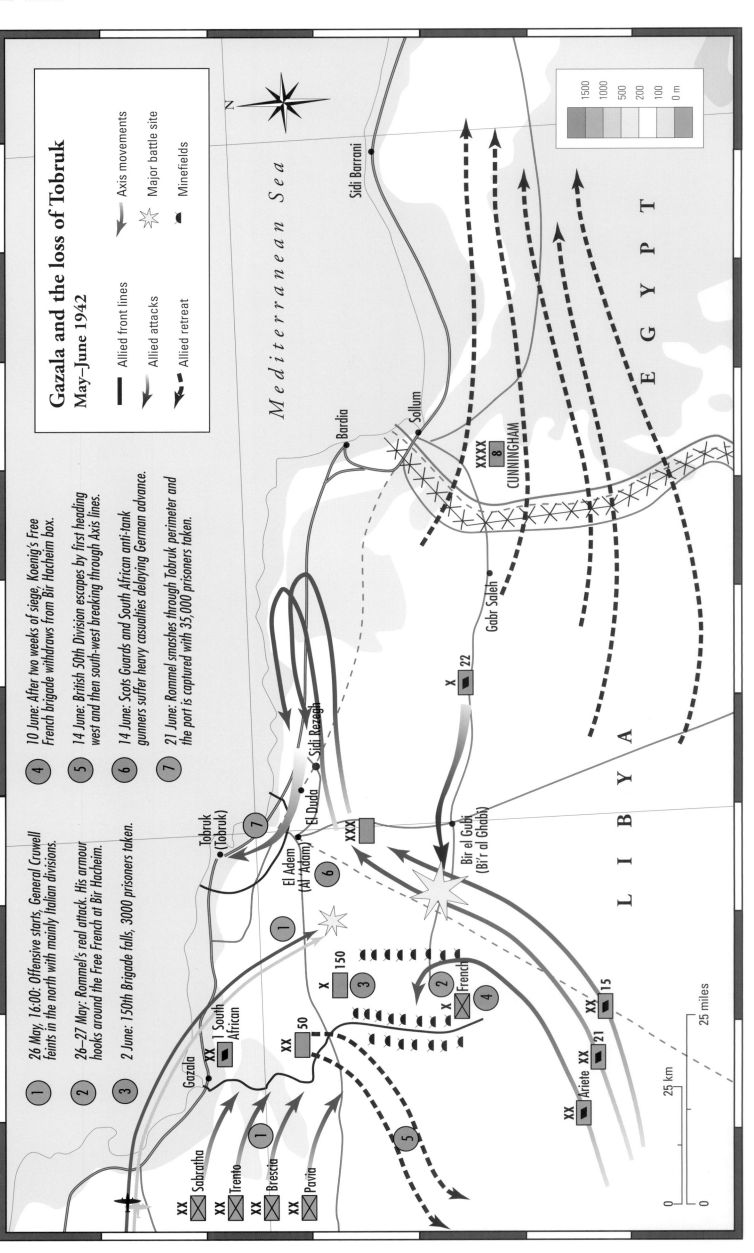

Gazala and the loss of Tobruk
May–June 1942

Allied front lines
Allied attacks
Allied retreat
Axis movements
Major battle site
Minefields

Operation Pedestal
11–13 August 1942

The delicate balance of the war in the Mediterranean depended on Malta. If the British could retain control of the island, aircraft and submarines could continue to threaten Rommel's lifeline in North Africa. If it could be neutralized, then the advantage would swing to the Axis side. The *Luftwaffe* pounded British convoys and Malta mercilessly, and the British fleet was short of the carriers which could counter German air power.

O N 10 AUGUST 1942, A LARGE CONVOY of 14 merchant ships left Gibraltar to perform a much-needed resupply mission to Malta, at that time under siege by the *Luftwaffe*. The supplies and oil the vessels carried were vital, so the convoy was escorted by three aircraft carriers, two battleships, four cruisers and 14 destroyers. Known as Operation Pedestal, the resupply mission came under heavy attack from the *Luftwaffe* and the *Regia Aeronautica* as well as from German U-Boats and Italian submarines. Inside a day, the convoy was within range of German aircraft. HMS *Eagle* was sunk on 11 August, and three cruisers and a destroyer were to follow the old carrier to the bottom. Losses continued to mount, but five supply vessels reached Malta on 13 August, including one precious oil tanker. Although losses had been high, enough got through to enable Malta to keep on fighting.

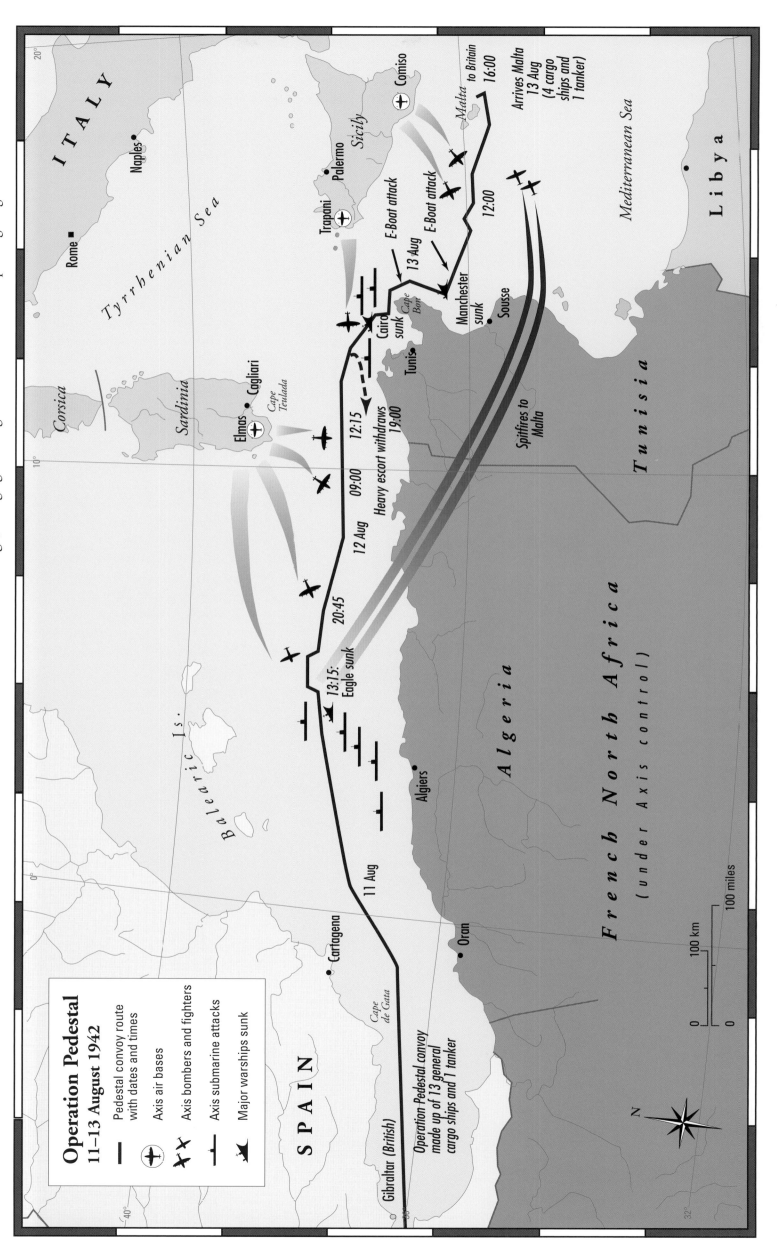

Operation Pedestal
11–13 August 1942

- Pedestal convoy route with dates and times
- Axis air bases
- Axis bombers and fighters
- Axis submarine attacks
- Major warships sunk

Operation Pedestal convoy made up of 13 general cargo ships and 1 tanker

The Eve of Battle
23 October 1942

The early summer of 1942 had been a period of almost constant retreat for British and Commonwealth forces in North Africa, but from their powerful defensive line at El Alamein, the Eighth Army held off two powerful Axis attacks in June and August. Now, massively reinforced and with the Germans and Italians exhausted, it was time to strike back.

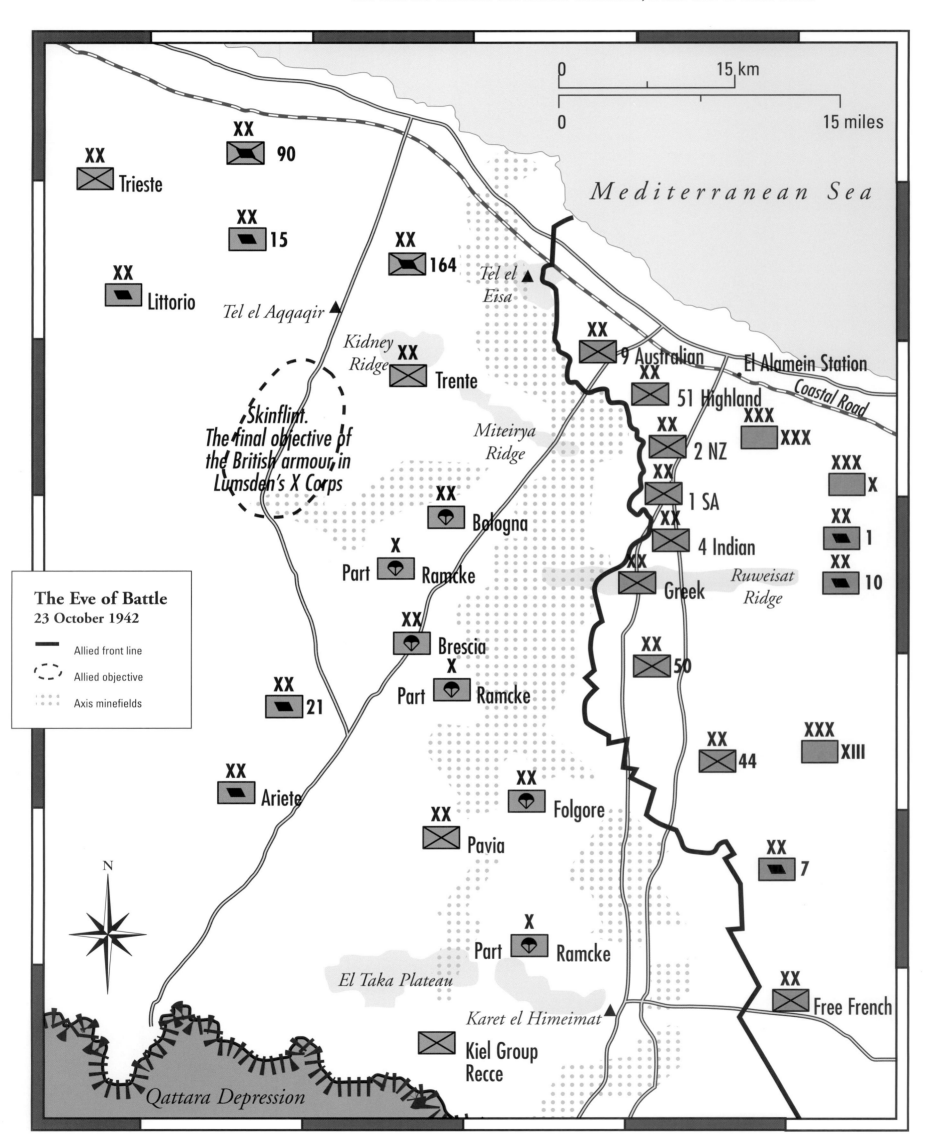

The Eve of Battle
23 October 1942

— Allied front line

- - - Allied objective

⋯ Axis minefields

El Alamein – Operation Lightfoot 24–29 October 1942

Safe behind strong defences, flanked to the north by the Mediterranean and to the south by the impassable sands of the Qattara Depression, the British could concentrate on building up forces for a major attack on the Axis armies. Under new commander General Bernard Law Montgomery, the Eighth Army soon had a massive materiel superiority over Rommel's command.

By October 1942, the newly reinforced British and Commonwealth forces could deploy 250,000 men, 1200 tanks and over 750 aircraft against an Axis force of 80,000 men, 489 tanks and 675 aircraft. The imbalance was made greater by the fact that Rommel's men were tired and poorly supplied, and most of his hard-used equipment was close to breakdown.

On the night of 23/24 October, Montgomery launched Operation Lightfoot, the first phase of a meticulously planned, multi-stage offensive. The British XIII Corps launched a diversionary attack in the south. After that had drawn Rommel's attention, XXX Corps at the north of the line cleared its way through German minefields towards Kidney Ridge, covered by the largest artillery barrage ever seen in North Africa. It was followed by the tanks of X Armoured Corps.

Battle in the dust

When the sun rose on 24 October, the infantry had gained most of its objectives, but the armour had been delayed in the night and were still under the guns of the German artillery. As a result, over the next eight days a grim battle was fought in the vast dust bowl between the sea and the Miteirya Ridge.

Meanwhile, Montgomery reconsidered his plans. Regrouping his armoured force, which had been reinforced with the 7th Armoured Division transferred from XIII Corps to the south, he planned another massive strike, which would be called Operation Supercharge.

Rommel had by now realized that he could not win such a set-piece battle, and began planning his withdrawal. Unfortunately for *Panzerarmee Afrika*, he received orders from Hitler to stand fast. Rommel probed forwards trying to find a weak spot in the British lines. But there were no weak spots, and by 2 November he had only 35 operational tanks left.

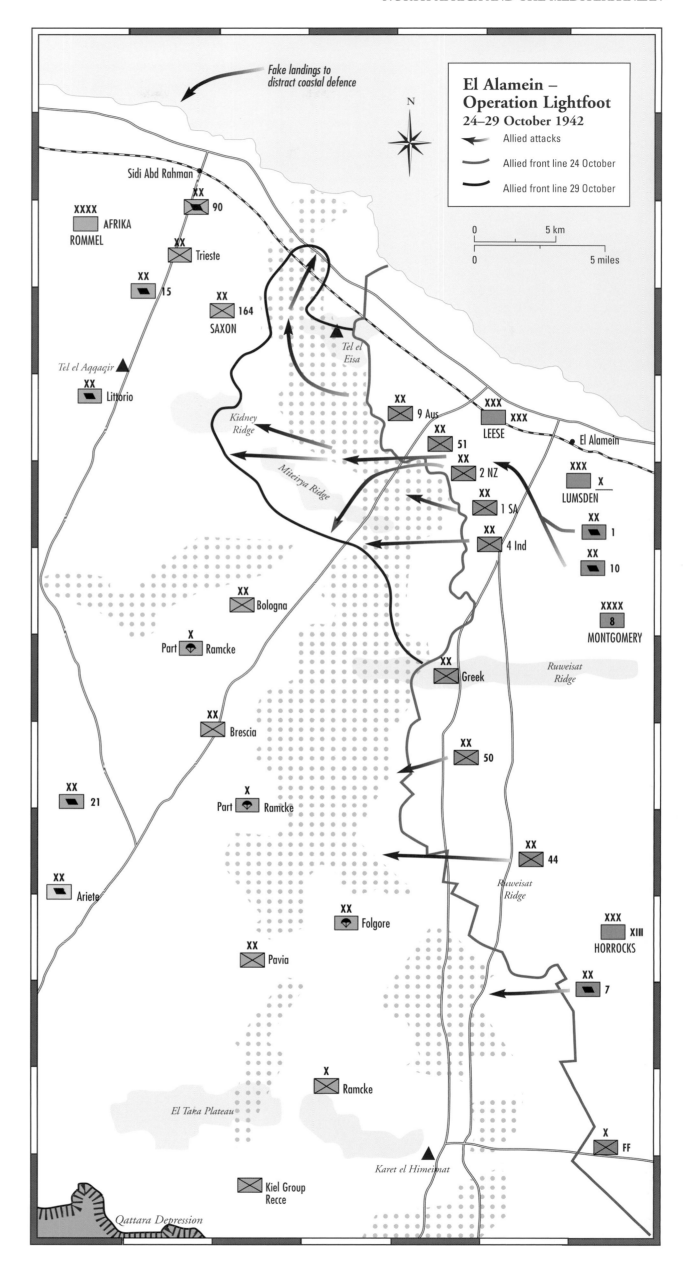

El Alamein – Operation Supercharge 2–4 November 1942

At 01:05 on the morning of 2 November, another massive artillery barrage signalled the start of Operation Supercharge. By dawn on 4 November, British reconnaissance patrols had passed south of Tel el Aqqaqir only to find that the expected Axis defences were not there. To save his army, Rommel had disobeyed his *Führer*, and the entire Axis force was now withdrawing westwards. The battle was over. Now it was time for the pursuit.

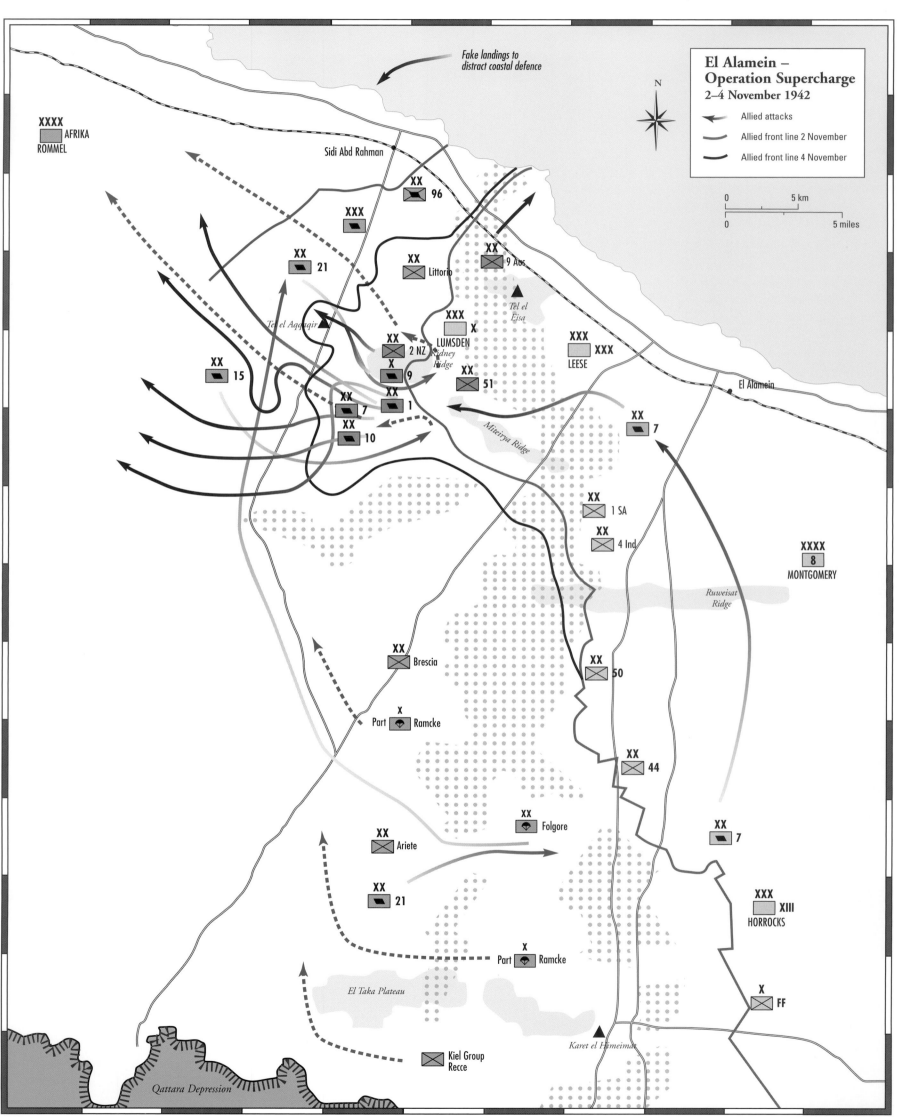

El Alamein – Operation Supercharge 2–4 November 1942

→ Allied attacks

Allied front line 2 November

Allied front line 4 November

The Mediterranean
Late 1942

Although generalship, heroism, armour and mobility all played their part in the Desert War, it could be argued with some justification that logistics was the deciding factor in the campaign. Both British and Axis supplies had to come by sea, and both sides did their best to ensure that the opposition's reinforcements were interdicted. The balance of power had originally favoured Italy, but aggressive action by the British fleet quickly achieved dominance.

ONCE THE GERMANS MADE THEIR PRESENCE FELT in the theatre with victories in Greece, Crete and North Africa, the balance was tipped against the British. The Germans countered Royal Navy sea power with *Luftwaffe* air power. Unlike the war in the Atlantic, practically all of the Mediterranean was within range of shore-based warplanes. The Axis controlled virtually all of the air bases in the central Mediterranean: with one exception the British were limited to the eastern and western ends of the sea. However, that one exception was to prove crucial. The British still controlled Malta, a little over 110 km (70 miles) from Sicily, and not much further away from Tunisia and Libya.

Bone in the Axis throat

Malta provided a base for both naval vessels and aircraft, which could strike at virtually every Axis supply route, and which took a heavy toll of Italian and German shipping. Both the *Luftwaffe* and the *Regia Aeronautica* did all they could to neutralize the threat, and Malta came under such heavy air attack that for a time only submarines could use its harbours. But resupply convoys were fought through to the island, and once carriers were able to deliver fighter reinforcements, the German and Italian air forces could be held at bay.

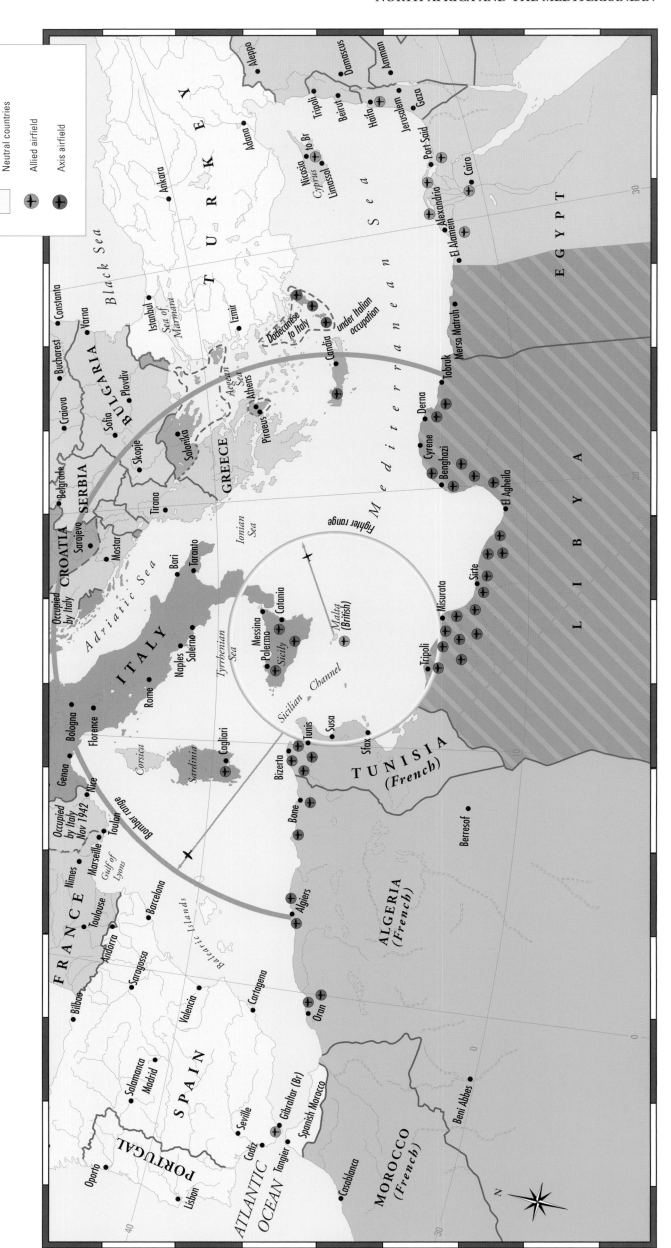

The Mediterranean
Late 1942

Under German or Axis occupation

Allied to Germany

Italian territory

Under Italian occupation

Allied or under Allied occupation

French, under Vichy control

Axis occupied

Neutral countries

Allied airfield

Axis airfield

Operation Torch
8 November 1942

As *Panzerarmee Afrika* retreated before the advancing Eighth Army, Rommel must have believed that this was simply another phase in the backwards and forwards North African campaign: before long, as he came closer to his bases, he would be reinforced, while as the British supply lines grew longer his opponents would eventually be weak enough for him to counter-attack. Any such thoughts must have been dashed on 8 November, when news came of a massive Allied landing at the other end of North Africa.

On 8 November 1942, British and American forces landed in Morocco and Algeria. It was the most ambitious amphibious operation up to that time: 35,000 US troops were shipped straight across from America; another 49,000 from their bases in Britain, together with 23,000 British and Commonwealth soldiers. Nearly 400 transport ships were involved, escorted by six battleships, eleven aircraft carriers, fifteen cruisers and over a hundred destroyers and anti-submarine vessels. The Allies landed in separate but coordinated actions at Algiers, Casablanca and Oran.

Vichy French opposition

Algeria was a French colony, administered by the Vichy regime. Only two years before, the British had attacked the French fleet in Algeria, killing over a thousand French sailors. The Allies were not exactly met as liberators. But in Algiers at the end of the first day all the men were ashore having swept away a none too determined resistance.

Opposition at Oran, scene of what many Frenchmen saw as British perfidy, was especially fierce. The initial plan to encircle the city had gone off well. The troops had all disembarked by evening, but it quickly became clear that the French had now organized a strong defence.

At Casablanca, the incomplete French battleship *Jean Bart* had to be overpowered by the USS *Massachusetts*, and several French submarines were sunk by US carrier aircraft as they attacked the troop transports.

But the French colonial army was too small, too poorly equipped and internally divided: it could only impose a brief delay before Algeria's ports were in Allied hands and Allied troops were heading east along the coastal plain. Ahead lay Tunisia and 1500km (930 miles) beyond, Libya.

By 12 November, British paratroopers had been dropped at Bone and captured the airfield there. Five days later they had arrived at Souk el Arba, 480km (300 miles) east of Algiers. Meanwhile, the 503rd US Parachute Regiment had dropped at Youks le Bains, 160km (100 miles) to the south and taken Gafsa airfield inside Tunisia. The Allies now commandeered every possible piece of transport to rush supplies forward to the isolated airborne bridgeheads.

Gradually, the Allied high command came to recognize the enormous difficulty of covering the 2100km (1300 miles) from Casablanca to Tunis, given the appalling state of the rudimentary African road system. They also realized that some serious fighting lay ahead. Hitler, who had for so long starved Rommel of troops when victory had seemed in his grasp, in extremis now poured in men and materials to bolster the Tunisian bridgehead.

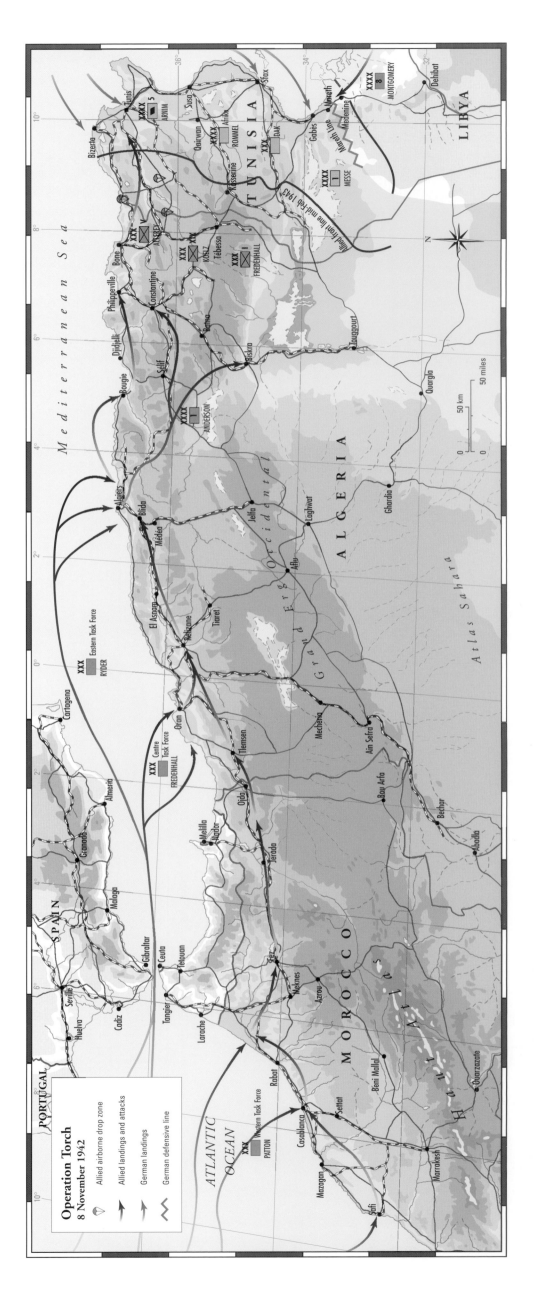

British Advance to Tunisia
November 1942–February 1943

The Germans that did manage to make it to Rommel's first makeshift defensive line at Fuka after the Battle of Alamein were worth little more than a battalion, and even when joined by the 90th and 164th divisions constituted in battle-ready terms a brigade only. Ramcke's parachute formation made its own way back to the German lines virtually intact, but received only Rommel's scorn. The slower-moving Italian Trieste and Littorio divisions were, however, destroyed, and many surrendered with scarcely a shot being fired.

Rommel's withdrawal from Alamein was not so much a retreat as 'a route march under slight enemy pressure'. Montgomery failed to press home the advantage and finish off the remnants of the *Afrika Korps*. The British general's caution, always a feature of his command, was exacerbated by the poor weather, his innate respect for the enemy, and his own administrative problems. At that moment, Rommel's force consisted of just 4000 men, 11 tanks, 24 of the feared '88s', 25 other anti-tank guns, and 40 assorted artillery pieces. However, he was able to hold off the advancing British, thanks to the arrival of the Italian Centauro Division at Antelat.

Rommel was finally able to relax at Mersa el Brega, due to the onset of winter. The roads dissolved, and the English supply lines went with them. He had an acrimonious meeting with Field Marshal Kesselring. Demanding supplies for his *Afrika Korps*, he was told that these were virtually all earmarked for for the troops in Tunisia. Rommel had met his match in Kesselring, politically more skilled and better connected than Rommel. He was also a better commander than Rommel gave him credit for, having stabilized the Tunis situation in just two weeks.

Kesselring had sewn up a deal with the Italians. Tunisia was to be given to Italy in exchange for their relinquishing Tripolitania. The new defence line was to be established at the Mareth Line, and Mersa el Brega was to be given up whenever Montgomery felt like advancing again.

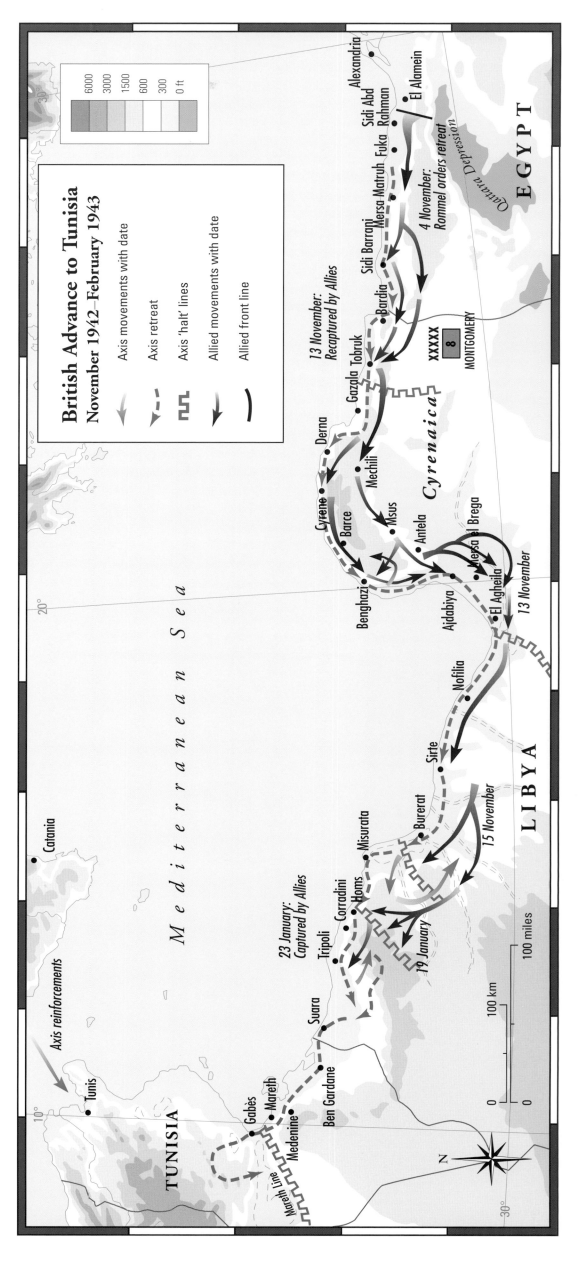

British Advance to Tunisia
November 1942–February 1943

Axis movements with date
Axis retreat
Axis 'halt' lines
Allied movements with date
Allied front line

Kasserine Pass
14–22 February 1943

The weather in North Africa was terrible that winter and campaigning came to an abrupt halt. Both sides used the opportunity to build up their supplies – a race that could only be won by the Allies. By early 1943, the Axis was being squeezed between the Eighth Army driving north and the Anglo-American armies driving east. Germany needed a miracle to avoid being swept from Africa.

Rommel did not favour being driven into the sea. Instead he planned to sweep the Allies from Africa before their strength became too overwhelming. He chose for his target the inexperienced Americans, whom he rightly assessed as still frighteningly green. His plan involved cutting off the leading British and American divisions with an all-out offensive that swept from Kasserine to the Mediterranean.

The attack was launched on 14 February, and on the 20th the Germans burst through the Kasserine Pass. The attack smashed into the US II Corps. For the last time Rommel was in the thick of battle. Piles of high-quality booty dropped into his hands, and bewildered American prisoners poured in. But it did not last. Given interception of Rommel's coded signals, the Allies could place just enough of a holding force against the German probing attacks. The delay gave the Allies time to rush up reserves, and by the evening of 22 February Rommel had to accept that his grandiose counter-stroke was not working. He called off the assault. Within days, the lost ground was recovered by the British and Americans. From then on, and with ever growing certainty, the noose around the remaining Axis forces in Tunisia began to tighten.

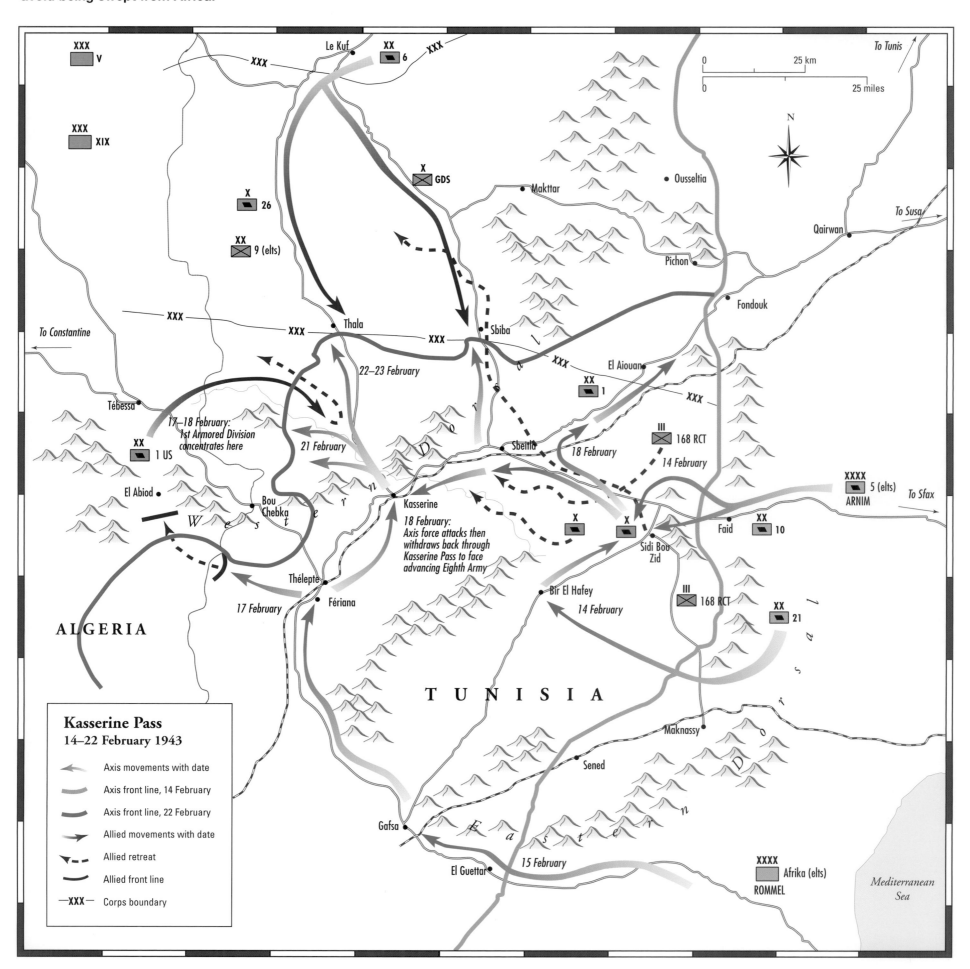

Kasserine Pass
14–22 February 1943

- Axis movements with date
- Axis front line, 14 February
- Axis front line, 22 February
- Allied movements with date
- Allied retreat
- Allied front line
- XXX — Corps boundary

Axis Defeat in Tunisia 20–29 March 1943

After Kasserine, command of all Axis troops in North Africa was given to Rommel, but he could do little in the face of Allied superiority in men and materiel.

Rommel launched an attack, a direct assault on Montgomery's positions at Medenine, but the British were waiting. The attack was smashed by massed tanks and anti-tank guns. Another assault against the British and Americans by von Arnim's forces in the north was equally unsuccessful. Even though Hitler had poured reinforcements into Tunisia, the Axis could not match Allied strength.

Montgomery opened the final Allied assault on Tunisia with a diversionary attack towards Enfidaville. Then the British First Army and Free French forces attacked the centre of the German defensive system. Further north, the US II Corps struck towards Bizerta.

The end in Africa

Constant Allied pressure meant that by May 1943, the remnants of the Axis forces had been compressed into a small enclave. Once the Allied Operation Vulcan was launched on 6 May, the remnants of the once mighty *Afrika Korps* disintegrated. Across the north of Tunis, Allied forces mopped up the last German resistance. When the dust had settled, more than 150,000 Axis troops had fallen into the hands of the Allies, in a defeat of Stalingrad proportions.

Axis Defeat in Tunisia 20–29 March 1943

- Front line 20 March
- Front line 29 March
- Axis attack
- Axis withdrawal
- British movement
- French movement
- New Zealand movement

26 March: Spoiling attack launched by Arnim becomes larger engagement than intended

German supply and evacuation by air

Rommel withdraws force from Kasserine area to reinforce Mareth Line defences

15 February: Eighth Army arrives

Capture of Tunis
April–May 1943

In Operation Vulcan, launched on 6 May 1943, the Allies outnumbered the Axis forces by six to one on the ground, and by fifteen to one in terms of armour and artillery. *Panzerarmee Afrika* had virtually no *Luftwaffe* support, the Allies having complete domination of the skies. With the collapse of German resistance following the launch of Operation Vulcan, British troops entered Tunis unopposed, while the American II Corps captured Bizerta without a fight. The surrender of Tunisia, recently so heavily reinforced by Hitler, was a massive morale boost for the Allies.

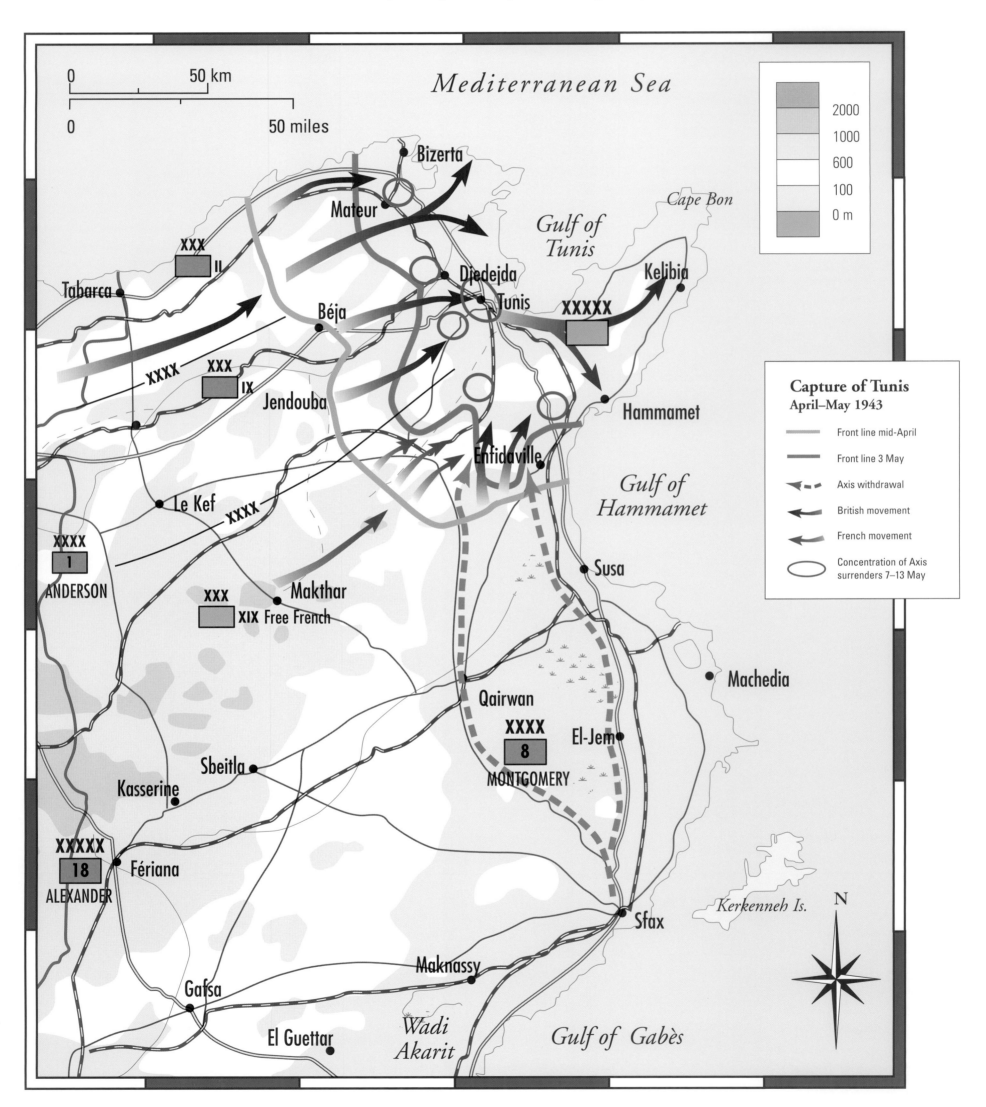

Legend:

Capture of Tunis
April–May 1943

- Front line mid-April
- Front line 3 May
- Axis withdrawal
- British movement
- French movement
- Concentration of Axis surrenders 7–13 May

Operational Plans
1942–43

① Operation Avalanche (US Fifth Army)

② Operation Baytown (British Eighth Army)

③ Operation Slapstick (British Eighth Army)

④ Other projected moves

Operational Plans
1942–43

With North Africa in Allied hands, the question of where to go next exercised the Anglo-American high command. The Russians were pressing for a second front in Europe, but the Allies lacked the capacity to mount an attack in Northern Europe. An attack on Sicily was decided upon, which would be followed by the invasion of the Italian mainland.

THE ATTACK ON SICILY was not the only invasion route considered by the Allies. The capture of Sardinia would allow Allied forces to strike either at Italy or the South of France, while Churchill was in favour of an attack on Greece. However, attacking Sicily was probably the least challenging logistically, and Operation Husky was set in train. The amphibious landings were to be supplemented by a massive airborne landing involving paratroopers and gliderborne troops. It was the first major airborne operation by the Allies, and many mistakes were made. Large numbers of gliders fell short of their targets, and many of the heavily laden paratroopers fell into the sea, where they drowned.

Amphibious assault

The landings took place on 10 July 1943, on 26 beaches along 150 miles (240 km) of Sicily's southeastern coast. Only half-hearted resistance was expected from the Italians: the real strength of the opposition would depend on how many German troops had been transferred to the island in recent weeks, and on just what orders they had been given by the *Führer*.

Invasion of Sicily
10 July–17 August 1943

As Montgomery's army advanced north towards Messina, racing Patton's army, which had burst through the centre of Sicily and was now driving along the north coast, the Germans decided to evacuate the island rather than make a last-ditch stand.

3–16 August: Italian forces evacuated

11–17 August: German forces evacuated. Allied air attacks ineffective

Amphibious landing attempts to outflank Axis positions

8–15 August: Amphibious attempts to outflank Axis positions

15 August

11 August

8 August

San Frattello Line

Santo Stefano Line 23 July

From Malta

Ionian Sea

Tyrrhenian Sea

Mediterranean Sea

Place names

San Giovanni
Reggio
Messina
Strait of Messina
Milazzo
Cape Milazzo
Gulf of Patti
Barcellona
Cape Calava
Cape Orlando
San Agata
Santa Stefano
Mistretta
Nicosia
Randazzo
Adrano
Palermo
Mount Etna
Catania
Gulf of Catania
Augusta
Gulf of Augusta
Siracusa
Gulf of Noto
Noto
Avola
Cape Passero
Ispica
Ragusa
Vizzini
Caltagirone
Gela
Gulf of Gela
Vittoria
Licata
Pozzallo
Comiso
Piazza Armerina
Enna
Caltanissetta
Canicatti
Agrigento
Cefalù
Termini
Corleone
Burgio
Sciacca
Castelvetrano
Mazara del Vallo
Marsala
Trapani
Cape S. Vito
Gulf of Castellamare
Alcamo
Partinico
Calatafimi
Vulcano I.
Caronie Mountains
Catania Plain
Cape Gallo
Palermo 22 July
Palermo

Unit labels

XXXX 8 MONTGOMERY
XIII DEMPSEY
78 (In Africa) Reserve
5
50
RM
231
51
1
206
1
XXXX LEESE
XXXX 15 ALEXANDER
505
504
45
1
1
1
4
3
2
3 Rangers
2 (Part)
2 (Afloat)
82
82 Reserve
9 (In Africa)
XXXX 7 PATTON BRADLEY
82
207 Coastal Division
15 (elts)
18
6 GUZZONI
136
19
1
Hermann Goering
XXX
208
202
Pz (elts)

Legend

Invasion of Sicily
10 July–17 August 1943

- Allied landings with dates
- Axis counter-attacks
- Allied front line 11 July
- Allied front line 15 July
- Allied front line 23 July
- Axis retreat line
- Axis retreat line
- Axis retreat line
- Axis retreat route
- Airfields constructed by Allies
- Allied airborne landings

Scale

2000
1500
1000
500
200
0 m

50 miles
50 km

10 July
11 July
Apr 11

N

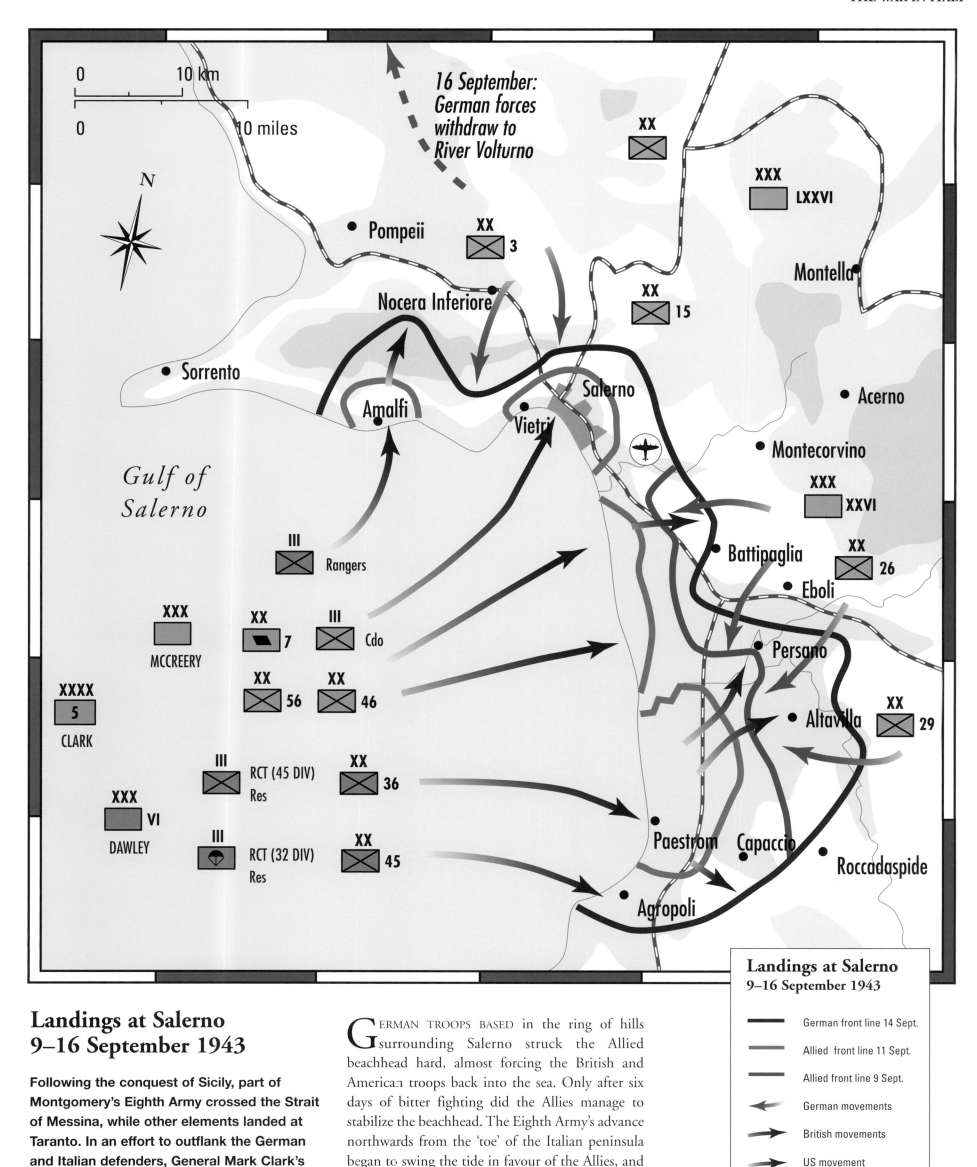

0   10 km

0   10 miles

16 September:
German forces
withdraw to
River Volturno

N

XX

XXX LXXVI

• Pompeii

XX 3

Montella •

Nocera Inferiore

XX 15

• Sorrento

• Acerno

Amalfi

Salerno

• Montecorvino

Gulf of
Salerno

Vietri

XXX XXVI

III Rangers

• Battipaglia

XX 26

XXX MCCREERY

XX 7   III Cdo

• Eboli

• Persano

XX 56   XX 46

XXXX 5 CLARK

• Altavilla   XX 29

III RCT (45 DIV) Res   XX 36

XXX VI DAWLEY

III RCT (32 DIV) Res   XX 45

• Paestrom   • Capaccio

• Roccadaspide

• Agropoli

Landings at Salerno
9–16 September 1943

**Following the conquest of Sicily, part of
Montgomery's Eighth Army crossed the Strait
of Messina, while other elements landed at
Taranto. In an effort to outflank the German
and Italian defenders, General Mark Clark's
Fifth Army made an amphibious landing at
Salerno – the most northerly point which
could be covered by Allied fighters.**

GERMAN TROOPS BASED in the ring of hills
surrounding Salerno struck the Allied
beachhead hard, almost forcing the British and
American troops back into the sea. Only after six
days of bitter fighting did the Allies manage to
stabilize the beachhead. The Eighth Army's advance
northwards from the 'toe' of the Italian peninsula
began to swing the tide in favour of the Allies, and
the German Tenth Army withdrew northwards to
the first of a series of holding positions across the
rugged river valleys of the Apennine mountains.

Landings at Salerno
9–16 September 1943

— German front line 14 Sept.

— Allied front line 11 Sept.

— Allied front line 9 Sept.

← German movements

→ British movements

→ US movement

Southern Italy 3 September– 15 December 1943

Slowly, the German forces gave ground, fighting a series of highly effective rearguard actions along the rocky defiles of the Apennines. With great skill, the Germans slowed the Allied advance to a crawl. At the same time, the Germans were preparing a powerful line of defences anchored on the ancient Benedictine abbey of Monte Cassino. The formidable defences of the Gustav Line were so powerful that the Allied advance ground to a halt as 1944 approached.

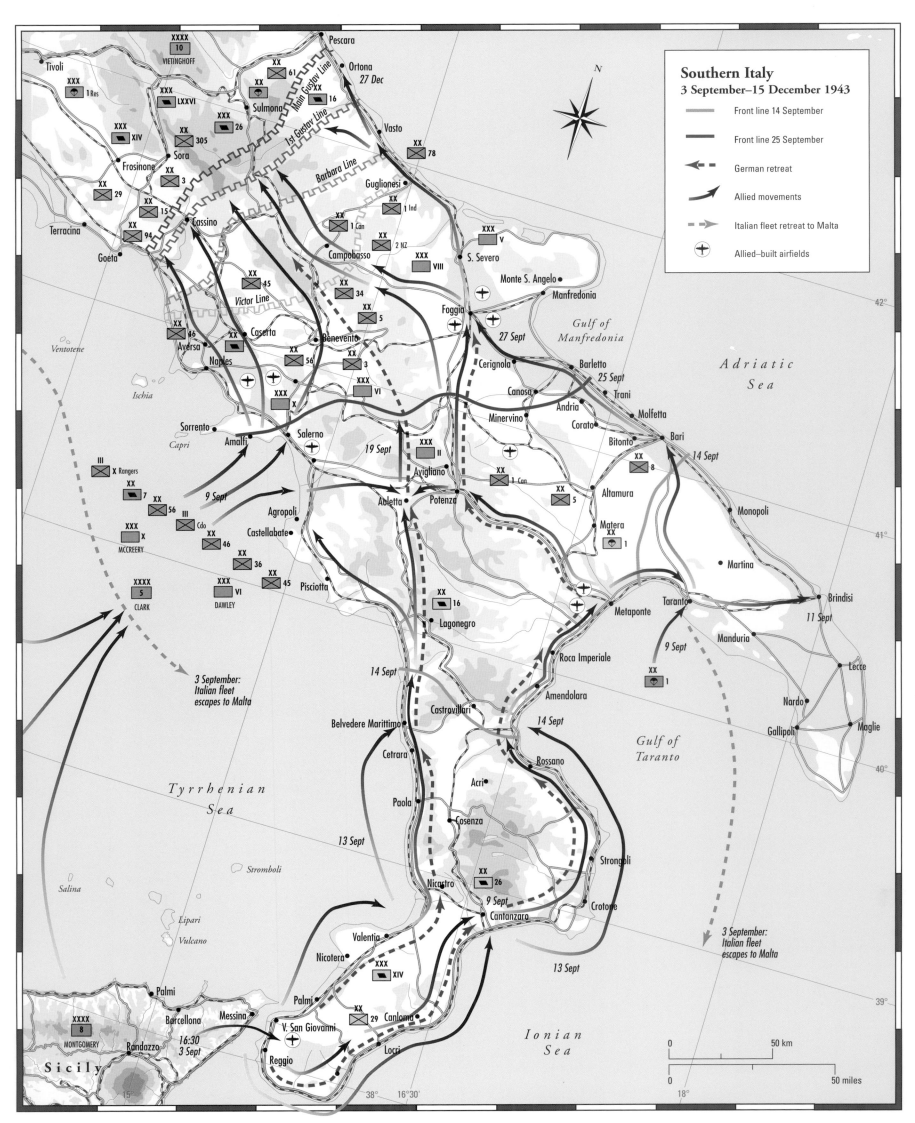

Southern Italy
3 September–15 December 1943

Front line 14 September
Front line 25 September
German retreat
Allied movements
Italian fleet retreat to Malta
Allied-built airfields

Monte Cassino

The Gustav Line was held by a variety of formations, including two panzer divisions.

Their powerful tanks could do little to influence the fighting directly – the terrain was just as hostile to them as it was to the Allies – so they were frequently used as pillboxes, often placed in strong buildings to provide added protection. The Germans also used a new ploy in the form of simplified Panther tank turrets set into steel boxes dug into specially chosen defensive positions.

The Allies soon learned that making headway would be difficult where either of these types of obstacle was situated.

Prominent in the German defence of Cassino was the *Luftwaffe*'s 1st Parachute Division, fighting on the ground as elite light infantry – as they had done since the invasion of Crete in 1941.

T HE FIRST ATTACKS were launched in January and February 1944. The Allies found themselves attempting to advance directly into a well-organized and stubborn defence. A direct frontal attack across the Liri by an American force in brigade strength turned into a major military disaster, and even when they managed to cross elsewhere the Allies found themselves faced with an almost sheer climb to the crest of Monte Cassino.

The rest of the battle evolved into a fierce round of infantry attacks met with strong defensive fire. In some cases, attackers and defenders got close enough for hand-to-hand combat. What Allied advances were made were later lost in the inevitable German counter-attacks. Only when the Free French broke through the German defences to the east did Cassino fall, after more than four months of the bitterest fighting of the war.

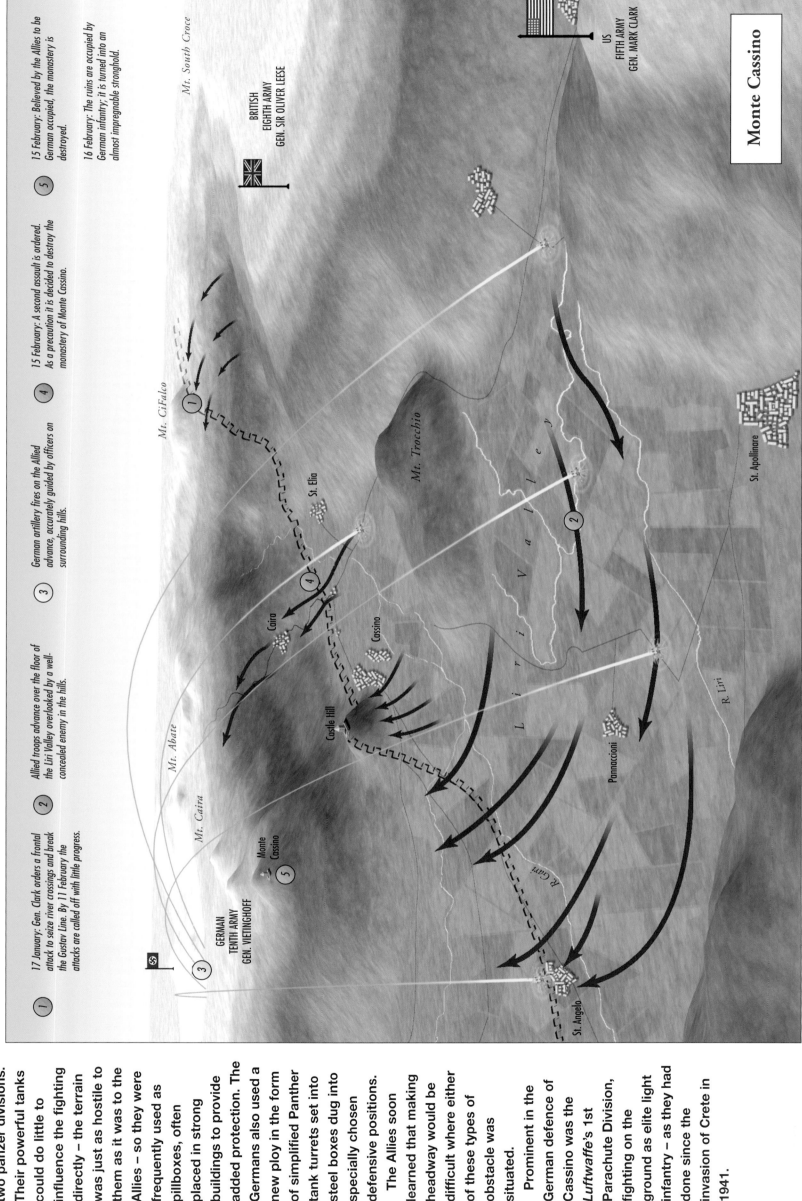

1. *17 January: Gen. Clark orders a frontal attack to seize river crossings and break the Gustav Line. By 11 February the attacks are called off with little progress.*

2. *Allied troops advance over the floor of the Liri Valley overlooked by a well-concealed enemy in the hills.*

3. *German artillery fires on the Allied advance, accurately guided by officers on surrounding hills.*

4. *15 February: A second assault is ordered. As a precaution it is decided to destroy the monastery of Monte Cassino.*

5. *15 February: Believed by the Allies to be German occupied, the monastery is destroyed.*

16 February: The ruins are occupied by German infantry; it is turned into an almost impregnable stronghold.

BRITISH
EIGHTH ARMY
GEN. SIR OLIVER LEESE

US
FIFTH ARMY
GEN. MARK CLARK

GERMAN
TENTH ARMY
GEN. VIETINGHOFF

Mt. South Croce

Mt. CiFalco

St. Elia

Mt. Trocchio

Mt. Abate

Mt. Caira

Caira

Cassino

Castle Hill

Monte Cassino

St. Angelo

St. Apollinare

Pannaccioni

L i r i V a l l e y

R. Liri

R. Cairi

Monte Cassino

Landings at Anzio
17 January–26 May 1944

WHILE THE ALLIED COMMANDERS HESITATED about what to do next, the German Fourteenth Army, initially caught by surprise, swiftly gathered forces for a counter-attack. From 3 to 19 February, the Germans attacked the Anzio beachhead. However, they failed to penetrate the Allied lines, thanks in part to the murderous fire support provided by Allied warships off-shore. After the Germans failed to drive the defenders into the sea, the fighting at Anzio degenerated into the kind of positional warfare more akin to 1917 than to 1944. However, once the Allies prised open the Gustav Line at Cassino, they could drive towards Anzio, breaking through to relieve the beachhead at the end of May.

While the attack on Cassino was stalled, General Clark attempted to outflank the German defences through an amphibious assault on the bay of Anzio. On the afternoon of 21 January 1943, 243 ships of all sizes sailed from the Bay of Naples, and under clear skies made for the beaches on each side of Anzio. By midnight the landing craft were loaded and moving in. To everybody's astonishment, there was no sign of German opposition.

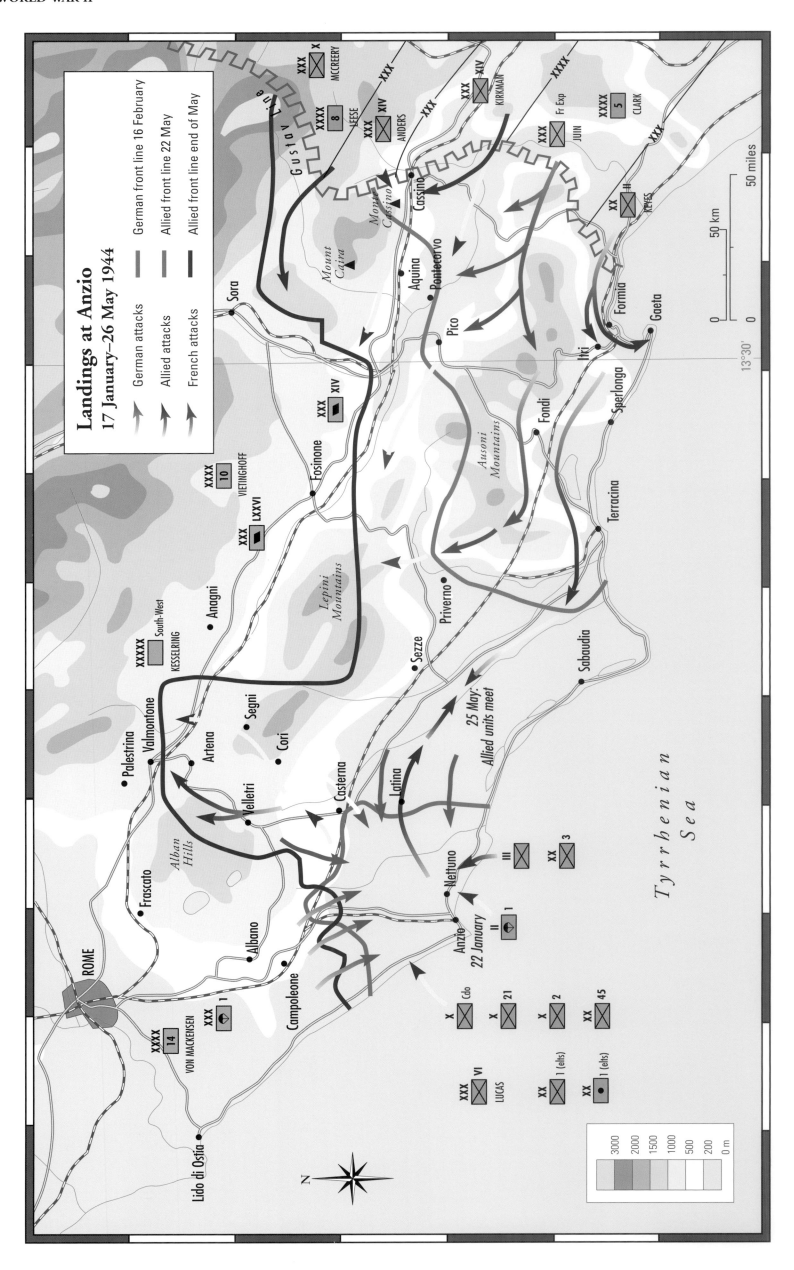

Landings at Anzio
17 January–26 May 1944

German front line 16 February
Allied front line 22 May
Allied front line end of May

German attacks
Allied attacks
French attacks

Liberation of Rome and Advance North June–December 1944

Rome was taken on 4 June, but for the next six months the Germans continued to fight a skilful delaying action up the Italian peninsula.

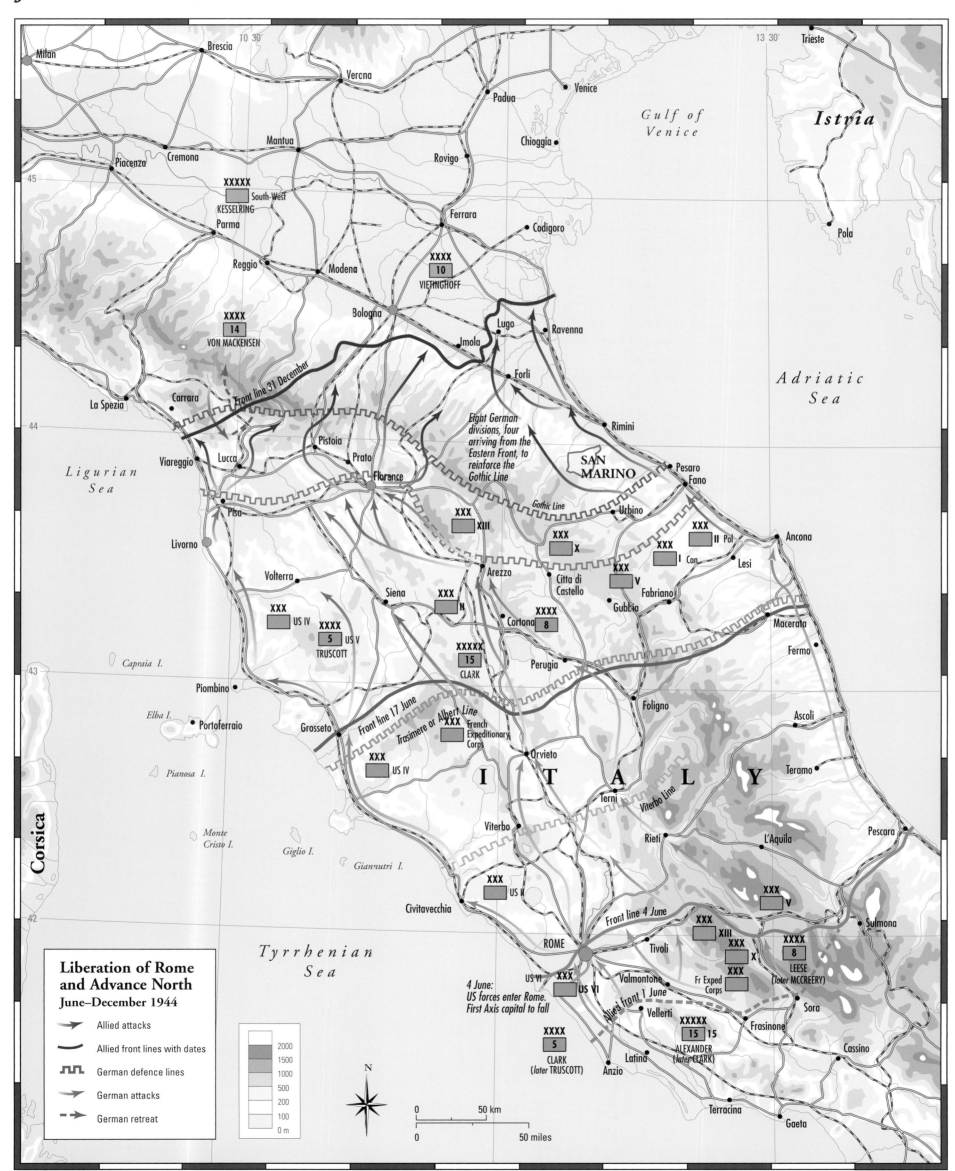

Milan
Brescia
Verona
Padua
Venice
Gulf of Venice
Istria
Trieste
Piacenza
Cremona
Mantua
Rovigo
Chioggia
Pola
Parma
Reggio
Modena
Ferrara
Codigoro
XXXXX South-West KESSELRING
XXXX 10 VIETINGHOFF
Bologna
Lugo
Ravenna
XXXX 14 VON MACKENSEN
Imola
Forli
La Spezia
Carrara
Front line 31 December
Adriatic Sea
Rimini
Viareggio
Lucca
Pistoia
Prato
Eight German divisions, four arriving from the Eastern Front, to reinforce the Gothic Line
SAN MARINO
Pesaro
Fano
Ligurian Sea
Pisa
Florence
Gothic Line
Urbino
XXX XIII
XXX II Pol
Ancona
Livorno
Volterra
Siena
Arezzo
XXX X
XXX I Can
Lesi
XXX US IV
XXX H
Citta di Castello
XXX V
Fabriano
XXXX 5 US V TRUSCOTT
Cortona
XXXX 8
Gubbia
Macerata
Capraia I.
XXXXX 15 CLARK
Perugia
Fermo
Piombino
Elba I.
Portoferraio
Grosseto
Front line 17 June
Trasimere or Albert Line
XXX French Expeditionary Corps
Orvieto
Foligno
Ascoli
Teramo
Pianosa I.
XXX US IV
Monte Cristo I.
Giglio I.
Giannutri I.
I T A L Y
Terni
Viterbo Line
Rieti
L'Aquila
Pescara
Viterbo
Corsica
XXX US II
Civitavecchia
Front line 4 June
XXX V
Sulmona
Tyrrhenian Sea
ROME
Tivoli
XXX XIII
XXX X
XXXX 8 LEESE (later McCREERY)
Sora
US VI
XXX US VI
4 June: US forces enter Rome. First Axis capital to fall
Valmontone
Fr Exped Corps
Allied front 1 June
Velletri
XXXXX 15 15 ALEXANDER (later CLARK)
Frasinone
Cassino
XXXX 5 CLARK (later TRUSCOTT)
Latina
Anzio
Terracina
Gaeta

Liberation of Rome and Advance North
June–December 1944

➤ Allied attacks

⌒ Allied front lines with dates

⊓⊓ German defence lines

→ German attacks

⇢ German retreat

2000
1500
1000
500
200
100
0 m

N

0   50 km
0   50 miles

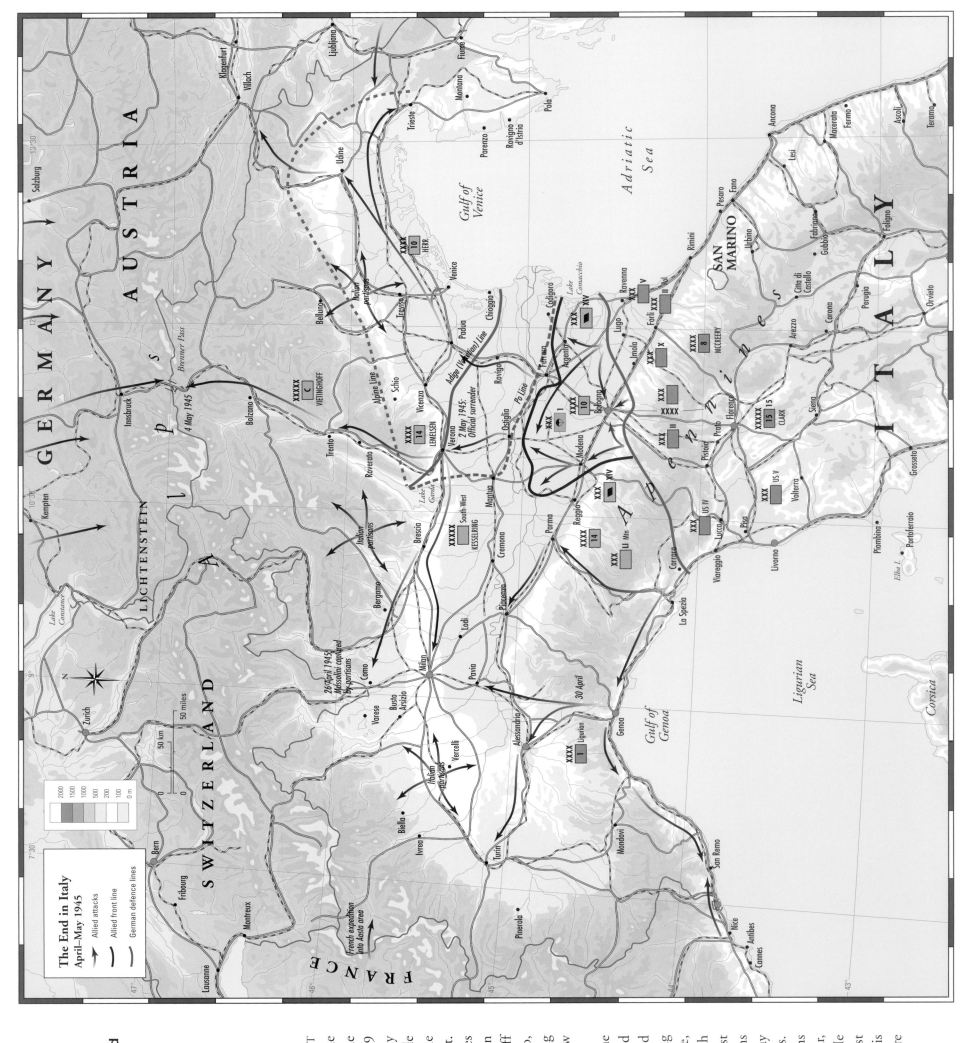

The End in Italy
April–May 1945

Although the Germans believed that they could hold the Gothic Line through the winter of 1944/45, the rapid Allied advances of September had forced a breach in the line. The Germans fell back to hold the rugged terrain south of Bologna.

IT WAS NOT UNTIL THE LAST months of the war that the Allies were able to make the decisive breakthrough. On 9 April 1945, the Eighth Army advanced east of Bologna, while the Americans shattered the German defences further west. Outnumbered and his forces lacking supplies, the German commander von Vietinghoff asked to retreat beyond the Po, but Hitler refused. Disobeying orders, Vietinghoff withdrew anyway.

However, at this stage in the war it was far too late. Allied armoured columns raced forwards, beating the retreating Germans to the river line, cutting them off. The Tenth Army had all but ceased to exist when Vietinghoff sought terms from the Allies, and on 2 May 1945, he surrendered his forces.

Mussolini, whose ambitions had brought Italy into the war, fled towards Switzerland. He was caught by communist partisans, executed alongside his mistress, and their bodies were strung up on meat hooks.

Operation Barbarossa
22 June–early October 1941

The scale of the invasion of the USSR was vast. The German armies massed along the Soviet frontier in the summer of 1941 represented the greatest concentration of military force the world had ever seen.

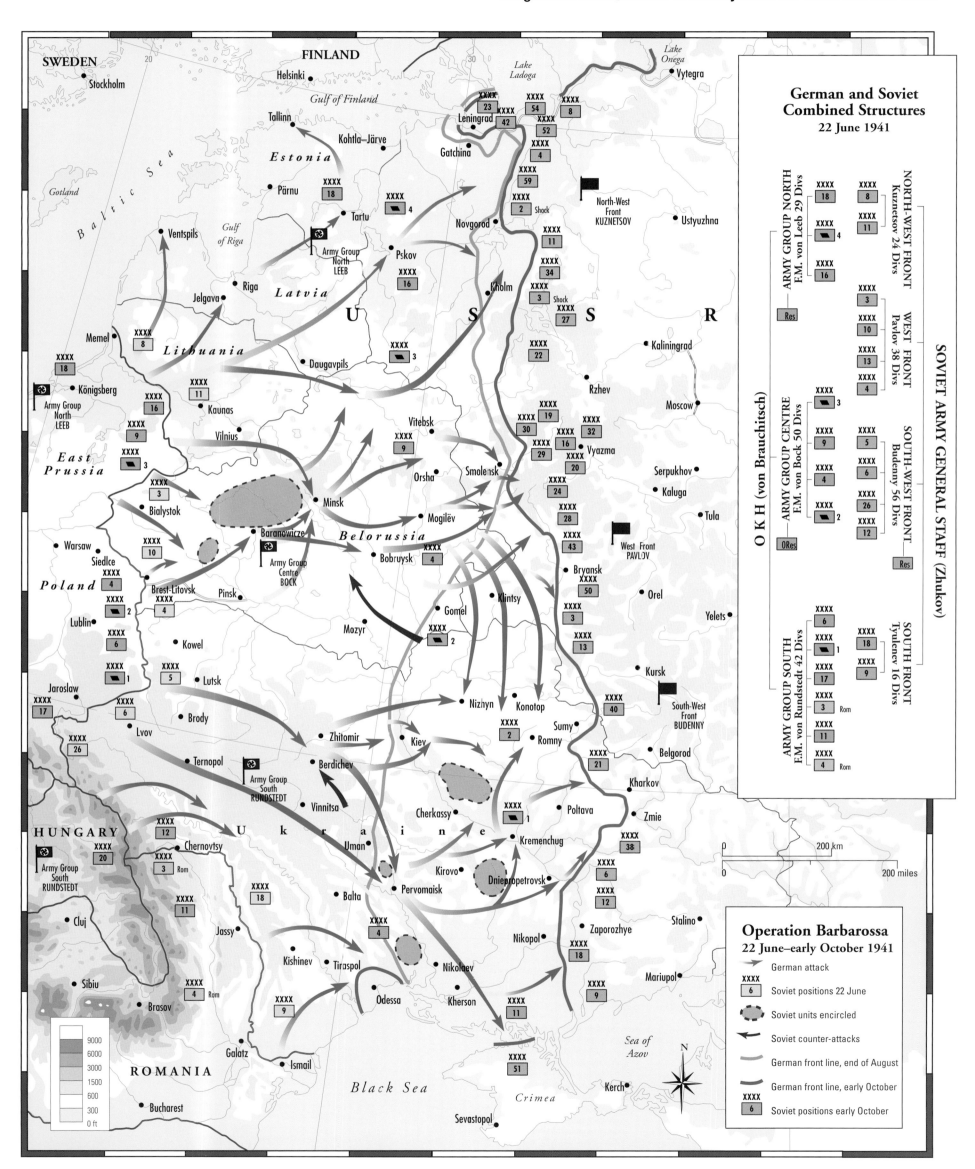

German and Soviet Combined Structures
22 June 1941

Operation Barbarossa
22 June–early October 1941

→ German attack

Soviet positions 22 June

Soviet units encircled

Soviet counter-attacks

German front line, end of August

German front line, early October

Soviet positions early October

Dispersion of Soviet Industry 1941–42

One of Stalin's major achievements as leader of the Soviet Union was the industrialization of his country – though this was achieved at a horrendous human cost. Nevertheless, without that industrial capacity, the USSR could never have fought off the German invaders. The various five-year plans of the 1930s saw heavy industries established to make use of the vast raw material wealth of Siberia. Most were set up beyond the Urals, which was well beyond the range of German bombers. However, lighter industries tended to be set up in European Russia, and these were vulnerable after the German invasion.

Within days of the German invasion in June 1941, the Soviet State Defence Committee ordered the dispersal of key war industries based in the western republics of the USSR. Within six months, more than 1500 factories had been dismantled and shipped eastwards. By early 1942, over 1200 of these plants were in full production, at a vastly greater rate than they had been in 1940. In that year, the Soviet munitions industry had produced some 63 million tonnes (62 million tons) of weaponry; in 1942, production had more than quadrupled, in spite of the need to move the factories. In spite of the fact that the USSR had access to about one third of the coal and steel supplies available to Germany in 1942, Soviet factories delivered twice as much war materiel as those of the Reich.

Industrial giant

In spite of the primitive nature of factory conditions, between 1943 and 1945 Soviet industry produced more than 80,000 aircraft, 73,000 armoured vehicles, and more than 300,000 artillery pieces. Britain and America also made a significant contribution to equipping the Soviet armies but apart from motor transport, the bulk of the Red Army's weapons were Soviet-made.

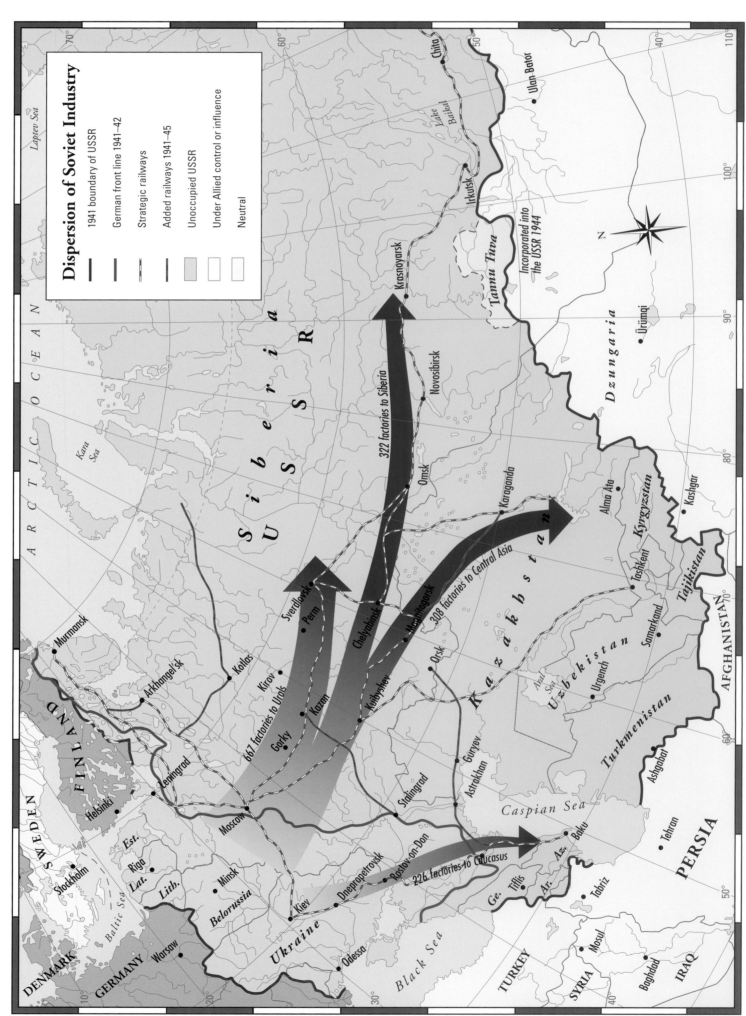

Operation Typhoon
September–December 1941

Following the diversion of much of its tank strength to Kiev during the summer, Army Group Centre resumed the advance on Moscow on 2 October 1941. However, the delay meant that the *Wehrmacht* still had not reached the Soviet capital when the icy Russian winter set in. The Germans had inflicted massive damage on the Red Army, but they had not taken their main objective, and lacking proper winter equipment they were being frozen in place.

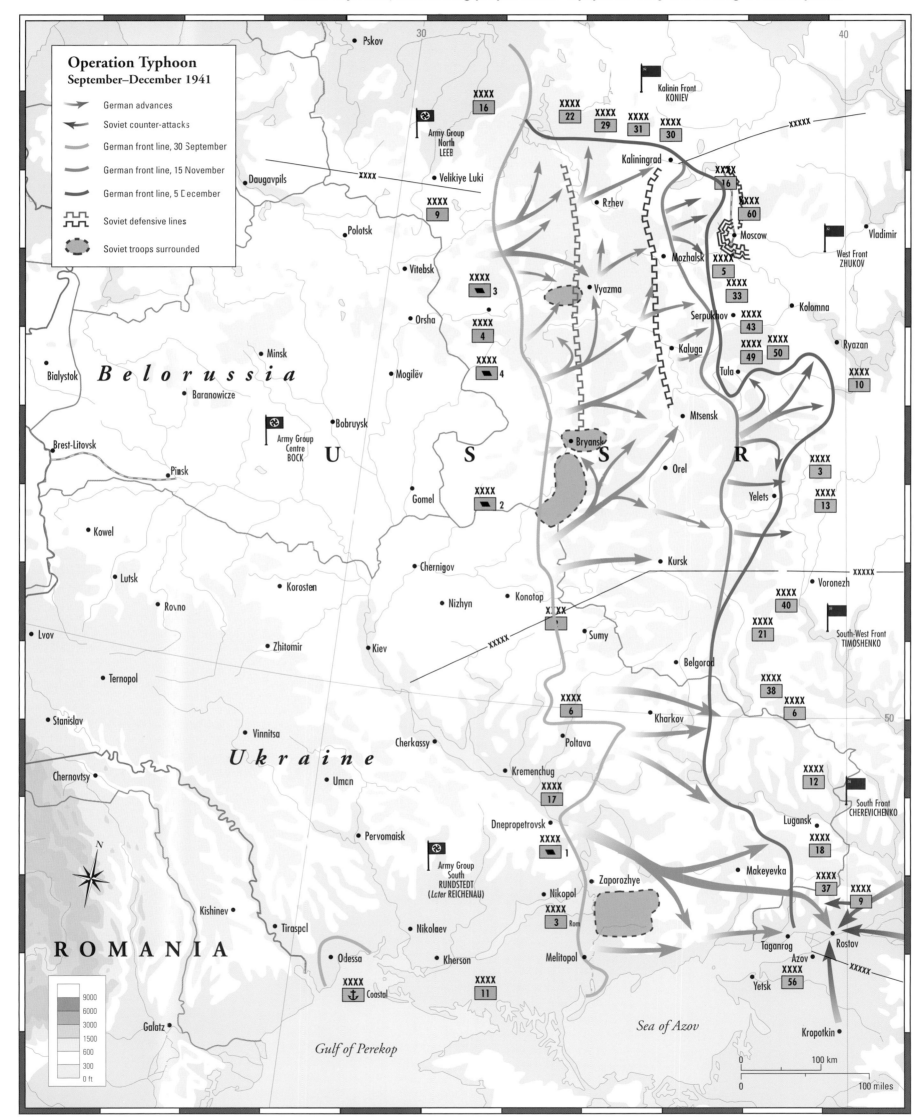

Operation Typhoon
September–December 1941

→ German advances
← Soviet counter-attacks
German front line, 30 September
German front line, 15 November
German front line, 5 December
Soviet defensive lines
Soviet troops surrounded

Siege of Leningrad September 1941– January 1944

As the birthplace of the Russian Revolution, Leningrad held a special significance to both the Soviets and to the Germans. Hitler made the city one of the *Wehrmacht's* key objectives in Operation Barbarossa, He confidently expected that Army Group North would be able to seize the city without difficulty once it had conquered the Baltic States. In the event, that took the *Wehrmacht* longer than expected, giving the city time to prepare its defences.

DRIVING UP THE WEST BANK of the Volkhov, the lead German panzers reached Ishora, only 17km (10.6 miles) from the centre of Leningrad. Motorized infantry swung up to the east towards the River Neva and the shores of Lake Ladoga. The old capital of Russia was now surrounded – but not occupied. The two leading divisions were soon enmeshed in a labyrinth of anti-tank ditches and straggling earthworks thrown up by the citizens while the Germans had paused to regroup. By the evening of 10 September the Germans had reached the Dugerdorf Heights, 10km (6.2 miles) southeast of the city.

But so many panzers had been hit or had broken down that the momentum of attack had been dissipated. German infantry crept up on their left during the following day, entered the Leningrad suburbs of Slusk and Pushkin, and in the evening occupied the Summer Palace of the Tsars at Krasnoye Selo. But the impetus had gone.

The Germans now settled in for a siege. For Leningrad, a precarious lifeline was provided by Lake Ladoga, a bare minimum of supplies coming by ship in summer and across the ice in winter.

The Germans did not manage to cut that line, which was enough to ensure that Leningrad survived over 900 days of siege – though more than half a million of its citizens did not.

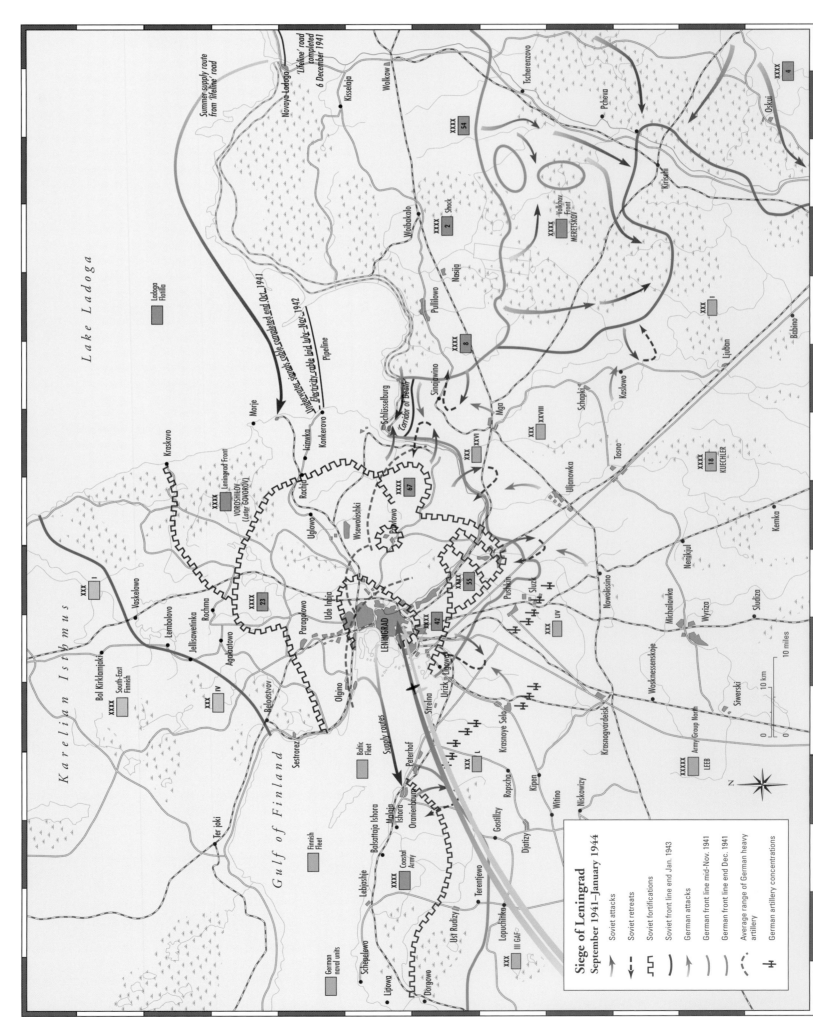

Siege of Leningrad
September 1941–January 1944

↗ Soviet attacks

⇠ Soviet retreats

⊔ Soviet fortifications

⌐ Soviet front line end Jan. 1943

↷ German attacks

⤻ German front line mid-Nov. 1941

⤻ German front line end Dec. 1941

⤸ Average range of German heavy artillery

✚ German artillery concentrations

Battle for Moscow January–June 1942

German reconnaissance units got to within sight of the spires of the Kremlin before a massive Soviet offensive burst over them. Launched on 5 December, it drove the Germans back from Moscow, and was followed by attacks all down the Eastern Front. Initially, the Germans retreated, but wherever conditions favoured defence, they stood and fought. By March, the Red Army had run out of steam. Soon, the Germans would be planning their own new offensive.

Battle for Moscow
January–June 1942

→ German advances
→ Soviet counter-attacks
‿ German front line end May
━ German front line January
⊓⊔ Soviet defensive lines
⬭ Soviet partisans operating behind enemy lines

Siege of Sevastopol
December 1941–July 1942

The Germans entered the Crimea in the summer of 1941. By December, the city of Sevastopol had been cut off. However, it was not until June 1942 that von Manstein's Eleventh Army made its final assault on the city, supported by the largest artillery pieces in history. After 24 days of devastating bombardment and close hand-to-hand combat, the city finally fell.

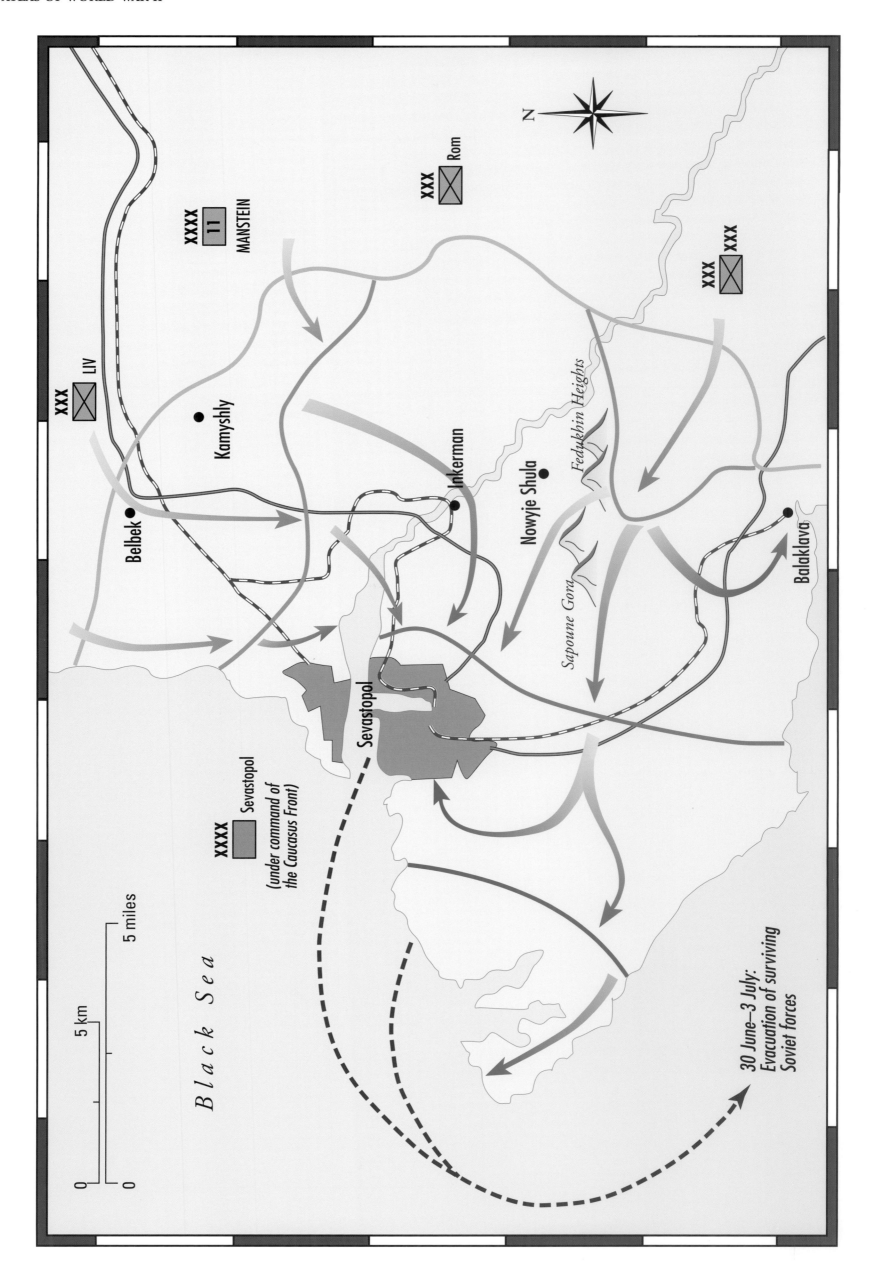

5 miles

5 km

0

0

Black Sea

XXXX
Sevastopol
(under command of the Caucasus Front)

Belbek

Kamyshly

XXX LIV

XXXX 11 MANSTEIN

XXX

XXX Rom

XXX

XXX

Inkerman

Nowyje Shula

Feduklin Heights

Sapoune Gora

Balaklava

Sevastopol

N

*30 June–3 July:
Evacuation of surviving
Soviet forces*

Yugoslavia 1941–43

The Germans might have thought that their rapid conquest of Yugoslavia in 1941 removed a potential problem from the southern flank of their war in the East, but in fact their problems were only just beginning.

The German occupation of Yugoslavia opened a vicious can of worms. In general, the Croats supported the Germans. Indeed Croatian Ustase nationalists conducted a genocidal campaign against the Serbs in Croatia and Bosnia.

Some Serbs, led by local quisling General Nedic, supported the Germans. Others – mostly pro-royalist fragments of the army and gendarmerie – took to the hills. Led by Draza Mihailovich, they adopted the old Serbian name of Chetnik, from *ceta*, or regiment.

Initial Serbian resistance brought savage reprisals from the Germans: the going rate was 100 Serbs executed for each German killed. But the Chetniks were also deadly foes of the Partisans – the communist rebels led by Tito. The Chetniks offered to come over to the German side to fight the communists – while continuing to fight the Croatian fascists who were being supplied by the Germans.

Internal rivalries were often more important than resisting the invaders. Serb fought Croat, Chetnik fought Partisan, and Muslims, Catholics and Orthodox Christians killed each other with unbridled enthusiasm.

Tito's Partisans

The Partisans were by far the most effective opposition to the Germans, and by the end of the war they claimed almost 200,000 men and women under arms. Although Tito himself was a Croat, he did more than any other Yugoslav to bring the war home to the Germans and their Croatian allies.

Tito's Partisan army won the support of the Western Allies in preference to the unreliable Serbian Chetniks, since by their actions they tied down no less than 35 German divisions. Partisans controlled large parts of the country, with some German garrisons being in a state of perpetual siege.

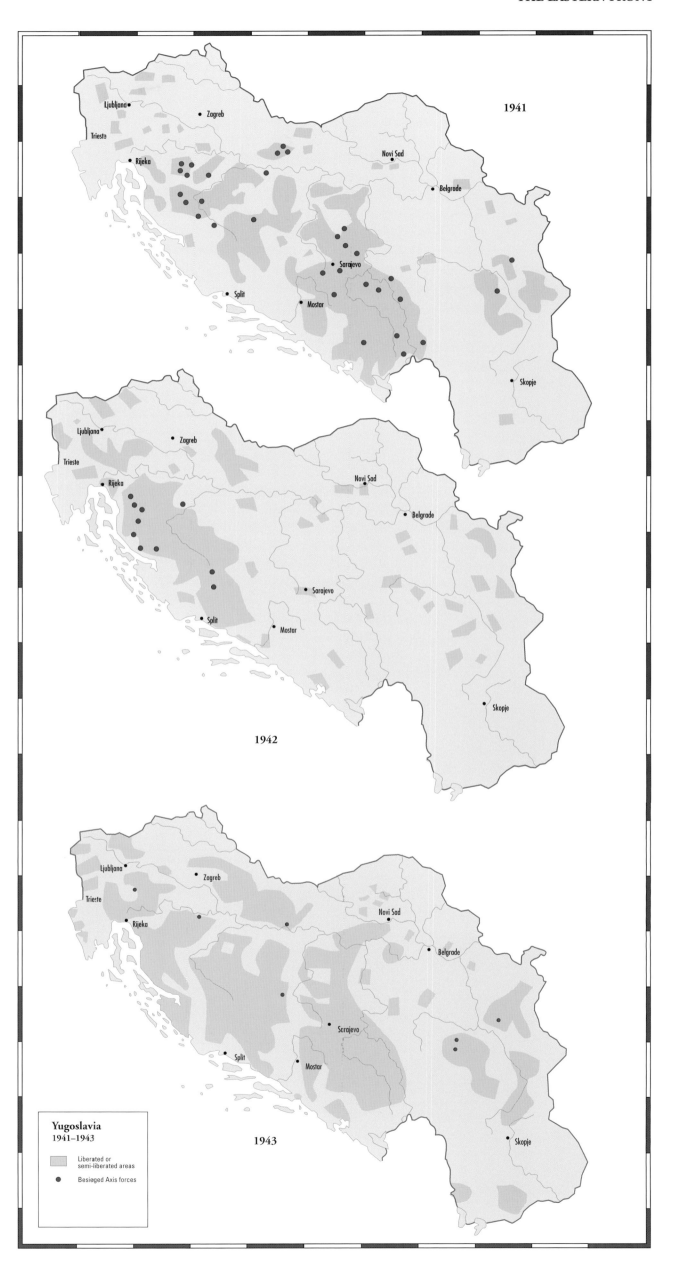

Yugoslavia 1941–1943

Liberated or semi-liberated areas

● Besieged Axis forces

The Caucasus
June–November 1942

The German summer offensive of 1942 had two main objectives. It was planned to destroy Soviet forces on the Don, moving on to Stalingrad before turning south to take the vital oil-producing areas of the Caucasus. Early successes led Hitler to order that both main objectives be attacked simultaneously, rather than in sequence. As a result, the Sixth Army commanded by General Paulus drove for Stalingrad while Army Group A advanced on the Caucasus.

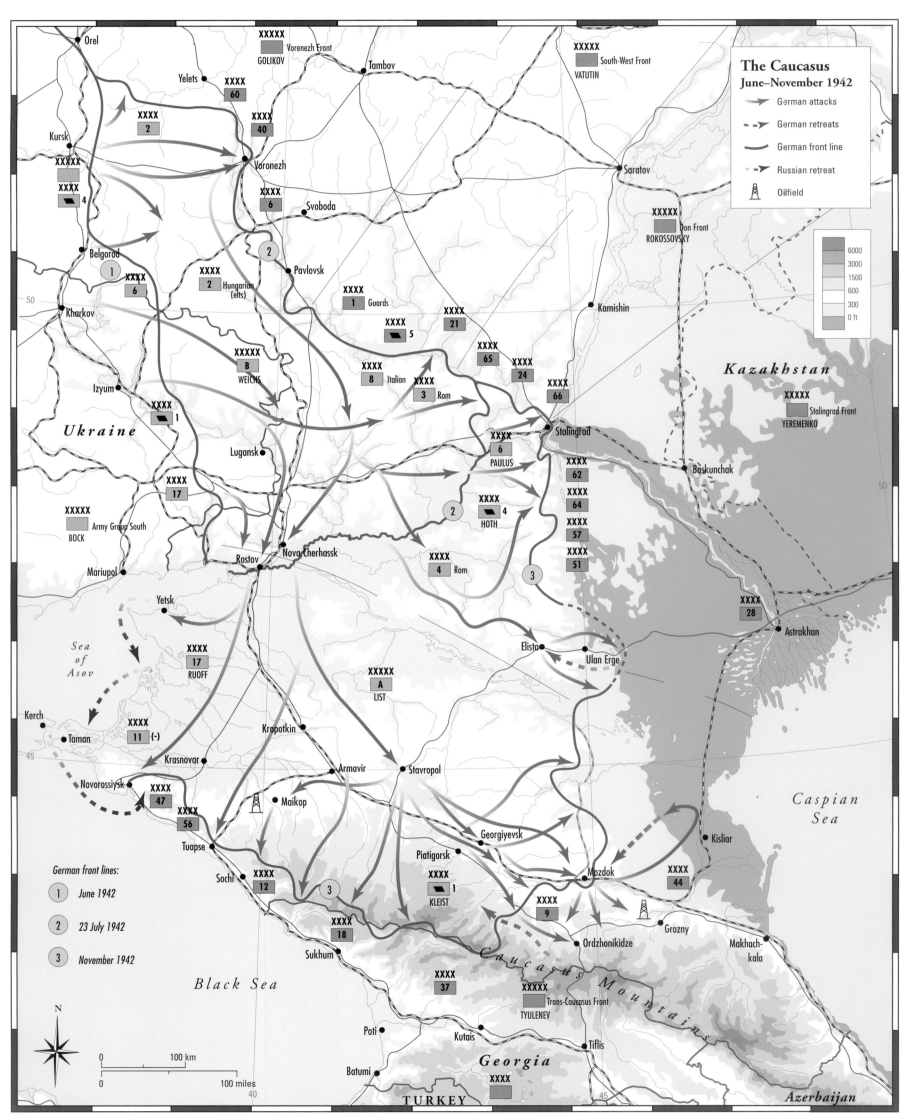

The Caucasus
June–November 1942

→ German attacks
⇢ German retreats
— German front line
⇠ Russian retreat
⚑ Oilfield

German front lines:
① June 1942
② 23 July 1942
③ November 1942

The Battle for Stalingrad September 1942–February 1943

Sixth Army launched its attack on Stalingrad in September 1942. In Berlin Hitler was already proclaiming victory.

However, the Russians fed in just enough troops to keep the Germans occupied, and to resist their best efforts.

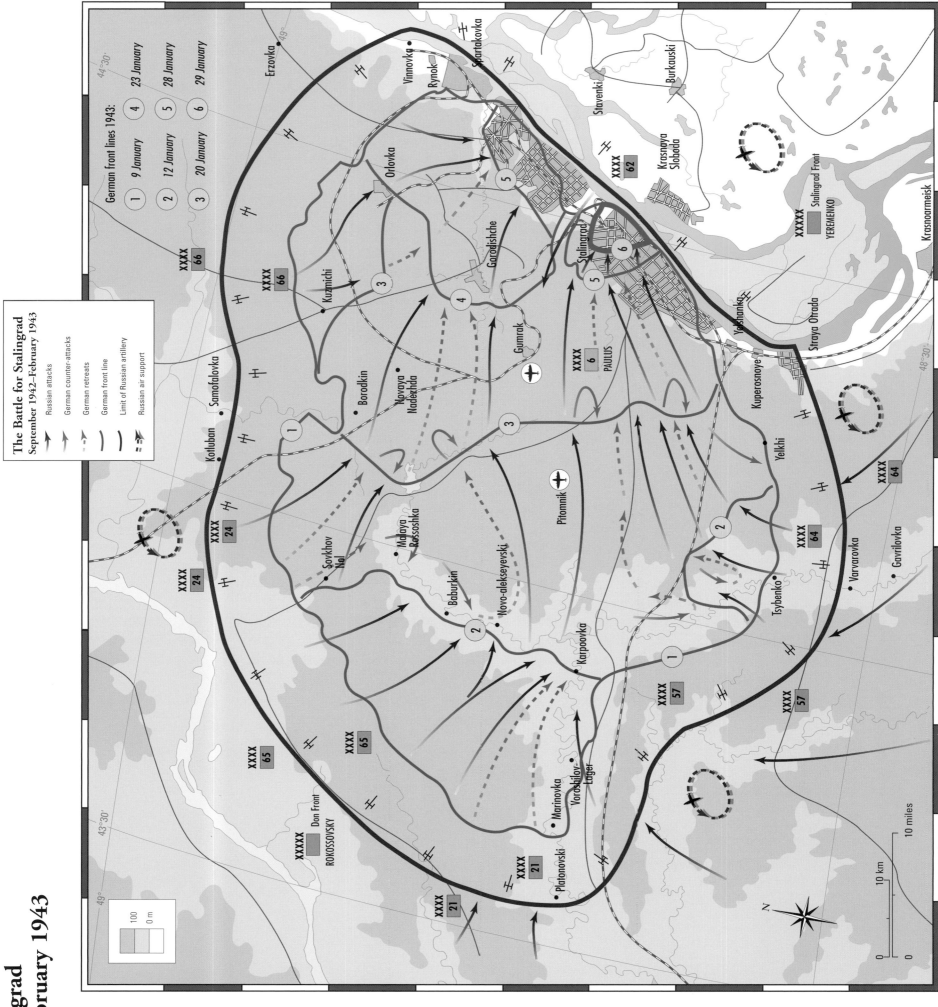

The Battle for Stalingrad
September 1942–February 1943

- Russian attacks
- German counter-attacks
- German retreats
- German front line
- Limit of Russian artillery
- Russian air support

German front lines 1943:
1. 9 January
2. 12 January
3. 20 January
4. 23 January
5. 28 January
6. 29 January

The huge mass of Red Army reserves were being held back for a different purpose. This was finally revealed on 19 November, after the last of six major attacks by the Sixth Army had been beaten off.

Surprise was near total when the Soviets unleashed massive barrages north and south of Stalingrad. German divisions were engulfed by wave upon wave of Soviet armour, heavily supported by aircraft and artillery. The next day the Soviets attacked in the south.

By 23 November, the encirclement was complete. Some 300,000 Axis soldiers were trapped inside Stalingrad. Stalin ordered the pocket crushed in January, and a renewed Soviet *blitzkrieg* broke into the perimeter west of the city. Some 25,000 sick and wounded were evacuated, but a far greater number of men died as frost-bitten limbs and wounds turned gangrenous. Of the 300,000 men in the pocket, 91,000 survived to surrender, of whom half would be dead before spring. Only 5000 would return from Soviet captivity.

The Russian winter still gripped the land when Paulus surrendered the Sixth Army at Stalingrad. Red Army elation at their victory and the good going provided by the frozen ground tempted the Soviets into widespread attacks. Any penetrations of the German lines were swiftly exploited.

WITHIN DAYS, Soviet tank battalions were racing across the open steppe west of the River Donets, overtaking scattered groups of retreating Germans. On 26 January they recovered Voronezh; by 8 February they were through Kursk and driving for the railway at Suzemka. The industrial city of Kharkov was abandoned by its SS garrison on 14 February, ignoring Hitler's orders to hold fast.

Field Marshal von Manstein had a clear plan for stabilizing the desperate situation in the East, and he persuaded the *Führer* to let him conduct the battle his way, instead of conducting the rigid defence which Hitler usually favoured.

Manstein let the Soviet advance continue while he assembled a powerful striking force on its flanks. There was massive support from a newly reinforced *Luftwaffe*.

Manstein sprang his first trap on 20 February. In what he dubbed his 'backhand blow', Manstein drove east to cut off all the Russian forces that had broken over the Donets.

Battle of Kharkov 29 January–20 February 1943

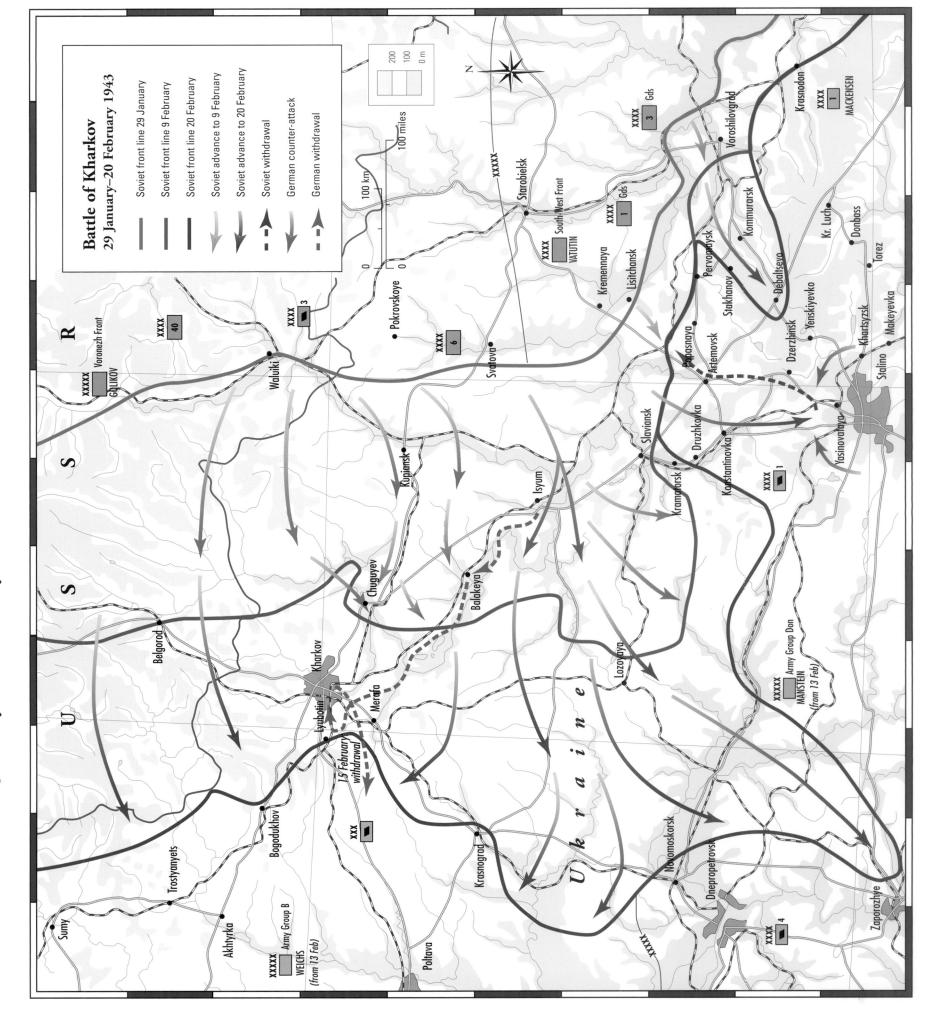

Battle of Kharkov
29 January–20 February 1943

- Soviet front line 29 January
- Soviet front line 9 February
- Soviet front line 20 February
- Soviet advance to 9 February
- Soviet advance to 20 February
- Soviet withdrawal
- German counter-attack
- German withdrawal

Eastern Front
Beginning of March 1943

The Battle of Kharkov improved the German position just as the spring thaw imposed its annual halt on military operations. The startling recovery of the *Ostheer* after the Stalingrad disaster unsettled Stalin, who made a tentative diplomatic approach to Hitler via Swedish diplomats. But the *Führer* was still set on decisive victory and the extermination of what he still regarded as the Jewish-Bolshevik threat.

HITLER'S ARMY WAS OUTNUMBERED two to one in men and five to one in tanks and guns, but the *Wehrmacht* knew that its training and tactical leadership were far superior to that of the Red Army. Although the Germans had taken a fearful battering over the winter, suffering massive losses at Stalingrad, they still held vast tracts of Soviet territory. Even though the odds did not favour a third successive large-scale summer offensive in 1943, the German Army high command was nevertheless determined on an attack.

The Soviets, too had suffered heavily. but the massive resources of the USSR were still coming into play. New, well-equipped divisions were being fielded, and the Red Army had been learning some hard lessons. It was fighting much more effectively than it had in 1942, partly as a result of a reorganization of its command structure.

New summer offensive

There was little thought of knocking Russia out of the war, however much Hitler clung to the dream of final victory. His generals were more pragmatic. They wanted to attack in order to cripple the Soviet Army. With the loss of North Africa, it was only a matter of time before the Allies attacked Italy or even landed in France. Unless the Red colossus could be smashed before then, a nightmare loomed: a two-front war that Germany could never win.

The front line had stabilized – running from just west of Rostov in the south, up to Velikiye Luki west of Moscow, then to Leningrad. However a huge Soviet salient protruded 80km (50 miles) westwards in front of Kursk, from just north of Belgorod up to the line of Ponyri. The salient was about 200km (125 miles) wide at its base.

This was the bulge on the map which drew all German eyes during the weeks which followed. It stuck out far more awkwardly than any sore thumb, and positively invited attack.

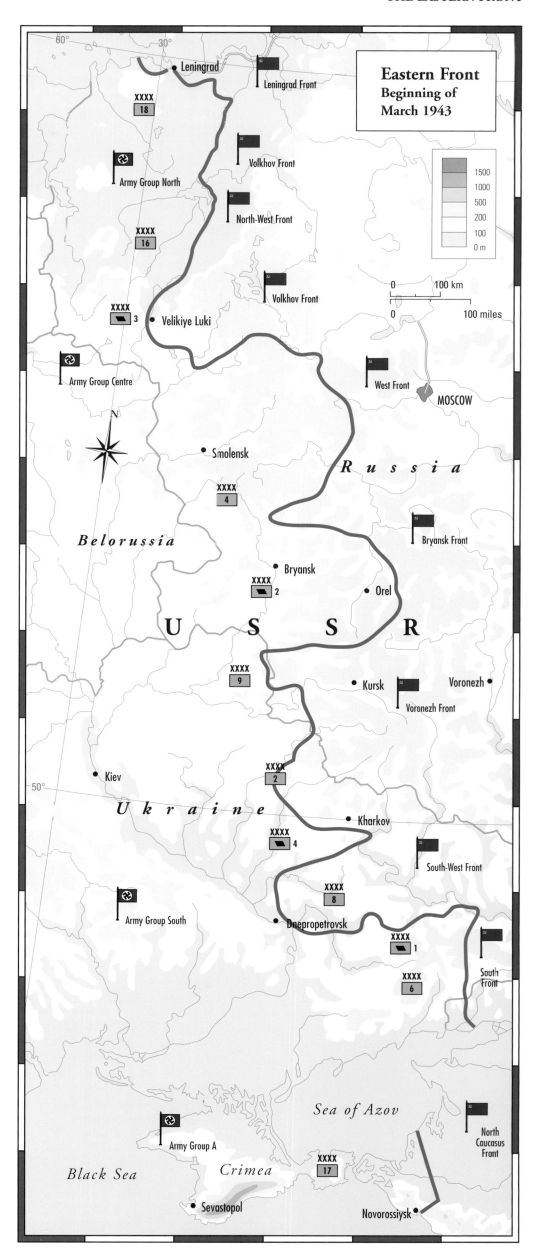

Battle of Kharkov
2–23 March 1943

By 3 March the Russians had had to abandon nearly 15,540 square kilometres (6000 square miles) of their recent gains. Kharkov was stormed in mid-March, and Belgorod was retaken. By month's end, the four Soviet tank corps were strung out between the Donets and Zaporozhye.

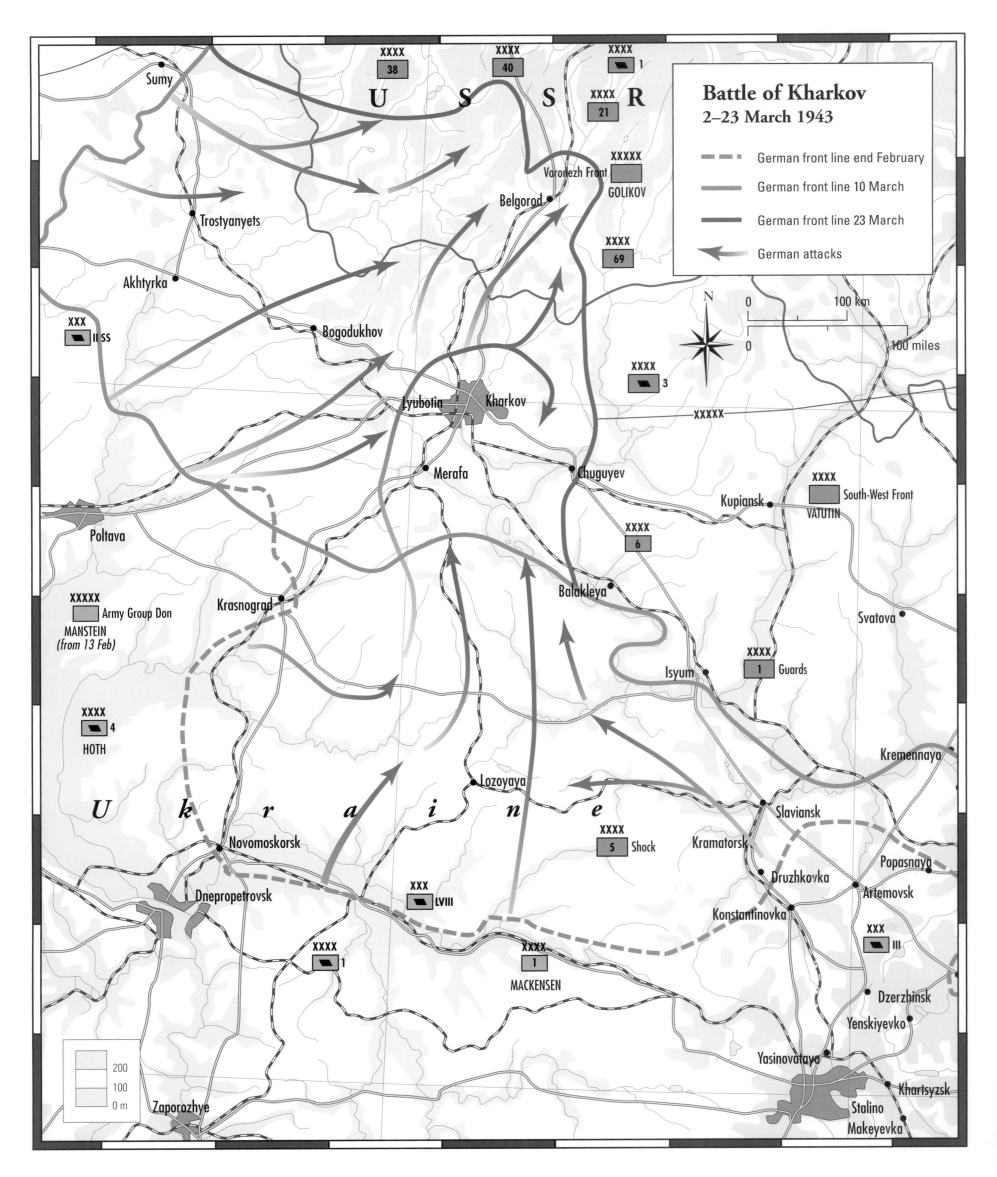

Battle of Kharkov
2–23 March 1943

- – – – German front line end February
- ——— German front line 10 March
- ——— German front line 23 March
- ←——— German attacks

Eastern Front
July 1943

Not only would the removal of the Kursk Salient flatten the line of the front, but it would provide a sound strategic base for a drive deep into Russia which would show the world that the German Army was still the most powerful military machine in the world.

INITIAL ORDERS FOR THE OFFENSIVE, code named Operation Citadel, were issued by OKH – the German Army high command – on 13 March 1943.

The outlines of the plan were quite simple. Army Group Centre would attack from the north with a massively reinforced panzer group, while Army Group South would strike northwards from the opposite side of the salient with even stronger forces.

The Soviets had never previously managed to halt a determined German summer assault without giving up hundreds of kilometres of territory. The German high command assumed — and the Soviet generals feared — that it would be no different this time.

The panzers had to break through little more than 100km (62 miles) to cut off all Soviet units in the salient. Further exploitation might take them back to the Don at Voronezh. Elimination of the Kursk bulge would also bring the *Wehrmacht* into a position to threaten Moscow.

In fact, the follow-up operation envisaged by OKH was Operation Parkplatz: the storming of Leningrad. Nine divisions were earmarked for the assault and the superheavy siege artillery used to batter Sevastopol into submission was en route north. It was not destined to arrive.

Kursk was such an obvious objective that the Russians began fortifying it almost as soon as the Germans decided to attack it. As early as March, Marshal Georgi Zhukov and his front commanders were presenting Stalin with their thoughts on likely German plans for the coming campaigning season. Their predictions proved to be remarkably accurate.

In addition, the Red Army planned new offensives of its own, scheduled to open the moment the German attack stalled. Stalin and his most senior commanders gambled that they could hold Kursk against the elite panzer divisions, absorb the full strength of the German blow, then unleash a multi-front offensive that would liberate the Ukraine.

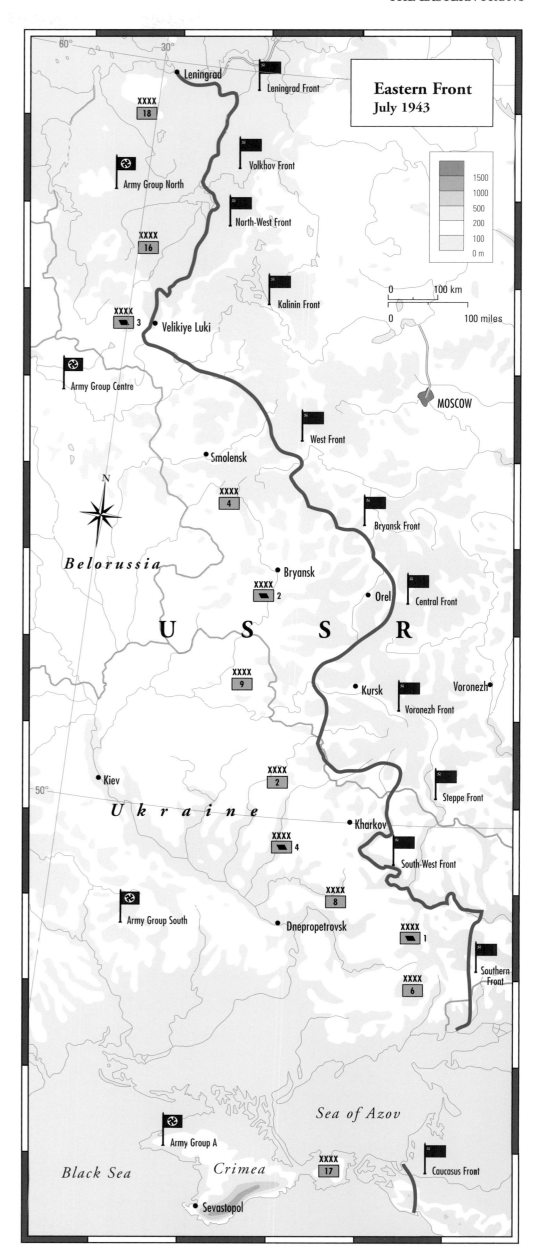

Operation Citadel
5–13 July 1943

Hitler postponed his attack several times in order to bring his forces up to maximum strength, and to employ the latest heavy tanks now in production. These delays were the cause of some debate in the German high command. Hitler himself was nervous: in a conversation with General Heinz Guderian in May he admitted that 'when I think of this attack my stomach turns over'.

A T 2.00 A.M. ON 5 JULY – an hour before the *Wehrmacht*'s opening barrage was due to launch the great offensive – hundreds of Soviet guns opened up. Soviet artillery blanketed the German assembly areas, killing hundreds of waiting troops and wrecking important communication networks.

German losses on that first day were reminiscent of those on the Western Front in 1916. By nightfall 200 panzers had been knocked out and 220 German aircraft shot down – and the days which followed increased the cost proportionately. Whole regiments were wiped out, batteries destroyed, squadrons crushed, before the leading formations broke clear of the defence belts – only to run into the waiting Russian armour and infantry.

Little progress is made

The German Ninth Army, commanded by the determined *Generaloberst* Model, made little headway into the northern shoulder of the salient. Citadel was more successful in the south. Hoth's panzers and Kempf's motorized infantry faced the Sixth Guards Army with the Seventh Guards Army on their left – all ready and waiting, all dug in behind belt after belt of murderous anti-tank defences.

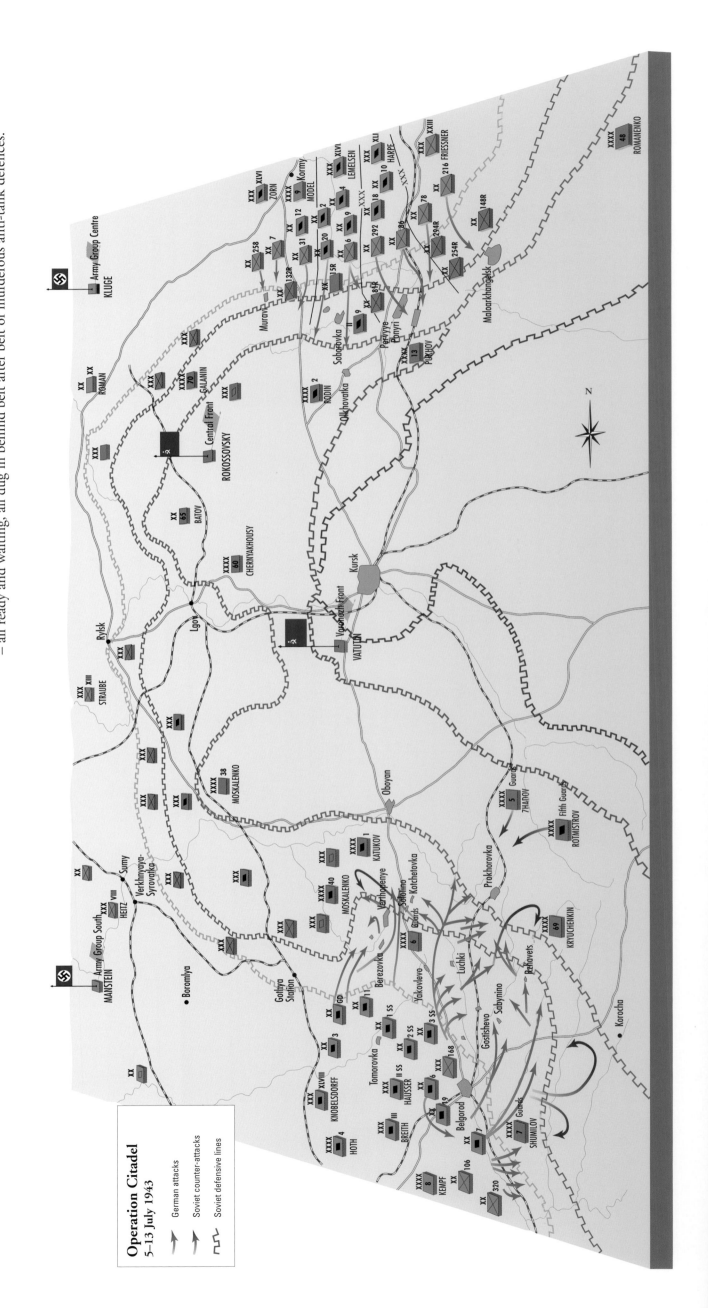

Operation Citadel
5–13 July 1943

→ German attacks
→ Soviet counter-attacks
⌐⌐ Soviet defensive lines

Battle of Prokhorovka
12 July 1943

At the beginning of the battle, the SS Panzer Corps smashed remorselessly through each line of defence. Again, the fighting went on 24 hours a day. The intense summer heat triggered thunderstorms by the end of each afternoon. Both sides were very active in the air, the *Luftwaffe* only being able to dominate selected areas of the front. The Soviets flew thousands of bomber sorties against German supply routes.

THE TANK BATTLES CULMINATED in the celebrated action near the small town of Prokhorovka. On 10 July the SS vanguard, led by *Totenkopf*, tore through the Soviet First Tank Army, overrunning the 71st Guards Rifle Division. Stalin sat at his desk in the Kremlin day and night, demanding hourly situation reports. He consented to the release of Fifth Guards Tank Army and the Fifth Guards Army from the reserve; they moved up, ready to counter-attack. Here they encountered the Germans in the largest and most bloody tank action of the whole battle.

The same day, to the north of the bulge, Army Group Centre was attacked by Soviet forces bent on liberating Orel. The ground won at such terrible cost had to be abandoned as Ninth Army pulled back to defend its own flank. Hitler called off Citadel and ordered the SS Panzer Corps to be transferred to the West. The *Ostheer* would go over to the defensive and contain the Russian drive on Orel.

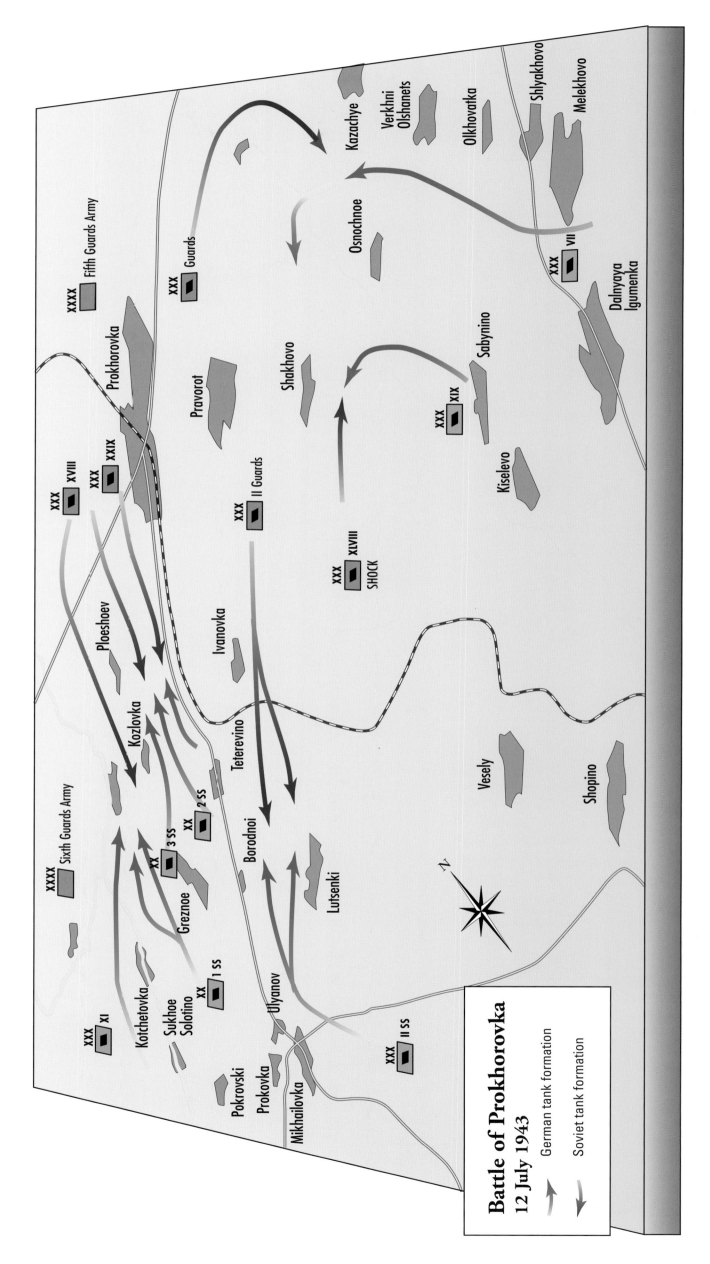

Battle of Prokhorovka
12 July 1943

→ German tank formation
→ Soviet tank formation

83

Soviet Advance to Dnieper 5 July–1 December 1943

Model's Ninth Army was unable to prevent the loss of Orel, which fell on 5 August. The Soviet Bryansk and Kalinin Fronts began new offensives in the north. Another major attack developed south of Kursk, forcing Manstein back to the scene of his triumph in the spring.

This time there was no power available for a backhand blow: all the Germans could do was fight a succession of rearguard actions as they withdrew, giving up Belgorod on 5 August and eventually abandoning Kharkov itself. On 23 August the city changed hands for the last time.

Army Group South retreated to prepared positions running from Zaporozhye to the Black Sea. The Soviets reached the isthmus connecting the Crimea to the mainland. The German Seventeenth Army was isolated.

As Kharkov fell in the south, General Popov launched an attack out of the newly won ground around Orel towards Bryansk. Further north, the Kalinin Front under Yeremenko drove down towards Smolensk. Two drives were launched in the direction of Kiev – from the Central Front under Rokossovsky and from the Voronezh Front under Vatutin. At the far south of the line, Tolbukhin's Southern Front crossed the River Mius, outflanked Taganrog (from which the last of Kleist's men hastily withdrew) and drove along the Azov coast to Mariupol.

By mid-September, the whole Soviet front from Smolensk down to the Black Sea was on the move. Within days, Central Front had swept through Sevsk as far as Konotop, Voronezh Front was through Piryatin, and Steppe Front had reached Poltava. South-West and Southern Fronts between them had cleared all enemy forces from the Donets Basin and were within striking distance of the Dnieper at Zaporozhye.

By the end of September the Red Army had reached the Dnieper north and south of Kiev.

Liberating the Ukraine and the Crimea January–May 1944

The Soviet offensives continued through the first months of 1944. Russian armies smashed through the Ukraine, retaking Kiev and reaching the River Bug near the Polish border.

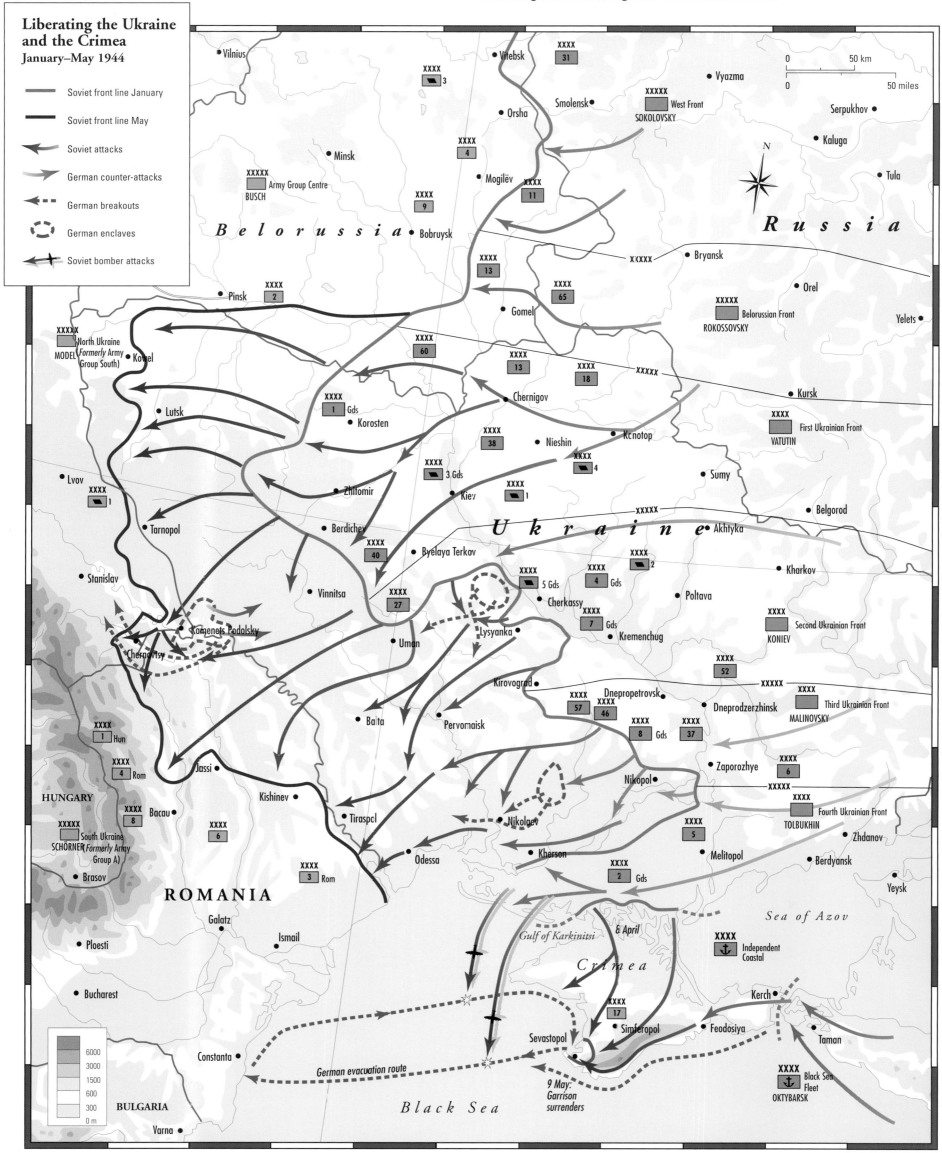

Liberating the Ukraine and the Crimea January–May 1944

- —— Soviet front line January
- —— Soviet front line May
- ◀— Soviet attacks
- ◁— German counter-attacks
- ◀-- German breakouts
- ⬭ German enclaves
- ◀✦ Soviet bomber attacks

Leningrad and the Karelian Front January–October 1944

By the beginning of 1944, Leningrad had been under siege for over two years. On the night of 13 January, General Govorov's Leningrad Front struck at the German forces around the city. On 20 January the Volkhov Front took Novgorod after flank attacks to the south across the frozen waters of Lake Ilmen. By the end of the month the Siege of Leningrad was over, and for the first time for 900 days the people of the city could walk their streets without fear of bomb or shell.

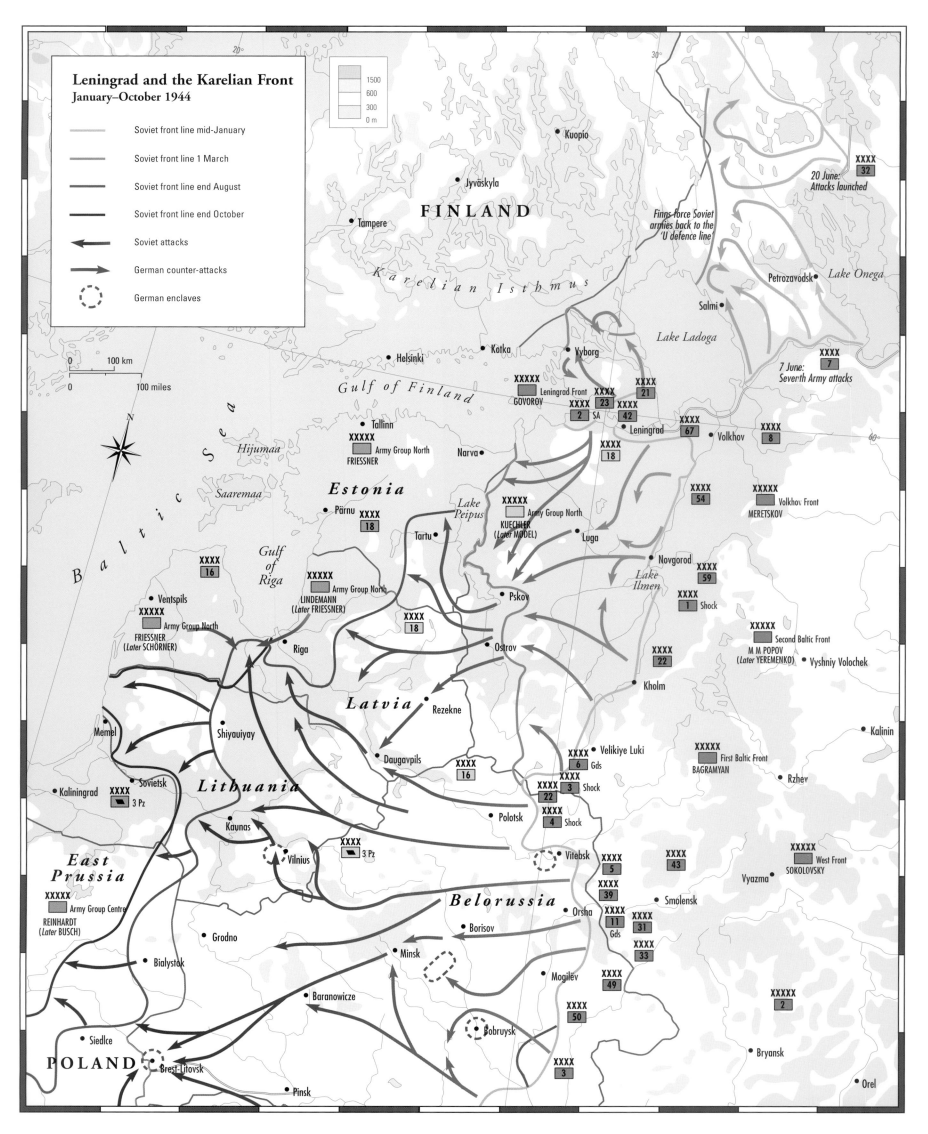

Leningrad and the Karelian Front
January–October 1944

— Soviet front line mid-January

— Soviet front line 1 March

— Soviet front line end August

— Soviet front line end October

← Soviet attacks

→ German counter-attacks

⬭ German enclaves

Karelian Front
September–October 1944

The northern offensive was not over with the relief of Leningrad. Luga fell on 12 February. Second Baltic Front under General Popov drove west below Lake Ilmen, and when on 1 March the Soviet high command called a halt, Soviet troops had reached Pskov and the shores of Lake Peipus.

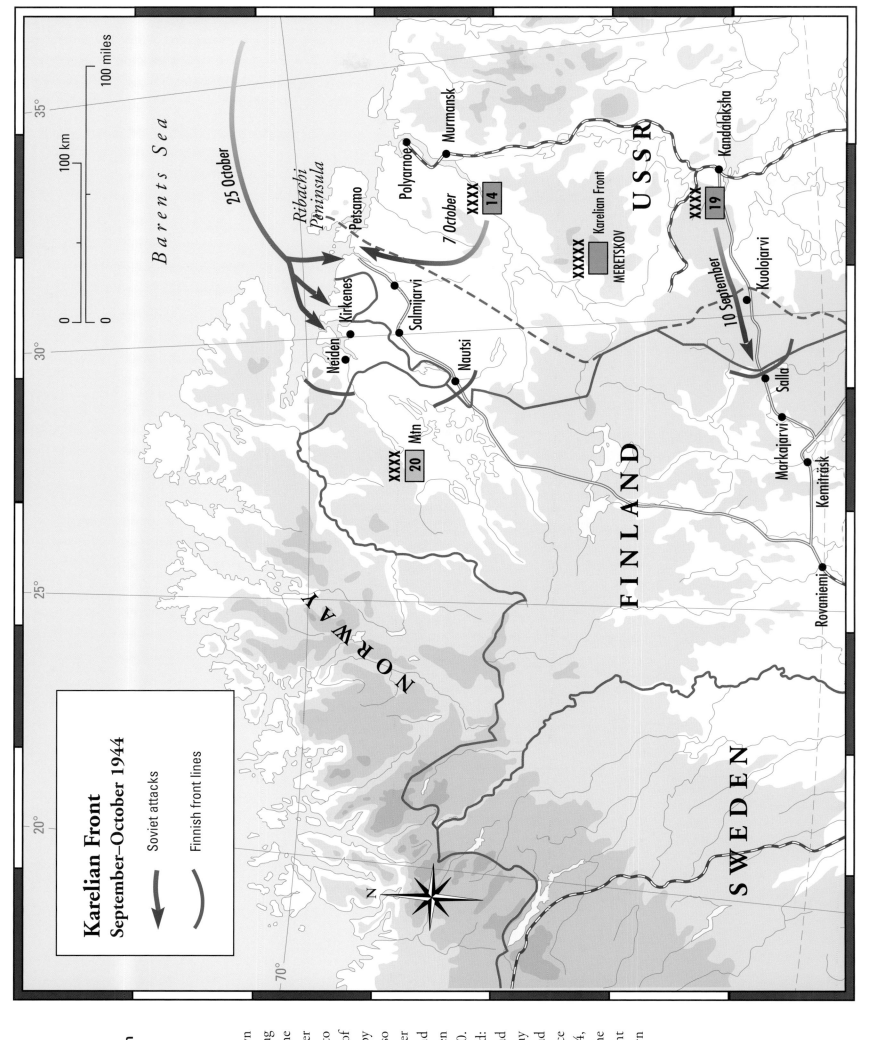

Further north, a little known campaign was also coming to a climax. Operations in the Karelian Isthmus and further into the Arctic were intended to finally knock the Finns out of the war. Vastly outnumbered by the Soviets, the Finns were also facing an enemy who was better trained, better equipped and better led than he had been during the Winter War of 1940.

Soviet pressure quickly told: not surprisingly, the Finns had to fall back as the Red Army retook territory which it had lost in 1941. An armistice followed on 4 September 1944, leaving German troops on the Arctic Front having to fight their way back to northern Norway.

Operation Bagration
June–July 1944

The Soviet summer offensive of 1944 was the most decisive campaign of the war. Launched three years to the day after the German invasion, and three weeks after the Western Allies landed in Normandy, the offensive saw the largest military force in history smash into German Army Group Centre. By the end of August, Soviet forces were in the Baltic States, across the Polish border and about to cross into Romania. And Army Group Centre had been annihilated.

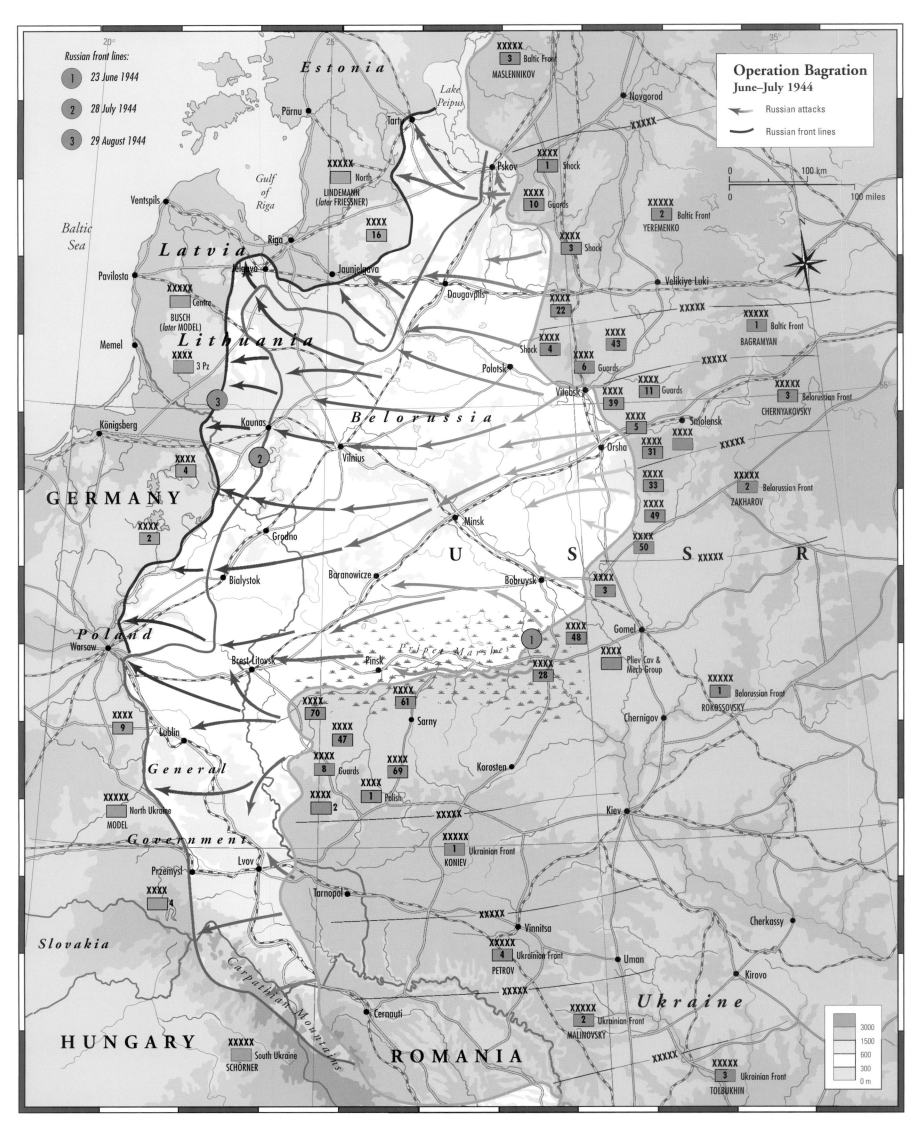

Soviet Advance into Poland July 1944

By the early summer of 1944, the Red Army was the biggest land force ever put into the field of battle. A very high proportion were combat troops, serving at what the Western Allies called 'the sharp end' – though the Soviet notion of a 'sharp end' was more like the head of a sledgehammer.

B REST-LITOVSK fell to Rokossovsky on 28 July and soon afterwards his forces reached the Bug north of Warsaw. Chuikov's Eighth Guards Army stormed out of Kowel, captured Lublin and reached the Vistula, which it crossed on 2 August.

On 13 July, Marshal Koniev's Ukrainian Front drove forward against very strong resistance from Army Group North Ukraine. This was where the *Wehrmacht* had expected the Soviet onslaught. It was not until two more tank armies had been brought up from reserve on 16 July, and this tremendous weight of men and firepower began to tell, that the defences cracked.

By the end of August, the Carpathians had been reached along their main length. The Red Army had now driven right through Poland and was closing on the pre-war borders with Czechoslovakia and Hungary.

In two months Soviet troops had advanced over 700km (435 miles) and now the time had again come to reorganize the supply lines. Their advance had been immensely costly – but it had inflicted even greater losses on the Germans.

Soviet Advance into Poland
July 1944

—— Soviet front line beginning of July

◄—— Soviet advances to 28 July

→ German counter-attacks

The Warsaw Rising
1 August–2 October 1944

The approaching Red Army prompted the Polish Home Army to rise against the German occupiers. The Red Army, which had just finished a major campaign with exhausted troops, low supplies and unserviceable equipment, stopped short of the city. Its reluctance to help the Poles may have come from Stalin himself: the Home Army was nationalist and anti-communist, and it was in the Soviet dictator's interest to see it wiped out – which it was, brutally.

The Warsaw Rising
1 August–2 October 1944

○ German isolated pockets 1–5 August

Polish attacks
1–5 Aug   30 Aug–2 Sept   26 Sept

German attacks
1–5 Aug   30 Aug–2 Sept   26 Sept

Polish attacks
30 Aug–2 Sept   26 Sept

Allied attempts to supply Polish Home Army by air drops

14–15 August: British aircraft from southern Italian bases drop supplies

5 August: Bomber raid on Wola district

30 August–2 September: Polish retreat

Soviet Advance into Romania and Hungary 8 August–15 December 1944

As the great Soviet summer offensive wound down, another campaign was about to open, with perhaps more political motivation than military. The Balkans were as great an attraction to Stalin as they had been for centuries to the Romanovs. By the end of August, Romania was in the process of being occupied by the Red Army, which then moved on Hungary, and Bulgaria was about to be invaded by one of Tolbukhin's armies driving down the Black Sea coast.

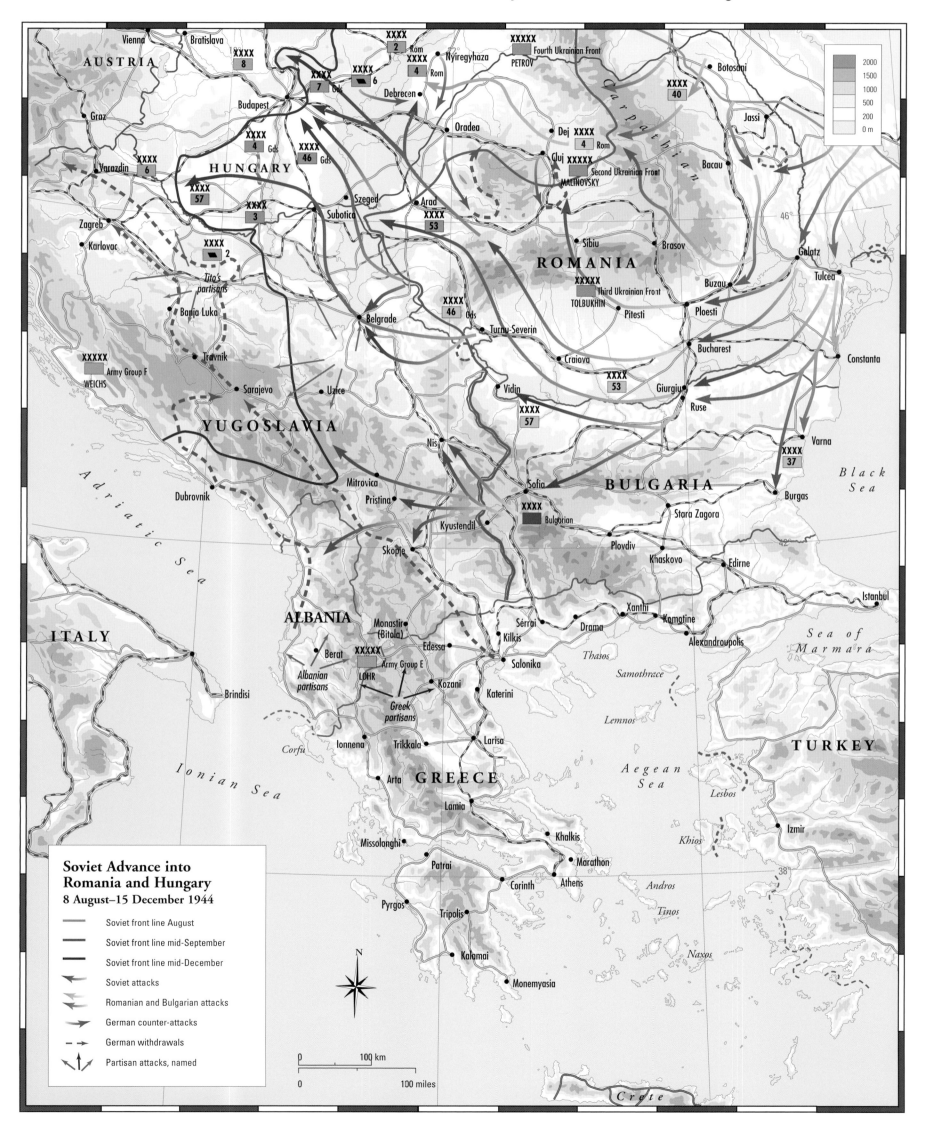

Soviet Advance into Romania and Hungary
8 August–15 December 1944

— Soviet front line August

— Soviet front line mid-September

— Soviet front line mid-December

← Soviet attacks

⇐ Romanian and Bulgarian attacks

→ German counter-attacks

-→ German withdrawals

↓ Partisan attacks, named

Liberation of Greece October–November 1944

In the aftermath of the Red Army's drive through Romania, the situation for German forces in the Balkans became precarious. To avoid being cut off in Crete, Greece and Albania, German units began withdrawing northwards in the early autumn of 1944. SS and other troops held open the Vardar Corridor, which allowed 350,000 troops of Army Group Lohr to escape through Macedonia and Bulgaria.

WITH THE WITHDRAWAL OF GERMAN forces from the region, the focus of the fighting in Greece switched to the struggle between communists and royalists. The royalists had the support of the British – British troops landed in Greece on 12 October 1944 with the intention of assisting the government in exile to return to power. They found themselves caught in the crossfire of a bitter civil war.

Civil conflict

Greek partisans had formed numerous anti-German groups during the years of occupation, but with the withdrawal of the Nazis the mutual antipathy between the groups spilled over into violence. The communists had hoped for support from Stalin, but the Soviet dictator had his eyes on other parts of the Balkans, and was quite happy for Greece to fall within the British sphere of influence. As a result, the communists were left to fend for themselves.

Although Greece had been officially declared liberated on 4 November 1944, the various partisan factions continued to fight each other with the enthusiasm they had formerly reserved for killing Germans: the civil conflict would continue well into the post-war years.

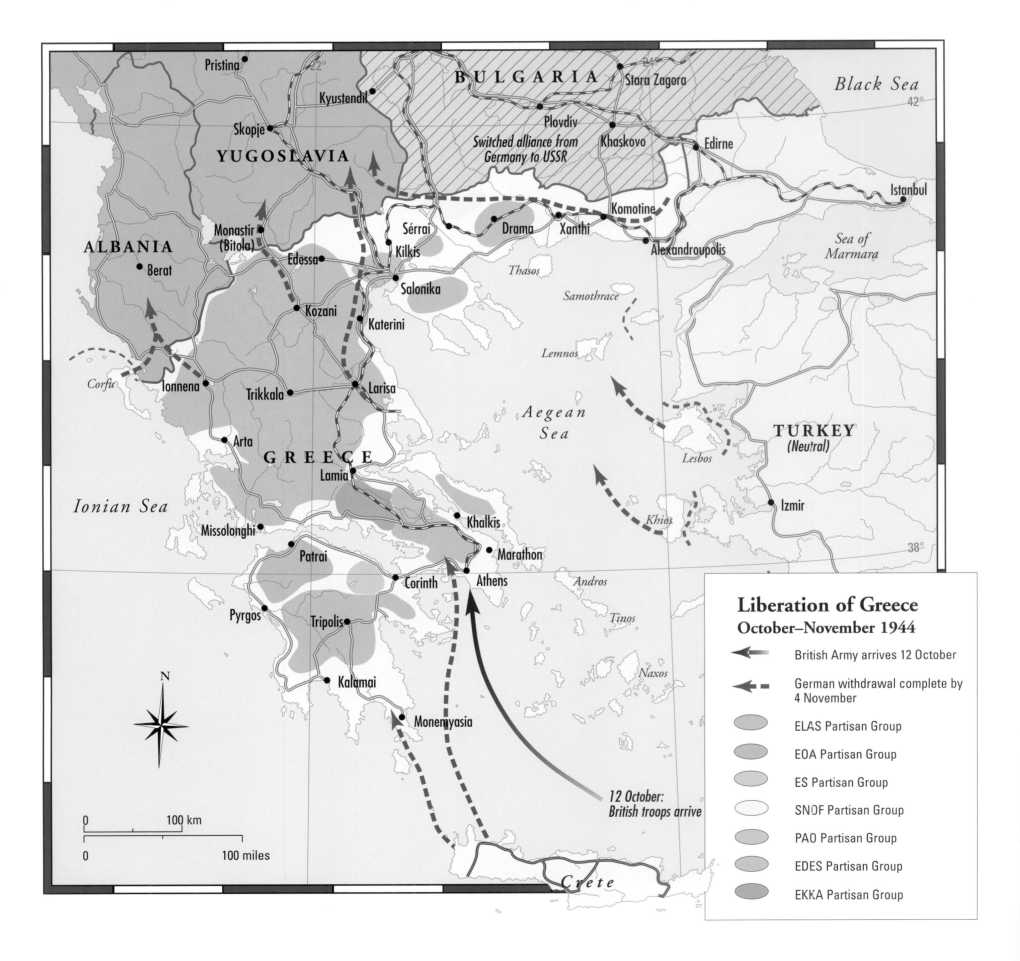

Liberation of Greece
October–November 1944

← British Army arrives 12 October

⇠ German withdrawal complete by 4 November

ELAS Partisan Group
EOA Partisan Group
ES Partisan Group
SNOF Partisan Group
PAO Partisan Group
EDES Partisan Group
EKKA Partisan Group

Battle of Budapest and Vienna December 1944–May 1945

When Hungary tried to withdraw from the Axis pact, Hitler had Admiral Horthy deposed and a puppet government was set up in his place. Hitler was determined to defend Budapest, hoping to prevent the Russians from pushing through Austria and southern Germany. The Hungarian capital was surrounded on 24 December 1944. In spite of German attempts to relieve the city, using some of the *Wehrmacht*'s last reserves, it fell on 13 February.

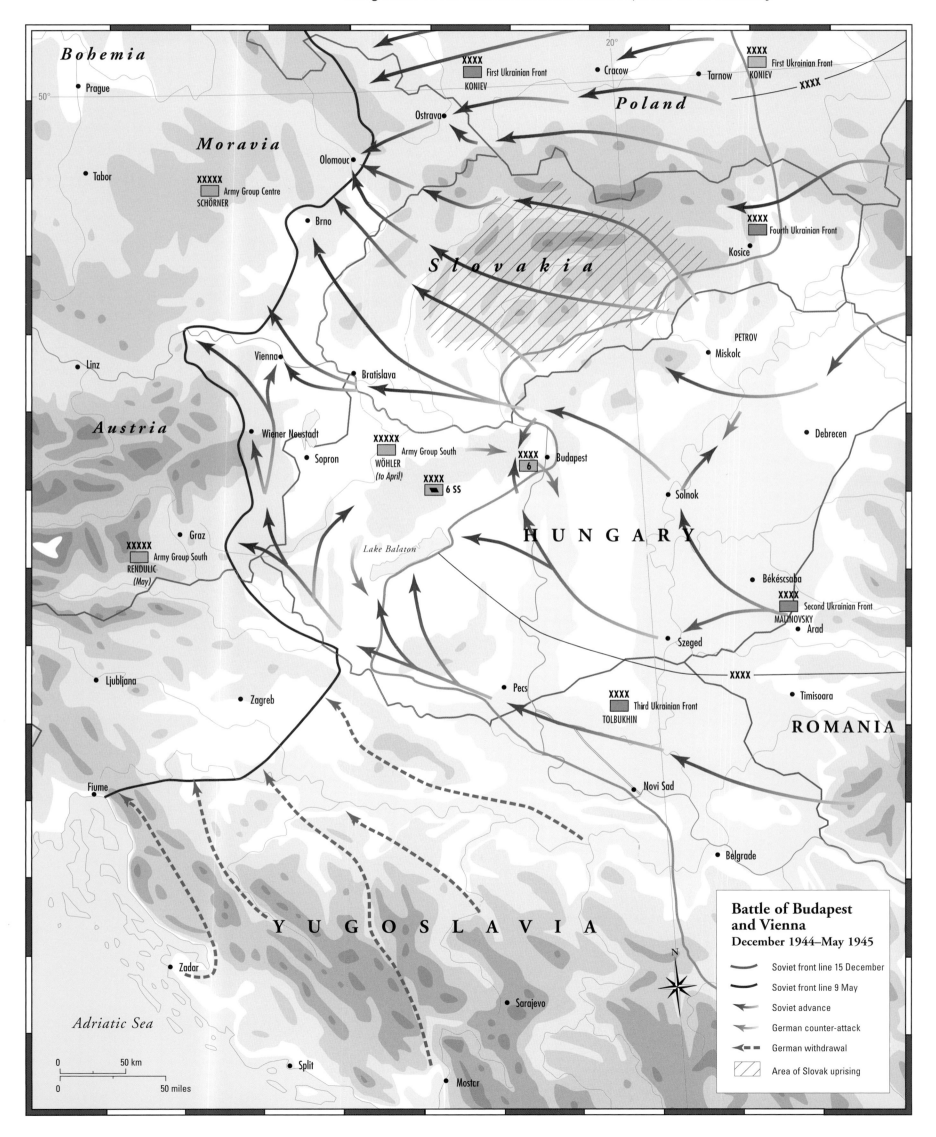

Battle of Budapest and Vienna
December 1944–May 1945

— Soviet front line 15 December
— Soviet front line 9 May
← Soviet advance
← German counter-attack
◄- - German withdrawal
▨ Area of Slovak uprising

Advance to the Oder
January–February 1945

Since Hitler had deployed the cream of the German armed forces in the Ardennes, the *Wehrmacht* had little to counter the new Soviet offensive which was launched on 12 January 1945. Attacking from the Vistula, the Red Army drove onto German soil for the first time. Silesia fell quickly, and by the end of January, Zhukov's First Belorussian Front was on the Oder. There Stalin called a halt, to allow time to prepare for the final attack on Berlin.

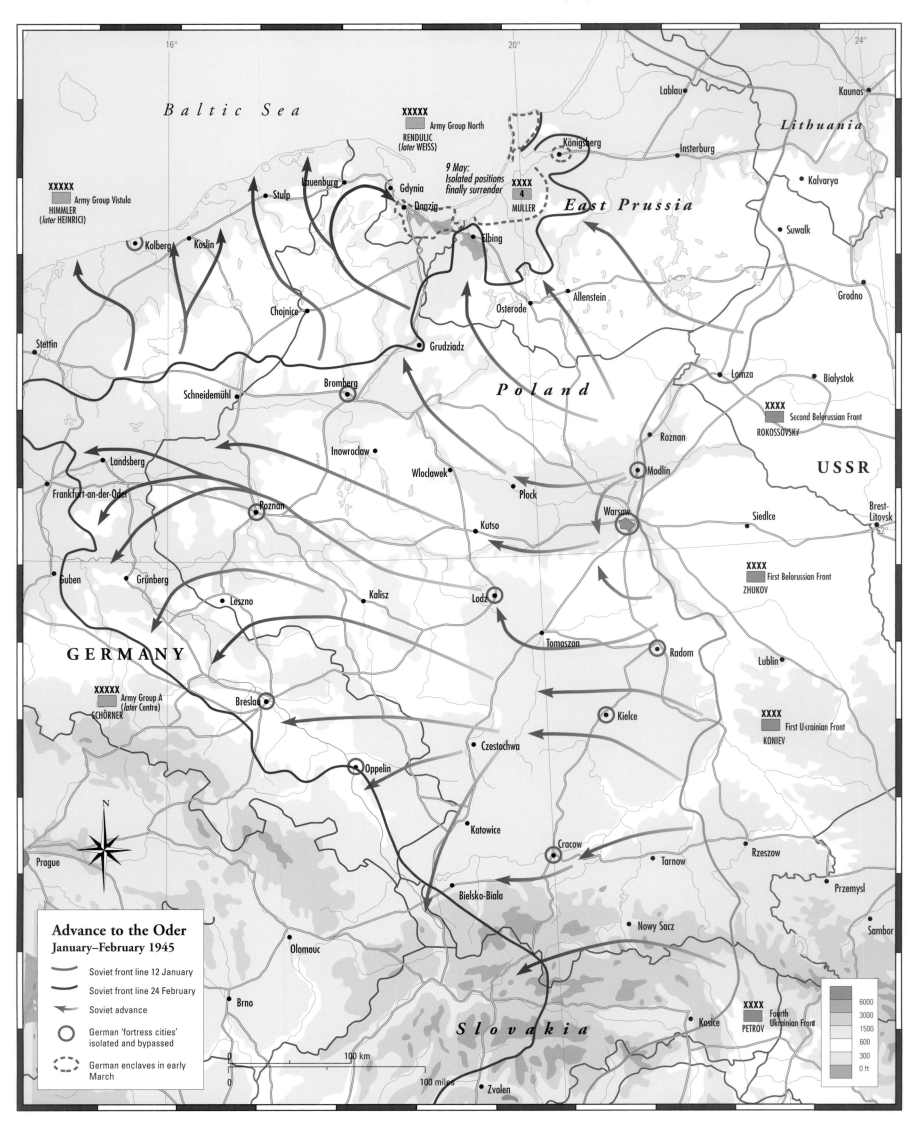

Advance to the Oder
January–February 1945

— Soviet front line 12 January

— Soviet front line 24 February

⟶ Soviet advance

◯ German 'fortress cities' isolated and bypassed

⌇ German enclaves in early March

Encirclement of Berlin
15 April–6 May 1945

Stalin ordered both Zhukov and Koniev to prepare for the attack on Berlin, counting on the rivalry between his two greatest marshals to spur their troops into the city before the Western Allies could snatch the prize. On 16 April 1945, a massive artillery bombardment launched the Soviet attack. By 21 April, Zhukov's troops were in the suburbs, and on 24 April troops of the First Belorussian and the First Ukrainian Fronts met on the River Havel. Berlin was surrounded.

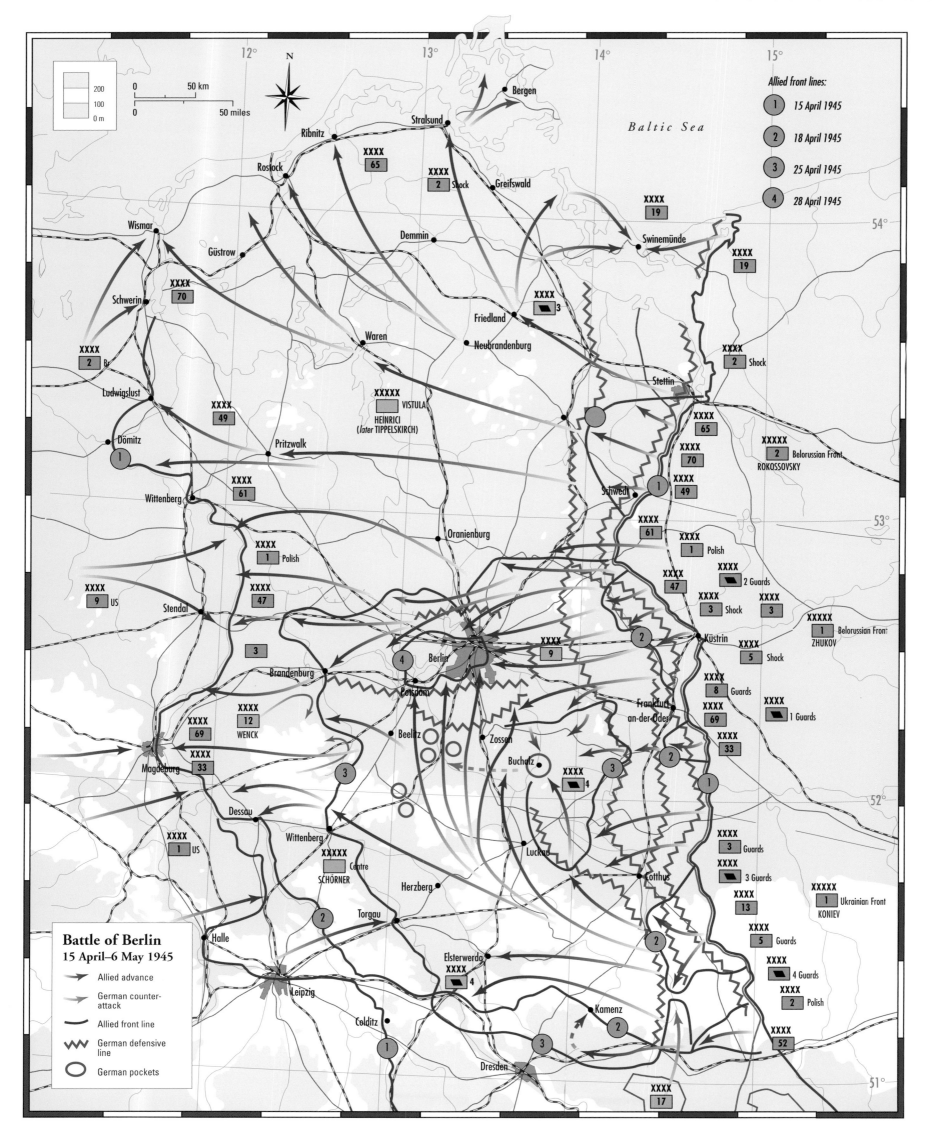

Allied front lines:

1 15 April 1945
2 18 April 1945
3 25 April 1945
4 28 April 1945

Battle of Berlin
15 April–6 May 1945

→ Allied advance
→ German counter-attack
— Allied front line
WW German defensive line
◯ German pockets

Battle for Berlin 26 April–2 May 1945

Although the defenders of Berlin fought with all the courage and professionalism of the German Army, the Soviet war machine was now an unstoppable juggernaut. Even though it was obvious that Berlin – indeed, the whole of the Third Reich – was doomed, Hitler resolved to stay in his capital, vowing to fight to the death against the hated communists.

By 22 April, Zhukov's troops were dividing into battle groups for urban combat: infantry companies with anti-tank guns, flamethrower teams and a tank platoon. The city of Berlin was surrounded and the troops swarmed forward to smash the last German resistance of the war.

A day later, Koniev's troops were making their final assault. They attacked under the cover of artillery packed at a density of more than 60 guns per kilometre of front. As the troops moved towards the centre of Berlin the guns followed. Field and heavy artillery blasted surviving German strongpoints over open sights at point-blank range.

Although a few die-hard Nazis continued to fight on in the cellars, resistance began to crumble. Troops from the Third Shock Army pressed on towards the *Reichstag*. The army command had issued nine victory banners before the battle: the first went up on the German parliament at 14:25 on 30 April.

Hitler committed suicide in his bunker beneath the Chancellery just as resistance around the *Reichstag* ceased. His successors attempted to open negotiations, as the last organized German units tried to fight their way out of the city, but by 5 May all fighting had ended.

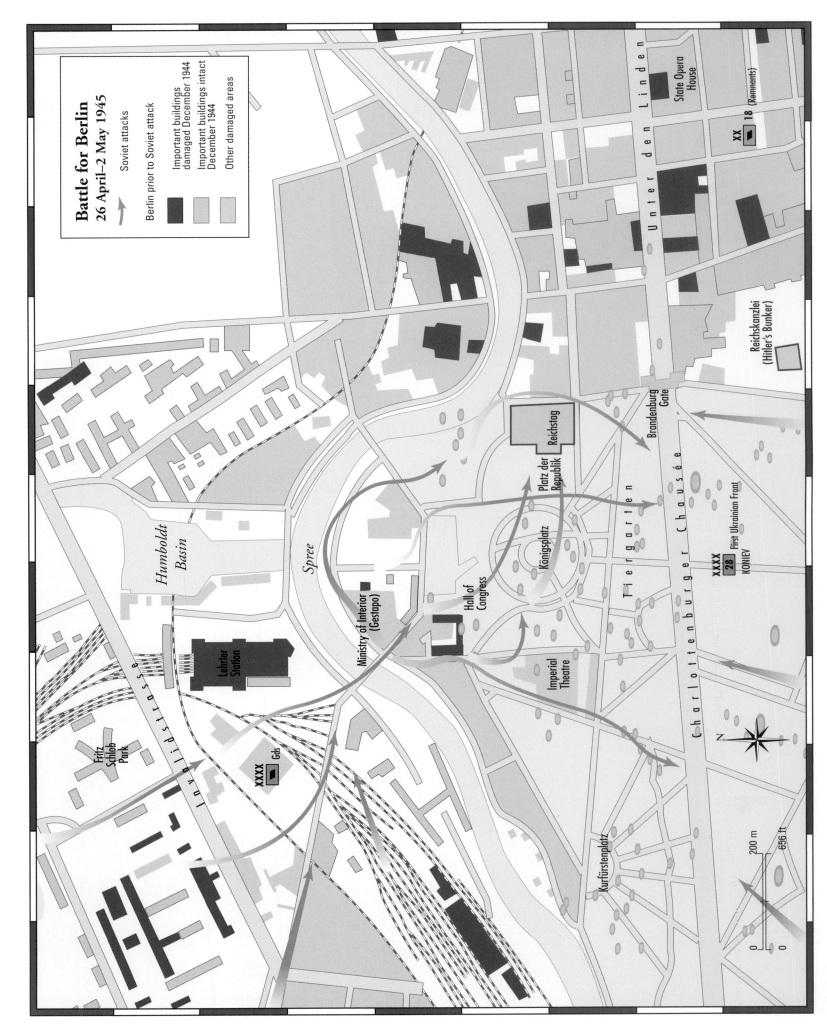

Battle for Berlin
26 April–2 May 1945

Soviet attacks

Berlin prior to Soviet attack

Important buildings damaged December 1944
Important buildings intact December 1944
Other damaged areas

Global Strategy 1941–45

World War II was not a global conflict in its early stages. However, in 1941 the war's scope increased tremendously. Germany's invasion of the USSR expanded the conflict eastwards and American involvement in the Battle of the Atlantic was growing. It was the Japanese attack on Pearl Harbor which finally saw battle erupt all over the planet.

T HE GEOGRAPHICAL EXTENT of World War II was unprecedented. Almost every part of the globe had some effect on strategy, with the sea routes between the Americas and Europe being of particular importance. The Allies had agreed that the defeat of Germany should be their first priority, but the war in the Pacific was not ignored.

The key to Allied strategy was the phenomenal industrial strength of the United States. The world's greatest economy had the capacity to be the arsenal of democracy, building the equipment and weapons used by all of the Allies. At the same time, American military might meant that it was fully capable of fighting two wars simultaneously: against the Germans in Europe and against the Japanese Empire across the vast distances of the Pacific.

Although Soviet industry also made a titanic contribution to the war effort, every tank, gun and aircraft it produced was needed on the Eastern Front. Even the Red Army was dependent on US aid, with American factories providing it with jeeps and trucks by the hundreds of thousands.

The agreement to concentrate on Germany first meant that the Battle of the Atlantic intensified as a massive build-up of American troops and equipment took place in Britain. Early operations in North Africa and the Mediterranean

achieved considerable success, but these were peripheral theatres. Stalin's insistence that the Allies open a second front meant that the Allies needed to mount an invasion of Europe as soon as possible. In May 1943, it was agreed by the Allies that a landing would be made on the European mainland some time in 1944.

Meanwhile, as the invasion of Europe was being planned, US forces began the long process of 'Island Hopping' across the Pacific. By using a massively expanded US Navy and its potent carrier strike power, the Americans were able to isolate and capture Japanese island garrisons all across the ocean. American submarines tightened a steel noose around Japan's seaborne trade, cutting off the vital supplies of raw materials which were the main reason that resource-poor Japan went to war in the first place. American long-range bombers began flying against the Japanese home islands from bases in China. As the US Navy advanced across the Pacific, one of its main aims was to capture island air bases from which giant new bombers would be able to attack Japan.

The Axis powers had reached their high point in 1941 and 1942. Now they were faced with the world's greatest military and industrial powers, they had nowhere to go but down into ruin.

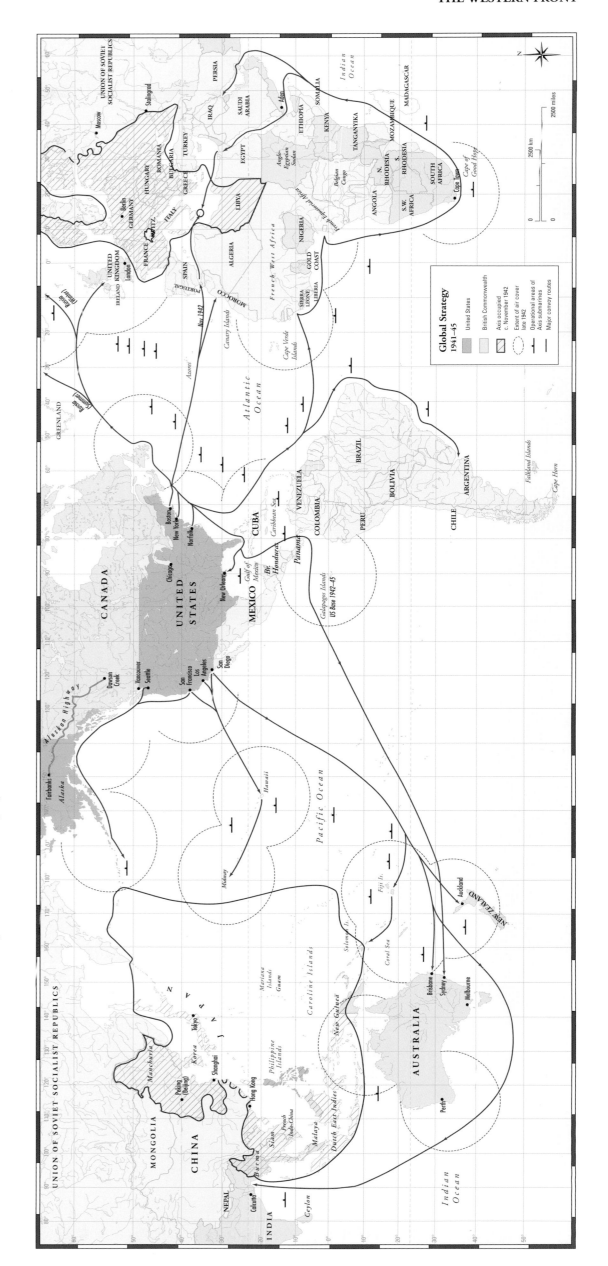

The Anglo-American conference in Casablanca in 1943 set the priority for future operations, and agreed that the unconditional surrender of Nazi Germany was the Allied goal in Europe.

THE AMERICANS wanted an invasion of Europe as soon as possible, much to British alarm. The disastrous raid on Dieppe in August 1942 convinced Allied commanders that a full-scale invasion would need more preparation.

Winston Churchill and Franklin D. Roosevelt agreed to set up a combined planning staff under General Sir Frederick Morgan, Chief of Staff to the Supreme Allied Commander, or COSSAC.

The first task was to decide where the invasion would take place. The Pas de Calais was the obvious choice, but it was also obvious to the Germans, and was the most heavily defended section of the European coast. Brittany was less well defended, but the coast was rocky and the area was subject to sudden violent storms.

In the end, COSSAC recommended that the landings be made in Normandy. It was a longer sea crossing than to the Pas de Calais, but there were good beaches, and it offered good routes into the interior of France.

COSSAC Plan
August 1943

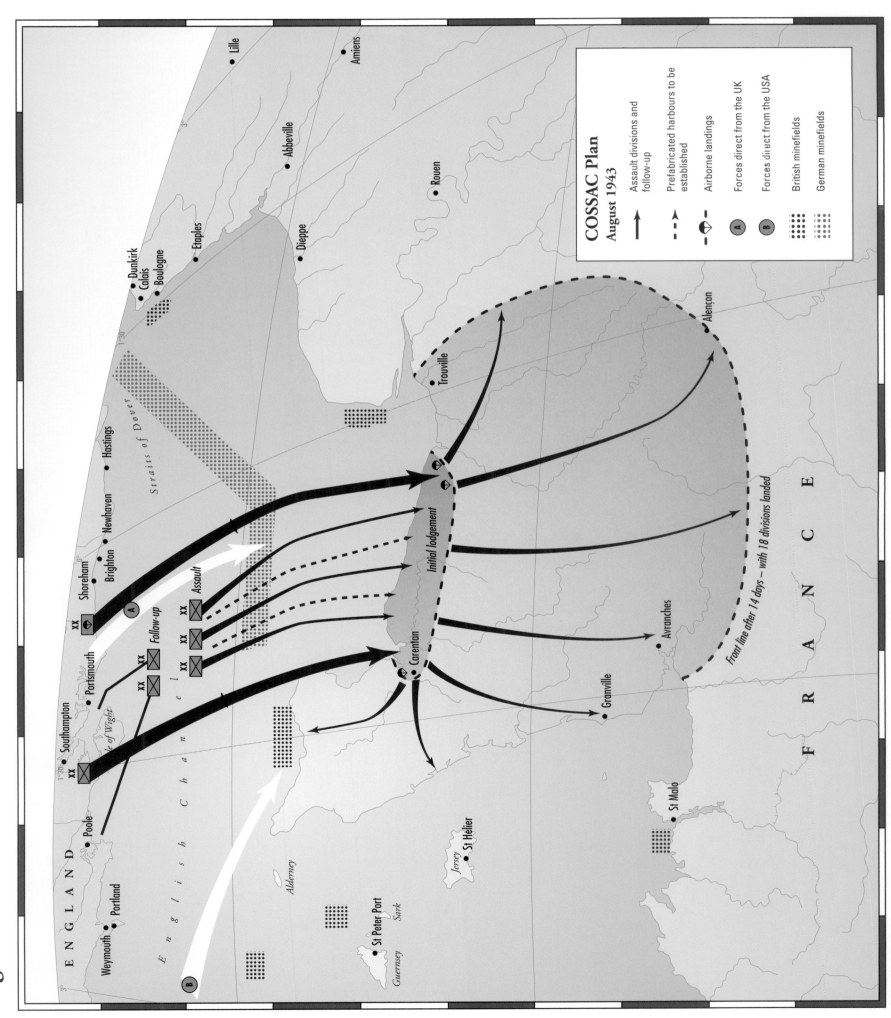

D-Day Landings: Plans and Objectives 6 June 1944

After a postponement because of bad weather in the Channel on 5 June, the Allied invasion of Europe was launched on D-Day, 6 June 1944. The plan for the invasion included an airborne assault to secure the flanks of the landing area, to be followed by a massive naval and aerial bombardment which covered the landing of five divisions on the first day. Commander of the ground troops was General Montgomery, under the overall command of General Dwight D. Eisenhower.

THE TIMING OF THE ASSAULT was dictated by the tides. The Allies had to land at low tide, when the German beach defences were exposed to view. Good weather was also critical for both the airborne and the amphibious landings. Three airborne divisions preceded the landings. The two American divisions were badly scattered on landing, but fortunately they were not counter-attacked by the Germans. The British 6th Airborne Division landed more favourably, taking the Orne crossings and knocking out the Merville battery.

The invasion fleet was vast: 4000 transport and landing craft, supported more than 1200 warships and thousands of combat aircraft. The British Second Army landed on three beaches along a 40km (25-mile front. By evening the 3rd Canadian Division was 11km (7 miles) inland, the 50th Division was within three kilometres (two miles) of Bayeux and the 3rd British Division had made contact with the 6th Airborne Division.

In the American sector, fortunes were more mixed. On Utah Beach, the US VII Corps quickly overwhelmed the defenders. However, on Omaha Beach the V Corps was in real trouble. Amphibious tanks had been launched too far from the beach and most were swamped. Stiff German resistance kept the Americans pinned down, and it was not until nightfall that the men could push inland. Now the race was on to reinforce the beachhead before the Germans could counter-attack the landings in force.

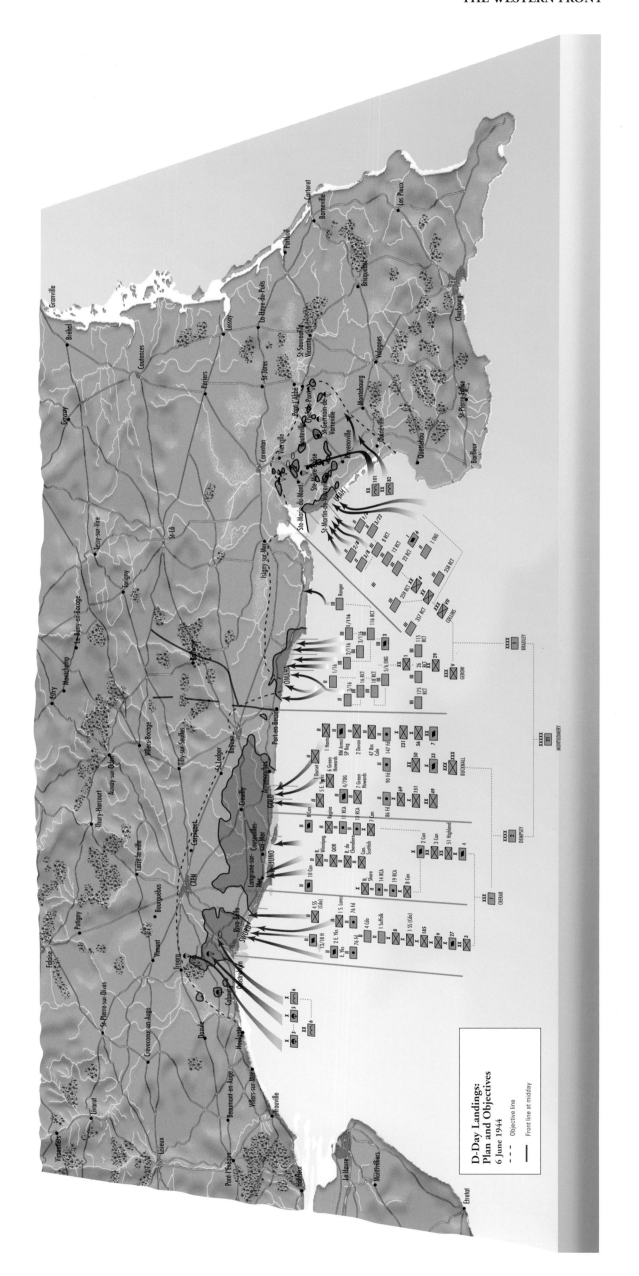

D-Day Landings:
Plan and Objectives
6 June 1944

- - - - Objective line

——— Front line at midday

Breakout Plan
22 July–6 August

Although the initial landings in Normandy had gone well, progress since then had been slow. In spite of Allied air supremacy and the potent support of naval gunfire, the British and Canadians encountered considerable opposition around Caen. While there was no denying that the delay in the British sector was a considerable setback, the bloody battle of attrition had the desired effect of sucking in German reinforcements, leaving much lighter opposition in the American sector.

WITH MORE THAN 875,000 TROOPS ASHORE by the end of June, it was clear that the Allies were on the European mainland to stay. However, it was not until 25 July that Operation Cobra, the American breakout from the beachhead began. They faced nine German divisions compared with the 13 in the British sector, and only two were panzer divisions. By 27 July, the US 2nd Armored Division had fought its way through to open country: the breakout had been achieved.

With American mobile forces fanning out through Normandy and Brittany, Hitler ordered a major attack against the US forces at Mortain. Four panzer divisions would smash through the Americans, driving across the base of the Cotentin Peninsula to split the US Third Army in two.

Panzer attack smashed

Hitler may have ordered the attack, but he did not take into account American resistance. Above all, he did not realize what effect Allied air supremacy would have. Although the attack reached Mortain, it was slowed by skilful American defensive fighting, and then it was stopped in its tracks by continuous attacks by British and American fighter bombers using rockets, cannon, machine guns and bombs.

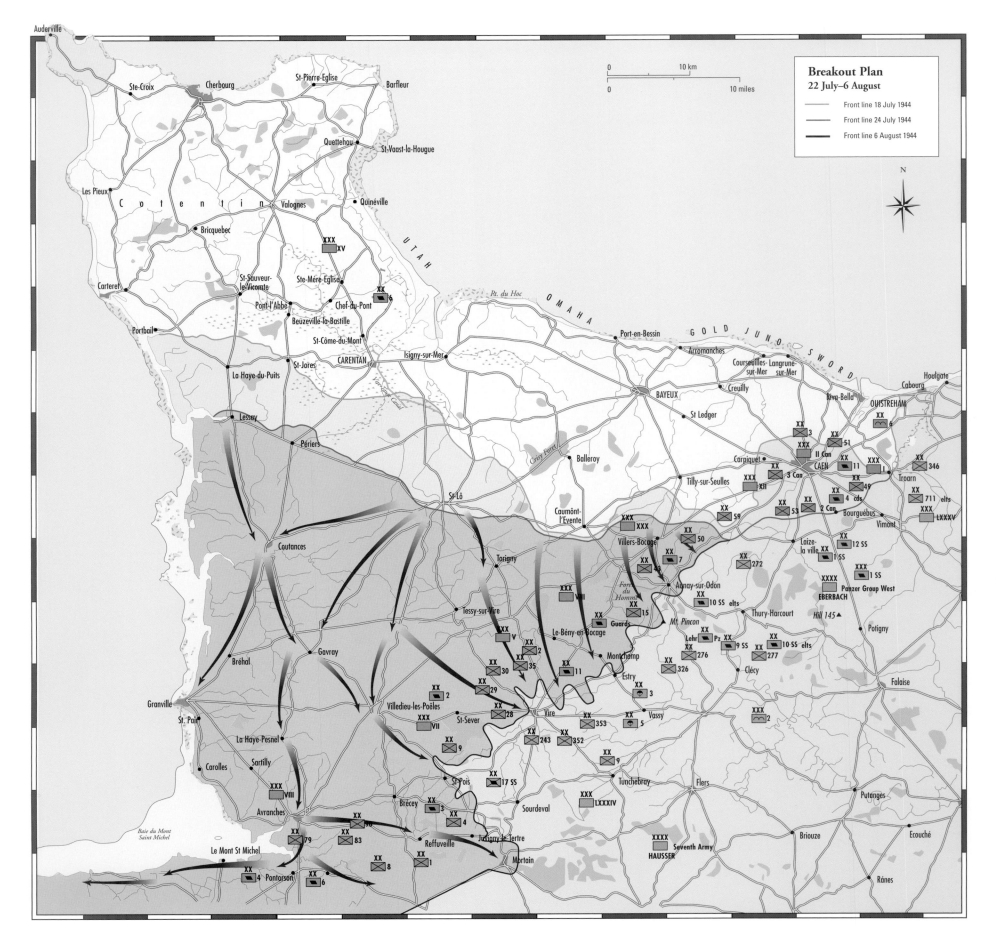

Falaise Pocket
6–19 August 1944

The failure of the German armoured counter-attack at Mortain gave the Allies the chance to win a smashing victory over the Germans in Normandy.

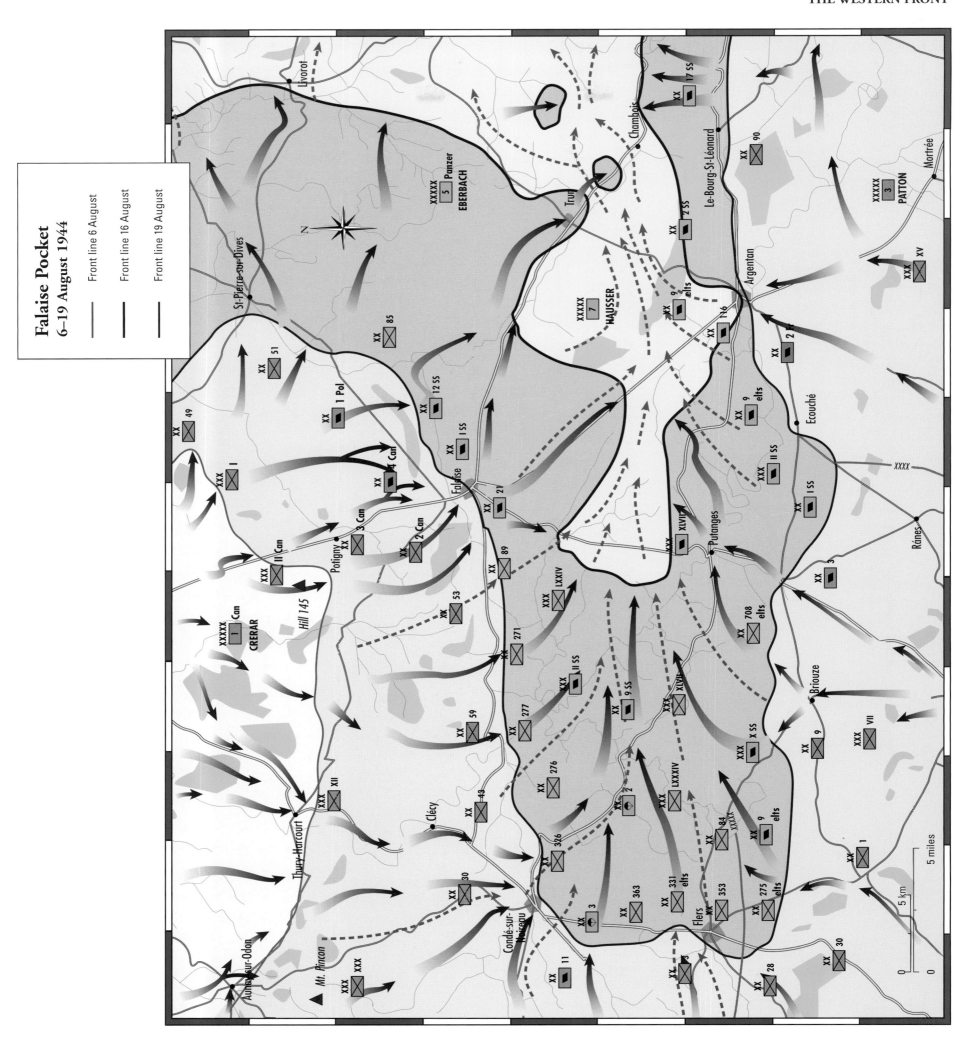

Falaise Pocket
6–19 August 1944

Front line 6 August
Front line 16 August
Front line 19 August

George S. Patton now raced the US Third Army deep into France. His troops reached Argentan on the 13th of August, and the Canadians punched through to Falaise three days later. The Fifth *Panzerarmee* and the composite force designated *Panzergruppe Eberbach* were caught in a trap with a narrow exit to the east.

Now Allied fighter bombers began to reap a bloody harvest. Most of the German combat troops were penned in a pocket 65km (40 miles) long and 20km (12 miles) wide. The tough Polish tank crews serving with the British 4th Armoured Division became the cork in the bottle of the shrinking Falaise Pocket. When the Canadians and Americans linked up with the Poles at the town of Chambois, the trap was shut.

Some Germans did manage to slip through the Allied lines at night, in bad weather, but between 25,000 and 50,000 were taken prisoner, leaving another 10,000 dead behind them in the killing ground. In Normandy the Germans had lost 1500 tanks, 3500 guns and 20,000 assorted vehicles. These were losses that they could never hope to replace.

The Liberation of Paris
14–25 August 1944

The Allied armies had finally shattered the ring of steel that had surrounded the Normandy beachhead for more than two months. The Germans had no other prepared defence lines inside France upon which to fall back, and throughout the summer and early autumn, they fought a well-organized but inevitable retreat back to the very borders of the Reich.

HITLER'S INSISTENCE that the German Army cling to its positions in Normandy until it was too late for an orderly withdrawal was catastrophic. Instead of the fighting retreat across France envisaged by his generals, the German Army collapsed in rout. US armoured columns fanned out in pursuit, Allied aircraft strafing and bombing every road east.

Between D-Day, 6 June, and the end of August 1944 the German Army lost 221,000 men killed, missing or captured in France. Another 67,000 were wounded. The *Westheer* began the campaign with 50 infantry divisions and 12 panzer divisions. By the time Field Marshal Model gathered up the wreckage, there were only 24 infantry divisions and 11 panzer divisions. All had been reduced to a fraction of their authorized strength.

The day before the Falaise Pocket closed, an uprising began in Paris. The city was not an important military target, but pressure from General de Gaulle and the danger of a communist take-over forced the supreme commander to change his mind. Forces were diverted to the French capital, led by the French 2nd Armoured Division.

The Allied armies had reached the Seine 11 days before they had expected to, and when the French troops entered Paris on 24 August, they were 55 days ahead of schedule.

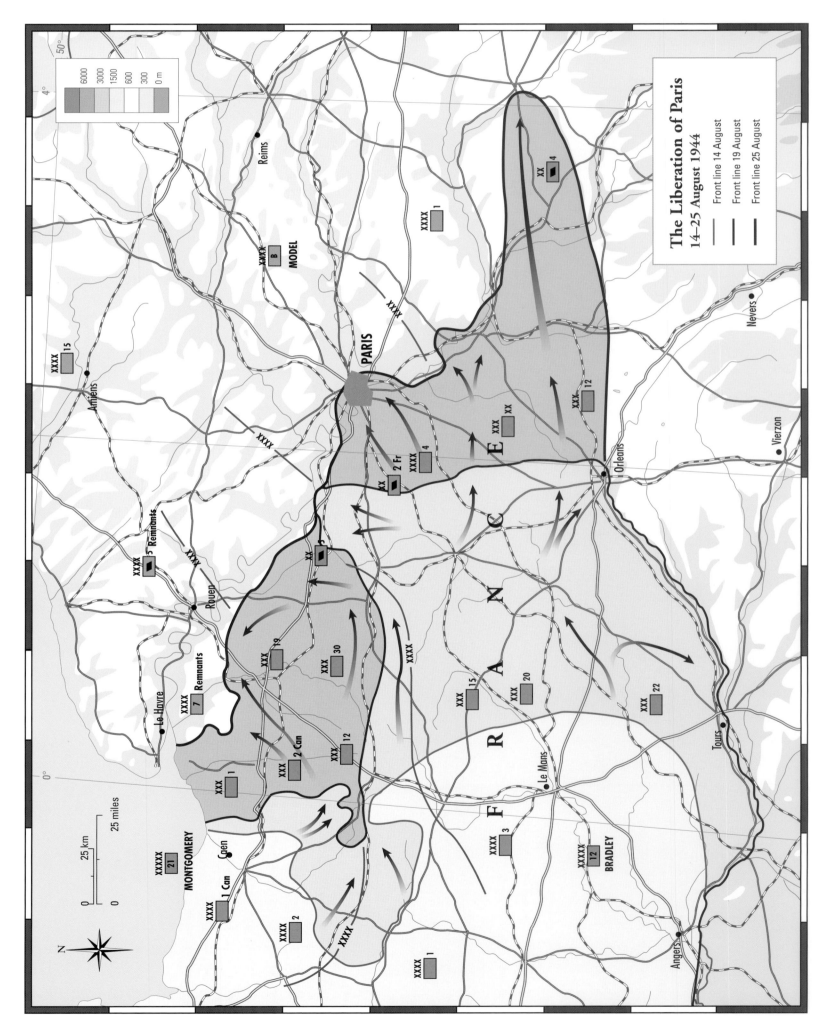

The Liberation of Paris
14–25 August 1944

Front line 14 August
Front line 19 August
Front line 25 August

Invasion of Southern France August 1944

The initial planning for Operation Overlord called for a near simultaneous landing in the South of France, with the aim of confronting the Germans with landings in two widely separated areas. By 10 August, the invasion fleet for Operation Anvil/Dragoon had been assembled in various Mediterranean ports, and the invasion itself started with commando landings on the night of 14 August. The main landings took place at dawn on 15 August.

Operation Anvil/Dragoon was driven more by the political necessity that a recognized authority was restored in the South of France, preventing communist elements in the Resistance from establishing an administration, than from any real military requirement. The invasion itself was a Franco-American effort, with limited British participation. Some 94,000 troops embarked from Naples to form the initial landing force, and they were able to come ashore with remarkably little resistance. German units barely put up a fight, and were ordered to retreat northwards where they would soon be needed to defend Germany itself. The Allied advance proceeded smoothly. Marseille surrendered on 28 August, and leading elements of General Lucian K. Truscott's VI Corps moved rapidly up the Rhone valley, entering Lyons on 3 September.

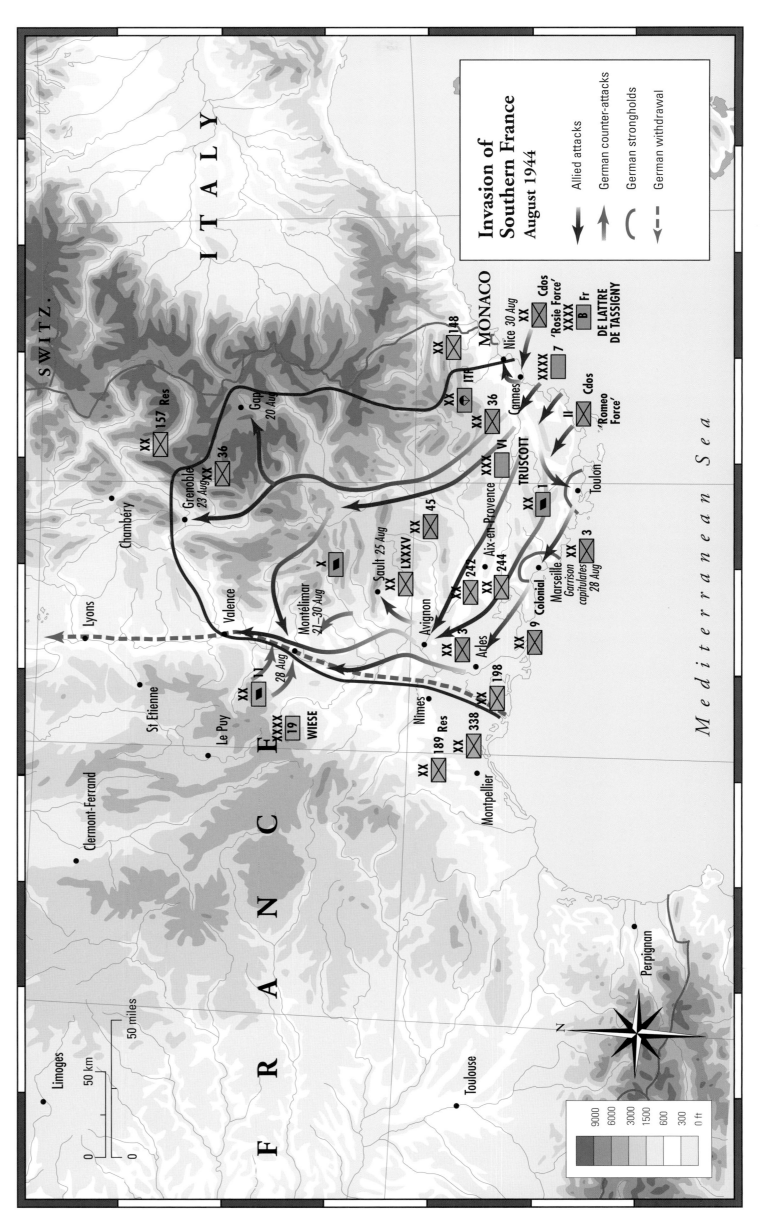

Allied Advance to 4 September 1944

The American Seventh Army advancing from the south linked up with Patton's forces by mid-September. The US First Army had closed on the German city of Aachen. But tenacious resistance by German garrisons in French ports was restricting Allied supplies; men were tired, and equipment worn out. The helter-skelter advance slowed, then stopped.

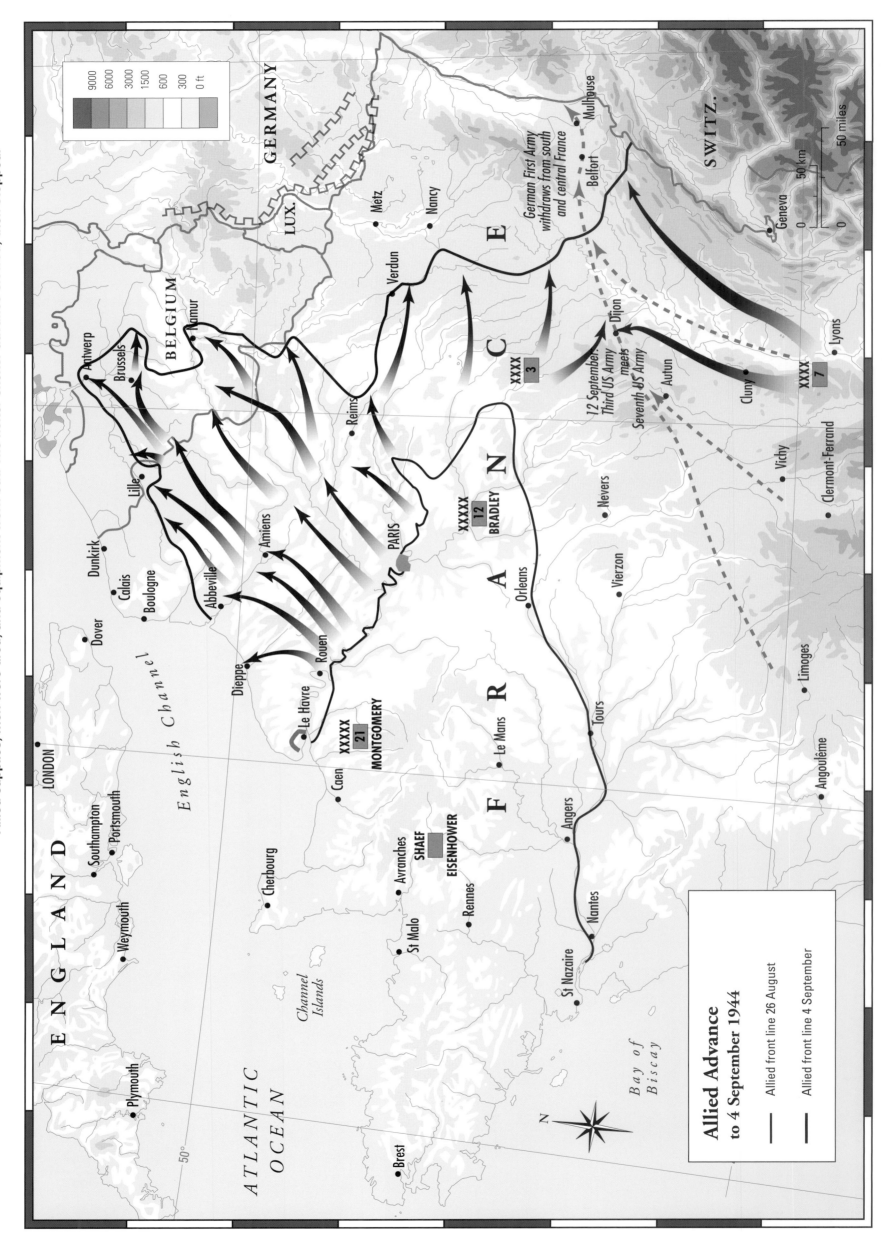

GERMANY

LUX.

BELGIUM

ENGLAND

FRANCE

SWITZ.

English Channel

Atlantic Ocean

Bay of Biscay

Channel Islands

German First Army withdraws from south and central France

12 September: Third US Army meets Seventh US Army

9000 6000 3000 1500 600 300 0 ft

Metz
Nancy
Verdun
Reims
Antwerp
Brussels
Namur
Lille
Amiens
Abbeville
Dunkirk
Calais
Boulogne
Dover
PARIS
Rouen
Dieppe
Le Havre
Caen
Cherbourg
Avranches
St Malo
Rennes
Le Mans
Orleans
Nevers
Vierzon
Tours
Angers
Nantes
St Nazaire
Brest
Weymouth
Plymouth
Southampton
Portsmouth
LONDON
Angoulême
Limoges
Clermont-Ferrand
Vichy
Lyons
Cluny
Autun
Dijon
Belfort
Mulhouse
Geneva

XXXX 3
XXXX 7
XXXXX 12 BRADLEY
XXXX 21 MONTGOMERY
SHAEF EISENHOWER

N

50 km
50 miles
0
0

50°

Allied Advance to 4 September 1944

— Allied front line 26 August

— Allied front line 4 September

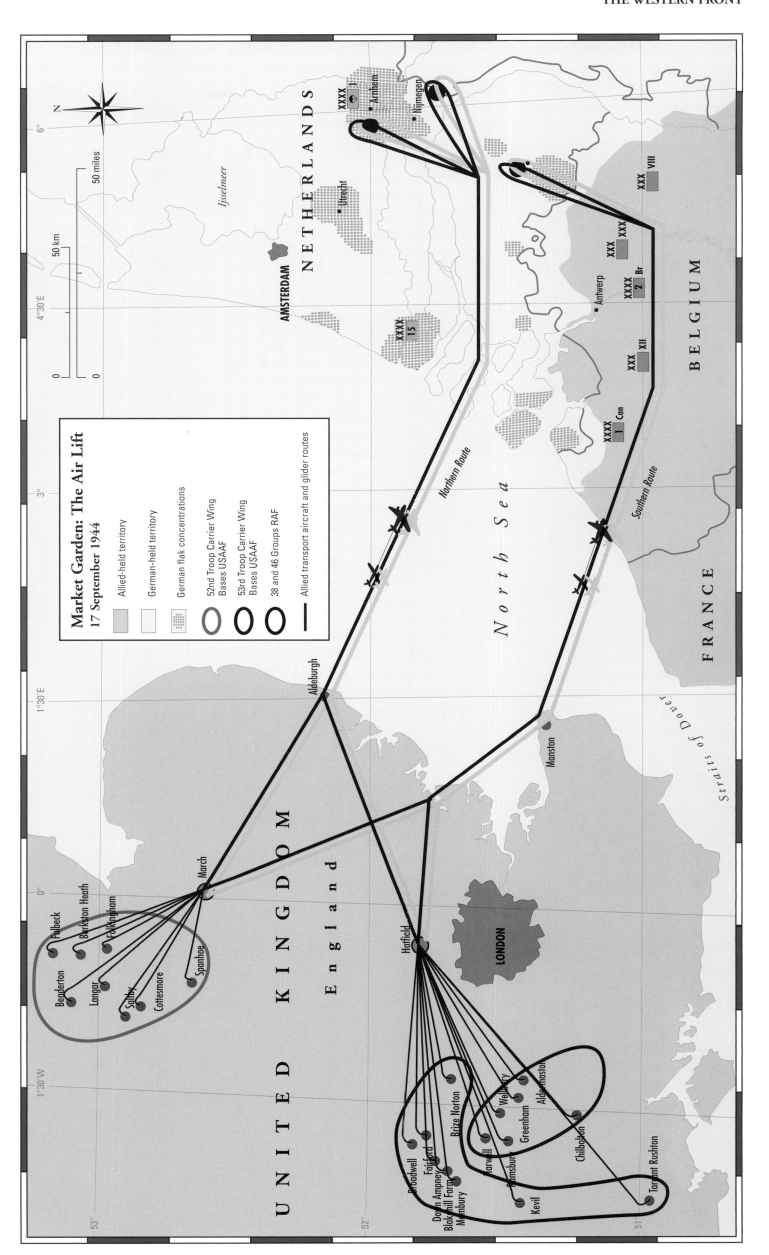

Market Garden: The Air Lift
17 September 1944

Field Marshal Sir Bernard Montgomery planned to break open the German defences in the north before they had the chance to solidify. His uncharacteristically daring idea was to land the British 1st Airborne Brigade and the Polish Parachute Brigade near the Dutch town of Arnhem, behind the German lines. The Allied Supreme Commander, General Dwight Eisenhower, expanded Montgomery's plan to include American troops. The US 82nd and 101st Airborne Divisions would also be committed.

O N SUNDAY 17 SEPTEMBER, the peoples of Britain and Holland looked skyward to an airborne armada heading southeast. A total of 1545 transports and 478 gliders were in the air, escorted by 1131 fighters: the formation was 16km (10 miles) across and 150km (93 miles) deep. Fewer than 50 *Luftwaffe* interceptors were available, and they made little impression. Flak caught some aircraft as they neared the landing zones, but within 80 minutes there were 20,000 paratroopers on the ground. Field Marshal Model himself fled his headquarters as Allied paratroops formed up nearby. At the same time, the British XXX Corps attacked along the road to Eindhoven. The advance of the tanks was preceded by a rolling artillery barrage that knocked out many of the German anti-tank guns that lay in wait in nearby woods.

Market Garden: The Air Lift
17 September 1944

Allied-held territory

German-held territory

German flak concentrations

52nd Troop Carrier Wing Bases USAAF

53rd Troop Carrier Wing Bases USAAF

38 and 46 Groups RAF

Allied transport aircraft and glider routes

Airborne Drop Zones September 1944

The British were confident of success. Military intelligence convinced them that the opposition to the elite paratroop formations would come only from second-rate German units consisting of old men, teenage conscripts and Dutch SS men who could not wait to change sides. But the Germans had received timely reinforcements.

THE 9TH AND 10TH SS Panzer Divisions had been sent to the Arnhem area to refit and re-organize. Curiously, British intelligence lost track of both divisions and their presence so near to the airborne landing zones upset the Allied plan from the very beginning.

The US 101st Airborne Division captured the bridge over the canal at Veghel. The US 82nd Airborne took the bridge at Grave. But the bridge at Nijmegen was held by the SS and although 2 Para, commanded by 34-year-old Major John Frost, seized one end of the bridge at Arnhem, his battalion was then isolated.

The rest of the British 1st Airborne Division was unable to get into Arnhem. Its way was blocked by determined German forces who had quickly formed ad hoc battle groups to blunt the British thrusts towards the bridge.

General Bittrich's II SS Panzer Corps may have been in urgent need of rest and replenishment, but it reacted with blistering speed. The Allies couldn't have known that their entire battle plan had been captured by the Germans in a crashed glider. The Germans knew every detail of 'Market Garden' before it happened.

By the afternoon of 18 September, tanks from the British Guards had linked up with the Americans at Eindhoven. A day later the ground troops were in Nijmegen: an advance of nearly 80km (50 miles) in 48 hours.

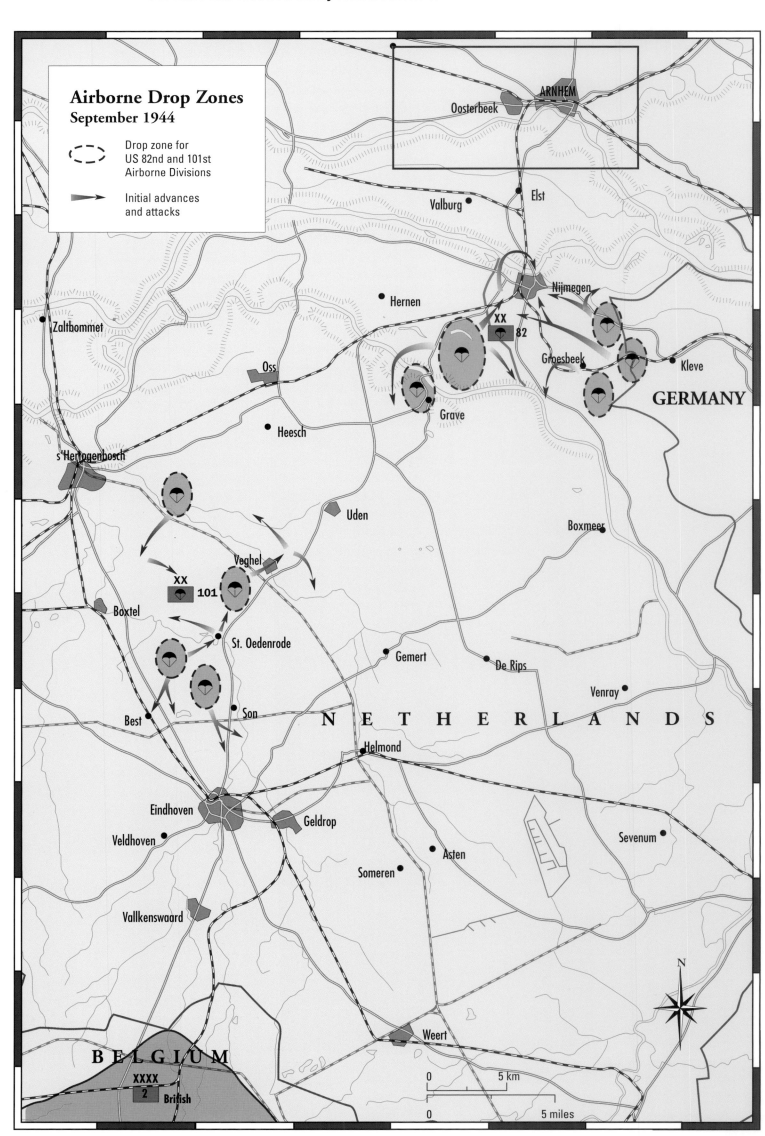

Airborne Drop Zones
September 1944

- - - Drop zone for US 82nd and 101st Airborne Divisions

➤ Initial advances and attacks

ARNHEM

Oosterbeek

Valburg

Elst

Nijmegen

Hernen

Zaltbommel

Groesbeek

Kleve

GERMANY

Oss

Grave

Heesch

s'Hertogenbosch

Uden

Boxmeer

Veghel

Boxtel

St. Oedenrode

Gemert

De Rips

Venray

Best

Son

N E T H E R L A N D S

Helmond

Eindhoven

Veldhoven

Geldrop

Asten

Sevenum

Someren

Vallkenswaard

Weert

B E L G I U M

British

0   5 km

0   5 miles

N

First Airborne Division Landing Zones, September 1944

Even as the ground forces pushed towards Nijmegen, the same day saw the British airborne forces at Arnhem in increasing difficulty. 4 Para established a defensive perimeter around Oosterbeek outside the town, but relief was not to come to the embattled 2 Para at the bridge, where they were enduring a series of increasingly heavy assaults. Meanwhile, the advancing XXX Corps was being held up by an SS Kampfgruppe which held the bridge at Nijmegen, clinging to their positions in the teeth of intense artillery barrages.

Two Para's last stand ended in surrender on 21 September. Officers and men of the II SS Panzer Corps were united in praise for Frost's men – and the rest of the division now pinned against the Rhine. A final effort to save the British position in Arnhem came on 21 September. The British landed the Polish Parachute Brigade south of the Rhine, but the Germans prevented them from breaking through to Arnhem. On 24 September the road was cut south of Veghel by the *Jungwirth* Battalion. The German battle groups suffered grievous losses, but they slowed the northward progress of XXX Corps just long enough for a new defensive line to be established north of Nijmegen. On 25 September the British survivors were withdrawn over the Rhine. Just over 2000 finally escaped. The Germans captured 6000 men from 1st Airborne – more than half of them wounded.

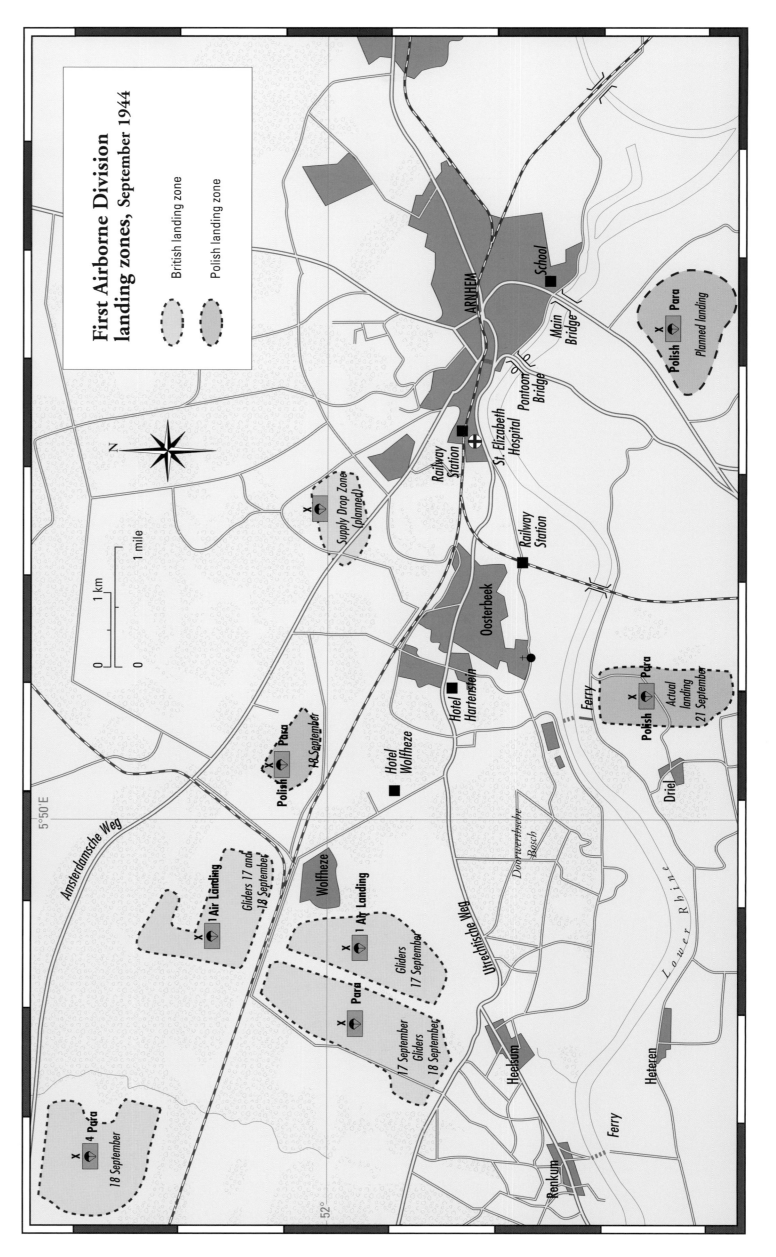

First Airborne Division landing zones, September 1944

British landing zone

Polish landing zone

Battle of the Bulge
16–24 December 1944

On 16 December 1944, to the astonishment of the Allies, the Germans launched a massive armoured offensive through the Ardennes. Hitler's plan was to use two panzer armies to drive for Antwerp, splitting in half the Allied armies threatening the Reich. Four thinly stretched American divisions were battered by the 16 divisions of the Fifth Panzer Army and the Sixth SS Panzer Army. German tanks by-passed St Vith in the north, and surrounded Bastogne in the south. However, news that SS men had massacred prisoners of war stiffened American resistance, and German progress slowed. By 20 December they were still 32km (20 miles) short of the Meuse, and Allied forces were moving to mount a counter-attack.

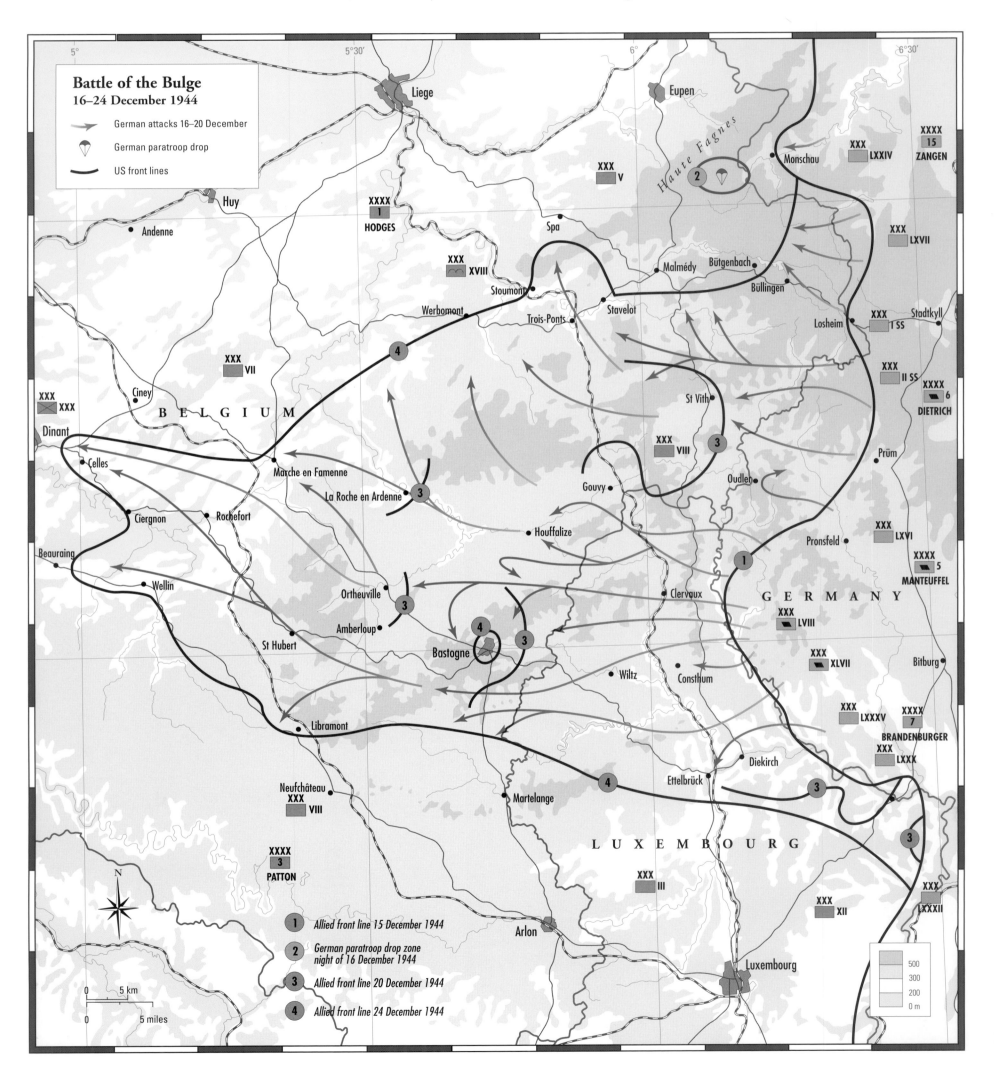

Battle of the Bulge
16–24 December 1944

→ German attacks 16–20 December

⛊ German paratroop drop

⌒ US front lines

① Allied front line 15 December 1944

② German paratroop drop zone night of 16 December 1944

③ Allied front line 20 December 1944

④ Allied front line 24 December 1944

Battle of the Bulge Counter-attack 26 December 1944– 7 February 1945

As Hasso von Manteuffel's panzers probed westwards, they came under heavy fire from American tank destroyers and artillery while US infantry fought doggedly into gaps or held on to isolated strongpoints. By Christmas day, the sting had been drawn from the German onslaught. The Fifth Panzer Army made a last attempt to take Bastogne but was fought off, and the next day elements of Patton's Third Army arrived to break the siege. Meanwhile, Montgomery deployed a British armoured brigade to hold the left flank of the American line, and authorised the troops caught in the St Vith salient to withdraw. The arrival of the US 2nd Armored Division brought the Germans crashing to a halt. As the Allies moved onto the offensive, the Germans were forced back, and all the ground they had gained had been retaken by the end of January. They had shocked the Allies, but American losses could be made good within days. the Germans lost 120,000 men and over 600 tanks, and those were irreplaceable.

Over the Christmas period the skies cleared, and Allied air forces were free to bring their weight to bear on the German panzer forces.

Losses began to mount as Field Marshal Montgomery was given command of all the troops north of the Bulge, reorganizing them to contain and then throw back the Germans. General Omar Bradley ordered elements of the US First Army to hold the flank of the German attack, and then to drive on St Vith. He ordered General Patton to send his crack 4th Armored Division to relieve Bastogne from the south. Patton complained about being diverted from his own objectives, but nevertheless, in a consummate manoeuvre, he swung the bulk of his army through 90 degrees in less than 48 hours.

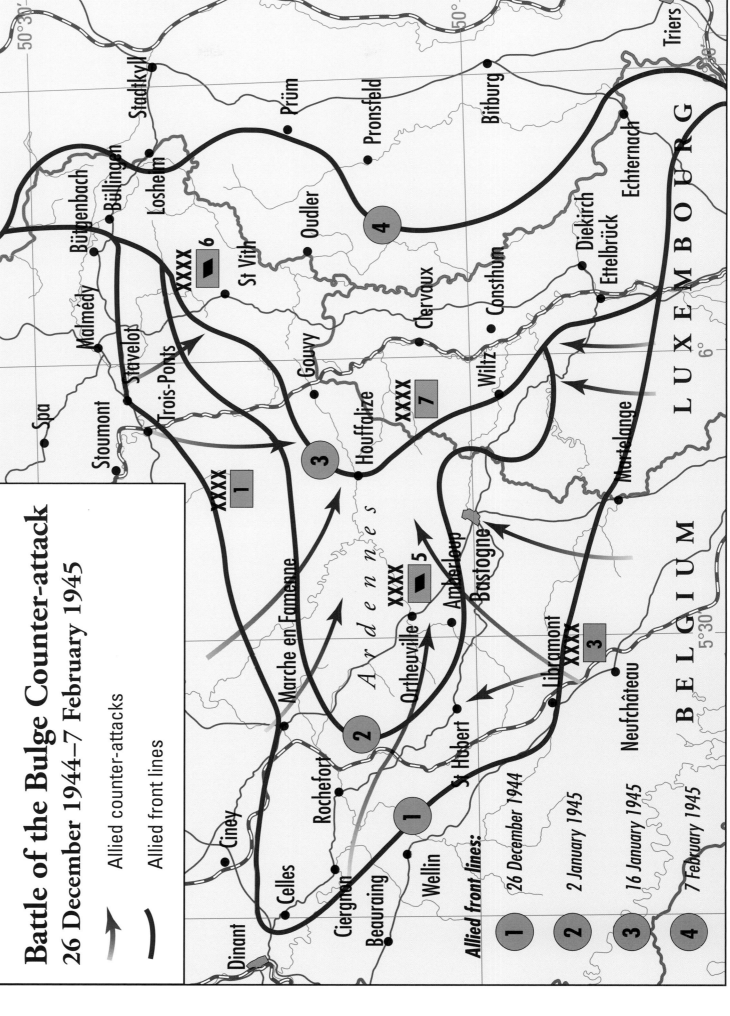

Battle of the Bulge Counter-attack 26 December 1944–7 February 1945

→ Allied counter-attacks

⌒ Allied front lines

Allied front lines:
1 26 December 1944
2 2 January 1945
3 16 January 1945
4 7 February 1945

Advance to the Rhine
8 February–21 March 1945

In February 1945, the task for the Canadian and British armies in the north, the four US armies stretching down to Strasbourg and the French army in the Vosges was to cross the Roer, Our and Saar Rivers and to reach the Rhine. By 21 February, Goch, Kleve and Calcar were in British and Canadian hands, and the Americans took Mönchengladbach on 1 March. Five days later, Cologne was in American hands.

O N 7 MARCH, the Ludendorff Bridge at Remagen was taken intact by the US First Army, and American troops were across the Rhine. The main assault crossings of the river were to take place two weeks later.

On 23 March, Montgomery's 21st Army Group stormed the Rhine at Wesel. They were preceded by two divisions of paratroopers. By nightfall, the ground troops had joined up with the paratroopers and the Rhine bridgeheads were secure.

Further south, the Americans launched their own crossings, mostly mounted by fewer men with smaller resources. Patton, eager to beat Montgomery across the river, had sent an assault regiment of the US 5th Division, part of his Third Army, to cross the Rhine in rubber boats between Nierstein and Oppenheim. Securing the far bank, they were joined by the rest of the division.

During the next few days, crossings were made at Boppard, St Goar, Worms and Mainz. By the end of March, Darmstadt and Wiesbaden were in American hands, and US armoured columns were driving for Frankfurt-am-Main. Further south, the French had put an Algerian division across the river at Gemersheim.

Most German troops knew that the war was lost and were ready to surrender, though a few young volunteers along with die-hard SS men continued to fight to the last.

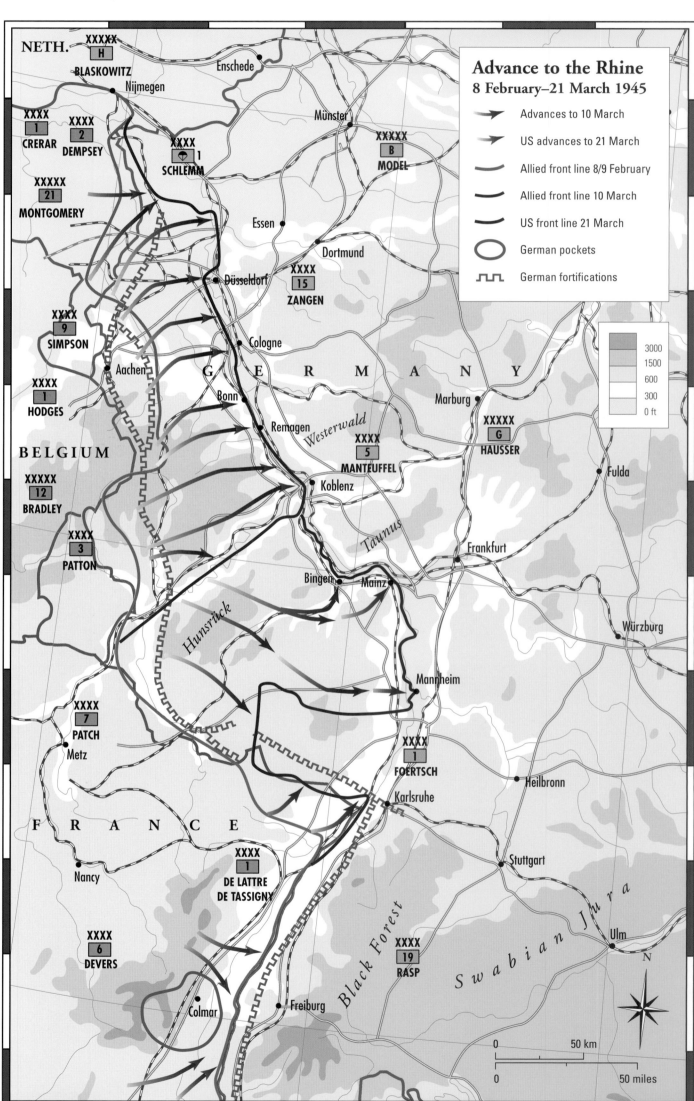

Advance to the Rhine
8 February–21 March 1945

→ Advances to 10 March
→ US advances to 21 March
— Allied front line 8/9 February
— Allied front line 10 March
— US front line 21 March
◯ German pockets
⊓⊔ German fortifications

Germany Defeated March–April 1945

Launching out of the huge bridgehead stretching up the east bank of the Rhine from Bonn, Allied troops drove deep into Germany. Elements of the US Ninth Army crossed the Weser on 4 April. By 11 April they were approaching the Elbe. On 24 April, the US First Army reached its stop line on the Mulde, and the next day made theo first link-up with Soviet forces at Torgau. Germany had been divided in two.

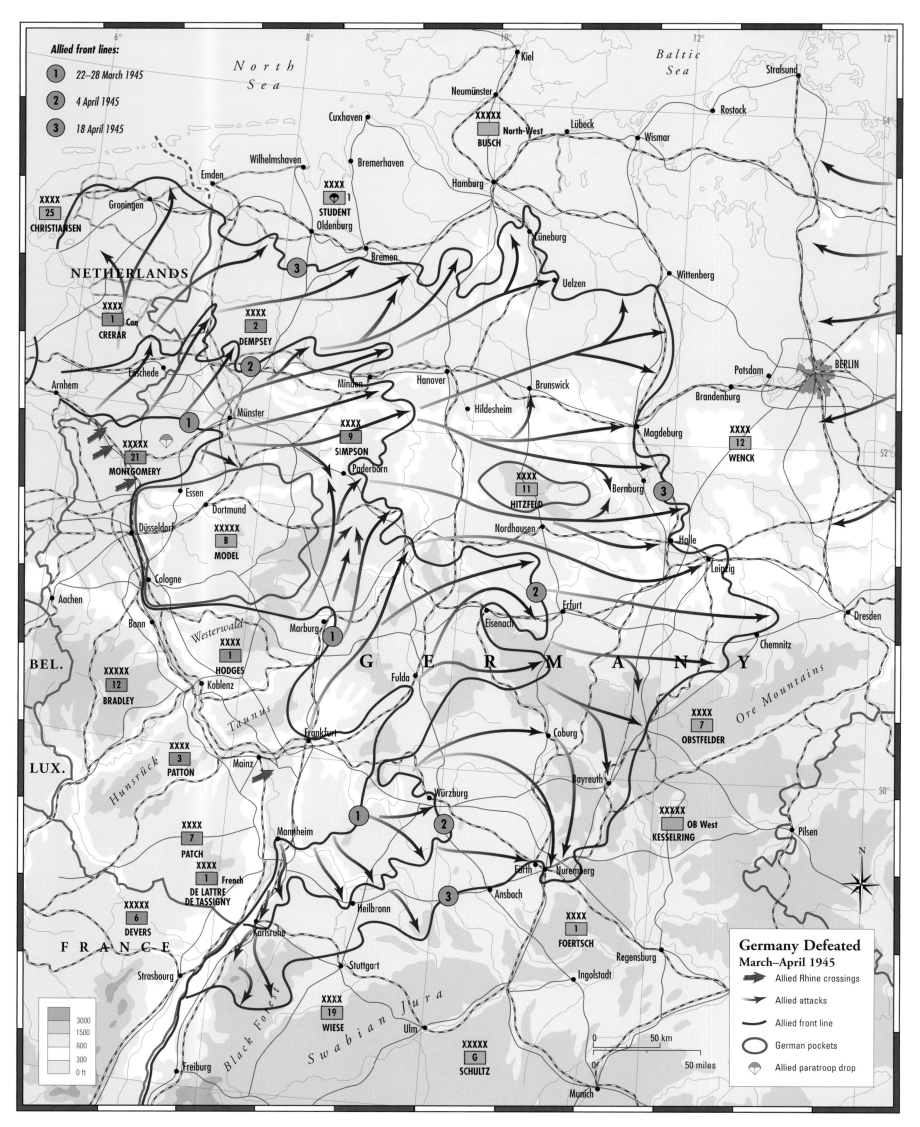

Allied front lines:
1 22–28 March 1945
2 4 April 1945
3 18 April 1945

Germany Defeated
March–April 1945
Allied Rhine crossings
Allied attacks
Allied front line
German pockets
Allied paratroop drop

0   50 km
0   50 miles

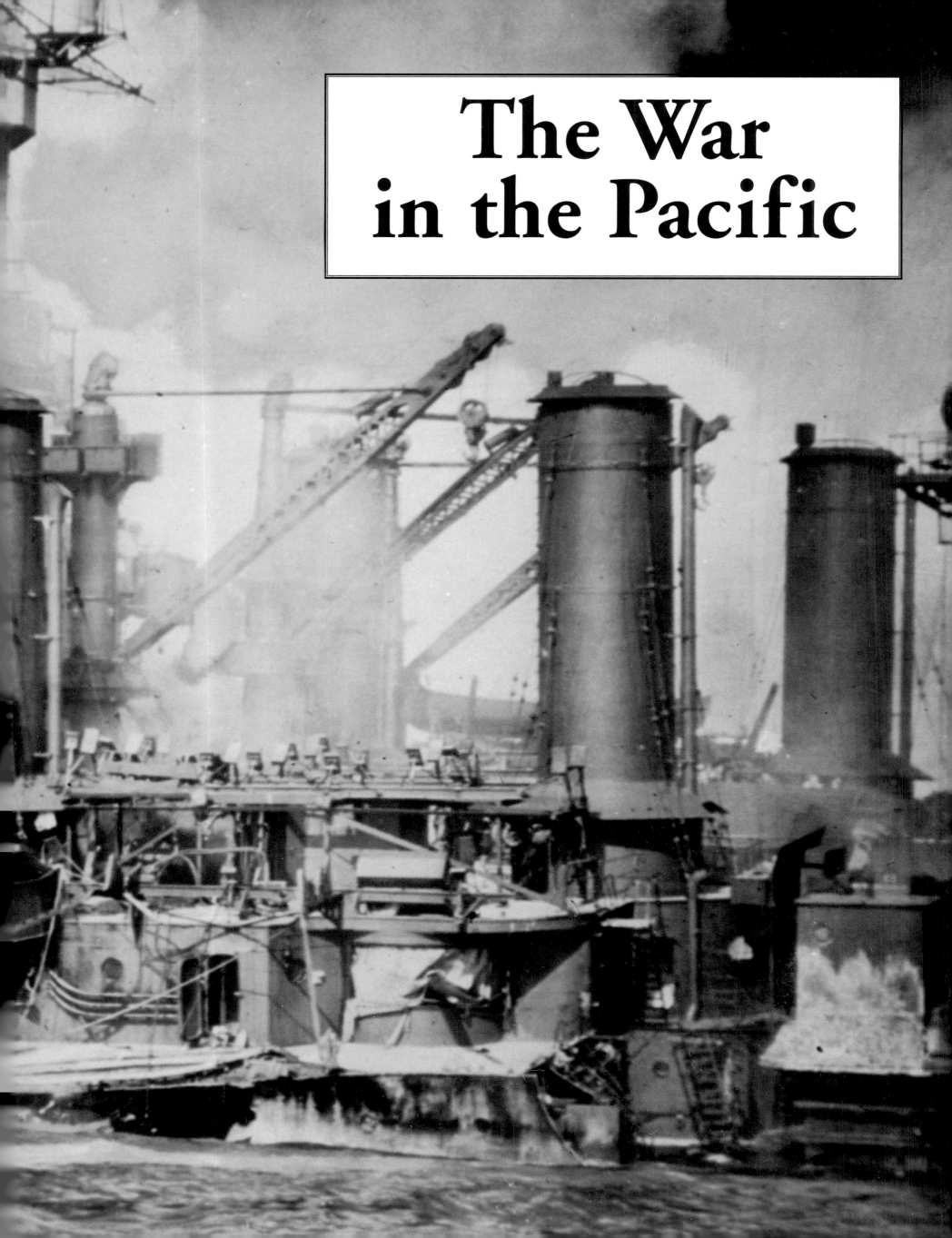

The War in the Pacific

Revolution in China 1912–35

For much of the nineteenth century, the Chinese Empire had been a pawn in the expansionist struggles of the imperial powers. The rise of Chinese Nationalism under Sun Yat Sen was followed by fragmentation, as rival warlords seized various parts of the country. Eventually, the Kuomintang gained control of the most populous and fertile provinces.

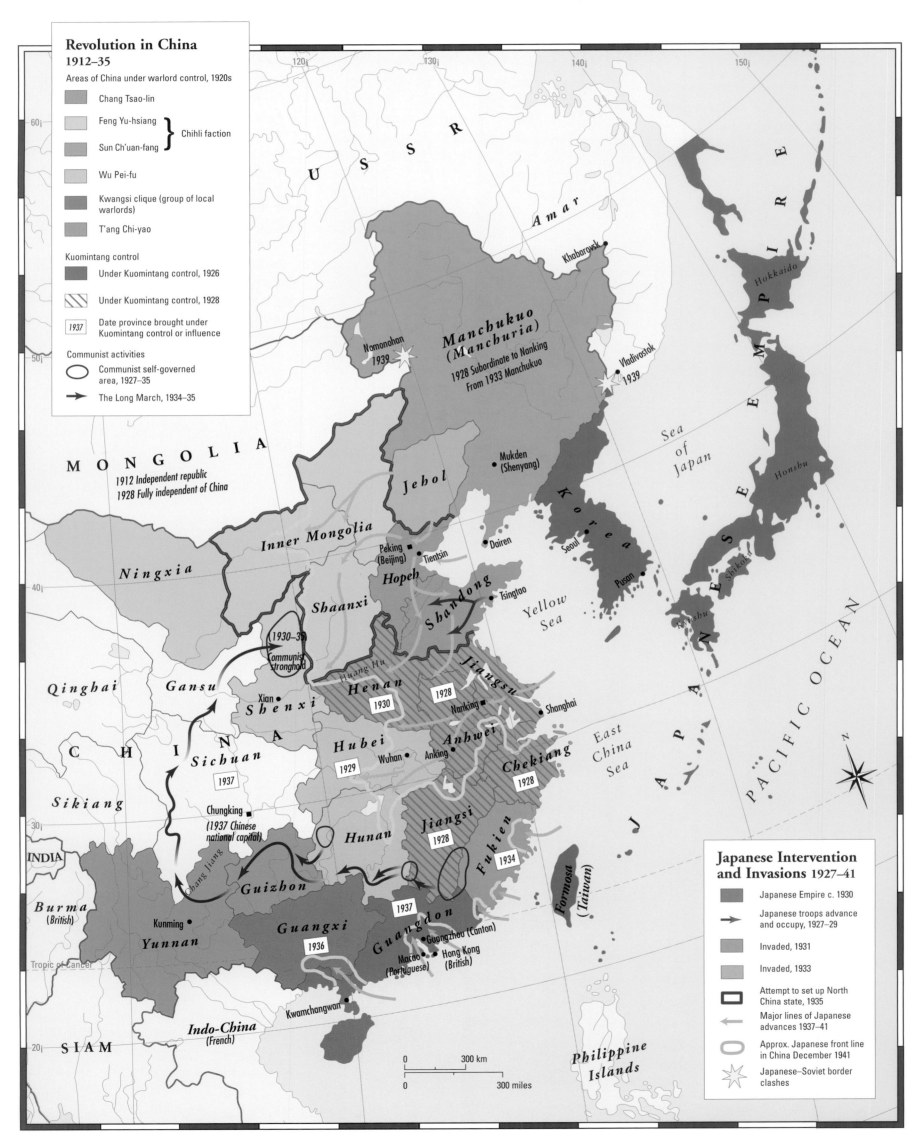

Revolution in China 1912–35

Areas of China under warlord control, 1920s

- Chang Tsao-lin
- Feng Yu-hsiang } Chihli faction
- Sun Ch'uan-fang } Chihli faction
- Wu Pei-fu
- Kwangsi clique (group of local warlords)
- T'ang Chi-yao

Kuomintang control

- Under Kuomintang control, 1926
- Under Kuomintang control, 1928
- 1937 Date province brought under Kuomintang control or influence

Communist activities

- Communist self-governed area, 1927–35
- The Long March, 1934–35

Japanese Intervention and Invasions 1927–41

- Japanese Empire c. 1930
- Japanese troops advance and occupy, 1927–29
- Invaded, 1931
- Invaded, 1933
- Attempt to set up North China state, 1935
- Major lines of Japanese advances 1937–41
- Approx. Japanese front line in China December 1941
- Japanese–Soviet border clashes

The Expansion of Japan 1920–41

THE OUTBREAK OF THE GREAT WAR in 1914 was seen by Japan as an opportunity to expand its power into the Chinese mainland. Declaring war on the side of the Allies, the Japanese seized German holdings in China and the Pacific. In just three decades, Japan had won control of Korea, the German treaty ports in China, and in 1931, the fiercely nationalist Japanese Army seized Manchuria without reference to the Tokyo government. Colonial ambitions and the rise of Japanese militarism in the 1930s now saw the Japanese cynically manipulating China into war.

The creation of the modern state of Japan was rapid after the Meiji Restoration of 1868. In less than 40 years, the Japanese Empire changed from being a feudal state into a country with a modern army and navy. These were tested in a war with China, fought over control of Korea, and were proved in a stunning triumph over the Russians in 1905. Both wars were settled by international treaty, and the Japanese felt that they had been cheated of their just rewards by the interference of the Great Powers.

The Expansion of Japan

Japanese Empire 1920	Colonial possessions 1941
Territory added by 1931	British
Territory added by 1933	United States
Territory added by 1937	Dutch
Territory added by 1941	French
Chinese Nationalist control 1937	Portuguese
Warlord control 1937	

Midway Is.

Gilbert Is.

Fiji

PACIFIC OCEAN

Aleutian Islands

USA
Alaska

Wake Is.

Marshall Is.

Caroline Islands
Japanese mandate

Bismarck Arch. • Rabaul

Guadalcanal

Coral Sea

Iwo Jima

Mariana Is.
Saipan

Yap

Guam (to US)

New Guinea

• Port Moresby

AUSTRALIA

Arafura Sea

Khabarovsk •

Vladivostok •

JAPAN

Tokyo •
Kyoto •

Sea of Japan

U S S R

Irkutsk •

Trans-Siberian Railway

Korea

Harbin •

Seoul •
Pusan •
Nagasaki

East China Sea

Taihoku

Shanghai •

Nanking •

Philippine Islands

Manila •

Timor

Celebes

Dutch East Indies

Java Sea

TANNU TUVA

Ulan Bator •

M O N G O L I A

Peking •

C H I N A

Chungking •

Kunming •

Canton •
Haiphong

Hong Kong

1940 Japanese established bases in the northern part of French Indo-China

N. Borneo

Sarawak

Borneo

Java

Sumatra

Batavia •

Palembang •

TIBET

Lhasa •

NEPAL
BHUTAN

Burma

Mandalay •

Rangoon •

SIAM

Bangkok

French Indo-China

Saigon

Malaya
Kuala Lumpur •
Singapore •

Hanoi •

INDIA

Delhi •

Calcutta •

Bombay •

Madras •

Colombo •

INDIAN OCEAN

N

Hawaii Operation, Track of Japanese Attack Force 26 November– 7 December 1941

Japan's colonial ambitions in the 1930s brought the empire into disagreement with Britain, France and the USA, all of whom had economic interests in Asia. In an attempt to rein in Japanese expansion, the USA pushed through an oil embargo.

RICH IN AMBITION but poor in natural resources, Japan was hit hard by the oil embargo. As a matter of preserving face, the Japanese government could not submit to foreign demands, and Japan saw war as the only answer to its problems. The army and navy planned a rapid war of conquest, after which it could bargain with the Western powers from a position of strength. The British and the Americans expected an attack into Southeast Asia, but neither anticipated a daring naval raid on Pearl Harbor, designed to destroy the US Navy's Pacific Fleet.

Departure from Hitokappu Bay
Tokyo time 06:00 26 Nov
Hawaii time 10:20 25 Nov
Washington time 16:00 25 Nov

Fleet concentrates 22 Nov
Sortie begins 26 Nov

West longitudinal date:
Japanese forces irrespective
of longitude always operated
on Tokyo time

(7 Dec East longitudinal date)
Attack launched 06:05–06:20 local time

Attack on Pearl Harbor
Tokyo time 03:25 8 Dec
Hawaii time 07:55 7 Dec
Washington time 13:25 7 Dec

7 Dec:
Heavy cruiser Minneapolis and the
destroyer-minesweepers Boggs,
Chandler, Hovey and Lamberton
were involved in gunnery exercises
south of Oahu

5 Dec:
Heavy cruiser Indianapolis and the old
destroyer-minesweepers Dorsey, Elliot,
Hopkins, Long and Johnson sailed
from Pearl Harbor for an amphibious
exercise of Johnston Island

5 Dec:
US carrier Lexington,
with the heavy cruisers
Astoria, Chicago and Portland
and the destroyers Porter,
Flusser, Drayton, Lamson, and
Mahan, sailed from Pearl Harbor
with aircraft for Midway

7 Dec: Two Japanese
destroyers shell Midway

4 Dec:
US carrier Enterprise,
in the company of the
heavy cruisers Chester,
Northampton and
Salt Lake City, and the
destroyers Balch, Gridley,
Craven, McCall, Maury, Dunlay,
Fanning, Benham and
Ellet, flew aircraft into Wake

**Hawaii Operation, Track of
Japanese Attack Force
26 November–7 December 1941**

→ Track of Japanese force

→ Track of Japanese submarines
in support of main force

Extent of US air patrol
before 7 December

Wind direction

42 Wind speed in miles per hour

Vis. 9.4 Visibility in miles

PACIFIC OCEAN

USSR

Manchukuo

Korea

JAPAN

Sea of Japan

Honshu

Bonin Islands

Aleutian Islands

Midway

Wake Island

Johnston Island

Hawaiian Islands

Philippine Islands

Pearl Harbor: The Japanese Attack 7 December 1941

The Far East forces of the warring European powers had been cut back to the bone, but the US Pacific Fleet based at Hawaii remained a significant threat to Japanese plans. British attacks on Taranto had confirmed the feasibility of air strikes against warships in harbour, and the Imperial Navy planned a similar surprise action against the Americans – without the formality of any declaration of war.

① Tender *Whitney* and destroyers *Tucker, Conyngham, Reid, Case* and *Selfridge*
② Destroyer *Blue*
③ Light cruiser *Phoenix*
④ Destroyers *Aylwin, Farragut, Dale* and *Monaghan*
⑤ Destroyers *Patterson, Ralph Talbot* and *Henley*
⑥ Tender *Dobbin* and destroyers *Worden, Hull, Dewey, Phelps* and *Macdough*
⑦ Hospital Ship *Solace*
⑧ Destroyer *Allen*
⑨ Destroyer *Chew*
⑩ Destroyer-minesweepers *Gamble* and *Montgomery* and light-minelayer *Ramsey*
⑪ Destroyer-minesweepers *Trever, Breese, Zane, Perry* and *Wasmuth*
⑫ Repair vessel *Medusa*
⑬ Seaplane tender *Curtiss*
⑭ Light cruiser *Detroit*
⑮ Light cruiser *Raleigh*
⑯ Target battleship *Utah*
⑰ Seaplane tender *Tangier*
⑱ Battleship *Nevada*
⑲ Battleship *Arizona*
⑳ Repair vessel *Vestal*
㉑ Battleship *Tennessee*
㉒ Battleship *West Virginia*
㉓ Battleship *Maryland*
㉔ Battleship *Oklahoma*
㉕ Oiler *Neosho*
㉖ Battleship *California*
㉗ Seaplane tender *Avocet*
㉘ Destroyer *Shaw*
㉙ Destroyer *Downes*
㉚ Destroyer *Cassin*
㉛ Battleship *Pennsylvania*
㉜ Submarine *Cachalot*
㉝ Minelayer *Oglala*
㉞ Light cruiser *Helena*
㉟ Auxiliary vessel *Argonne*
㊱ Gunboat *Sacramento*
㊲ Destroyer *Jarvis*
㊳ Destroyer *Mugford*
㊴ Seaplane tender *Swan*
㊵ Repair vessel *Rigel*
㊶ Oiler *Ramapo*
㊷ Heavy cruiser *New Orleans*
㊸ Destroyer *Cummings* and light-minelayers *Preble* and *Tracy*
㊹ Heavy cruiser *San Francisco*
㊺ Destroyer-minesweeper *Grebe*, destroyer *Schley* and light-minelayers *Pruitt* and *Sicard*
㊻ Light cruiser *Honolulu*
㊼ Light cruiser *St. Louis*
㊽ Destroyer *Bagley*
㊾ Submarines *Narwhal, Dolphin* and *Tautog* and tenders *Thornton* and *Hulbert*
㊿ Submarine tender *Pelias*
51 Auxiliary vessel *Sumner*
52 Auxiliary vessel *Castor*

AFTER INTENSE BUT very secret preparation, the Japanese Combined Fleet sailed from the Kuriles on 26 November 1941. In the lead was a carrier force commanded by Admiral Chuichi Nagumo.

Nagumo's six carriers launched their first wave of 183 aircraft at 05:30 Hawaii time on 7 December 1941. They found clear weather over the target, and attacked just before 8.00 a.m.

The American fleet, together with six targeted air bases and other military facilities, were at a low state of readiness, it being a Sunday morning. All six airfields were dive-bombed and then strafed. At the same time, 140 aircraft fell on the Pacific Fleet, virtually without opposition.

Battleship Row

All of the seven battleships on Battleship Row were hit, and only the *Nevada* managed to get up steam before the second Japanese wave came in to complete the destruction. *Arizona* blew up, *Oklahoma* capsized, and *West Virginia* and *California* settled to the bottom.

For the loss of under 30 aircraft, the Japanese had ripped the heart out of the US battle fleet. But while the attack was a tactical triumph, it was a strategic disaster, bringing Japan into conflict with the world's greatest power.

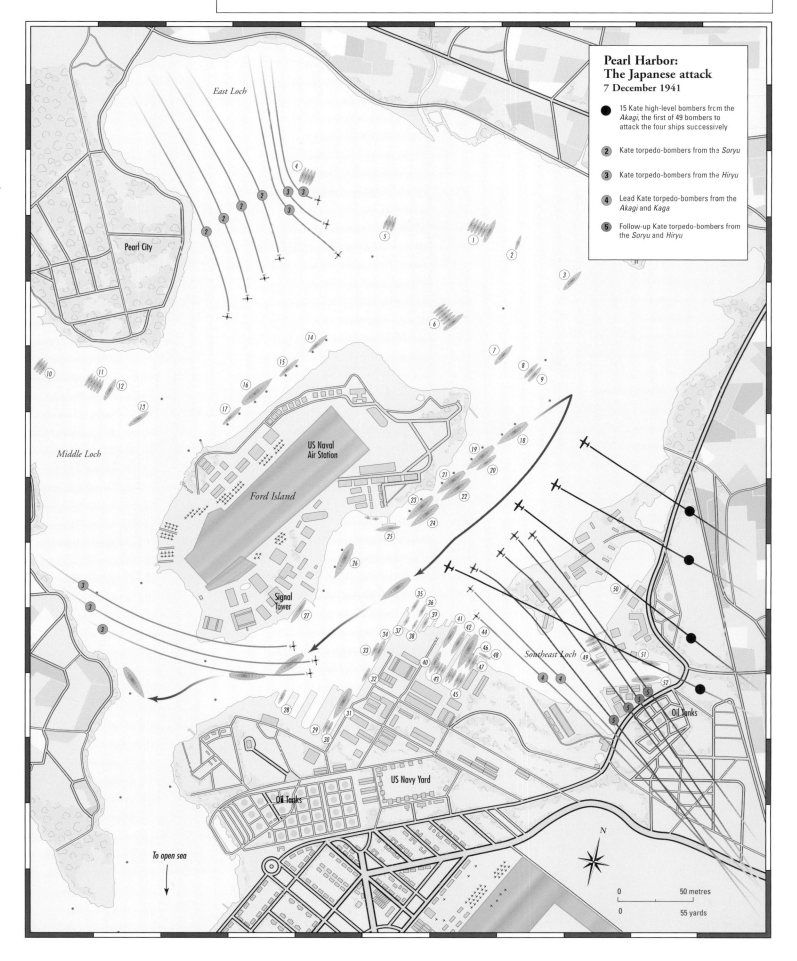

Pearl Harbor: The Japanese attack 7 December 1941

● 15 Kate high-level bombers from the *Akagi*, the first of 49 bombers to attack the four ships successively

② Kate torpedo-bombers from the *Soryu*

③ Kate torpedo-bombers from the *Hiryu*

④ Lead Kate torpedo-bombers from the *Akagi* and *Kaga*

⑤ Follow-up Kate torpedo-bombers from the *Soryu* and *Hiryu*

Japanese Expansion
December 1941–July 1942

Pearl Harbor was only one part of a complex and far reaching plan. At the same time as the US Navy was being gutted, Japanese forces were launching a *blitzkrieg* campaign across the Pacific and through Southeast Asia. These were intended to give Japan the territory and resources the empire required to maintain its expansion.

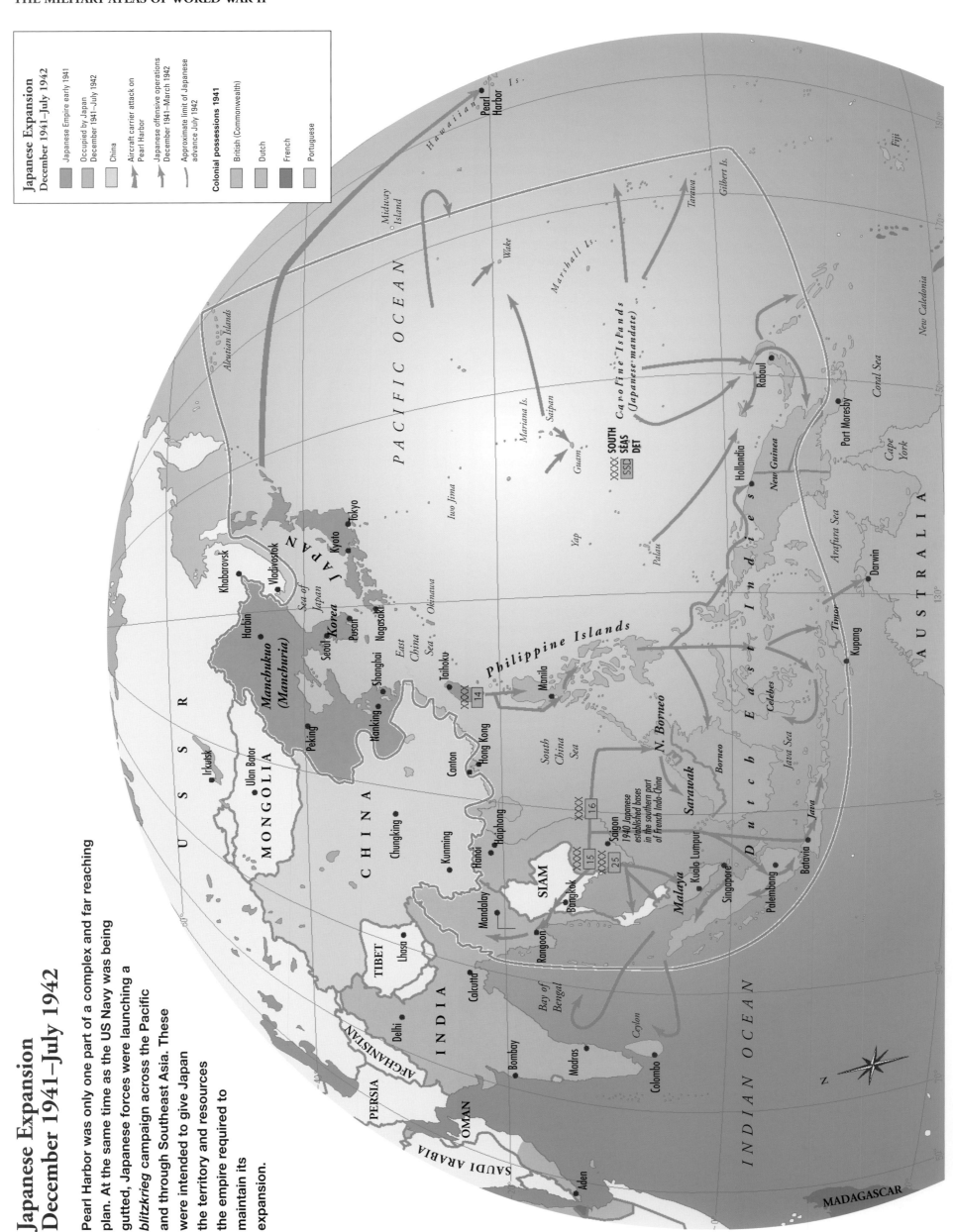

Japanese Expansion
December 1941–July 1942

Japanese Empire early 1941
Occupied by Japan December 1941–July 1942
China
Aircraft carrier attack on Pearl Harbor
Japanese offensive operations December 1941–March 1942
Approximate limit of Japanese advance July 1942

Colonial possessions 1941
British (Commonwealth)
Dutch
French
Portuguese

Invasion of Malaya 8 December 1941– 31 January 1942

Japan had already occupied Indo-China earlier in 1941, and with the outbreak of war Japanese forces moved on British possessions in Southeast Asia. Malaya was a vital source of raw materials, and Singapore was Britain's great bastion in the region. However, the British had grossly underestimated Japanese capabilities, and the Commonwealth forces in the region were ill-prepared to counter the Japanese landings.

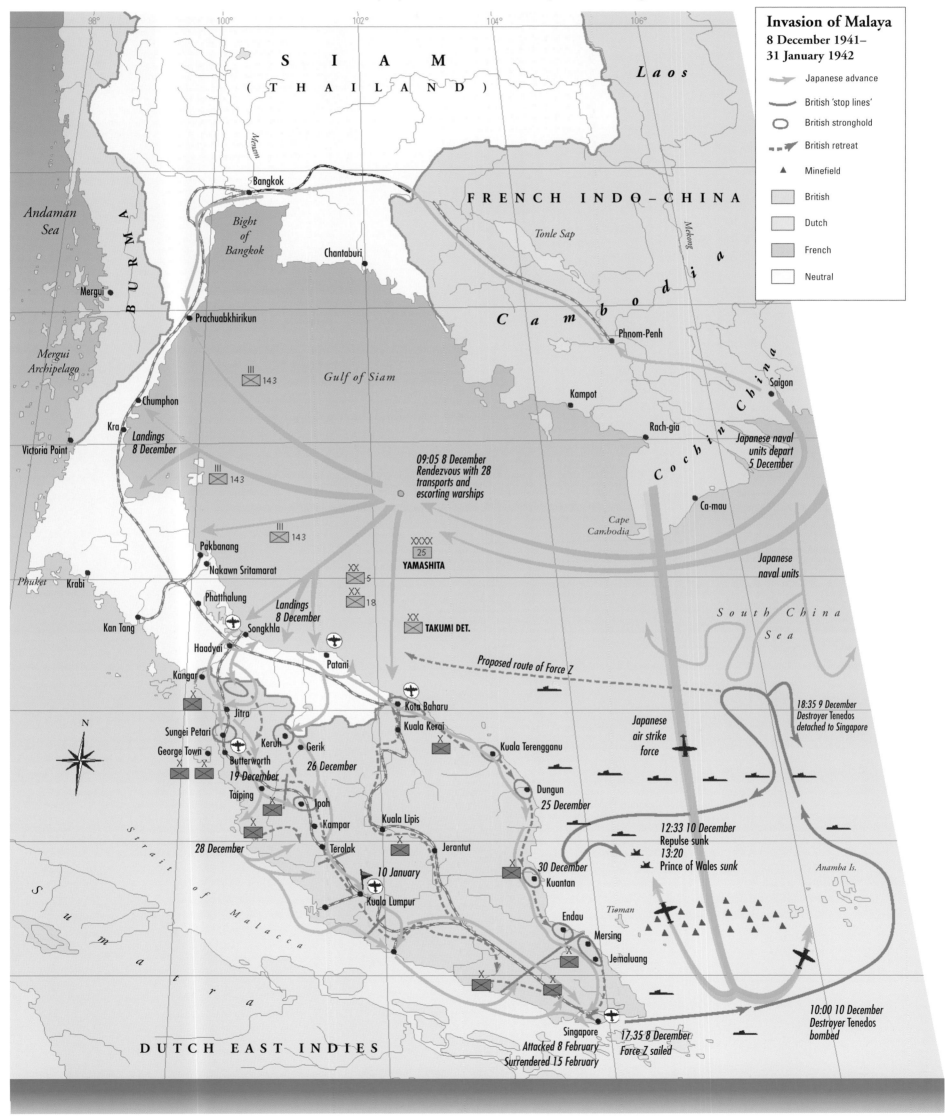

Invasion of Malaya
8 December 1941–
31 January 1942

→ Japanese advance

⌐ British 'stop lines'

○ British stronghold

⇠ British retreat

▲ Minefield

☐ British

☐ Dutch

☐ French

☐ Neutral

BRITISH FORCES in Malaya were forced to retreat as the Japanese pushed their way down the east and west of the peninsula. After initial stiff resistance on the landing beaches, the Japanese pushed forward and captured the airfield at Singoran, With their own fighters now on the peninsula, the Japanese quickly won air superiority.

Every time the British tried to make a stand, the Japanese outflanked their positions with a new landing further south. British morale suffered as the Japanese surged forwards. By the end of January, General Perceval realized that the British position in Malaya was untenable, and surviving troops were withdrawn to Singapore.

Fall of Singapore

Singapore was intended to be Britain's fortress in the Far East, but most of its defences were designed to counter an attack from the sea. But the Japanese were not coming by sea.

The Japanese crossed the narrow Johore Strait on 8 February, and the British were swiftly pushed back. By 13 February, some 80,000 men were trapped in and around the city of Singapore. Two days later General Perceval surrendered. It was one of the greatest humiliations in British military history. Winston Churchill was shocked, and morale in the hard-pressed United Kingdom reached a new low.

Capture of Singapore 8–15 February 1942

Once the Japanese had established a firm foothold on the Malayan peninsula, their advance was inexorable. A British attempt to intercept the invasion force with the capital ships *Prince of Wales* and *Repulse* ended in tragedy when both were sunk by Japanese bombers. RAF Buffalo fighters were completely outclassed by Japanese land-based and naval fighters, and could nothing to hinder the Japanese advance.

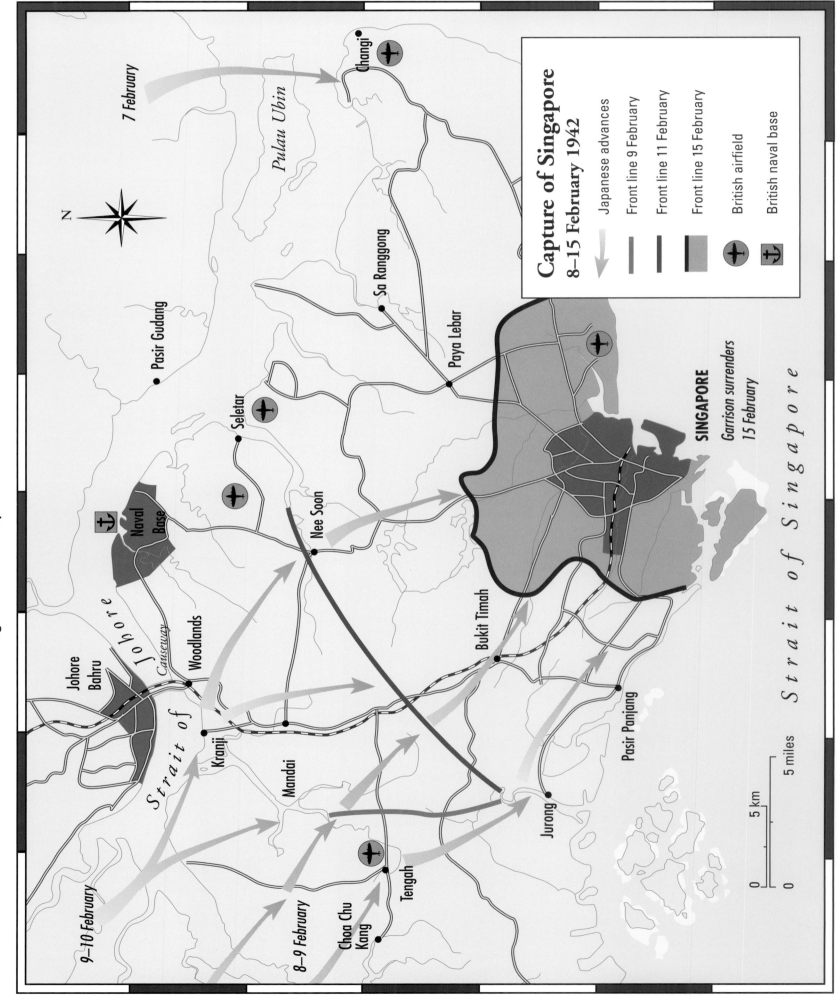

Capture of Singapore 8–15 February 1942

Legend:
- Japanese advances
- Front line 9 February
- Front line 11 February
- Front line 15 February
- British airfield
- British naval base

Japanese Invasion of the Philippines 8 December 1941– June 1942

The Americans had reinforced the Philippines with Boeing B-17 bombers, expecting to use the island group as a base from which to attack Japan. However, like the British, the US Army had grossly underestimated Japanese military capacity. The Japanese invasion was swift and ruthless. General Douglas MacArthur, the former commander of the Philippine Army and now US commander in the area, had to retreat from Manila to the Bataan Peninsula.

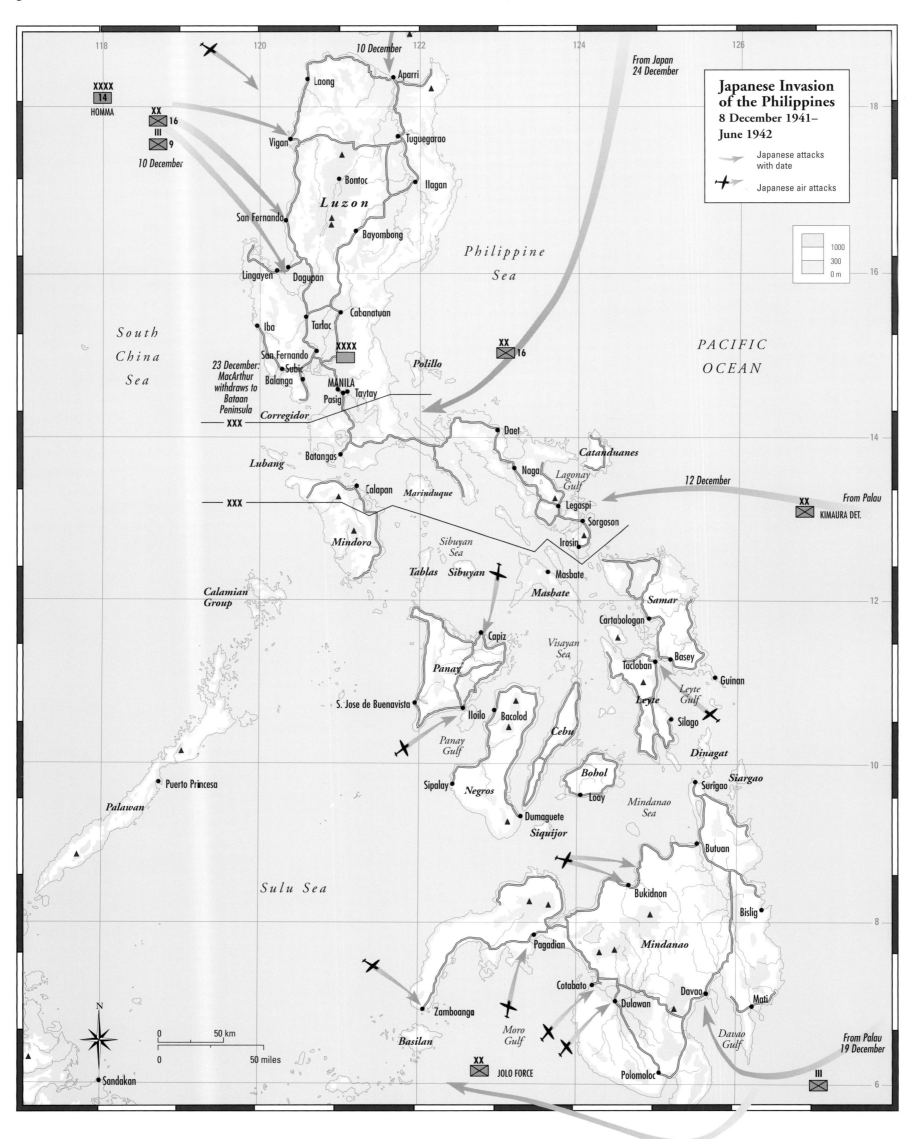

Japanese Invasion of the Philippines 8 December 1941– June 1942

→ Japanese attacks with date

✈ Japanese air attacks

Manila and Bataan 10 December 1941– 9 April 1942

The Philippines were defended by 19,000 US troops, 12,000 Philippine regulars and around 100,000 conscripts. Early Japanese landings diverted the defenders from the main Japanese assault, which arrived on 22 December. The Japanese gained ground quickly against the partly trained Philippine Army, presenting MacArthur with the choice of retreat or being crushed by the advancing Japanese in a pincer action. The flamboyant American general chose retreat.

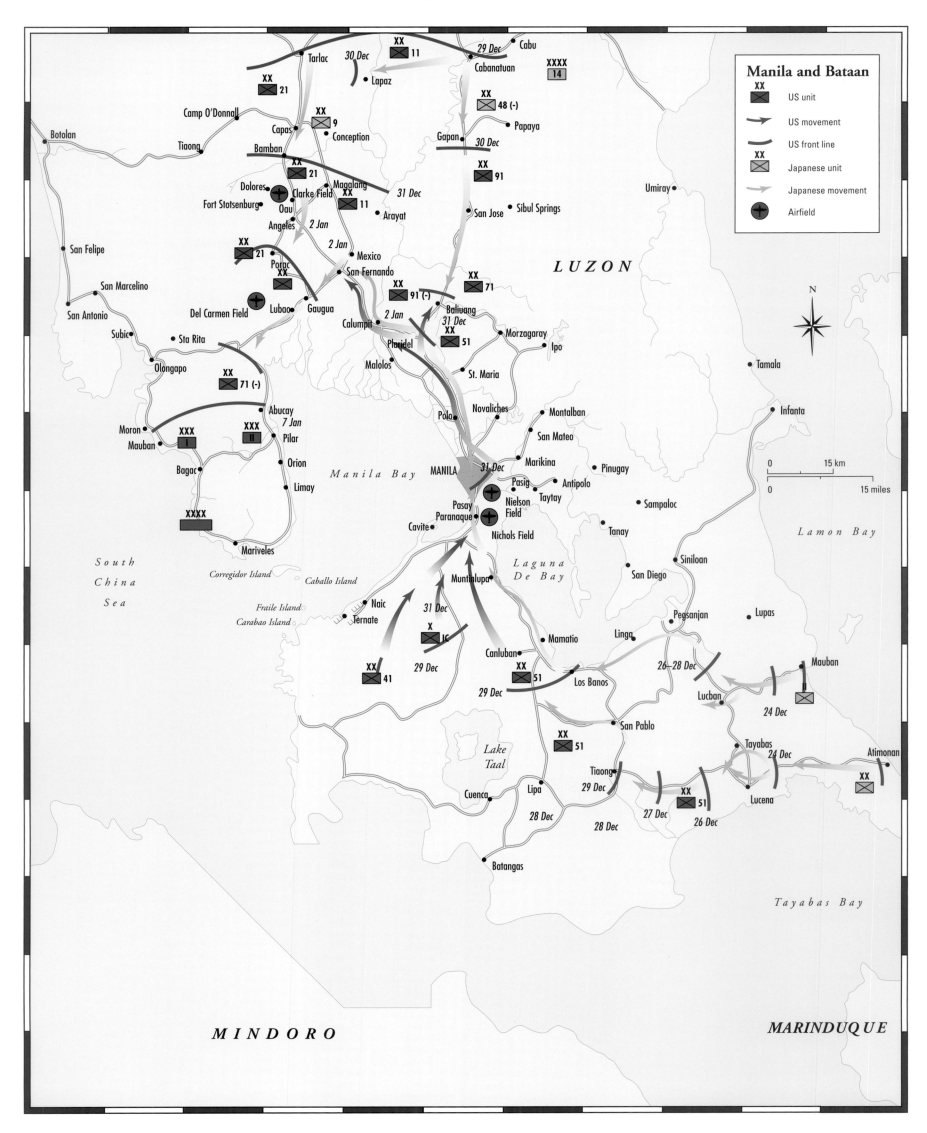

Manila and Bataan

- XX — US unit
- → US movement
- ⌒ US front line
- XX — Japanese unit
- → Japanese movement
- ● Airfield

Bataan and Corregidor

After a series of Japanese frontal assaults, an attempt to outflank the first American defensive line on the Bataan Peninsula was made. However, these amphibious landings were beaten back after savage fighting. General Homma, the Japanese commander, decided not to try again until reinforcements arrived from Japan. Meanwhile, General MacArthur was ordered to leave the Philippines by President Roosevelt.

MACARTHUR WAS RELUCTANT TO LEAVE, saying 'I shall return' after he and his staff had been spirited away in PT Boats. Meanwhile, the defenders of Bataan were in an increasingly difficult situation. Fighting men were surviving on quarter rations, and disease was beginning to seriously deplete the number of able-bodied soldiers. However, the casualties were not all one-sided: Japanese losses to tropical diseases were also high, and the stubborn American defence was also proving costly. On 3 April, after three months of fighting, the reinforced Japanese broke through Bataan's defences, and advanced swiftly down the peninsula. The last defenders surrendered on 9 April, leaving only the island of Corregidor and a few other isolated islands in American hands.

Corregidor is a small fortified island at the mouth of Manila Bay. While the other islands were being taken care of, the Japanese mounted a series of shattering bombardments which smashed most of Corregidor's defences. The Japanese followed the bombardment with troops, which quickly overwhelmed the defenders. On 6 May, MacArthur's successor, General Wainwright, surrendered. Many of the defenders died on the infamous 'Death March' across Bataan and into captivity.

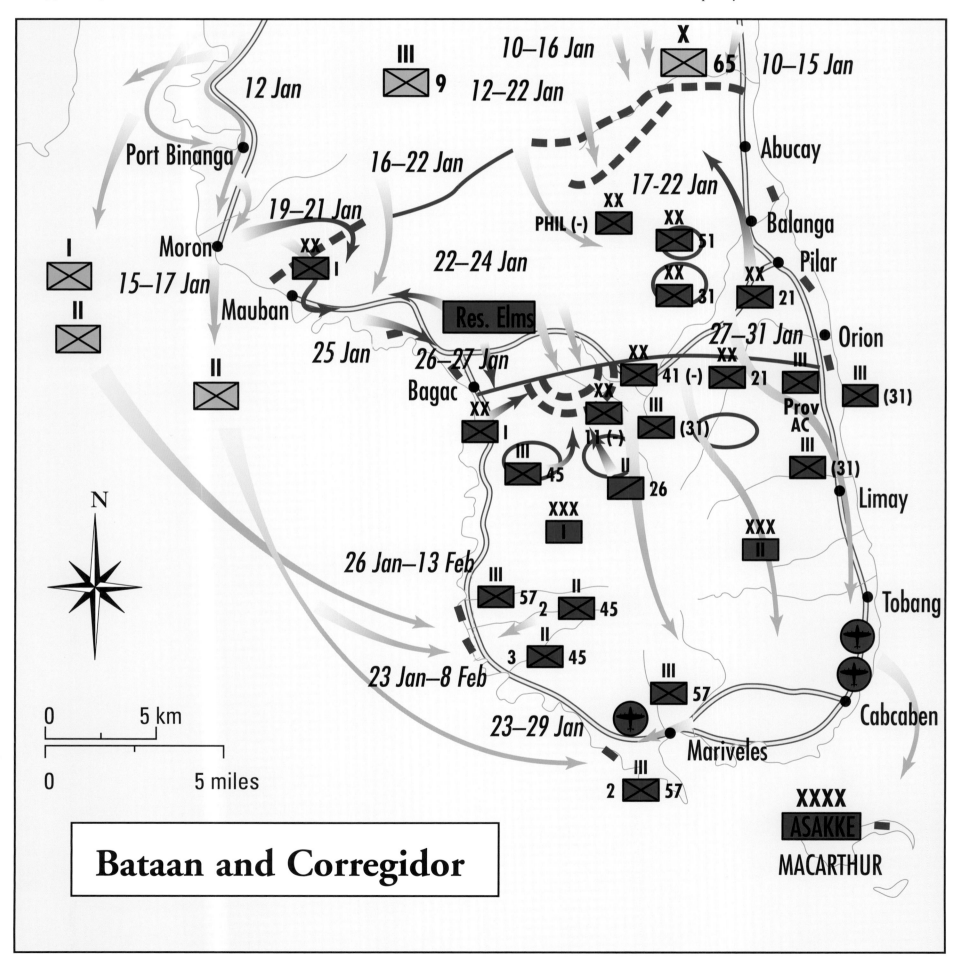

Bataan and Corregidor

Japanese Invasion of the Dutch East Indies January–March 1942

The oilfields of the Dutch East Indies were among Japan's primary targets for conquest. Once again, the Japanese attack advanced at a startling rate. Allied efforts to disrupt the advance were largely naval, but the thrown together ABDA force (American, British, Dutch and Australian) could offer little resistance to the powerful Japanese cruiser squadrons which protected the Imperial invasion convoys.

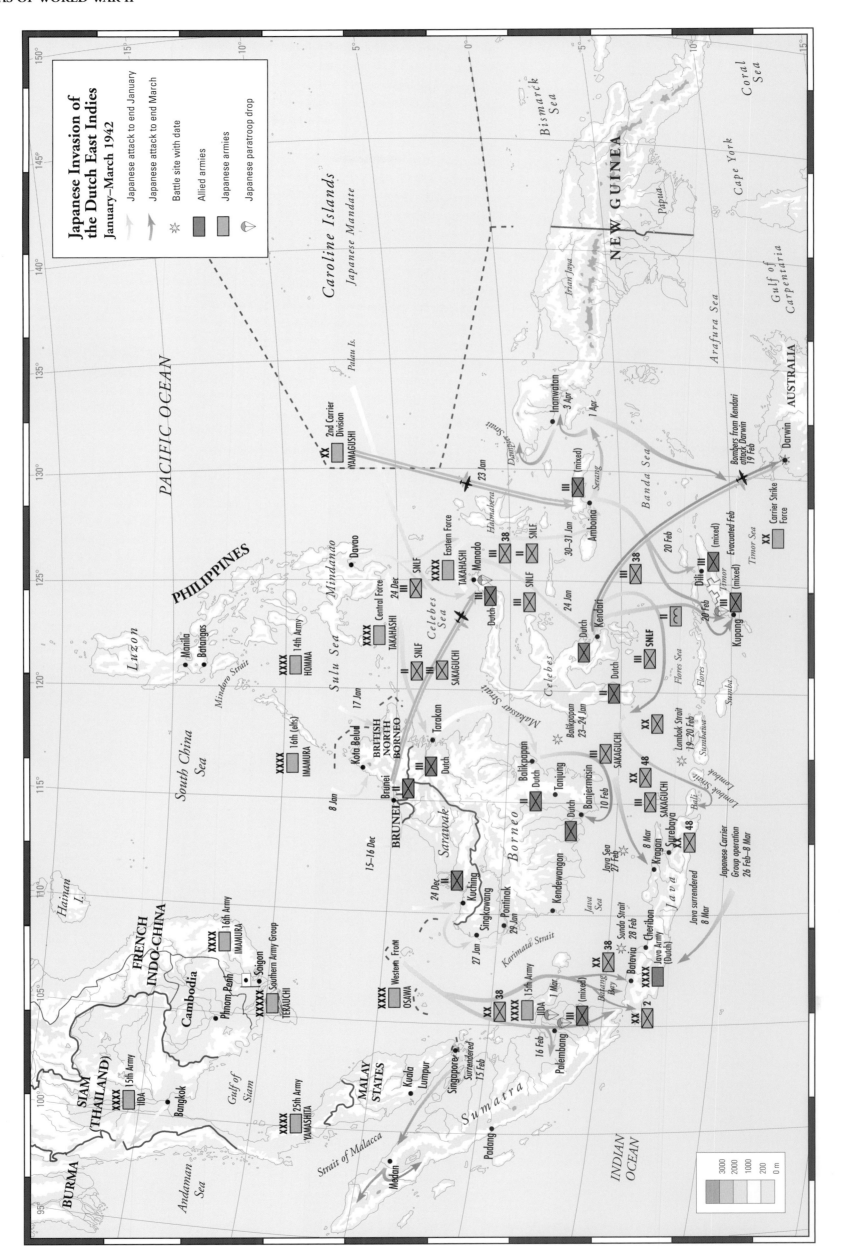

Japanese Invasion of the Dutch East Indies
January–March 1942

Japanese attack to end January
Japanese attack to end March
Battle site with date
Allied armies
Japanese armies
Japanese paratroop drop

Japanese Invasion of Burma January–May 1942

Japan invaded Burma on 15 January 1942. The initial attacks seized airfields which would be used to support the drive on Rangoon. The city was taken on 8 March. British defensive plans were not put into effect until it was too late, and by the end of April British forces in Burma had been ordered to withdraw to India, leaving the Japanese victorious.

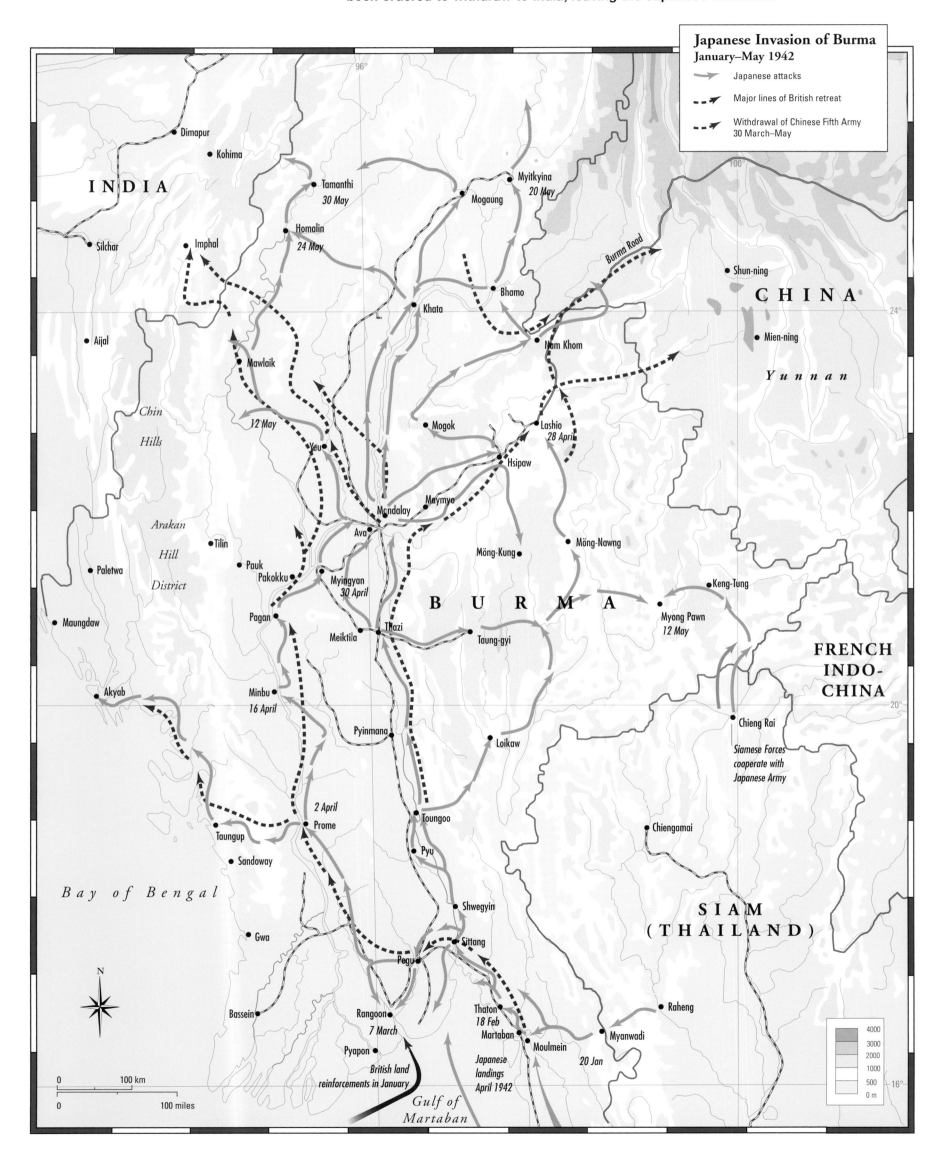

Japanese Invasion of Burma
January–May 1942

→ Japanese attacks

⇢ Major lines of British retreat

⇢ Withdrawal of Chinese Fifth Army
30 March–May

INDIA

CHINA

BURMA

SIAM (THAILAND)

FRENCH INDO-CHINA

Bay of Bengal

Gulf of Martaban

Yunnan

Chin Hills

Arakan Hill District

Dimapur
Kohima
Silchar
Imphal
Aijal
Tamanthi *30 May*
Homalin *24 May*
Mawlaik
12 May
Yeu
Khata
Mogaung
Myitkyina *20 May*
Bhamo
Shun-ning
Nam Khom
Mien-ning
Mogok
Lashio *28 April*
Hsipaw
Maymyo
Mandalay
Ava
Möng-Kung
Möng-Nawng
Keng-Tung
Tilin
Paletwa
Pauk
Pakokku
Myingyan *30 April*
Pagan
Meiktila
Thazi
Taung-gyi
Myong Pawn *12 May*
Maungdaw
Minbu *16 April*
Pyinmana
Loikaw
Chieng Rai
Akyab
Taungup
Sandoway
Gwa
2 April
Prome
Toungoo
Pyu
Chiengamai
Shwegyin
Sittang
Pegu
Bassein
Rangoon *7 March*
Pyapon
Thaton *18 Feb*
Martaban
Moulmein *20 Jan*
Myanwadi
Raheng

Burma Road

Siamese Forces cooperate with Japanese Army

British land reinforcements in January

Japanese landings April 1942

N

0   100 km

0   100 miles

4000
3000
2000
1000
500
0 m

Indian Ocean Raid March–April 1942

Having dealt with the US Navy at Pearl Harbor, Nagumo's carrier force raided the Indian Ocean, after bombing Darwin. Carrier aircraft raided Trincomalee and Colombo, losing several planes. The old battleships of the British Eastern Fleet could not catch the Japanese. However, Imperial Navy reconnaissance aircraft found the cruisers *Dorsetshire* and *Cornwall* and the old carrier *Hermes*, and all three ships were sunk by devastating dive-bombing attacks.

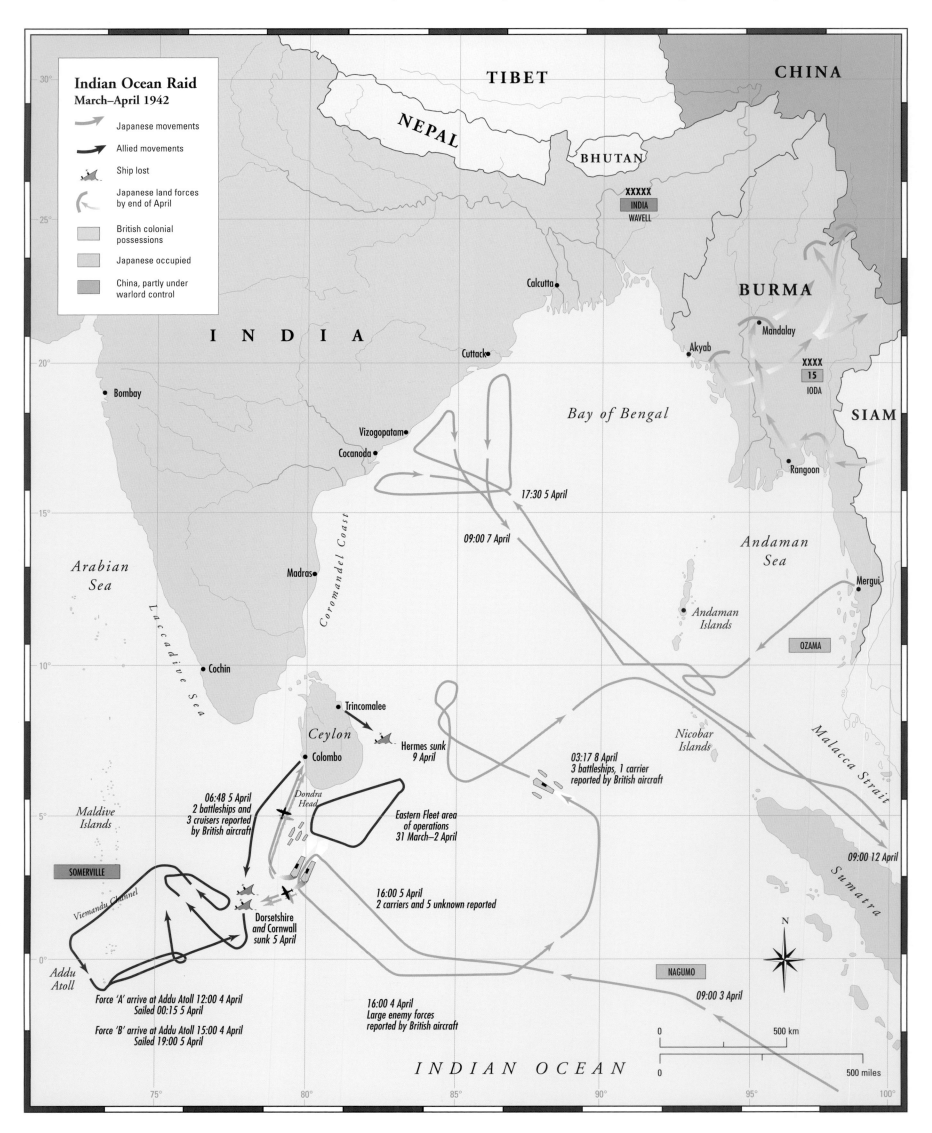

Indian Ocean Raid
March–April 1942

Japanese movements

Allied movements

Ship lost

Japanese land forces by end of April

British colonial possessions

Japanese occupied

China, partly under warlord control

TIBET

CHINA

NEPAL

BHUTAN

XXXXX
INDIA
WAVELL

Calcutta

INDIA

BURMA

Mandalay

Cuttack

Akyab

XXXX
15
IODA

Bombay

Vizogopatam

Cocanoda

Bay of Bengal

SIAM

Rangoon

17:30 5 April

09:00 7 April

Andaman Sea

Arabian Sea

Madras

Coromandel Coast

Mergui

Laccadive Sea

Andaman Islands

Cochin

OZAMA

Trincomalee

Nicobar Islands

Malacca Strait

Ceylon

Hermes sunk 9 April

03:17 8 April
3 battleships, 1 carrier reported by British aircraft

Colombo

Maldive Islands

Dondra Head

06:48 5 April
2 battleships and 3 cruisers reported by British aircraft

Eastern Fleet area of operations 31 March–2 April

09:00 12 April

Sumatra

SOMERVILLE

16:00 5 April
2 carriers and 5 unknown reported

Viemandu Channel

Dorsetshire and *Cornwall* sunk 5 April

N

NAGUMO

09:00 3 April

Addu Atoll

Force 'A' arrive at Addu Atoll 12:00 4 April
Sailed 00:15 5 April

Force 'B' arrive at Addu Atoll 15:00 4 April
Sailed 19:00 5 April

16:00 4 April
Large enemy forces reported by British aircraft

0   500 km

0   500 miles

INDIAN OCEAN

Battle of the Coral Sea
28 April–11 May 1942

To further Imperial intentions of cutting the lines of communication between Australia and the USA, Japan launched 'Operation MO', aimed at seizing Port Moresby on the southern coast of New Guinea. Up until this point, Japan's *blitzkrieg* through Asia and the Pacific had met with nothing but stunning success. This time, however, they encountered more serious opposition. Getting wind of Japanese plans through code breakers, Admiral Chester Nimitz sent a carrier task force to the Coral Sea, which was in position by the beginning of May.

EARLY ON 7 MAY BOTH CARRIER FORCES staged air searches. US aircraft located an enemy carrier force heading for Port Moresby and the Task Force commander, Admiral Fletcher, launched a strike which sank the small carrier *Shoho*. The next day, reconnaissance aircraft from both fleets located each other's opponents, and both fleets launched carrier strikes at a range of 200 miles (320 km). American dive bombers hit the fleet carrier *Shokaku*, knocking it out of action. The Japanese strike hit both American carriers, the *Lexington* and the *Yorktown*, causing damage but not enough to prevent the recovery of returning aircraft. However, fires aboard the *Lexington* got out of control, and the vessel was destroyed in a series of huge explosions. American losses were more serious than those of the Japanese in the first sea battle in history in which the main combatants never saw each other. However, the Battle of the Coral Sea was a setback for the Japanese, who had to abandon their plan to take Port Moresby.

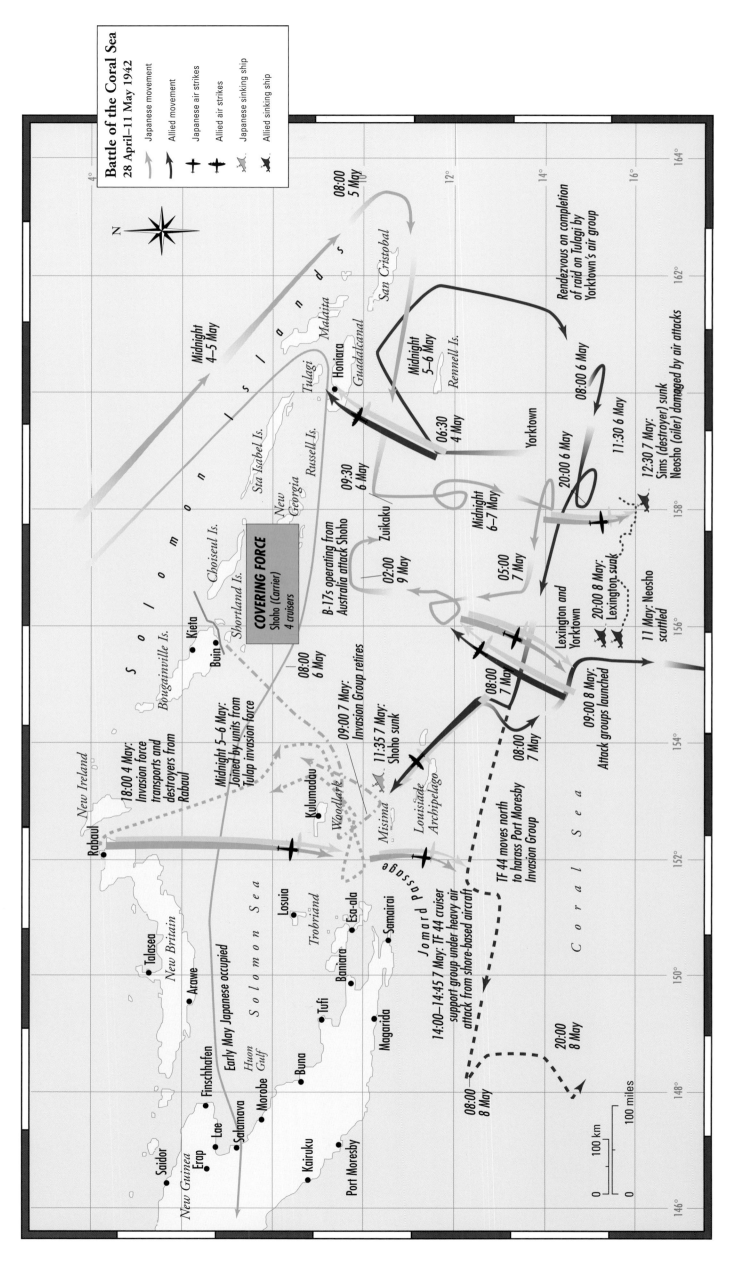

Admiral Yamamoto's Plans to Seize Midway May–June 1942

The Imperial Japanese Navy was nurtured on the concept of winning wars at sea by fighting one 'Great Decisive Battle', in which the enemy's fleet was annihilated. In order to draw the carriers of the US Navy's Pacific Fleet into such a battle, Admiral Isoroku Yamamoto devised the 'MI' operation. The complex plan called for landings to be made in the Aleutian Islands, which would draw the Americans northward. This would be followed by an amphibious attack on Midway Island, a key US outpost only 1,150 miles (1850 km) from Hawaii.

T HE CAPTURE OF MIDWAY would pose such a threat to Hawaii that Admiral Chester Nimitz, the American Commander-in-Chief Pacific, would be forced to throw his weakened fleet against the invasion force. As he did so, a third Japanese force – Vice-Admiral Nagumo's First Carrier Striking Force supported by the Imperial Navy's main battle fleet – would mount a colossal ambush to destroy the Americans.

Yamamoto's plan was excessively complex, and required that at least nine separate formations dispersed across thousands of miles of ocean should act with perfect timing. Crucially, the Japanese were also unaware that their American code breakers had at least partially cracked Japanese naval codes, and that Admiral Nimitz had a chance to mount an ambush of his own.

On the face of things, the Japanese had much the more powerful force. Nagumo's veteran and battle-tested force included the carriers *Akagi*, *Kaga*,

Hiryu and *Soryu*. About 480km (300 miles) astern of the carriers was the battle fleet, with Yamamoto himself flying his flag in the giant new battleship *Yamato*, the largest warship in the world.

US carriers

American carrier strength was currently under pressure. USS *Enterprise* and USS *Hornet* under Rear-Admiral Raymond Spruance were at Pearl Harbor. The badly damaged USS *Yorktown*, carrying Admiral Frank Fletcher, arrived from the Coral Sea on 27 May. She was repaired enough to fight in a remarkable three days. By the end of May, all three carriers were on their way from Hawaii to a position about 565km (350 miles) northeast of Midway. There they waited as the Japanese approached Midway on 4 June, the would-be ambushers were about to be ambushed themselves.

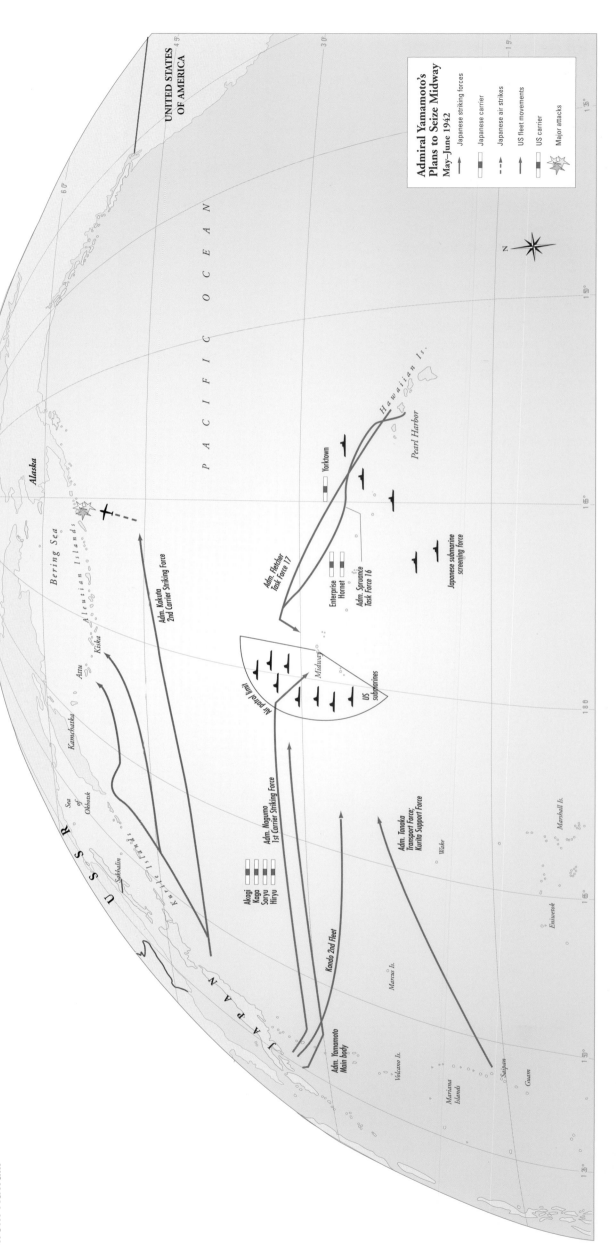

Battle of Midway
4–5 June 1942

At 04:30 on 4 June, Admiral Nagumo launched the first strike of 72 bombers and 36 fighters against the island of Midway. He was about 385km (240 miles) from the target and was closing at high speed. A powerful screen of fighters was retained, to protect the carriers against American aircraft based at Midway. At 05:30, Nagumo's force was sighted by a Consolidated PBY Catalina. At 06:16, the radar station on Midway detected the incoming Japanese planes at a range of 120km (74 miles), and Midway's fighter force and anti-aircraft defences were brought to action stations. Marine Corps Brewster Buffaloes and Grumman Wildcats raced to intercept the Japanese, though their aircraft were no match for the nimble Mitsubishi Zeros escorting the Japanese strike force.

THE INITIAL SIGHTING REPORT FROM THE US NAVY PBY had galvanized the Americans on Midway into action. Long before the first Japanese aircraft arrived, the slow and vulnerable PBY Catalina flying boats had lumbered off the lagoon, heading eastwards to orbit in safety. These were followed by all of the attack aircraft on Midway. First off were six of the Navy's brand new TBF Avenger torpedo bombers, followed by four equally new Martin B-26 Marauders of the US Army. A second wave of 16 Marine SBD Dauntless dive bombers, Army B-17 Flying Fortresses and Marine Vindicator torpedo bombers followed, heading northwest towards the Japanese fleet.

Between 06:30 and 07:00 Japanese strikes caused significant damage to Midway, destroying the seaplane hangar, several oil tanks and the hospital. Seventeen Marine fighters were shot down, but the Japanese strike leader, Lieutenant Tomonaga, signalled that a second wave would be needed since his force had not been able to hit the runways on Midway. Ten minutes after Tomonaga's signal, the first Midway-based aircraft attacked. Attacking at low level, with no fighter protection, the Avengers and B-26 bombers pressed home their attacks bravely, but to no effect. Japanese anti-aircraft fire and additional Zeros which had been quickly scrambled knocked most of the attackers out of the sky. The B-17 attacks scored no hits.

Nagumo was worried: he had lost 67 aircraft destroyed or damaged already, mostly to the anti-aircraft defences on Midway, and he had no idea where the American carriers were. Clearly another strike on Midway was necessary, but his aircraft had been armed with torpedoes and armour-piercing bombs in anticipation of engaging the US Navy. He did not know whether he had time to change the warloads.

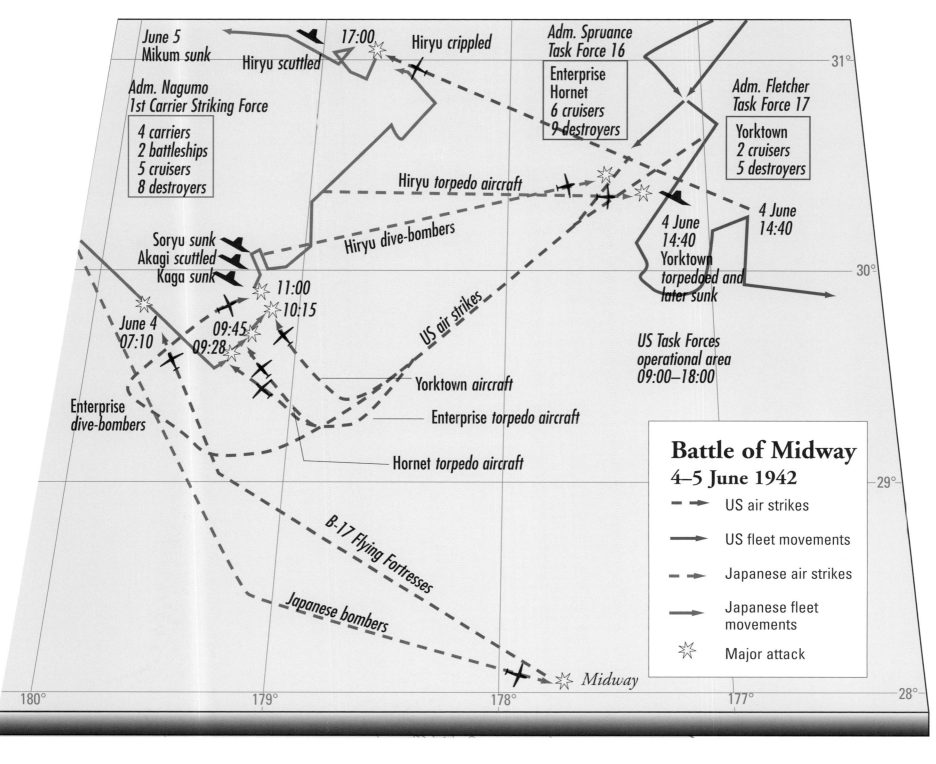

Battle of Midway I
4 June 1942 04:00–10:30

If Admiral Nagumo was worried about the location of the American carriers, his opponents, Admirals Fletcher and Spruance, had no such doubts. They knew that the enemy carriers could be attacked while they were recovering their aircraft from the first Midway strike, hitting them when they were at their most vulnerable. Between them, the two US Navy carrier groups had at 08:00 launched a 151-aircraft strike against the Japanese fleet. This was still on its way when a reconnaissance floatplane from the heavy cruiser *Tone* finally located the American carriers.

The first signals from the *Tone's* floatplane caused some confusion aboard the Japanese carriers, which had just finished switching the weapons load aboard their aircraft from anti-ship to high-explosive weapons for the second strike at Midway, and now had to switch back to torpedoes and armour-piercing bombs. The ships were in this process when the Marine dive bombers from Midway arrived. The attack scored no hits, but did manage to throw the Japanese carrier force into confusion. Nagumo decided that the aircraft returning from the first Midway strike should be landed, refuelled and rearmed before any attempt to attack the US carriers could be made. It was while the Japanese decks were the scene of this frantic activity that the US carrier aircraft arrived.

Carrier strikes go in

First to attack were the TBD torpedo bombers. Coming in low and slow, they proved easy meat for the Japanese fighter cover diving down from above, and 35 out of 41 aircraft were shot down. However, since the Zero fighters were now down at sea level, they could not interfere with the 49 SBD dive bombers which now arrived 3040m (10,000ft) above the four Japanese carriers. Attacking with deadly accuracy, *Yorktown's* bombers smashed the *Soryu*, while those of the *Enterprise* set *Akagi* and *Kaga* ablaze.

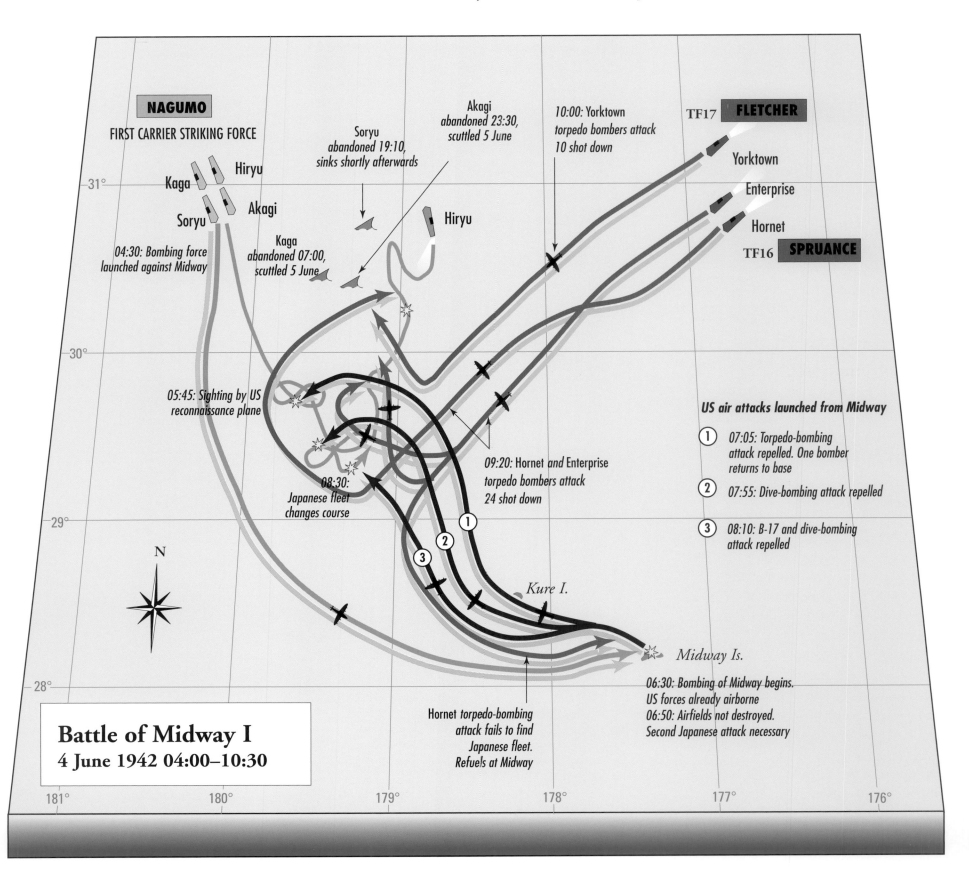

NAGUMO

FIRST CARRIER STRIKING FORCE

Kaga · Hiryu

Soryu · Akagi

04:30: Bombing force launched against Midway

Soryu
abandoned 19:10, sinks shortly afterwards

Akagi
abandoned 23:30, scuttled 5 June

Hiryu

Kaga abandoned 07:00, scuttled 5 June

10:00: Yorktown torpedo bombers attack 10 shot down

TF17 · **FLETCHER**

Yorktown

Enterprise

Hornet

TF16 · **SPRUANCE**

05:45: Sighting by US reconnaissance plane

US air attacks launched from Midway

① *07:05: Torpedo-bombing attack repelled. One bomber returns to base*

② *07:55: Dive-bombing attack repelled*

③ *08:10: B-17 and dive-bombing attack repelled*

09:20: Hornet and Enterprise torpedo bombers attack 24 shot down

08:30: Japanese fleet changes course

N

Kure I.

Hornet torpedo-bombing attack fails to find Japanese fleet. Refuels at Midway

Midway Is.

06:30: Bombing of Midway begins. US forces already airborne
06:50: Airfields not destroyed. Second Japanese attack necessary

Battle of Midway I
4 June 1942 04:00–10:30

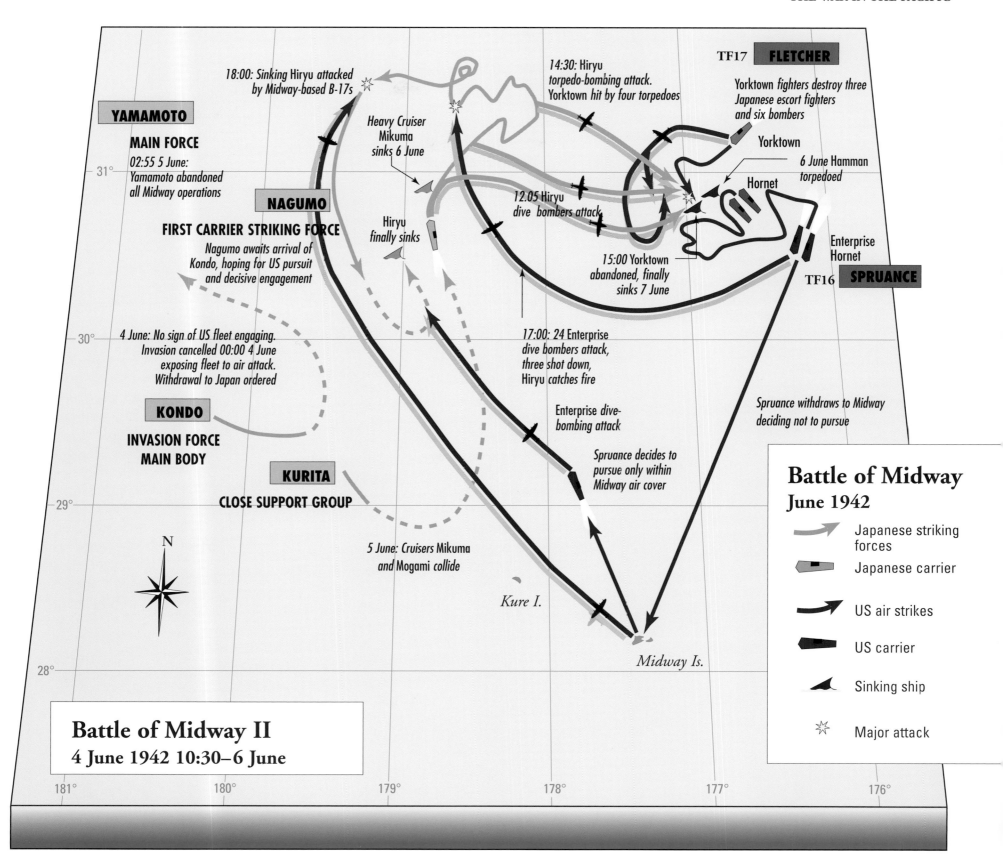

18:00: Sinking Hiryu attacked by Midway-based B-17s

14:30: Hiryu torpedo-bombing attack. Yorktown hit by four torpedoes

TF17 **FLETCHER**

Yorktown fighters destroy three Japanese escort fighters and six bombers

Yorktown

6 June Hamman torpedoed

YAMAMOTO

MAIN FORCE

02:55 5 June: Yamamoto abandoned all Midway operations

Heavy Cruiser Mikuma sinks 6 June

Hornet

NAGUMO

FIRST CARRIER STRIKING FORCE

Nagumo awaits arrival of Kondo, hoping for US pursuit and decisive engagement

Hiryu finally sinks

12.05 Hiryu dive bombers attack

Enterprise
Hornet

SPRUANCE

TF16

15:00 Yorktown abandoned, finally sinks 7 June

4 June: No sign of US fleet engaging. Invasion cancelled 00:00 4 June exposing fleet to air attack. Withdrawal to Japan ordered

17:00: 24 Enterprise dive bombers attack, three shot down, Hiryu catches fire

Spruance withdraws to Midway deciding not to pursue

KONDO

INVASION FORCE MAIN BODY

Enterprise dive-bombing attack

Spruance decides to pursue only within Midway air cover

KURITA

CLOSE SUPPORT GROUP

N

5 June: Cruisers Mikuma and Mogami collide

Kure I.

Midway Is.

Battle of Midway
June 1942

→ Japanese striking forces

◣ Japanese carrier

➤ US air strikes

◤ US carrier

◥ Sinking ship

✳ Major attack

Battle of Midway II
4 June 1942 10:30– 6 June

31°
30°
29°
28°

181°   180°   179°   178°   177°   176°

Battle of Midway II
4 June 1942 10:30–6 June

The devastating attack by the US Navy dive bombers had smashed three of Japan's first-line aircraft carriers. *Soryu*'s fires were uncontrollable, and the crew were ordered to abandon ship after 20 minutes. *Kaga* blazed for the rest of the day, and the order to abandon came at 5.00 p.m. Nagumo transferred his flag from *Akagi* before 11.00 a.m., but it was not until 7.30 p.m. that the crew was ordered to abandon ship. The carrier was still ablaze in the early hours when it was despatched by a destroyer. Of the four carriers which had been Japan's pride that morning, only *Hiryu* remained.

*H*IRYU HAD BEEN SOME DISTANCE from the other Japanese carriers, and had not been hit by the American dive bombers. She launched her own strike at 11:00, which found the *Yorktown* as she recovered her aircraft. Hit three times, *Yorktown* was soon ablaze, but excellent damage control put out the fire and enabled the American carrier to make 37km/h (20 knots) by 13:30. However, a second strike launched from *Hiryu* slammed in two more torpedoes and, listing dangerously, she had to be abandoned. The hulk refused to sink, and was taken in tow, but she did not survive long. The next day, *Yorktown* was torpedoed by a Japanese submarine and sank.

Hiryu hunted down

Before the second strike on *Yorktown*, she had sent 10 SBDs to find the remaining Japanese carrier. Even as their own ship was being abandoned, the Dauntlesses found *Hiryu* only about 175km (110 miles) from the US force. *Enterprise* and *Hornet* sent off 40 SBDs, which arrived high above *Hiryu* at about 5.00 p.m. Attacking immediately, they hit the Japanese carrier with four bombs and four near misses. Completely gutted, the *Hiryu* was later scuttled. The US Navy's carrier aircraft had ripped the heart out of Japan's carrier force in one of the key battles in history. From now on, the Pacific War would be a carrier war.

US Landings and the Battle of Savo Island
August 1942

In 1942, the Solomon Islands became a key strategic position in the developing war in the South Pacific. In Japanese hands, they would threaten the supply routes between the USA and Australia. Occupation by the Allies would counter that threat, and would additionally provide a springboard for an Allied campaign against Japanese positions in the Southwest Pacific. The Japanese made the first move, capturing Tulagi. They then moved on to Guadalcanal, where they began to construct an airfield near Lunga Point.

A<small>N AIRFIELD ON</small> G<small>UADALCANAL</small> would allow Japanese bombers to attack Allied shipping over a wide area. In a surprise assault, 19,000 US Marines under Major-General Alexander Vandegrift landed on Tulagi and Guadalcanal on 7 August, and chased the Japanese airfield construction workers into the jungle. The Japanese reaction was swift and devastating. Admiral Mikawa, the naval commander at Rabaul, led a force of five heavy cruisers and two light cruisers at flank speed down the slot – the passage through the middle of the Solomons which separated the outer islands of Choiseul and Santa Isabel from the larger island of New Georgia. In the early hours of 9 August Mikawa's cruisers rounded Savo Island, and came upon the heavy cruisers HMAS *Canberra* and USS *Chicago*. Opening fire at point-blank range, the Japanese cruisers knocked out *Canberra* and drove off *Chicago* in under 10 minutes. Rounding the island, they encountered another Allied cruiser group, and quickly sank the *Vincennes*, the *Quincy* and the *Astoria*. It was the heaviest defeat in US naval history, but it could have been much worse had the Japanese gone on to sink the amphibious transports: instead, Mikawa broke off his attack.

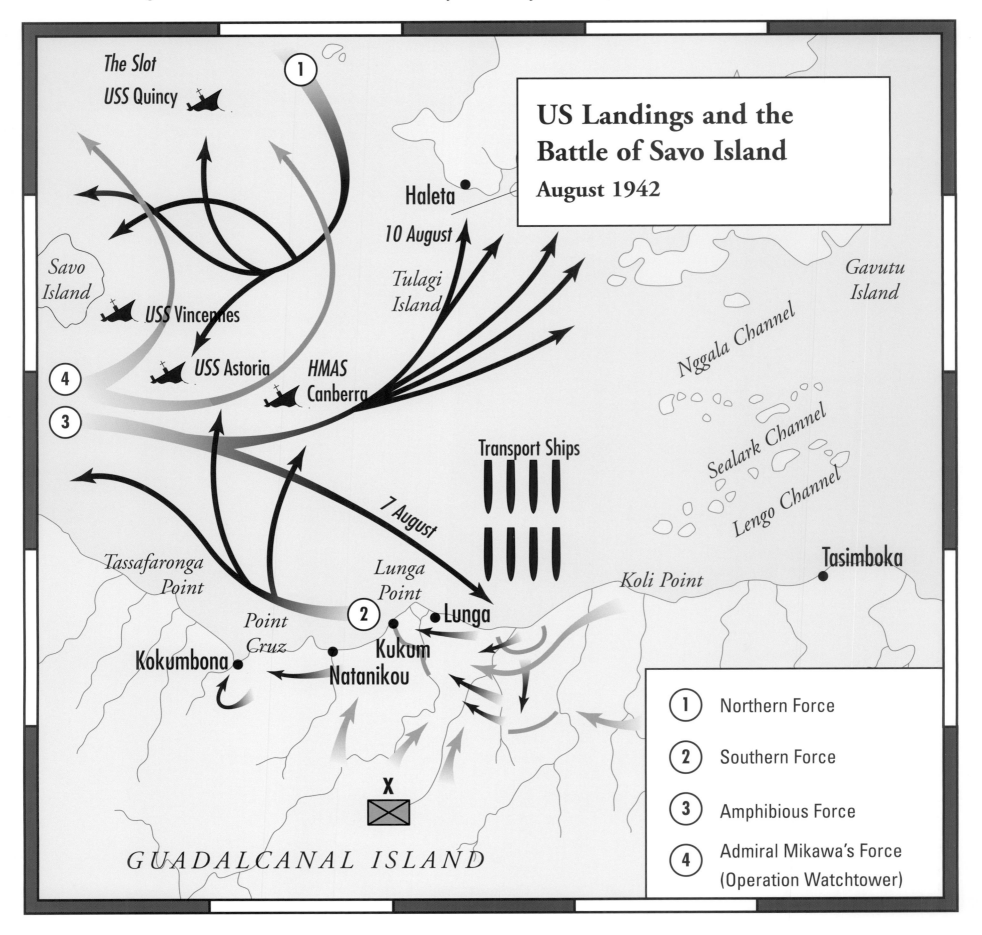

US Landings at Guadalcanal August 1942

By 8 August, US engineers had completed the airfield, renamed Henderson Field. Admiral Turner, the amphibious force commander, continued landing troops and supplies even after the Japanese success at Savo Island, but a heavy morning air raid forced him to withdraw with 1000 Marines and most of the landing force's artillery still aboard his ships. Admiral Yamamoto ordered Mikawa to reinforce Japanese positions at Guadalcanal, and ordered Admiral Kondo's battleships and Admiral Nagumo's carriers to make for the Solomons.

THE JAPANESE DID NOT REALIZE just how many Marines were on Guadalcanal. A Japanese destroyer force under Admiral Raizo Tanaka raced down the Slot by night to land 1000 men of Colonel Kiyano Ichiki's regiment at Taivu, 20km (12 miles) to the west of the Americans. On the night of 19 August, Ichiki led 6000 troops in an attack on what he believed to be the 2000 Marines defending Henderson Field. The Americans had been given time to set up a series of defences around the airfield. The Japanese repeatedly charged with fixed bayonets, only to be cut down by American machine-gun fire and by Marine light tanks. Ichiki himself led the attacks from the west, while a further force which had been landed at Tassafaronga attacked from the east. By dawn the Japanese attack had been beaten off, and dusk of the same day found Ichiki and a handful of survivors making a last stand at the mouth of the Tenaru River. Only 35 US Marines were killed in the battle.

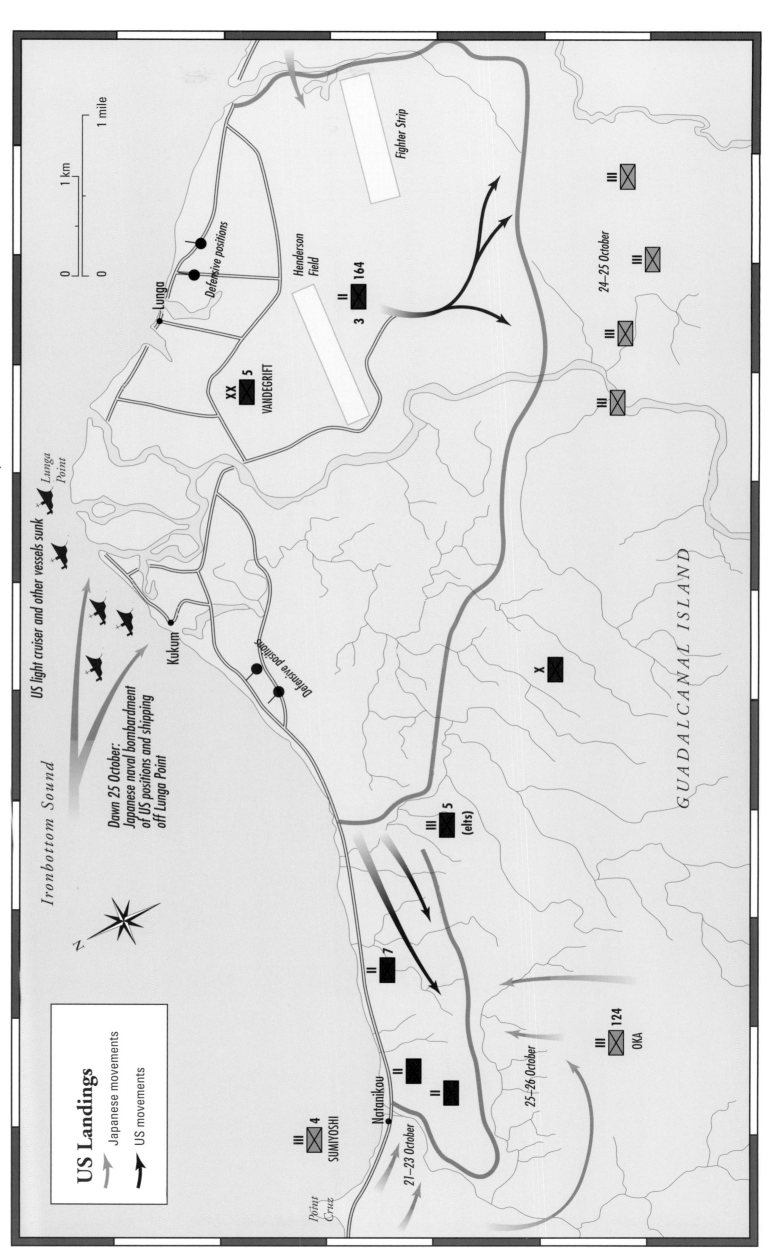

Guadalcanal
September–October 1942

Every naval battle which took place along the Slot was fought between the Japanese who wanted to land more troops on Guadalcanal to fight the increasingly bitter struggle for Henderson Field, and the Americans who aimed to stop them from doing that. The fast destroyer transports commanded by Admiral Tanaka had been named the Tokyo Express by the Americans. In the month up to 13 September, more than 8000 Japanese troops had been landed – and 1200 of those were killed that night in an assault on high ground near the airfield which came to be known as Bloody Ridge.

A MONTH AFTER THE SLAUGHTER at Bloody Ridge, and after the naval battle off Cape Esperance, Japanese strength on Guadalcanal had risen to 22,000 men facing 23,000 Marines on the main island with a further 4500 on Tulagi. Japanese destroyers and cruisers raced down the Slot by night to bombard American positions. In the middle of October, the battleships *Kongo* and *Haruna* bombarded Henderson Field, destroying fuel stocks and many of the aircraft on the field. However, land attacks on the Marine positions at the end of October were again beaten off, with Japanese casualties running into the thousands. The Marines, fighting from well-positioned and well-dug defensive positions, lost only a few hundred.

On the night of 14/15 November, during which seven of Admiral Tanaka's destroyers were sunk, only 4000 of an 11,000-strong Japanese reinforcement actually reached Guadalcanal. They were quickly sent into action, only to find that the Americans had gone onto the offensive. By the end of the month, the American perimeter had been expanded, and the Marines had been massively reinforced by the arrival of the 2nd Marine Division, the 25th Infantry Division, and the Americal Division.

By now, even the most bellicose officers at the Imperial Japanese Headquarters were beginning to count the cost. Since 7 August, Japan had lost 65 naval vessels and more than 800 aircraft in the Solomons. Losses of troops had been in the tens of thousands, and the survivors, by now opposed by more than 50,000 fresh American troops, were on less than half rations. Hunger and disease were now killing as many Japanese soldiers as the Americans. In January 1943, it was decided to withdraw, and in the first week of February the last runs of the Tokyo Express managed to evacuate over 11,000 troops.

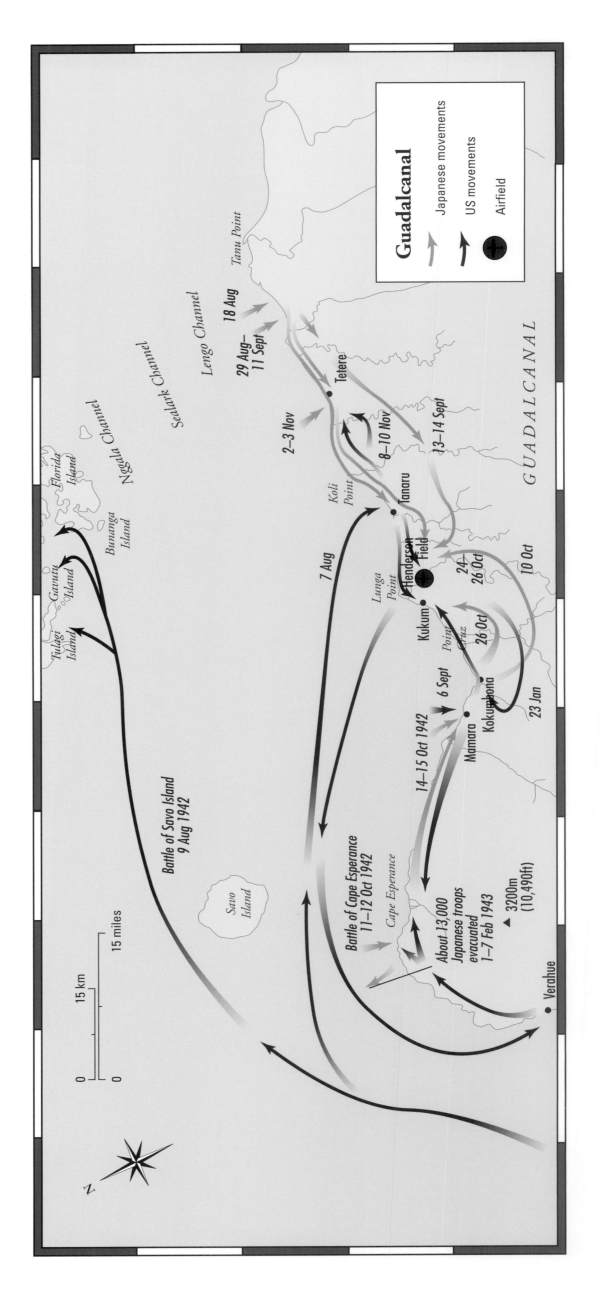

Solomon Islands Sea Battles August–November 1942

The American landings on Guadalcanal marked the first stage in a long Pacific struggle. The Marines on the island soon came under pressure from the sea, as the Japanese Navy threw its weight behind the attempt to defeat the landings. The virtual annihilation of an American cruiser force off Savo Island showed up American inexperience, as well as demonstrating Japanese mastery of night fighting at sea. The four cruisers which sank to the bottom of 'Ironbottom Sound' were the first of many vessels to be lost in these crowded waters. The sea battles in the Solomons would eventually draw in every type of naval vessel, from carriers and battleships through cruisers and destroyers to submarines and PT Boats.

The passage down the centre of the Solomons chain was known as the Slot. The Japanese were dominant by night, but American air power commanded the area by day. The campaign soon developed into one of move and counter-move. The Japanese sent resupply convoys racing down the Slot in what became known as the Tokyo Express, timing their runs so that the final approach to Guadalcanal came by night. Marine Corps and US Army aircraft based on Henderson Field together with Navy carrier aircraft attacked the Japanese convoys by day, hitting them as they moved at speed up and down the Slot.

The Imperial Navy saw the Solomons battles as a way to draw the American carriers into striking range of a Combined Fleet force under the command of Admiral Chuichi Nagumo, who had led the attack on Pearl Harbor. Both sides achieved some successes: in the Battle of the Eastern Solomons, the Japanese light carrier *Ryujo* was sunk, while the USS *Enterprise* was put out of action. Later, USS *Saratoga* was torpedoed and sidelined for months, while on 14 September the submarine *I-19* torpedoed and sank the USS *Wasp*.

Cruiser action

A US cruiser force attacked a Japanese convoy off Cape Esperance on the night of 11/12 October, and in a confused night action the US Navy vessels got the better of the escorting Japanese cruisers, but at the cost of allowing the Japanese convoy through. Two nights later the Japanese sent the

battleships *Hiei* and *Kirishima* to shell Henderson Field, the only American response being an attack by four PT Boats.

On 25 October, US reconnaissance aircraft spotted three Japanese carriers moving down the Slot. After a typical carrier battle off the Santa Cruz Islands – the main combatants never set eyes upon each other – the Japanese light carrier *Zuiho* had been sunk, the carriers *Zuikaku* and *Shokaku* had been damaged, the USS *Enterprise* had been hit and the USS *Hornet* had to be abandoned after a torpedo strike.

Sea battles of Guadalcanal

The climactic naval actions off Guadalcanal came in the middle of November. The largest Tokyo Express ever was detected coming down the Slot, preceded by a heavy Japanese bombardment force. A sacrificial US Navy action on the night of 12/13 November forced the Japanese battleships to retire after sinking or badly damaging several heavy cruisers. At mid-morning on 14 November, US reconnaissance aircraft spotted 11 fast transports escorted by 12 destroyers and five heavy cruisers. A carrier strike from the repaired *Enterprise* sank two cruisers and damaged two more, and then a continuous series of American air attacks by Marine and Navy dive and torpedo bombers sank or damaged several of the transports and seven of the destroyers. Only 4000 of 11,000 Japanese troops landed on Guadalcanal, with many of the troops being too shocked to be of any great fighting value.

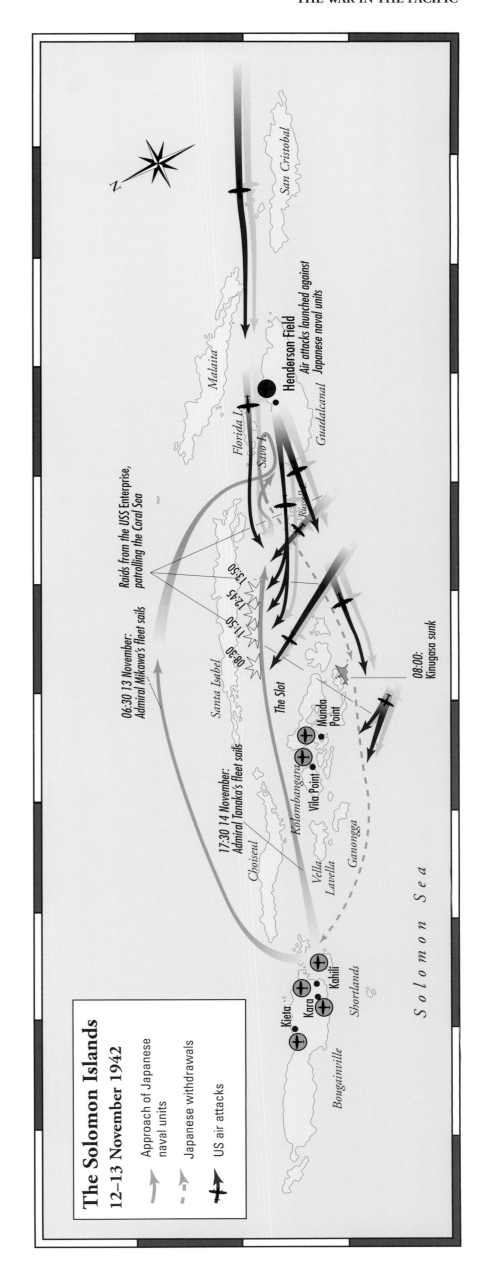

The Solomon Islands 12–13 November 1942

→ Approach of Japanese naval units

⇢ Japanese withdrawals

✈ US air attacks

Guadalcanal
13 November 1942

The decisive naval actions of Guadalcanal began when the US Navy intercepted a powerful Japanese force in Ironbottom Sound. In a confused night action, the Japanese sank three destroyers and two cruisers, but failed to land troops on Guadalcanal.

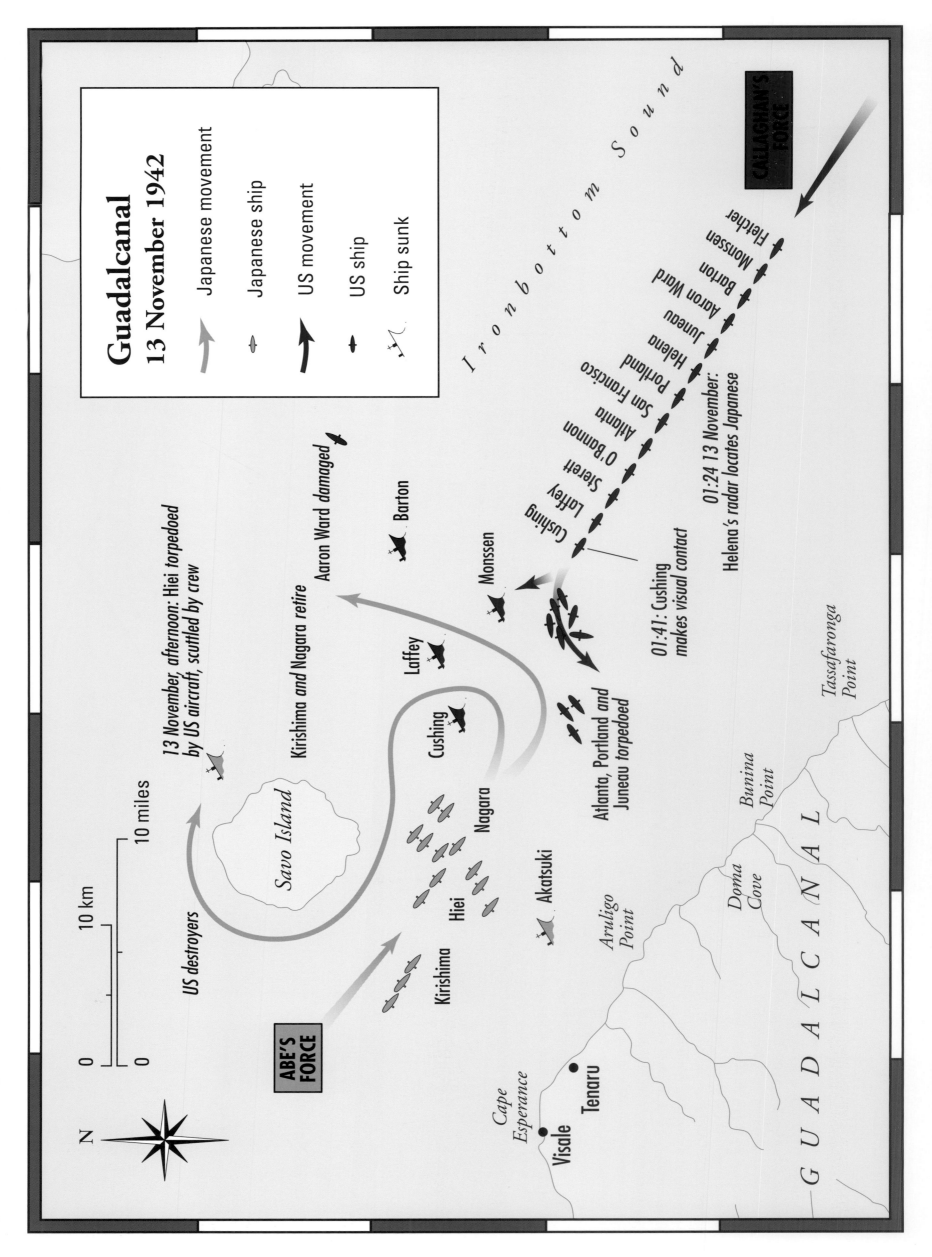

Guadalcanal
13 November 1942

- Japanese movement
- Japanese ship
- US movement
- US ship
- Ship sunk

CALLAGHAN'S FORCE

Fletcher
Monssen
Barton
Aaron Ward
Juneau
Helena
Portland
San Francisco
Atlanta
O'Bannon
Sterett
Laffey
(Cushing)

01:24 13 November:
Helena's radar locates Japanese

01:41: Cushing
makes visual contact

Atlanta, Portland and
Juneau torpedoed

Monssen

Barton

Aaron Ward damaged

Cushing

Laffey

Kirishima and Nagara retire

13 November, afternoon: Hiei torpedoed
by US aircraft, scuttled by crew

US destroyers

Savo Island

Nagara

Hiei

Akatsuki

Kirishima

ABE'S FORCE

10 miles

10 km

Ironbottom Sound

Tassafaronga
Point

Bunina
Point

Doma
Cove

Aruligo
Point

Cape
Esperance

Visale

Tenaru

G U A D A L C A N A L

N

Guadalcanal
14–15 November 1942

The next night, the Japanese sent a battleship and four cruisers to shell Henderson Field. This time, the US Navy was waiting in strength, with the new battleships *Washington* and *South Dakota*. *South Dakota* suffered a systems failure and took more than 40 hits, but *Washington* took *Kirishima* by surprise and sank the Japanese battleship in under seven minutes.

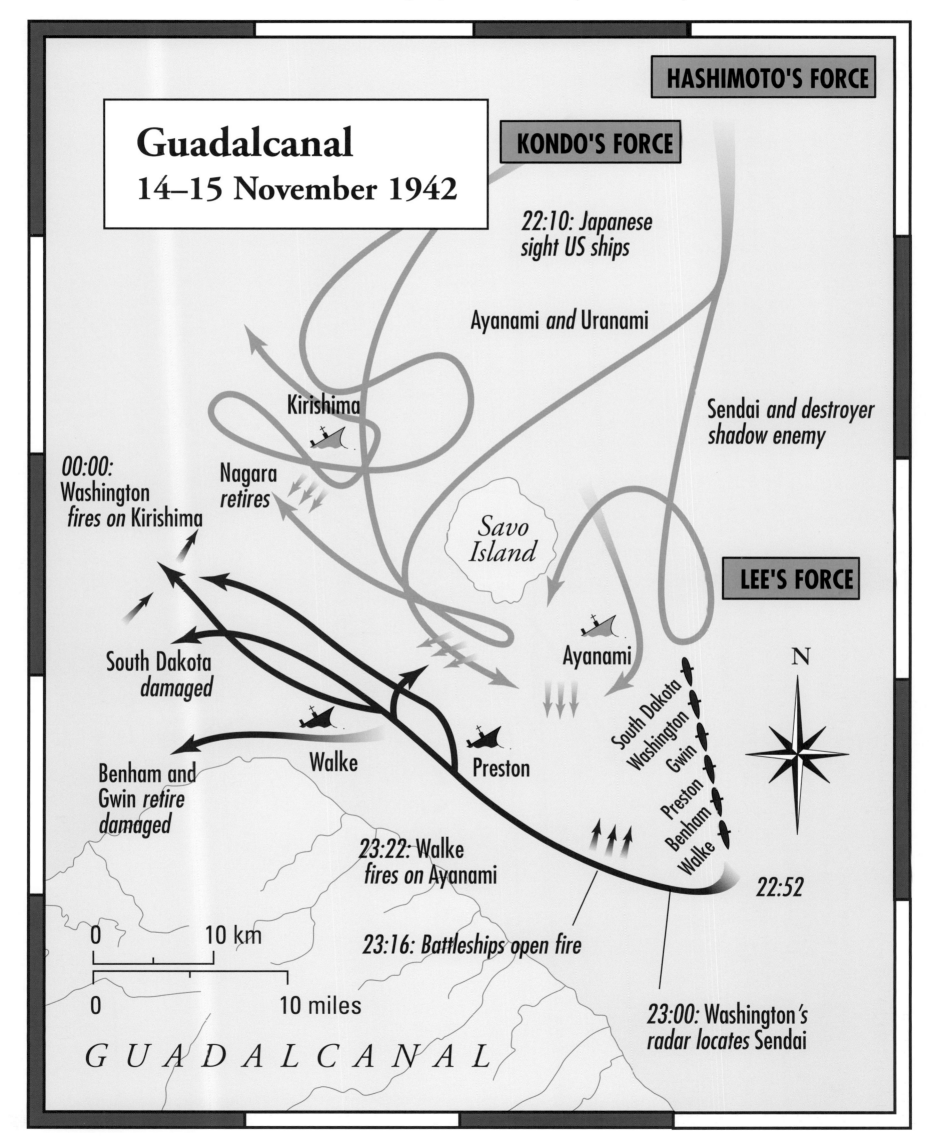

Guadalcanal
14–15 November 1942

HASHIMOTO'S FORCE

KONDO'S FORCE

22:10: Japanese sight US ships

Ayanami *and* Uranami

Sendai *and destroyer shadow enemy*

Kirishima

00:00: Washington *fires on Kirishima*

Nagara *retires*

Savo Island

LEE'S FORCE

South Dakota *damaged*

Ayanami

South Dakota
Washington
Gwin
Preston
Benham
Walke

Benham and Gwin *retire damaged*

Walke

Preston

N

23:22: Walke fires on Ayanami

22:52

23:16: Battleships open fire

0   10 km

0   10 miles

23:00: Washington's radar locates Sendai

G U A D A L C A N A L

New Guinea
August 1942–September 1943

New Guinea's geographical location made the huge island of strategic importance both to the Allies and the Japanese. Japan could use it as a base to attack Australia and to interdict American communications in the Southwest Pacific. The Allies could use it as a platform to attack Japanese conquests in the Dutch East Indies. Early in 1942 Japan decided to occupy the island, landing on the north coast. However, attempts to take Port Moresby by sea were thwarted at the Battle of the Coral Sea.

JAPAN DECIDED TO ADOPT A LAND STRATEGY, and decided to attack across the Owen Stanley mountains along the Kokoda Trail. The heavily forested mountains rising over 3960m (13,000ft) in places provided some of the toughest terrain in the world, and though they pushed to within 56km (35 miles) of Port Stanley, they were stopped by the Australians. At the end of a long and fragile supply line, the Japanese troops suffered grievously from disease and starvation, and they were forced to withdraw back to their bases on the north coast. The Australians retook Kokoda on 2 November, and the Japanese made a last stand at Buna on 21 January 1943. Australian and American reinforcements were now pouring over the trail, and more Allied troops were landed in amphibious operations.

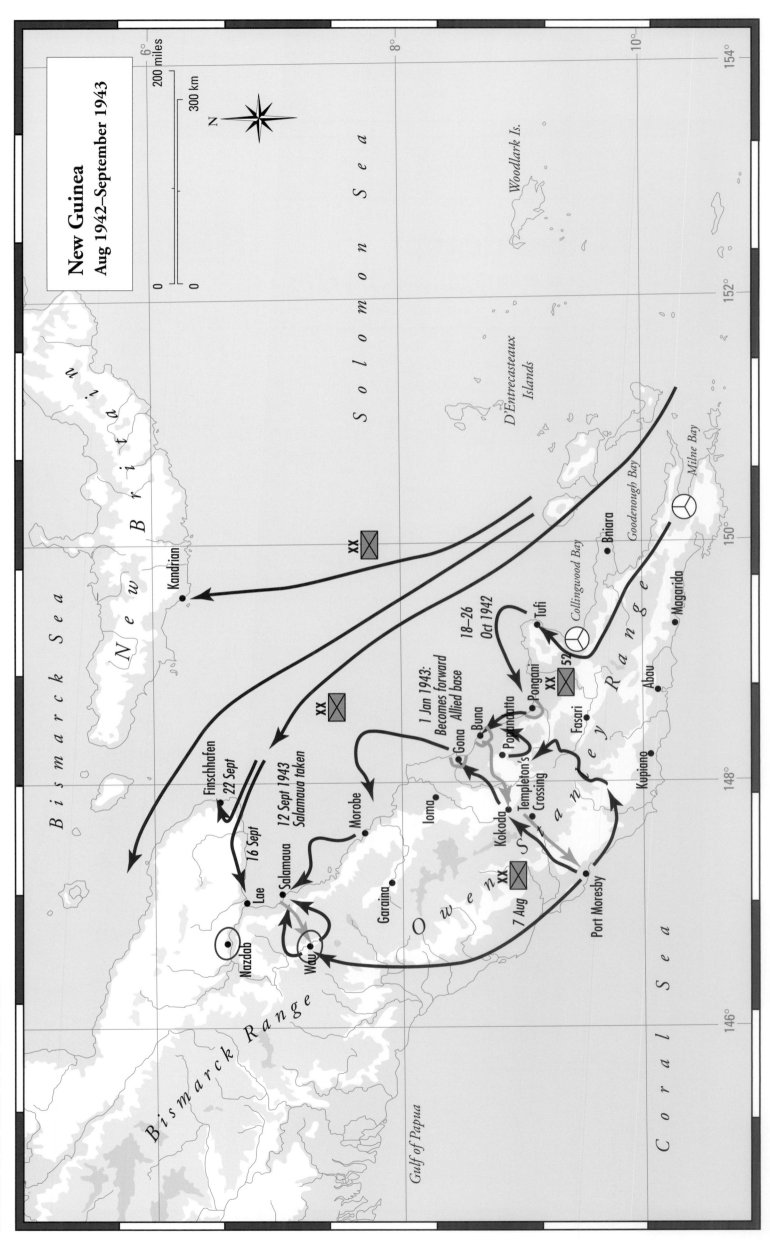

New Guinea
Aug 1942–September 1943

Operation Cartwheel
March 1942–November 1943

After victories in the Solomons and New Guinea, the Americans planned a two-pronged assault on Japan. One, led by Admiral Nimitz, would push through the Central Pacific, while the other, under General MacArthur, would maintain the pressure in the Solomons and New Guinea. The two advances would meet in the Philippines and Formosa.

MACARTHUR WAS READY TO LAUNCH Operation Cartwheel by May 1943. This was intended to consolidate the advances of 1942 by isolating the major Japanese base at Rabaul on New Britain. Competition for resources between MacArthur and Nimitz meant that the original scope of the operation was reduced, but Cartwheel nevertheless was the proving ground for the later 'Island Hopping' campaigns.

A major Japanese effort to reinforce their troops on New Guinea was dealt a shattering blow at the Battle of the Bismarck Sea. The troop convoy was wiped out by land-based bombers and attack aircraft, the USAAF's B-25 Mitchells being especially effective in low-level attacks using the new skip-bombing technique. Only 100 soldiers out of the entire division

carried in the convoy ever reached New Guinea. The Japanese responded by launching an air offensive of their own, but despite its large scale the I-Go offensive achieved little in the face of improved Allied aircraft and tactics.

Allied advance

By using a mix of amphibious assaults, conventional ground advances and even airborne assaults, Allied forces advanced through the Solomons and along the New Guinea coast. By November of 1943, the primary aim of neutralizing the threat posed by the powerful Japanese base at Rabaul had been achieved. The Imperial high command, knowing that it could not win a war of attrition with the Americans, withdrew its forces to Truk.

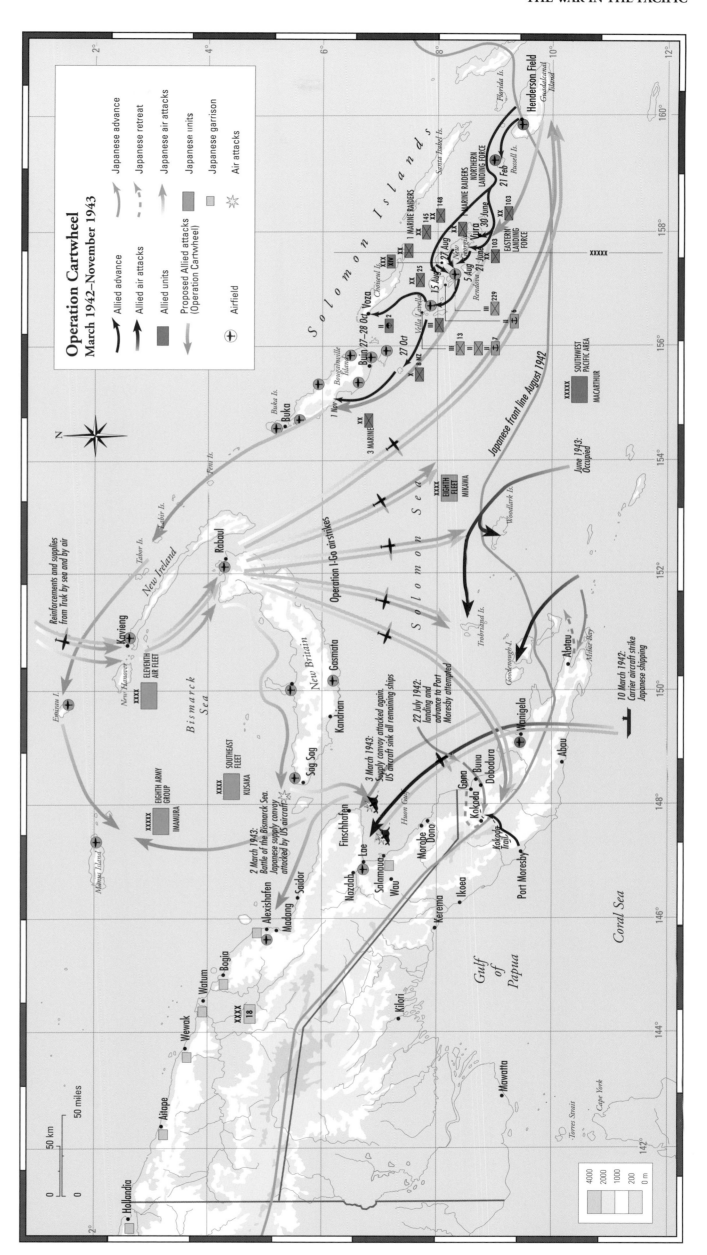

The Aleutians
June 1942–May 1943

Japan's attack on the Aleutian Islands had been part of the massively complex Midway operation in June 1942. Two light carriers launched an air attack on Dutch Harbor, and then provided support for the occupation of Attu and Kiska. The landings went ahead as planned – the only aspect of the Midway operation which did – and the Japanese garrison prepared to defend these far-flung outposts from any American counter-attack (though the appalling weather presented more of a threat than enemy action).

EVEN AT THE HEIGHT OF SUMMER, the weather in the Aleutians hampered military operations, and it was almost a week before an American reconnaissance flight discovered the Japanese presence on the formerly uninhabited islands. There was some initial concern among the American commanders that the landings might be a prelude to a larger operation aimed at Alaska. Some reinforcements were sent to counter such an operation, but forces necessary to retake the islands were not available in 1942. As a result, the Americans simply bombed and blockaded the Japanese positions on the islands.

One unintended consequence of the Aleutian operation came after the raid on Dutch Harbor, when a Mitsubishi A6M 'Zero' fighter was forced to crash land on Akutan Island. It was recovered almost intact by the Americans, who returned it to flying condition, enabling the USAAF and

the US Navy to develop tactics to deal with its agility, and to develop improved new aircraft which would outperform the Japanese fighter.

Plans to retake the islands began to take shape early in 1943. Japanese positions were regularly bombarded from January. In March, a Japanese cruiser force in the Kuriles was ordered to escort a reinforcement convoy, and on March 26 it encountered an American cruiser squadron off the Komandorski Islands. After a four-hour gun battle, the Japanese withdrew.

Attu was assaulted by a US amphibious force on 11 May 1943, and after two weeks' hard fighting, often in atrocious weather, it was back in American hands. Ten weeks later, an armada of over 100 ships assembled at Kiska, landing 34,000 American and Canadian troops on 15 August. There they found that the Japanese, recognizing the futility of their position, had withdrawn at the end of July.

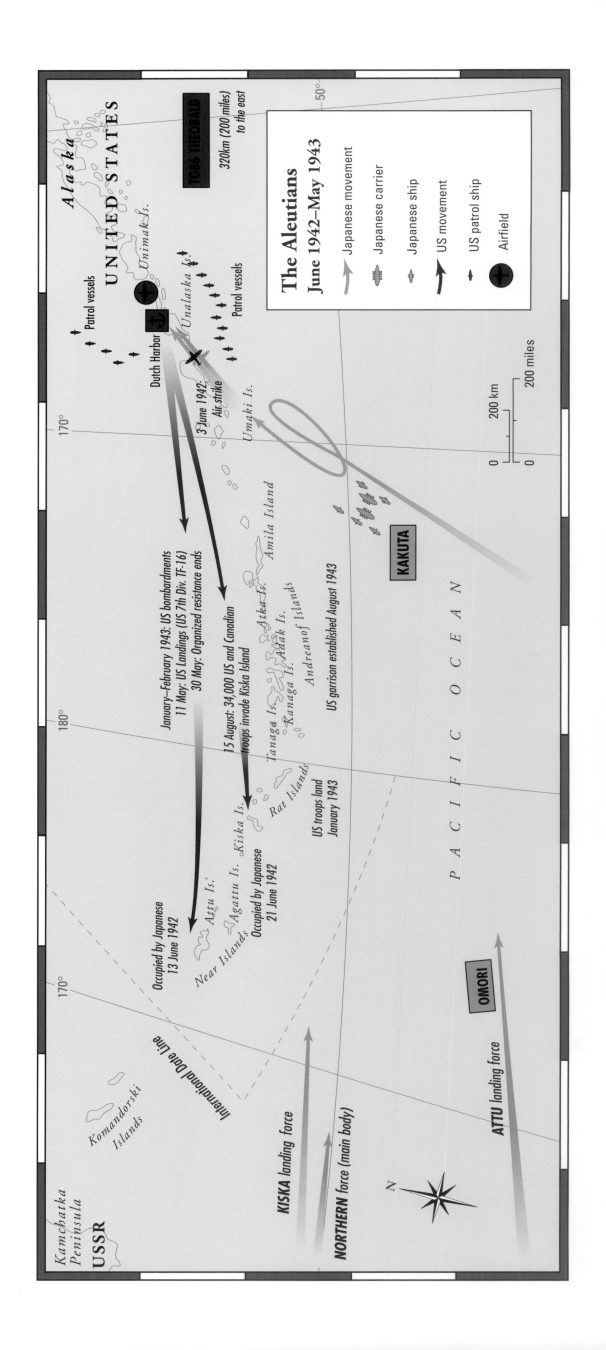

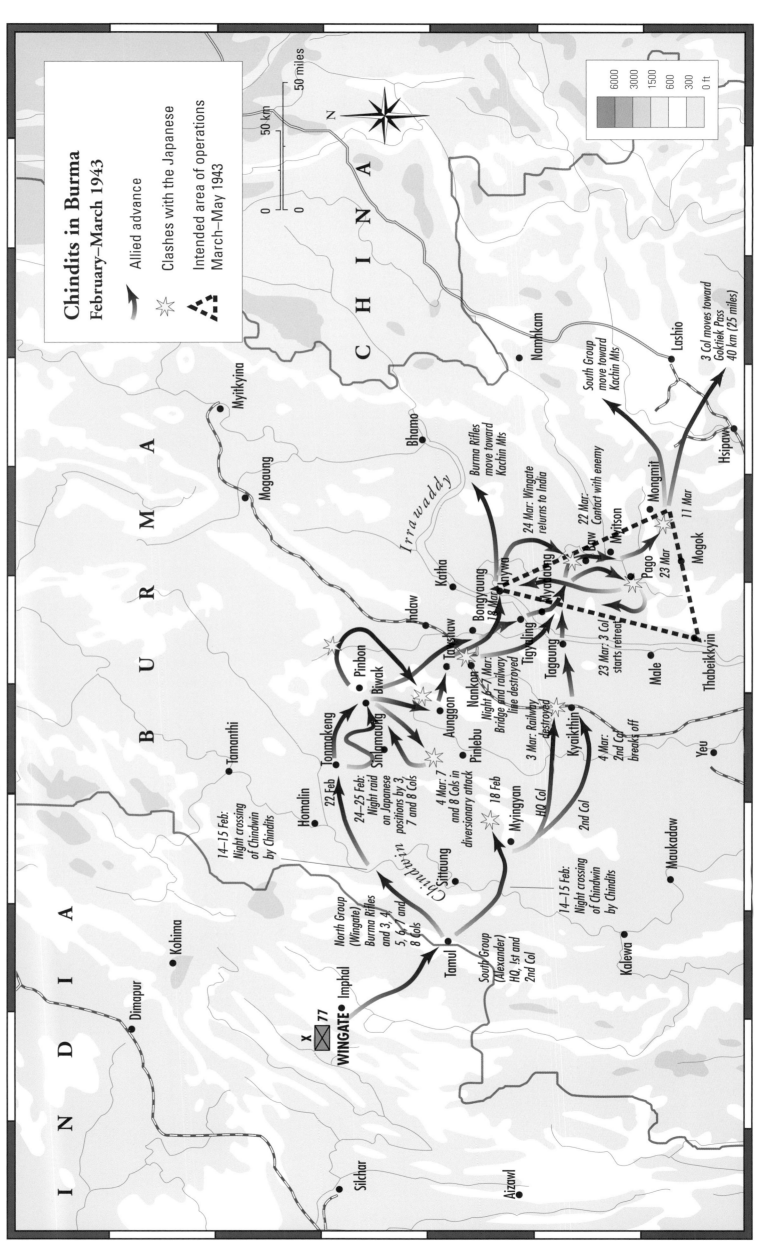

Chindits in Burma
February–March 1943

Created by Brigadier Orde Wingate, an unconventional soldier with a background in counter-insurgency operations in Palestine, the Chindits were precursors of modern-day special forces units. Officially the 77th Indian Brigade, the Chindits were a long-range penetration group intended to operate deep behind Japanese lines, being supported from the air. Formed in 1942, the Chindits were ready for operations early in 1943, and on 8 February they crossed the Chindwin River into Burma, catching the Japanese by surprise.

THE INITIAL CHINDIT ATTACKS on Japanese supply lines were very successful, forcing the Japanese to deploy large numbers of troops to protect their logistics routes. Spurred on by this success, Wingate ordered his men across the Irrawaddy River. This was a mistake: the Chindits were now operating in more open country, making them more vulnerable to Japanese attacks. They had also moved beyond the range of RAF resupply. Wingate decided to retreat back across the Irrawaddy, only to find a Japanese blocking force in his way. The Chindits scattered, making their way back to India in small groups. Although a failure – over 30 per cent of the men were lost – the Chindit campaign was a morale booster as it proved that British and Empire soldiers could take on the Japanese in the jungle.

Chindits in Burma
February–March 1943

→ Allied advance

✳ Clashes with the Japanese

◣ Intended area of operations March–May 1943

Tarawa Atoll
20–23 November 1943

Operation Galvanic, the attacks on the Tarawa and Makin Atolls in the Gilbert Islands, marked the opening of the American drive through the Central Pacific. The attack on Tarawa saw 18,000 men of the 2nd Marine Division launched against 4000 defenders of Betio, the largest island in the atoll. It took the Marines 75 hours and 45 minutes of the bitterest fighting in Marine Corps history to secure Betio, at a cost of 1300 dead. The 4000 Imperial Japanese Marines under Admiral Shibasaki were under orders to defend to the last man and most did: only 17 survivors surrendered or were found wounded, most of whom were Korean labourers.

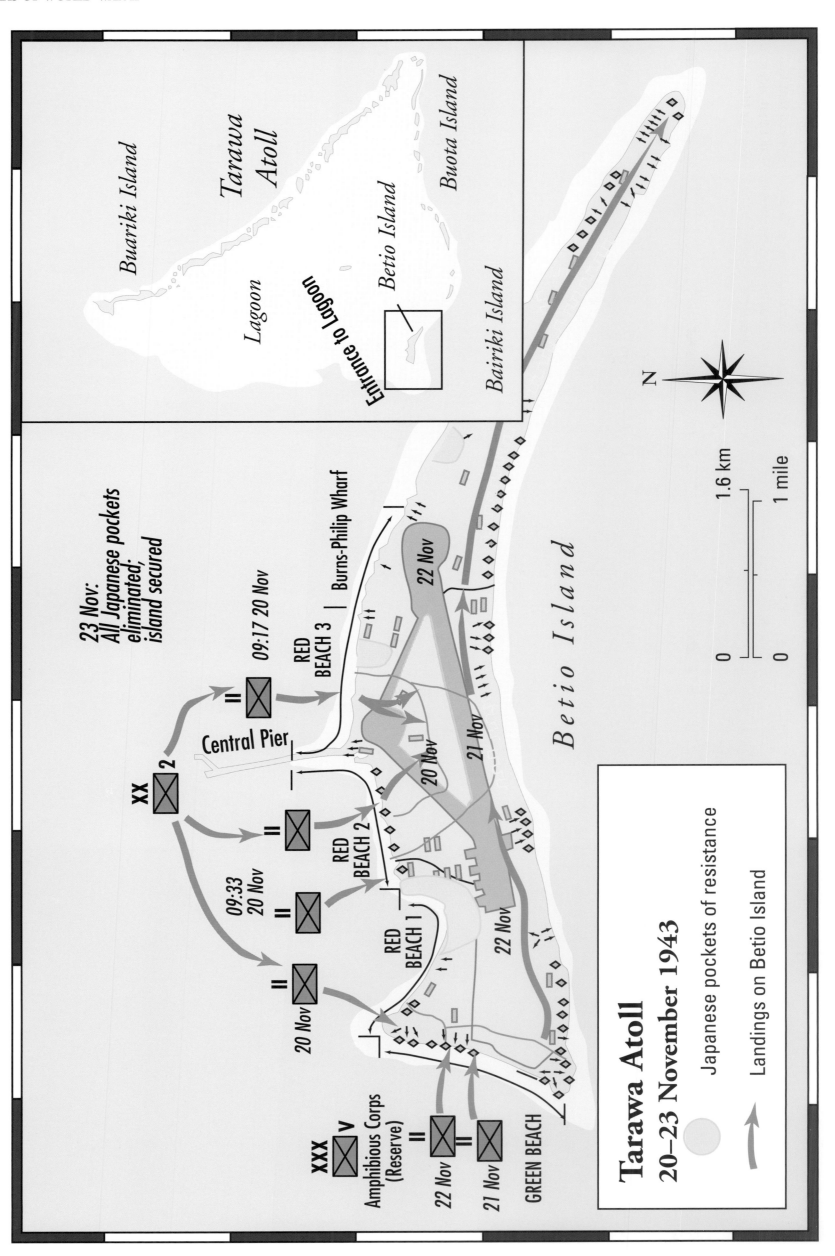

Makin Atoll
20–23 November 1943

The simultaneous attack on Makin Atoll, about 160km (100 miles) to the north of Tarawa, was easier since the Japanese garrison was smaller. Nevertheless, it took three days of bitter fighting by 6700 troops of the US Army's 27th Division to overcome 800 Japanese defenders. US losses were 64 killed and 150 wounded. Only one Japanese soldier survived. Operation Galvanic showed that the drive through the Central Pacific was possible – but that unless the lessons of the Gilberts were learned, the cost would be high.

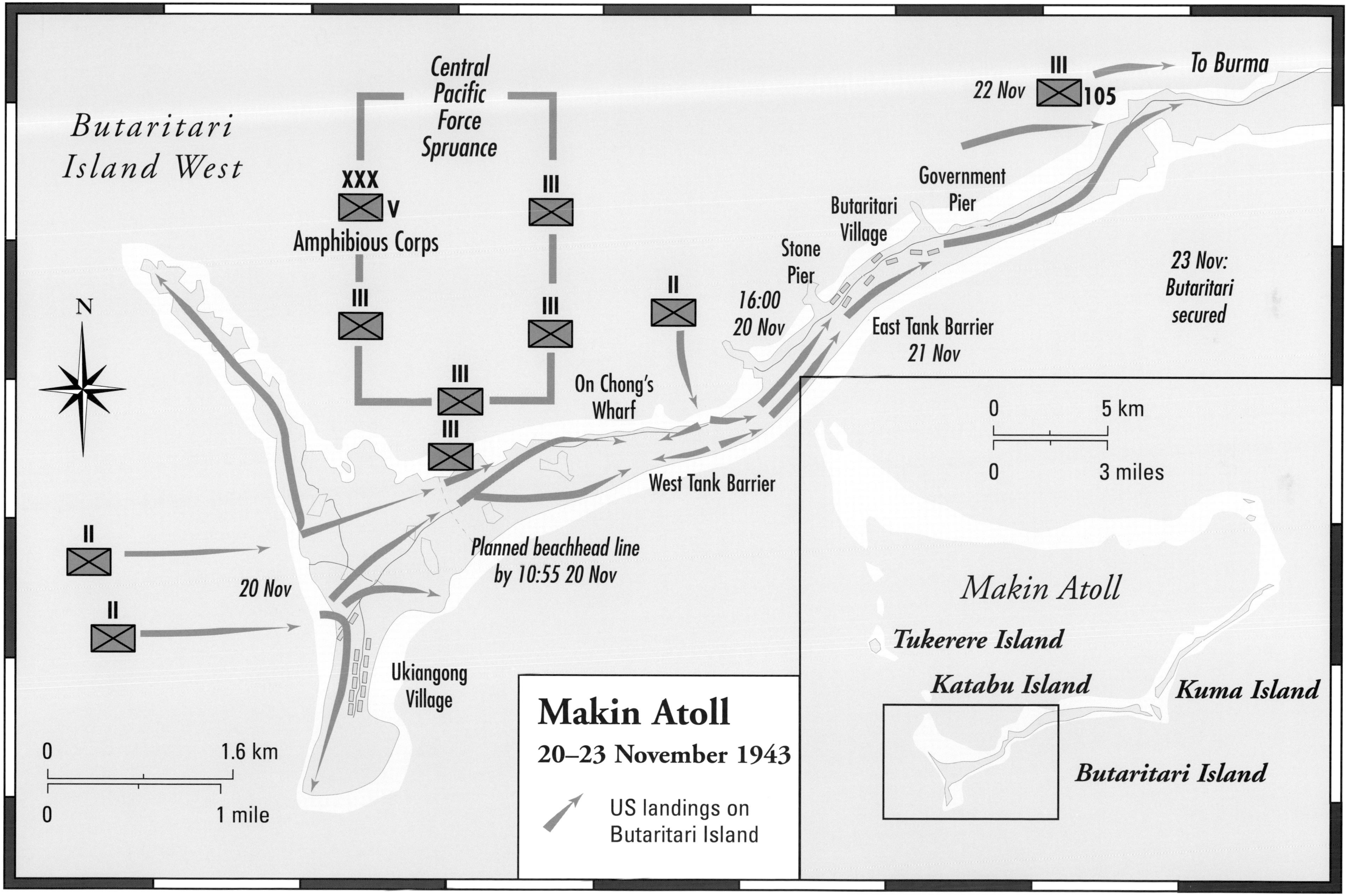

Butaritari
Island West
Central
Pacific
Force
Spruance
XXX
V
Amphibious Corps
III
III
III
III
III
II
II
II
III
105
22 Nov
To Burma
N
20 Nov
Planned beachhead line
by 10:55 20 Nov
West Tank Barrier
On Chong's
Wharf
16:00
20 Nov
Stone
Pier
Butaritari
Village
Government
Pier
East Tank Barrier
21 Nov
23 Nov:
Butaritari
secured
Ukiangong
Village
0
1.6 km
0
1 mile
Makin Atoll
20–23 November 1943
US landings on
Butaritari Island
0
5 km
0
3 miles
Makin Atoll
Tukerere Island
Katabu Island
Kuma Island
Butaritari Island

Second Arakan Campaign
December 1943–April 1944

The Second Arakan Campaign was part of a general Allied offensive intended to clear the Japanese out of northern Burma. Attacking out of India into the Arakan region of northwest Burma, the British/Indian XV Corps achieved some success before the Japanese invasion of eastern India meant that further advances had to be delayed.

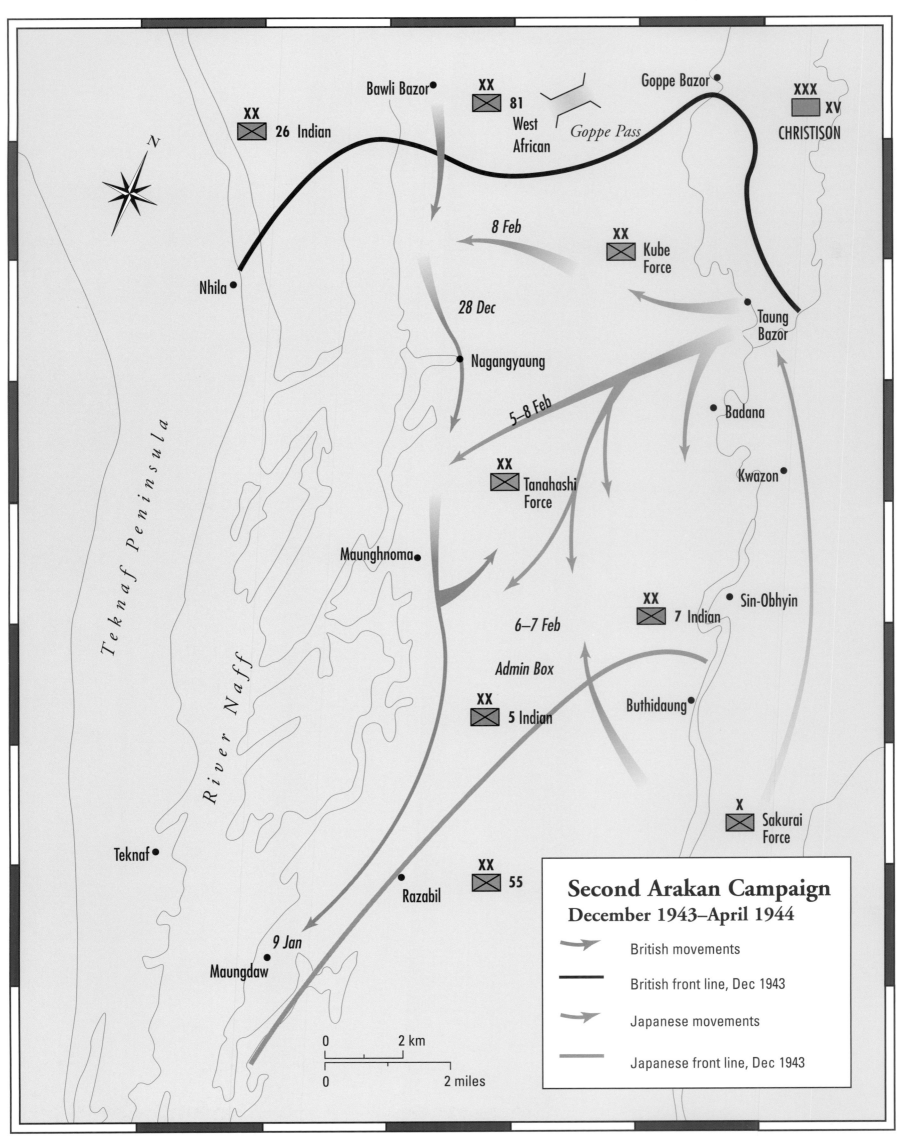

Second Arakan Campaign
December 1943–April 1944

British movements

British front line, Dec 1943

Japanese movements

Japanese front line, Dec 1943

Japanese Invasion of India
March–June 1944

On the night of 7/8 March 1944, 100,000 men of the Japanese Fifteenth Army under Lieutenant-General Renya Mutaguchi crossed the River Chindwin. Their aim was to take Imphal and Kohima before driving further into India in the direction of Dimapur. The Japanese 33rd Division attacked Imphal, the 15th was tasked with cutting the Imphal to Kohima road, while the 31st Division advanced on Kohima.

ALL THREE PRONGS OF THE JAPANESE ADVANCE came close to success, and by late March both Imphal and Kohima were under siege. Lieutenant-General William Slim, commander of the Fourteenth Army, airlifted the 5th Indian Division from the Arakan into Kohima. He ordered the British 2nd Infantry Division to relieve Kohima from the north. As the Japanese around Imphal were successfully beaten off, a major battle developed at Imphal, with the two sides at one stage fighting across the width of a tennis court. However, by late May the Japanese were running desperately short of supplies, and after the British and Indian troops seized key positions, they were ordered to withdraw. By early June, this had developed into a general Japanese retreat. By November, Slim's army had driven the Japanese back beyond the Chindwin.

Japanese Invasion of India
March–June 1944

→ Japanese advance
→ Allied airlift
⊕ Allied parachute drop
◯ Allied pockets

Pacific Situation to October 1944

The situation in the Pacific changed decisively after Midway and Guadalcanal. Japanese forces had been stopped at the height of their expansion, and the incredible industrial power of the United States was just getting into its stride.

THE DECISION WAS MADE to bypass any large Japanese strongholds on islands of little strategic value, leaving them to be dealt with later in detail. The aim of the American planners was to advance as fast as possible on the Japanese home islands themselves.

Although the Allies had moved onto the offensive, the Japanese were still far from beaten. Although the Allies were on the advance in the Pacific and in Burma, the Japanese Empire remained large, and areas still under occupation included the Dutch East Indies, Malaya, Burma, and large parts of eastern and northern China.

The Allied approach to Japan only increased Japanese determination to resist. Fighting became more and more ferocious. Allied planners began to worry just how much it was going to cost in terms of lives when the inevitable final attack on Japan came about.

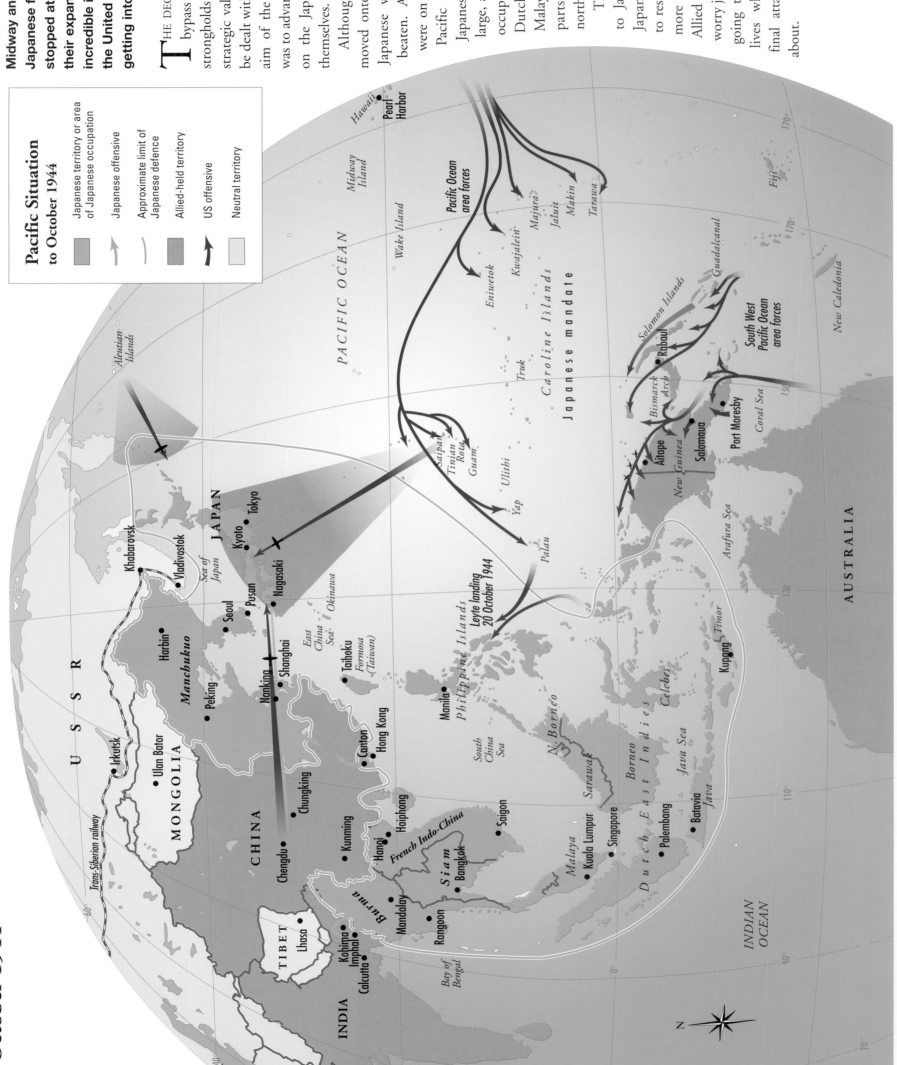

Pacific Situation
to October 1944

- Japanese territory or area of Japanese occupation
- Japanese offensive
- Approximate limit of Japanese defence
- Allied-held territory
- US offensive
- Neutral territory

Carrier Raids in the Central Pacific to October 1944

As American and other Allied forces advanced through the Central and Southwest Pacific regions, they were preceded by fast carrier task forces equipped with the new fleet carriers and new aircraft coming off American production lines in ever increasing numbers.

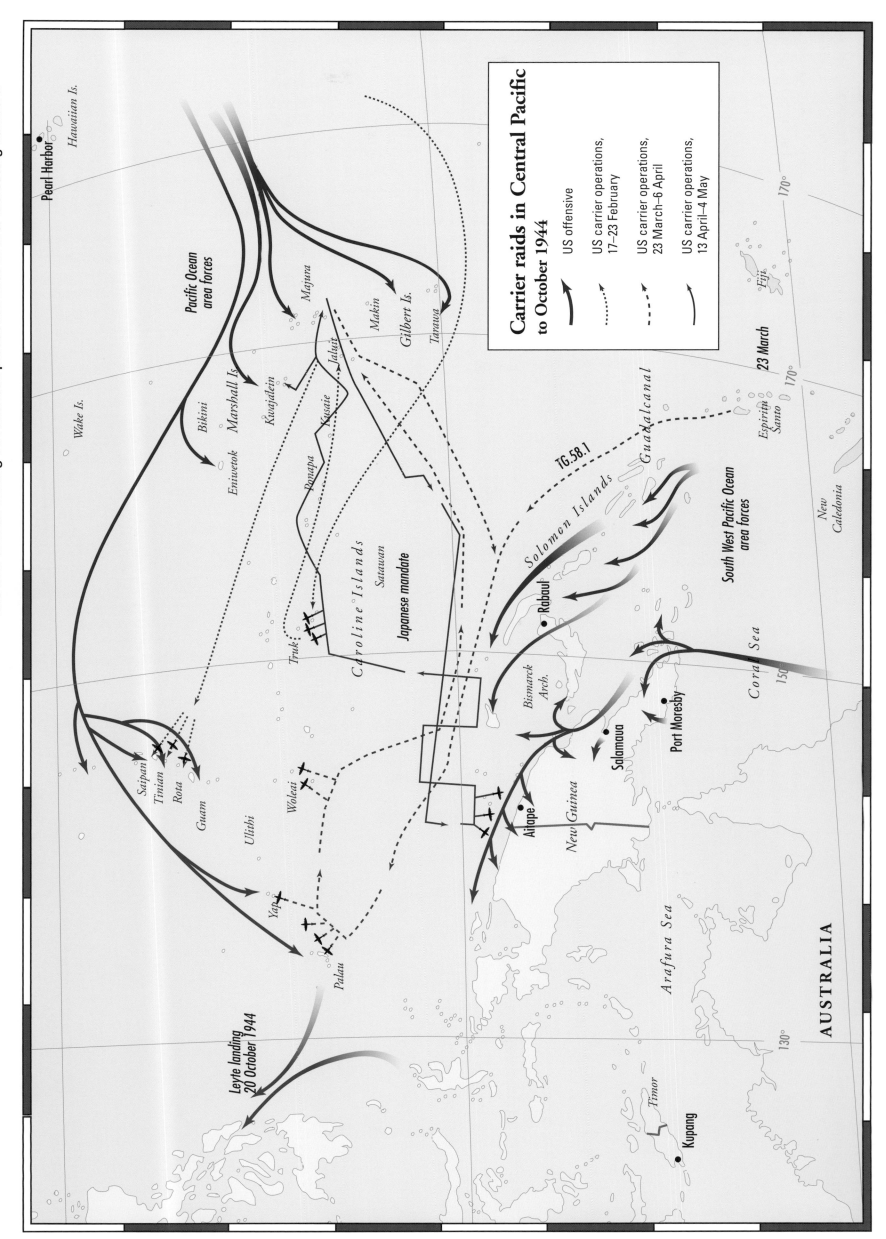

Pearl Harbor

Hawaiian Is.

Pacific Ocean area forces

Majuna

Makin
Gilbert Is.
Tarawa

Wake Is.

Bikini
Marshall Is.
Kwajalein
Kusaie
Jaluit

Eniwetok

Ponapa

Fiji

Caroline Islands

Satawan

Japanese mandate

Truk

TG.58.1

Guadalcanal

Solomon Islands

Espiritu
Santo

New Caledonia

23 March

Saipan
Tinian
Rota
Guam

Ulithi

Woleai

Yap

Palau

Rabaul

Bismarck Arch.

South West Pacific Ocean area forces

Salamaua

Port Moresby

Coral Sea

Aitape

New Guinea

Arafura Sea

Timor

Kupang

AUSTRALIA

Leyte landing 20 October 1944

Carrier raids in Central Pacific to October 1944

→ US offensive

⋯▸ US carrier operations, 17–23 February

--▸ US carrier operations, 23 March–6 April

⌒ US carrier operations, 13 April–4 May

Battle of the Philippine Sea I
19 June 1944

The invasion of the Mariana Islands in June 1944 compelled the Japanese to react in strength, since possession of Saipan, Tinian and Guam would allow the USAAF to base heavy bombers – including the massive new Boeing B-29 Superfortress – within striking distance of the home islands themselves.

THE THREAT WAS SO GREAT that the Japanese Navy decided to commit what was left of its carrier force into the fight to defeat the Americans. The first attack was made by shore-based aircraft – but most had already been destroyed by carrier raids, and the few which managed to attack were knocked out of the sky. On 19 June, 69 Japanese aircraft were launched in the first wave from three fleet carriers and six light carriers. Over 40 were shot down by American fighters and by the massed AA guns of US Navy battleships. Minutes after 110 further aircraft were launched, the large new carrier *Taiho* was torpedoed. The air strike was again shot to pieces. The last two strikes of the day had little effect, by which time another US submarine had torpedoed the fleet carrier *Shokaku.*

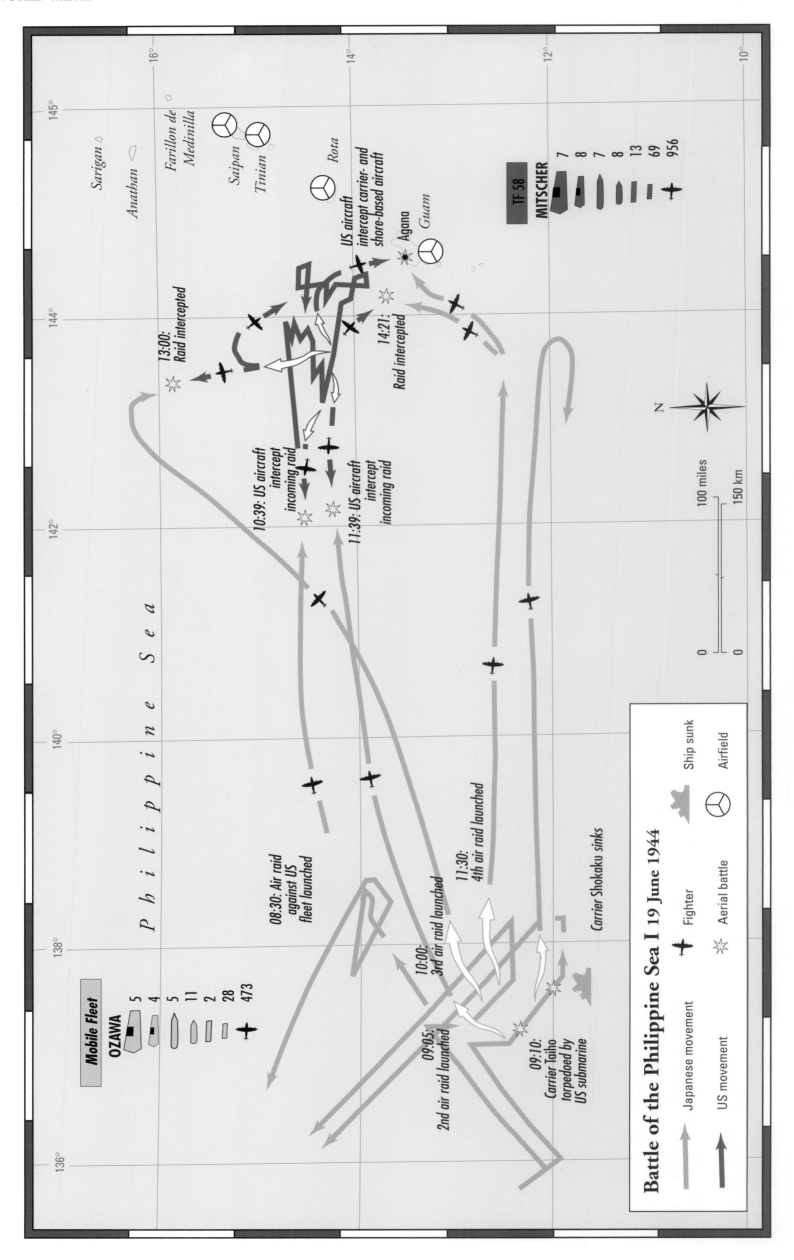

Battle of the Philippine Sea 19 June 1944

Japanese movement	US movement
Fighter	Aerial battle
Ship sunk	Airfield

Mobile Fleet
OZAWA
5
4
5
11
2
28
473

TF 58
MITSCHER
7
8
7
8
13
69
956

09:05: 2nd air raid launched

09:10: Carrier *Taiho* torpedoed by US submarine

10:00: 3rd air raid launched

11:30: 4th air raid launched

08:30: Air raid against US fleet launched

10:39: US aircraft intercept incoming raid

11:39: US aircraft intercept incoming raid

13:00: Raid intercepted

14:21: Raid intercepted

US aircraft intercept carrier- and shore-based aircraft

Carrier *Shokaku* sinks

Philippine Sea

Sarigan
Anathan
Farillon de Medinilla
Saipan
Tinian
Rota
Guam
Agana

100 miles
150 km

Battle of the Philippine Sea II
20–21 June 1944

A T 15:40 ON 20 JUNE Ozawa's carriers were located by a Douglas SBD from the USS *Enterprise*. The Japanese were 275 miles (445 km) from the US Navy's Task Force 58, right at the edge of attack range, but Admiral Marc Mitscher did not hesitate. He had 210 aircraft aloft within 10 minutes, and was following at full speed to reduce the length of their return flight. Although 20 aircraft were lost to Japanese anti-aircraft fire, the strike force sank a light carrier and two fleet oilers and damaged the carriers *Chiyoda* and *Zuikaku*, the last Japanese survivor of Pearl Harbor. With dry tanks and overtaken by darkness, 80 American aircraft had to ditch short of their carriers, though many of the crews were rescued by flying boats the next day.

Incredibly, Vice-Admiral Jisaburo Ozawa seemed unaware of his losses and believed the inflated reports of success relayed to him by his pilots and by the commanders on the Marianas. With barely 100 aircraft remaining, he withdrew westwards to refuel ready to resume action the next day. In fact, the Imperial Navy's carrier arm had been annihilated, losing a total of 346 aircraft and two fleet carriers against US Navy losses of 30 aircraft.

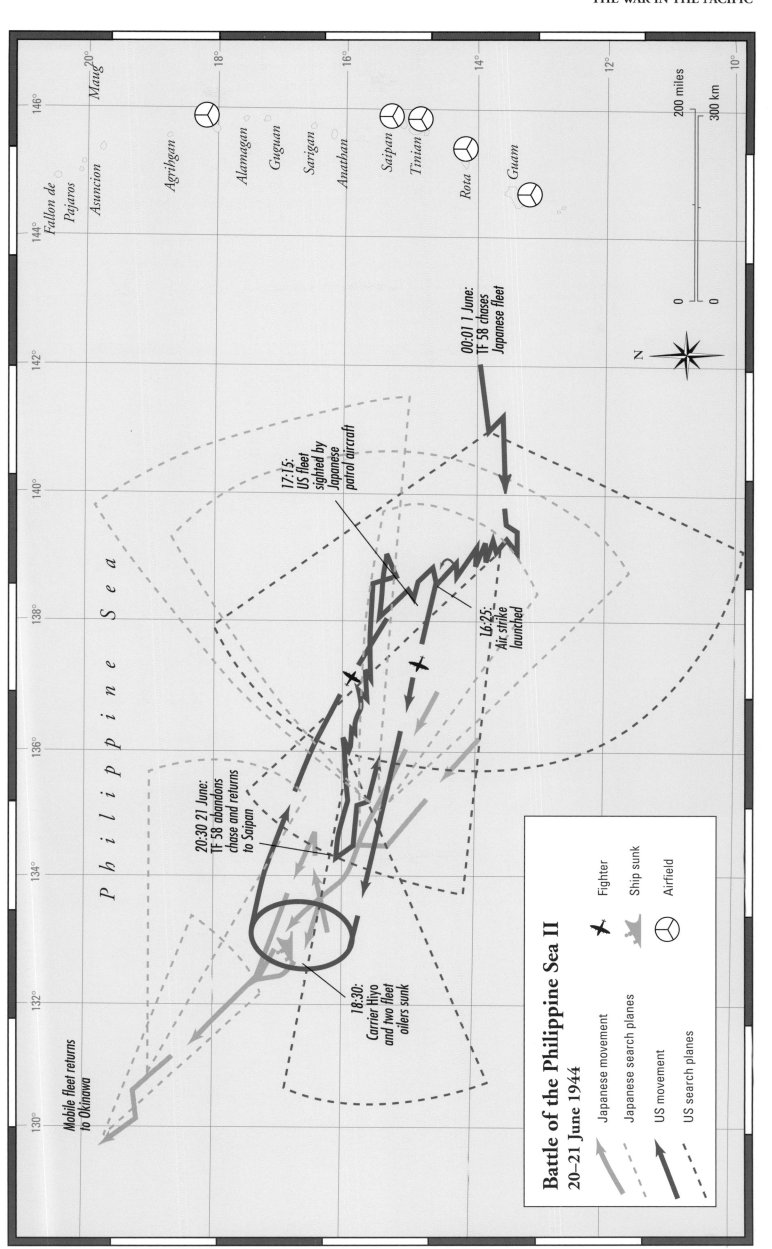

Mobile fleet returns to Okinawa

20:30 21 June: TF 58 abandons chase and returns to Saipan

18:30: Carrier Hiyo and two fleet oilers sunk

17:15: US fleet sighted by Japanese patrol aircraft

16:25: Air strike launched

00:01 1 June: TF 58 chases Japanese fleet

Philippine Sea

Maug
Fallon de
Pajaros
Asuncion
Agrihgan
Alamagan
Guguan
Sarigan
Anathan
Saipan
Tinian
Rota
Guam

N

200 miles

300 km

Battle of the Philippine Sea II
20–21 June 1944

Japanese movement
Japanese search planes
US movement
US search planes

Fighter
Ship sunk
Airfield

The Saipan Landings
15 June–9 July 1944

The capture of the Mariana Islands offered numerous advantages to the United States in the summer of 1944. They could dominate Japanese sea and air routes in the western Pacific, they could be used to attack the major Japanese naval base at Truk, they would provide a support base for operations against the Philippines, and they would allow bombers to be based within range of the Japanese home islands.

OPERATION FORAGER HAD AS ITS AIM the capture of the southern Marianas, including the islands of Saipan, Tinian and Guam. On 11 June, the US Navy's Task Force 58 began a heavy bombardment of the Marianas, beginning with air attacks which destroyed over 150 Japanese aircraft on the ground. On 13 June, US Navy battleships, cruisers and destroyers began shelling shore positions, reducing many Japanese fortifications to wreckage – though many of the more heavily built positions remained operational. The first Marines went ashore at Saipan early on the morning of 15 June 1944 and by nightfall they had managed to establish two beachheads in the face of heavy Japanese resistance. After 10 days, US troops had occupied most of the island, but resistance continued for more than three weeks.

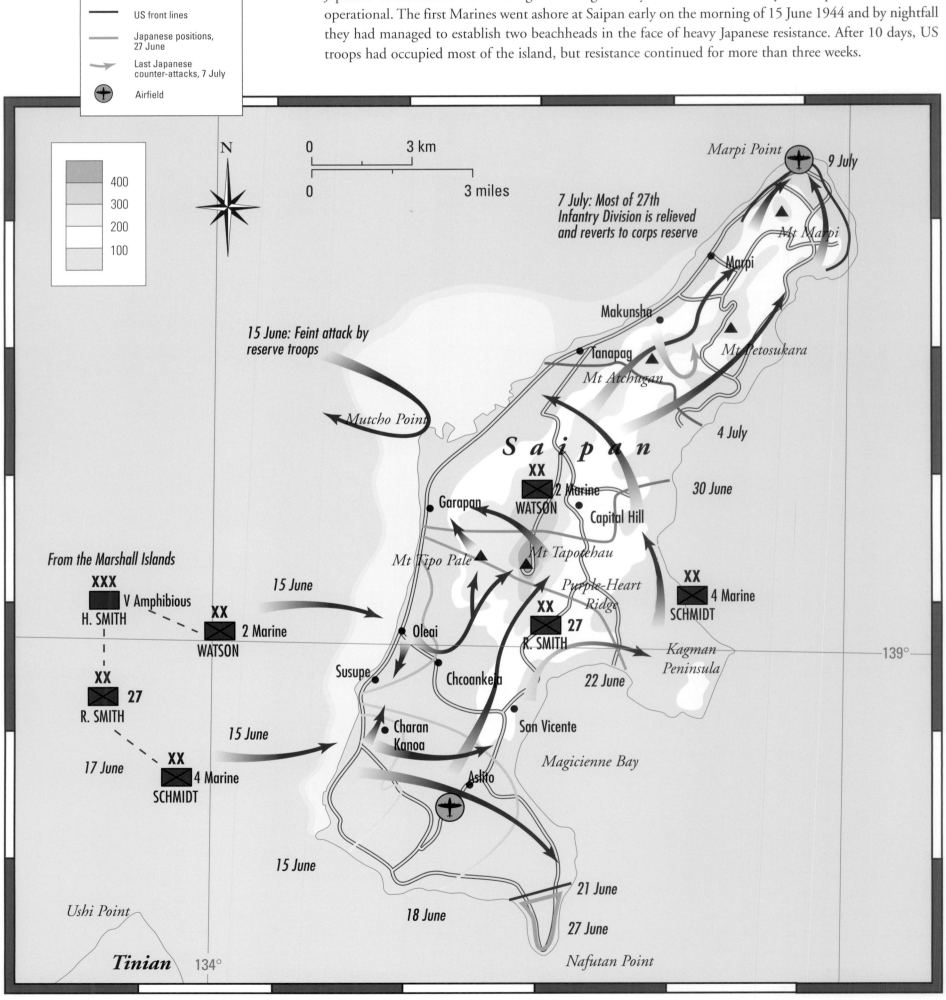

The Saipan Landings
15 June–9 July 1944

- → US movement
- — US front lines
- — Japanese positions, 27 June
- → Last Japanese counter-attacks, 7 July
- ⊕ Airfield

7 July: Most of 27th Infantry Division is relieved and reverts to corps reserve

Marpi Point — 9 July

Mt Marpi

Marpi

Makunsha

Mt Petosukara

Tanapag

Mt Atchugan

4 July

15 June: Feint attack by reserve troops

Mutcho Point

S a i p a n

30 June

XX 2 Marine
WATSON

Garapan

Capital Hill

Mt Tipo Pale

Mt Tapotchau

Purple-Heart Ridge

XX 4 Marine
SCHMIDT

From the Marshall Islands

XXX V Amphibious
H. SMITH

15 June

XX 2 Marine
WATSON

XX 27
R. SMITH

XX 27
R. SMITH

Oleai

Kagman Peninsula

139°

Susupe

Chcoankeja

22 June

17 June

XX 4 Marine
SCHMIDT

15 June

Charan Kanoa

San Vicente

Magicienne Bay

Aslito

15 June

21 June

18 June

27 June

Nafutan Point

Ushi Point

Tinian 134°

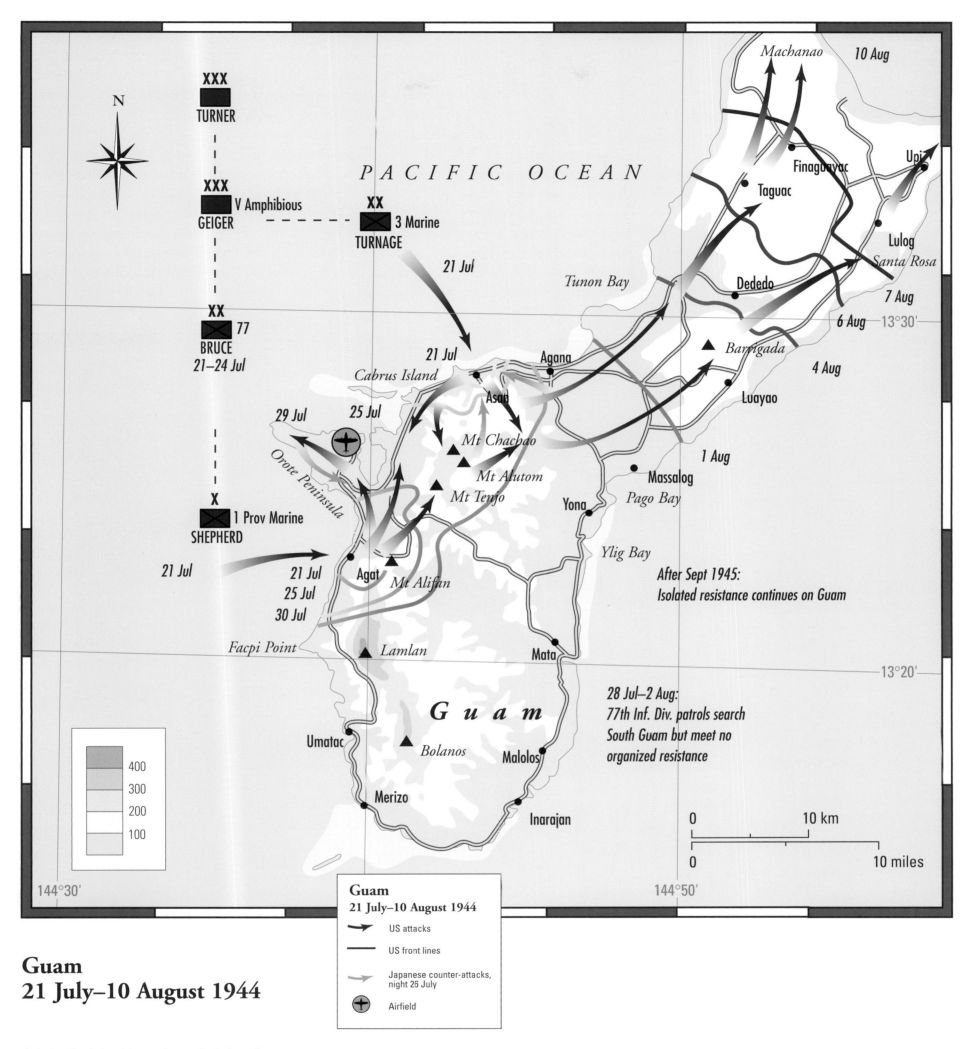

N

XXX
TURNER

PACIFIC OCEAN

XXX
GEIGER ☐ V Amphibious

XX
TURNAGE ☒ 3 Marine

21 Jul

XX
BRUCE ☒ 77
21–24 Jul

21 Jul

21 Jul

Tunon Bay

10 Aug

Machanao

Finagayac

Taguac

Dededo

▲ Barrigada

Luayao

4 Aug

7 Aug

Upi

Lulog
Santa Rosa

6 Aug — 13°30'

Cabrus Island

Agana

29 Jul

25 Jul

Asan

Mt Chachao

▲

Mt Alutom

▲ *Mt Tenjo*

1 Aug

Massalog

Yona

Pago Bay

Orote Peninsula

X
SHEPHERD ☒ 1 Prov Marine

21 Jul

21 Jul
25 Jul
30 Jul

Agat
Mt Alifan ▲

Ylig Bay

After Sept 1945:
Isolated resistance continues on Guam

Facpi Point

▲ *Lamlan*

Mata

13°20'

G u a m

Umatac

▲ *Bolanos*

Malolos

28 Jul–2 Aug:
77th Inf. Div. patrols search
South Guam but meet no
organized resistance

Merizo

Inarajan

0   10 km

0   10 miles

400
300
200
100

144°30'

144°50'

Guam
21 July–10 August 1944

→ US attacks

— US front lines

→ Japanese counter-attacks,
night 26 July

⊕ Airfield

Guam
21 July–10 August 1944

Originally, it had been intended that the landings on Guam should follow close on the heels of the Saipan landings. However, the 27th Infantry Division, originally intended to be the landing force's reserve, had to be diverted to reinforce the Marines on Saipan. Then the intervention by the Japanese fleet forced the Navy to move westwards to protect the landings, destroying Japanese carrier air power in the Battle of the Philippine Sea – the Great Marianas Turkey Shoot.

Without a reserve force, and with limited air cover, any landings on Guam would prove to be extremely risky, and it was decided to delay the landings until 21 July. As at Saipan, Japanese resistance was fierce, but lacked the numbers and equipment to do anything but delay the overwhelming strength of the American attack. Japanese troops did manage to mount a major counter-attack on the night of 25/26 July, but the Americans stood firm and repelled the onslaught. By the end of the month, after 10 days of fighting, US forces were in control of the island. However, not all of the Japanese soldiers were killed or surrendered: several retreated into the hilly jungles of Guam's interior. Small parties of soldiers and individuals held out for months, even years: the last survivor, Sergeant Shoichi Yokoi, unaware that the war was long over, did not give himself up until 1972!

Tinian
24 July–1 August 1944

The island of Tinian was the final target for the US invasion force, and the Marines stormed ashore on 24 July. By nightfall, 15,000 Marines, rested after action on Saipan, had been landed, and although there was some opposition from a Japanese defensive force some 9000 strong, only 15 Americans were lost on the first day. Tinian was secured within nine days, some 394 American lives having been lost. Most of the Japanese garrison lost their lives.

T HE SUCCESSFUL INVASION OF TINIAN hinged on a fake landing staged near 'Tinian Town' (presently known as San Jose village). While the 2nd Marine Division pretended to ready an attack on the southern part of the island, even going so far as to lower boats and men into the water, the 4th Marine Division was launching a full-blown invasion on Tinian's north side. The US Marine Landing Force overcame the numerically superior Japanese force on 1 August in what is considered to be the best-executed amphibious operation of the war. Marine casualties were 328 dead and 1571 wounded. As had happened on Saipan, many Japanese not killed by US military forces opted to commit suicide by jumping off cliffs rather than be caught by the Americans. Even before the island had been secured, aviation engineers and naval construction battalions were hard at work constructing the huge air bases necessary for the B-29 strategic bombers. As part of the 13-day naval bombardment of Tinian US forces used napalm bombs against the Japanese. It was the first time napalm had been used in combat.

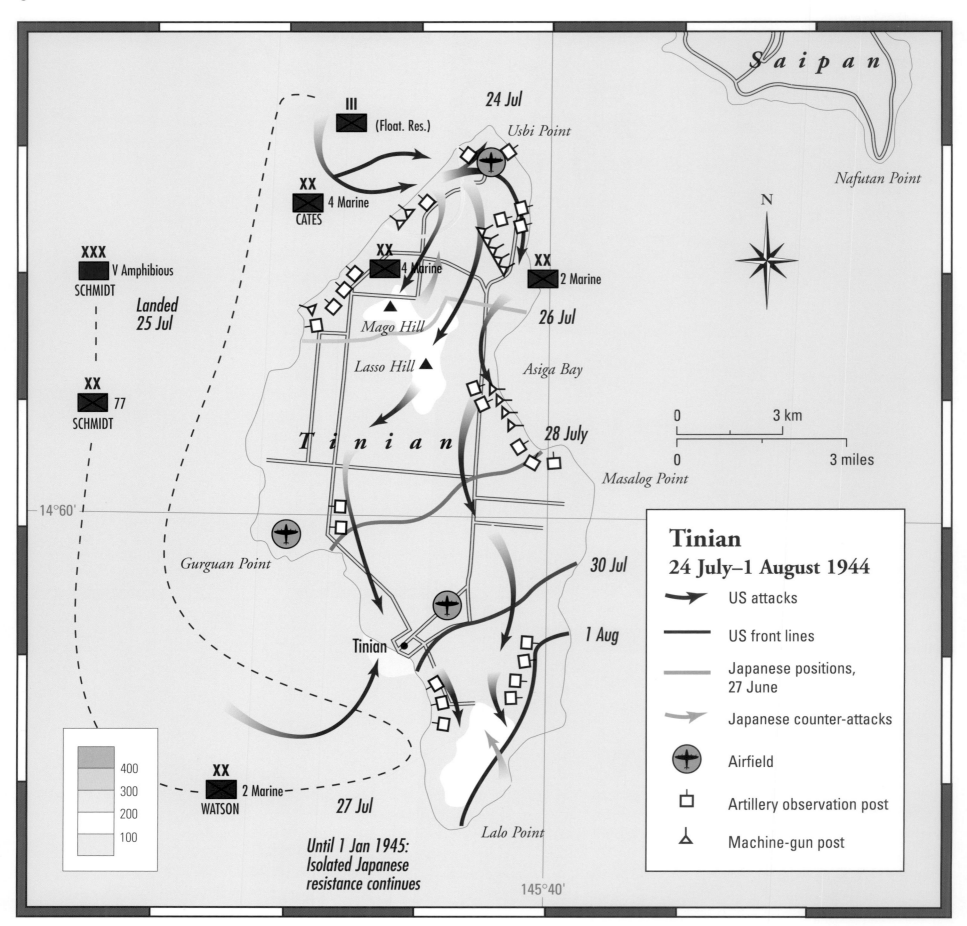

The Battle of the Philippines – Leyte Gulf 20–27 October 1944

The largest sea battle in history saw the destruction of Japan's last carriers in the action of Cape Engano, the last battleship-versus-battleship action in history in the Surigao Strait, the sinking of *Musashi*, the world's largest battleship, by US Navy aircraft in the Sibuyan Sea, the heroic defence of the American invasion force by three escort carrier groups against a powerful Japanese surface force off Samar, and the first recorded *kamikaze* attacks.

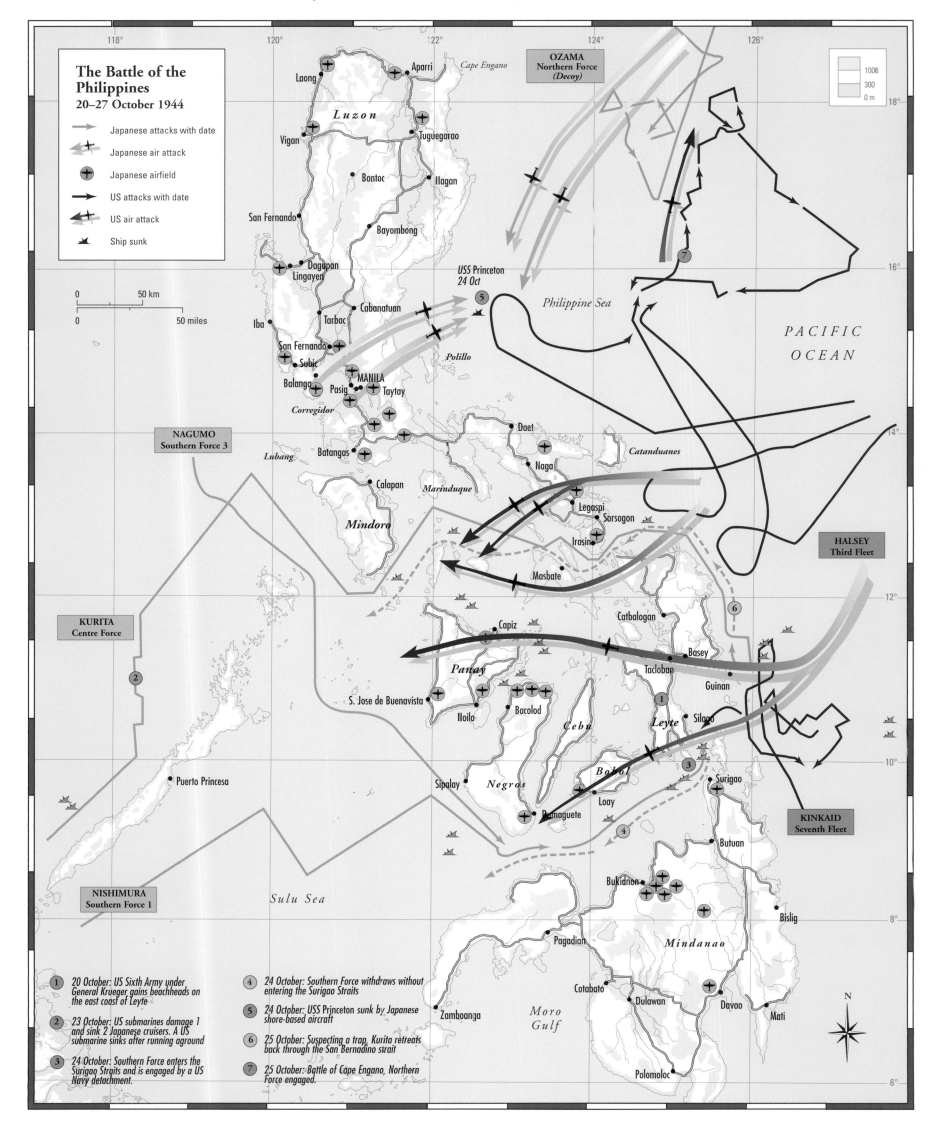

The Battle of the Philippines 20–27 October 1944

- Japanese attacks with date
- Japanese air attack
- Japanese airfield
- US attacks with date
- US air attack
- Ship sunk

1. 20 October: US Sixth Army under General Krueger gains beachheads on the east coast of Leyte

2. 23 October: US submarines damage 1 and sink 2 Japanese cruisers. A US submarine sinks after running aground

3. 24 October: Southern Force enters the Surigao Straits and is engaged by a US Navy detachment.

4. 24 October: Southern Force withdraws without entering the Surigao Straits

5. 24 October: USS Princeton sunk by Japanese shore-based aircraft

6. 25 October: Suspecting a trap, Kurita retreats back through the San Bernadino strait

7. 25 October: Battle of Cape Engano, Northern Force engaged.

Liberation of the Philippines January–August 1945

Although the US Navy saw little point in a campaign to liberate the Philippines, seeing the islands as no threat to the Allied advance on Japan, General MacArthur insisted that it be undertaken. After all, he had promised to return. After the capture of Leyte and Mindoro, US attention turned to Luzon. Resistance was fierce around Manila, which fell on 4 March 1945. Pockets of Japanese resistance continued to fight until the general surrender on 15 August 1945.

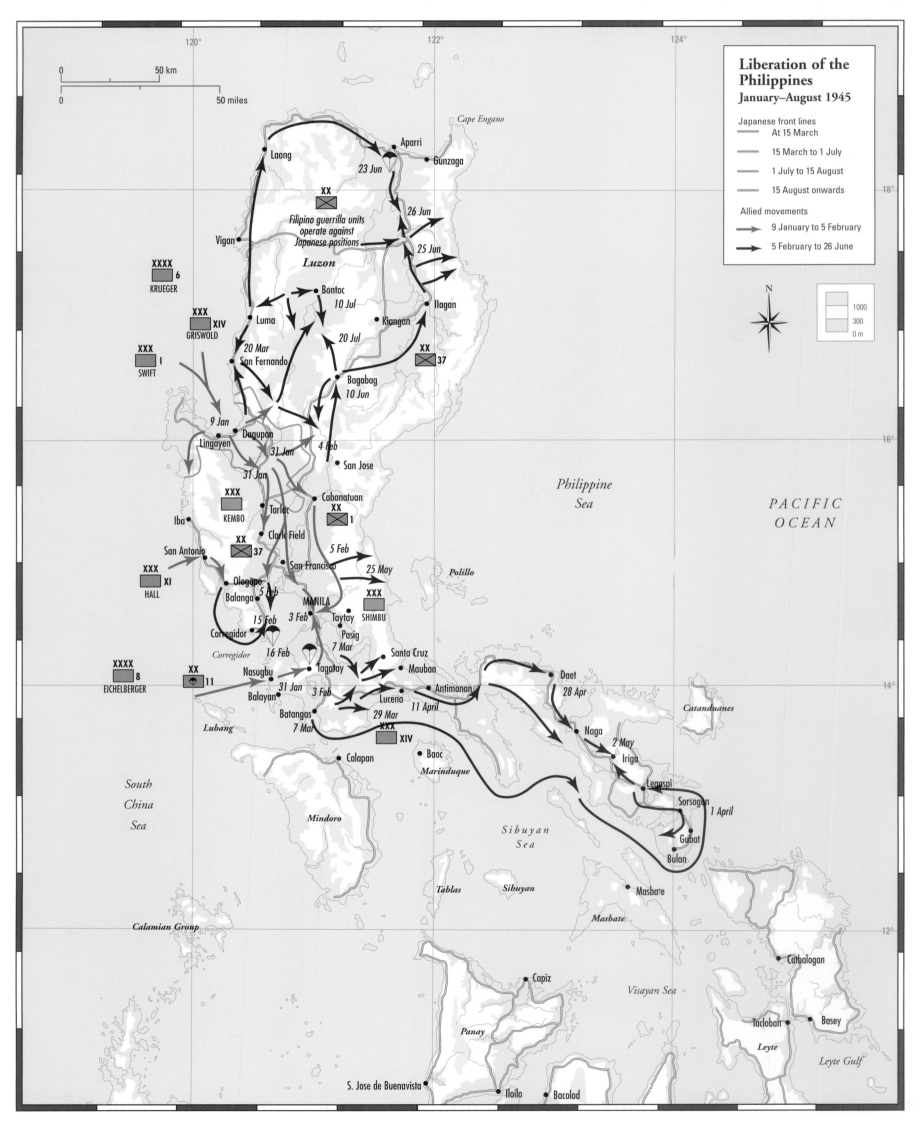

Liberation of the Philippines January–August 1945

Japanese front lines
- At 15 March
- 15 March to 1 July
- 1 July to 15 August
- 15 August onwards

Allied movements
- 9 January to 5 February
- 5 February to 26 June

War in China
July 1937–December 1944

Japan's war with China had started in 1937, though it saw more serious action with the USSR in border clashes in 1938 and 1939. The war with China was a desultory affair. Fierce clashes were interspersed with long periods of relative quiet. The nationalist Kuomintang, or KMT, were more concerned with the Communist threat. The last major Japanese offensive was in 1944, striking at US bomber bases – which by then had largely been superseded by bases on the Marianas.

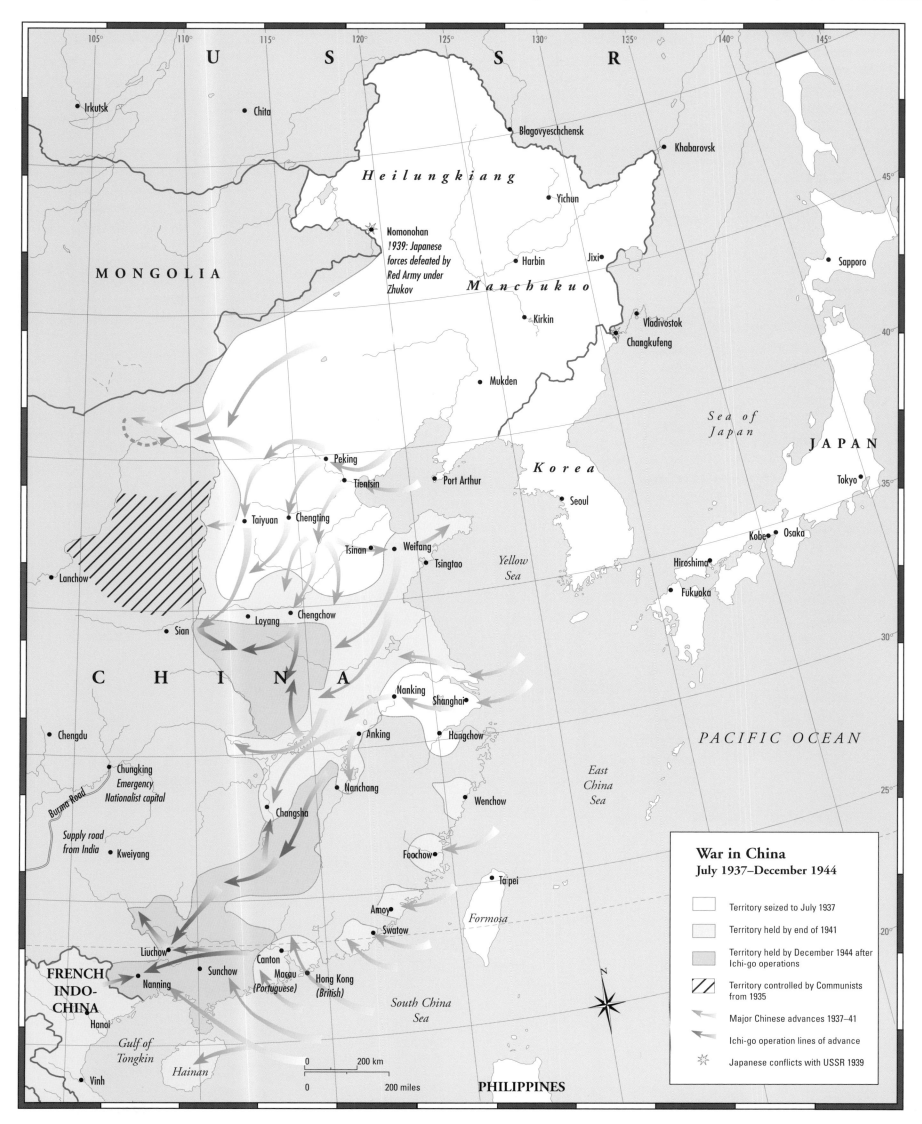

Nomonohan
1939: Japanese
forces defeated by
Red Army under
Zhukov

War in China
July 1937–December 1944

- Territory seized to July 1937
- Territory held by end of 1941
- Territory held by December 1944 after Ichi-go operations
- Territory controlled by Communists from 1935
- Major Chinese advances 1937–41
- Ichi-go operation lines of advance
- Japanese conflicts with USSR 1939

Allied Recapture of Burma
August–December 1944

Chasing the retreating Japanese Army through the jungles, mountains and rivers of Burma was a nightmare task, especially in the torrential rain of the monsoon, but General William Slim's Fourteenth Army now had the upper hand.

B Y THE END OF AUGUST 1944, the exhausted and near starving remnants of the Japanese Fifteenth Army were making their way back from Imphal and Kohima to relative safety east of the Chindwin. The British/Indian Fourteenth Army followed slowly, all movement being hampered by weeks of torrential rain.

Slim's primary task was to destroy the Japanese Burma Area Army, commanded by Lieutenant-General Hoyotaro Kimura. Slim wanted to bring the Japanese to battle between the Chindwin and Irrawaddy Rivers, probably in the huge loop of the Irrawaddy between Myinmu and Mandalay

Fourteenth Army advances
Slim sent the 19th Indian Division across the Chindwin at Sittaung. To their south the British 2nd and Indian 20th Divisions were to cross at Kalewa, attacking towards Monywa and Myinmu. The Japanese would then be caught, after a long and difficult retreat, with their backs to the Irrawaddy.

By 15 December, 19th Indian Division were at Indaw, ready to turn south. However, Slim had by now discovered that Kimura had decided not to fight, and had already withdrawn across the Irrawaddy, protecting the Yenanyaung oilfields and the rice fields of the Irrawaddy Delta. Slim would have to come up with a new plan.

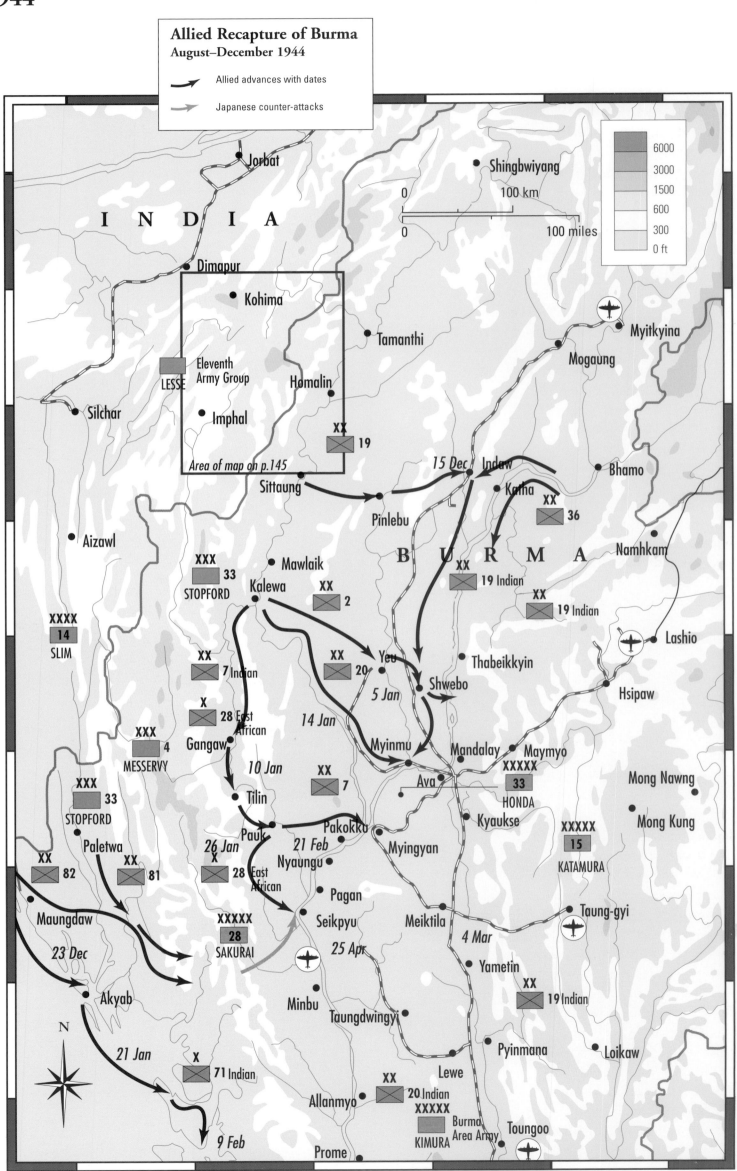

Allied Recapture of Burma
August–December 1944

→ Allied advances with dates

→ Japanese counter-attacks

Allied Recapture of Burma
December 1944–May 1945

Slim's new plan was to cross the Irrawaddy and to advance south of Mandalay. 19th Indian Division crossed at Thabeikkyin. Believing this to be the main British attack, the Japanese reacted by hurrying troops to the bridgehead and launching a fierce series of attacks.

ON 12 FEBRUARY, 20TH Indian Division crossed at Myinmu, triggering a further series of Japanese counter-attacks. However, this was really another feint: while the Japanese were occupied, the remainder of IV Corps was advancing stealthily down the Chindwin.

On 14 February 1945, IV Corps crossed the Irrawaddy at Nyaungu, catching the Japanese completely by surprise. Two mechanized brigades and a tank brigade headed for Meiktila. Two weeks later, the airfield at Thabutkon was overrun. By 4 March, after some of the fiercest fighting of the campaign, the 17th Indian Division was in Meiktila, and the whole east bank of the Irrawaddy was held by Fourteenth Army. With the British located in strength between the Irrawaddy and the Karen Hills, the Japanese Fifteenth and Thirty-third Armies were trapped.

Japanese counter-attack

The Japanese cut the road behind the British forces in Meiktila, who had to be supplied by air. However, the full weight of IV Corps came to their relief. By the end of March, the Japanese were in full retreat towards Rangoon.

Rangoon was shelled by the Royal Navy on 30 April, which was followed by an airborne landing on 1 May and an amphibious assault on 2 May. They found an empty city, as the Japanese had evacuated the day before. Although isolated pockets of resistance remained, the war in Burma was over.

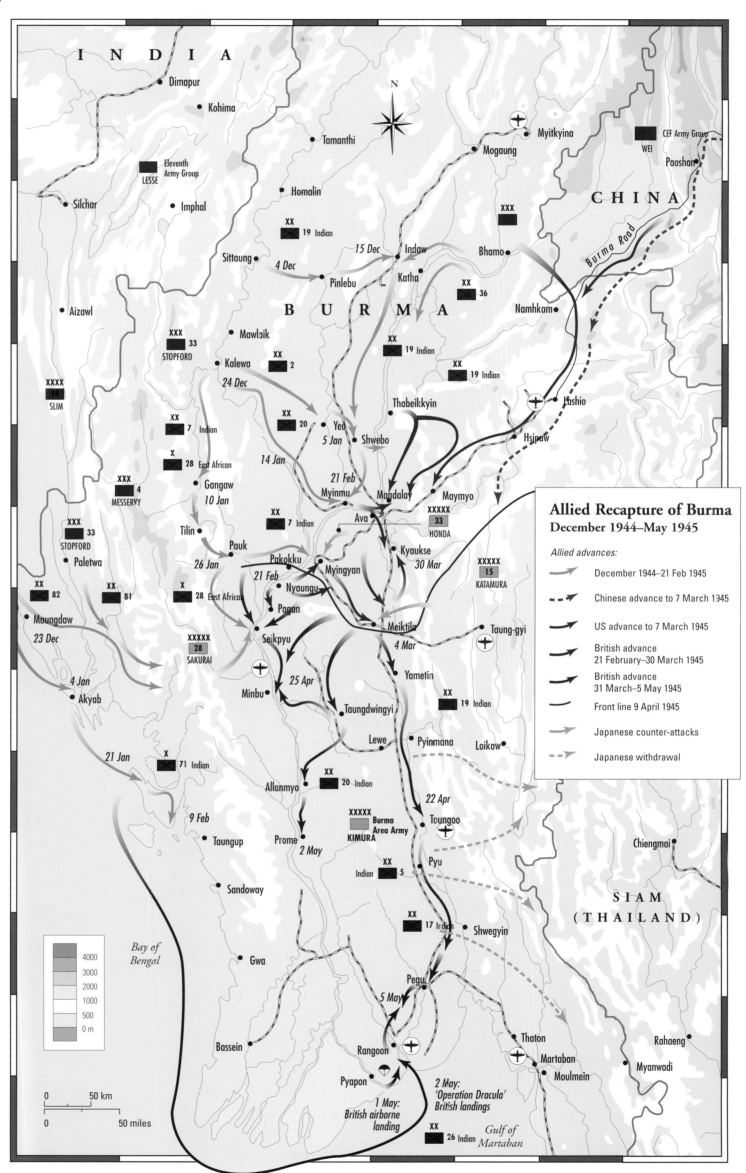

Allied Recapture of Burma
December 1944–May 1945

Allied advances:

→ December 1944–21 Feb 1945

⇢ Chinese advance to 7 March 1345

➤ US advance to 7 March 1345

➤ British advance 21 February–30 March 1945

➤ British advance 31 March–5 May 1945

— Front line 9 April 1945

➤ Japanese counter-attacks

⇢ Japanese withdrawal

Landings on Iwo Jima 19 February–26 March 1945

By the end of 1944, US planners had decided to take the island of Iwo Jima. Only 1060km (660 miles) from Tokyo, it would offer air bases which would enable P-51 Mustangs to escort B-29 bombers in raids over Japan.

HEAVY BOMBERS ATTACKED the island for 72 days, and in the three days before the assault the defences were shelled by seven battleships and seven cruisers. On the morning of 19 February 1945, two Marine divisions hit the beach in what was to become the bloodiest day in Marine Corps history.

Eight battalions deployed along a frontage of little more than 1.6km (1 mile) of beach. The 4th Marine Division landed in the centre of the island, flanked by the 5th Marines to the left near the foot of Mount Suribachi. As they breasted the low ridge, the Japanese defence, much of which had survived the bombardment, opened fire.

The Marines reached the west coast of the island on the first day, but it took another 35 harrowing days of hand-to-hand fighting to root the defenders out of their network of tunnels. US forces lost 6821 men to capture an island eight kilometres (five miles) long. Only 216 of the 23,000 Japanese defenders survived.

Landings on Iwo Jima 19 February–26 March 1945

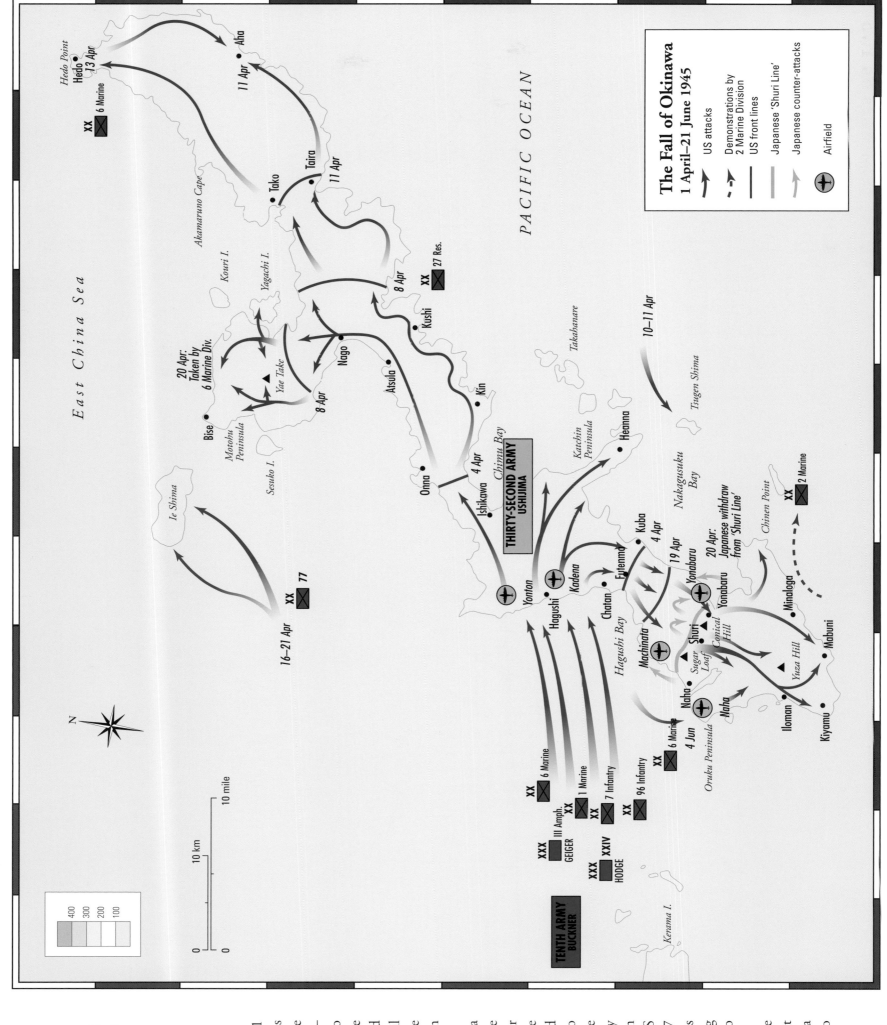

The Fall of Okinawa
1 April–21 June 1945

US attacks

Demonstrations by
2 Marine Division

US front lines

Japanese 'Shuri Line'

Japanese counter-attacks

Airfield

The Fall of Okinawa
1 April–21 June 1945

The island of Okinawa was the penultimate Allied target before the invasion of Japan itself. The Japanese high command stationed the veteran 62nd Infantry Division on the island, with orders to fight to the death.

THE LANDINGS BEGAN ON 1 April 1945, and key targets including airfields fell on the first day. Resistance was light – the Japanese had decided not to defend the coast against the awesome American air and naval power. It was not until they advanced inland that the Marines encountered the main Japanese defences.

The fighting on Okinawa changed from an easy advance into a savage, close-quarter struggle. Japanese positions were cunningly sited, well concealed and mutually supporting. No major counter-attacks were made, but even so, during May US casualties rose at an alarming rate. Eventually US power began to tell, and by 17 June the Japanese defensive lines had been broken, and surviving troops had been isolated into three small pockets.

Calculations based on the fighting in Okinawa meant that the Allies could expect over a million casualties if they had to invade Japan.

Pacific Situation up to August 1945

By the end of 1944, the Allies were advancing inexorably across the Pacific. Although the Japanese Empire still covered a massive area, it was steadily being reduced in size.

IN THE AUTUMN OF 1944, MacArthur's forces began the liberation of the Philippines. Early in 1945, British and Indian forces began the drive which would force the Japanese out of Burma. The next stage would be the reoccupation of Malaya and Singapore, which would isolate the widely dispersed Japanese forces in the Dutch East Indies.

The American liberation of the Philippines was followed by the capture of Iwo Jima and Okinawa, and the end of the war in Europe raised the prospect of a massive Allied reinforcement of the Pacific Theater. Large Japanese forces remained in China, but these were unlikely to be moved unless they were needed to defend Japan's home islands. And it was the invasion of those islands which occupied the minds of Allied planners.

Concerns began to mount about the potential casualties which would be sustained by both sides, since it was clear that the Japanese would fight for every inch of their homeland.

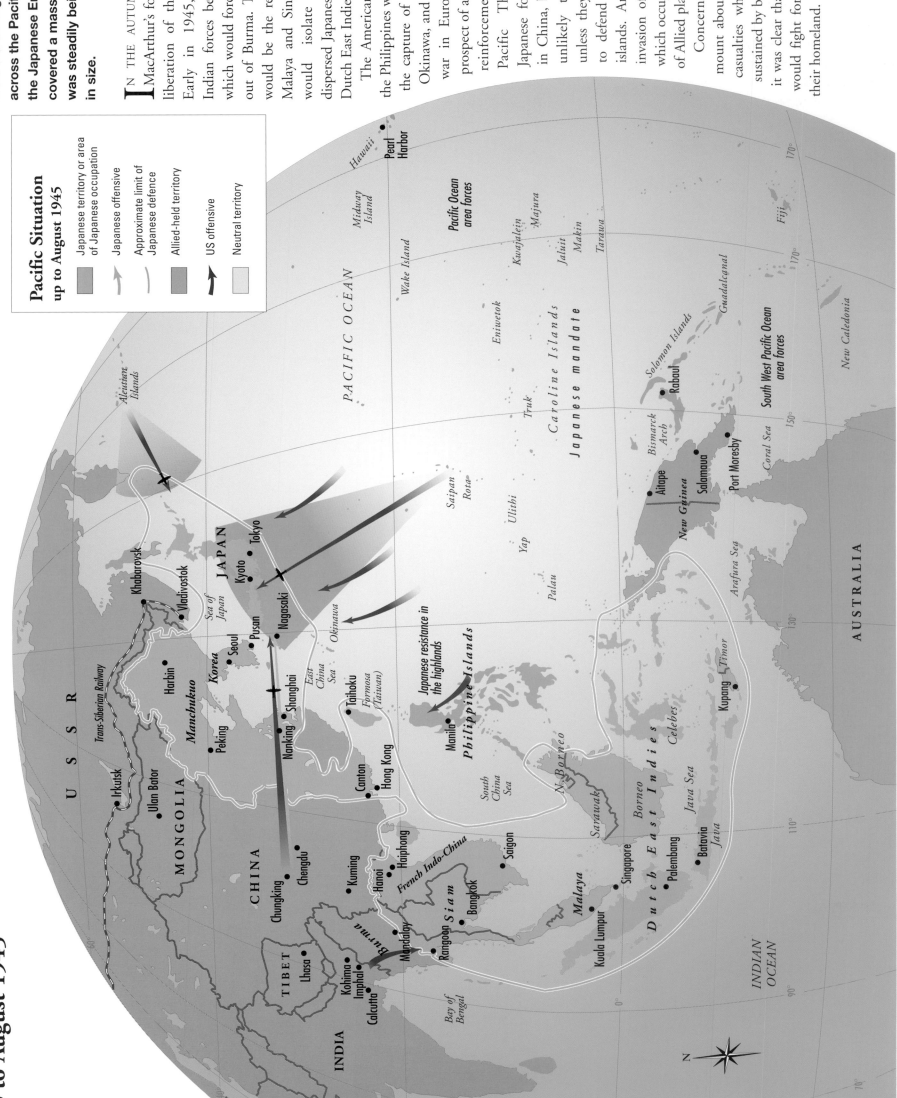

Pacific Situation up to August 1945

Japanese territory or area of Japanese occupation

Japanese offensive

Approximate limit of Japanese defence

Allied-held territory

US offensive

Neutral territory

Bombing of Japan
June 1944–August 1945

From the beginning of the war, the US military realized that a strategic bombing campaign against Japan would be an essential component in the ultimate defeat of the enemy. The specification for the giant new Boeing B-29 Superfortress was designed to make such a campaign possible.

The first operations against the Japanese homeland were carried out from bases in China, beginning on 15 June 1944. As the 'Island Hopping' campaign through the Pacific moved closer to Japan, the American strategic bombing offensive increased dramatically. Once the Marianas were captured five bases were established on Saipan, Tinian and Guam. Each base could accommodate 180 of the new bombers. The intensive phase of the attacks on Japan began on 24 November 1944, when a raid targeted an industrial area near Tokyo. Early attacks had limited success, but a switch from high-level daylight attacks to low-level night fire-bombing raids immediately produced results. In an attack on Tokyo and Yawata on the night of 9/10 March 1945, 41 square kilometres (16 square miles) of Tokyo were destroyed. Further raids were even more destructive, and by July more than 500,000 Japanese civilians had been killed and 13 million made homeless. In the process, Japanese industry had been almost completely destroyed.

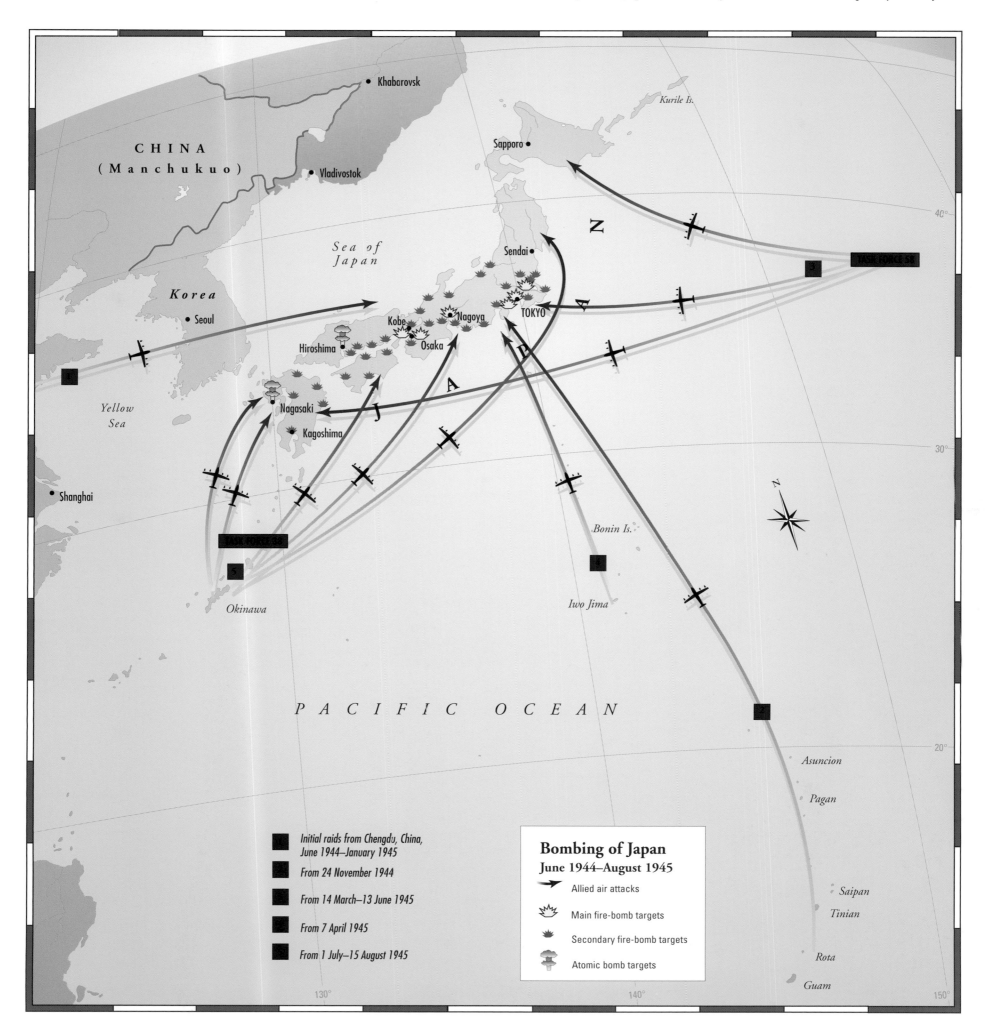

Initial raids from Chengdu, China, June 1944–January 1945
From 24 November 1944
From 14 March–13 June 1945
From 7 April 1945
From 1 July–15 August 1945

Bombing of Japan
June 1944–August 1945
Allied air attacks
Main fire-bomb targets
Secondary fire-bomb targets
Atomic bomb targets

Operations Against Japan February–August 1945

From 14 March 1945, the devastating B-29 raids on Japan were accompanied by attacks launched by US Navy carrier aircraft. With the Japanese Navy all but destroyed, fast carrier task forces sent hundreds of aircraft on sweeps over Japan, while the USAAF bombers continued to pound Japanese industry. Bombers, now escorted by Iwo Jima-based fighters, were now flying by day, and by early August the XXI Bomber Command was running out of targets.

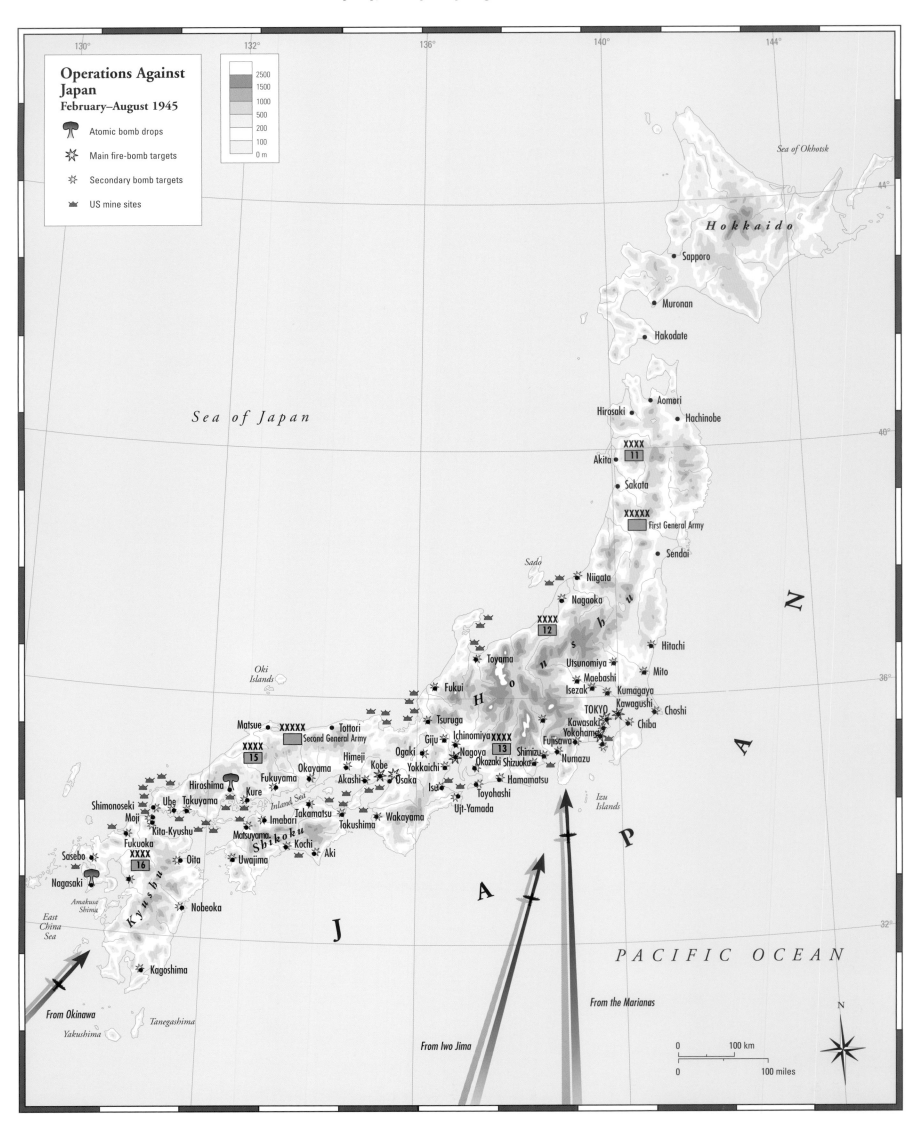

Japanese Merchant Shipping Routes, 1941–45

Japanese strategy had been based on the idea of a short, victorious war, followed by a negotiated peace settlement.

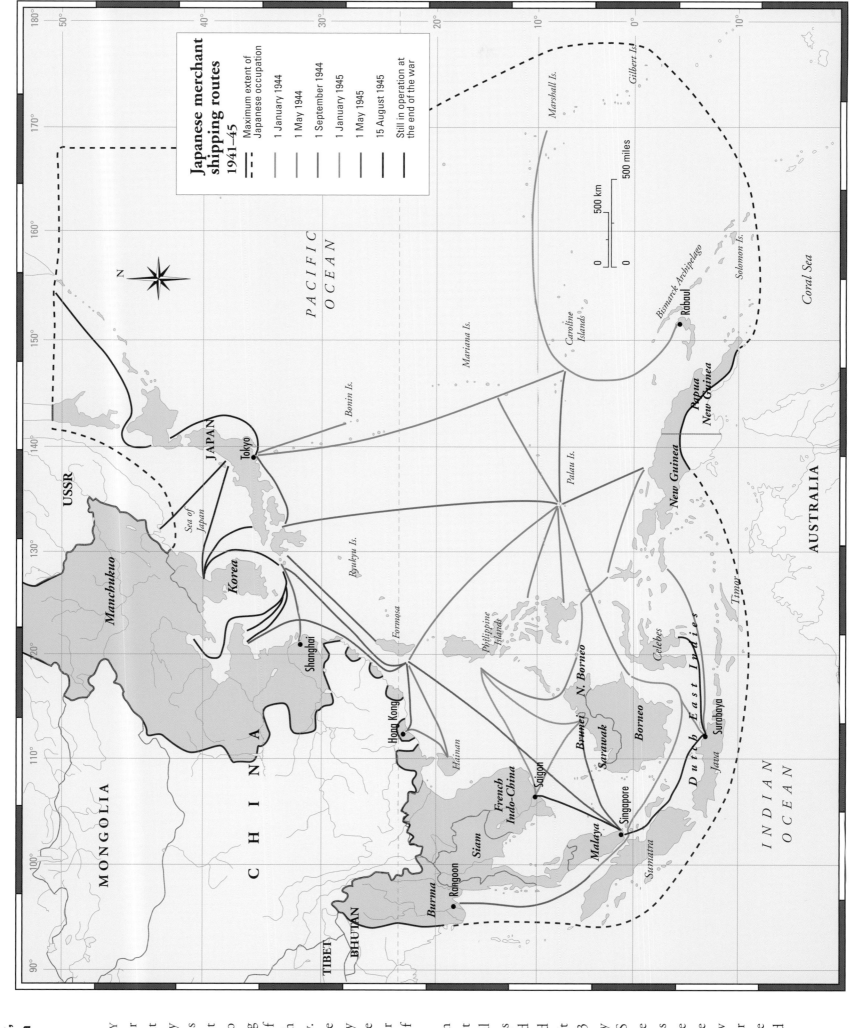

The Japanese plan to acquire a vast oceanic empire had been meticulous, and the power of the Imperial Navy had ensured that the conquest of much of the Pacific was achieved in an astonishingly short time. But the subsequent problems of sustaining that empire with a large merchant marine had scarcely been considered. Even though the US Navy had a substantial submarine arm, Japan went to war with no convoy plans and few anti-submarine vessels.

Given that the primary reason for Japan's war aims was to ensure that Japanese industry had a steady supply of strategic materials like oil, rubber and tin, it would have seemed logical to take steps to protect the long and vulnerable sea lines of communication over which such material would flow. However, the idea of commerce protection is inherently defensive, and defence to the military overlords of pre-war Japan was not worthy of consideration.

Losses were relatively light in the first months of the war, but heavy losses in the Guadalcanal campaign were a sign of things to come, as new, longer-ranged American submarines entered service in greater numbers. It was not until November 1943 that Japan introduced a convoy system, by which time US submarine attacks were expanding into the waters around the Philippines and the Dutch East Indies. Japanese shipping losses were now exceeding 200,000 tonnes per month, which was far more than Japanese shipyards could replace.

A LL THROUGH THE WAR, the growing US submarine force was employed in attacks on Japanese merchant shipping as well as on the Japanese fleet. In both these tasks, the American submarine force was aided by Magic – intelligence derived from broken Japanese codes. The Japanese Navy, obsessed as it was with the idea of the 'Decisive Battle', had done little to prepare for commerce protection, convoy operations or anti-submarine warfare. As a result, the US Navy won a spectacular victory. The Japanese merchant marine lost 8.2 million tonnes (8.1 million tons) of vessels during the war, with submarines accounting for 60 per cent of the losses. US submarines also sank 711,000 tonnes (700,000 tons) of naval vessels, about 30 per cent of the total.

Japanese merchant shipping losses 7 Dec 1941–1943

The Japanese attack on Pearl Harbor resulted in a significant loss of strength for the US Navy in the Pacific, forcing the United States onto the defensive from the outbreak of war. The only weapon immediately available to take the war to the Japanese was the US submarine force. Indeed, President Roosevelt had decided even before the start of the war that unrestricted submarine warfare would be undertaken in the event of hostilities with Japan.

Japanese merchant shipping losses 1943

- ○ 1 January–30 April
- ◑ 1 May–31 August
- ● 1 September–31 December
- ── Japanese territory

Total losses: 157 ships

Japanese merchant shipping losses 7 Dec 1941–31 Dec 1942

- ○ 7 Dec 1941–30 April 1942
- ◑ 1 May–31 August 1942
- ● 1 Sept–31 December 1942
- ── Japanese territory

Total losses: 89 ships

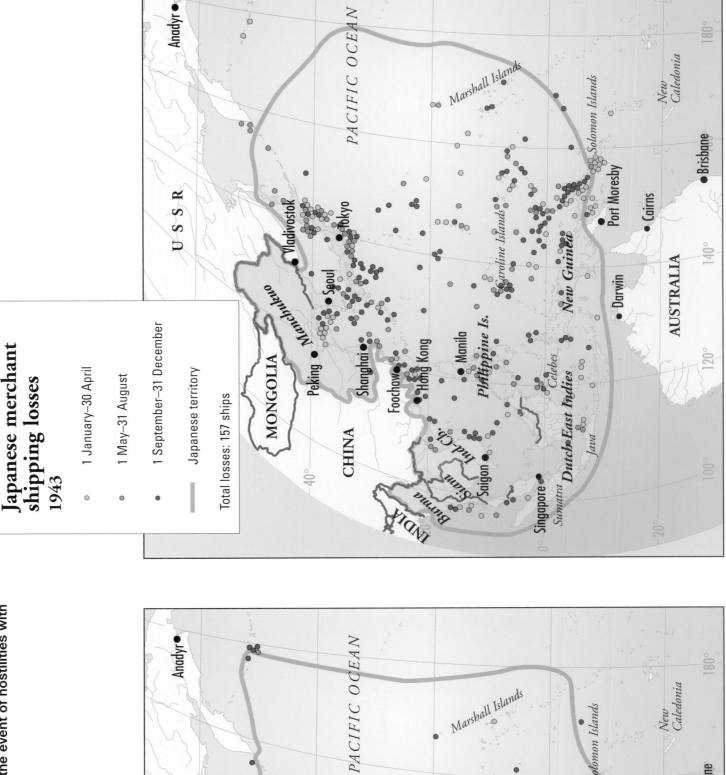

Japanese merchant shipping losses 1944–45

JAPAN'S EMPIRE WAS LARGE, but it was extremely vulnerable to war against commerce. Air power and surface vessels played their part in the campaign, but the submarine was the predominant factor in the destruction of Japanese trade and the strangling of the Japanese economy. US submarines accomplished three main achievements. Firstly, Japanese shipping losses cut off the supply of raw materials vital to allow Japanese industry to generate military power. Secondly, destruction of Japanese merchant marine and naval forces significantly reduced Japan's ability to project power over the vast distances of the Pacific. Thirdly, use of the submarine enabled the US Navy to take the offensive in Japanese-controlled waters and inflict heavy losses at a relatively small cost in American lives.

A total of 288 US Navy submarines were deployed operationally during World War II, including a relatively small number which were stationed in the Atlantic. Fifty-two were lost in action, 48 of which were destroyed in the Pacific war zone. American submariners made up less than two per cent of naval personnel, but with 22 per cent being killed in action they suffered the highest proportional loss rate in the US Armed Forces.

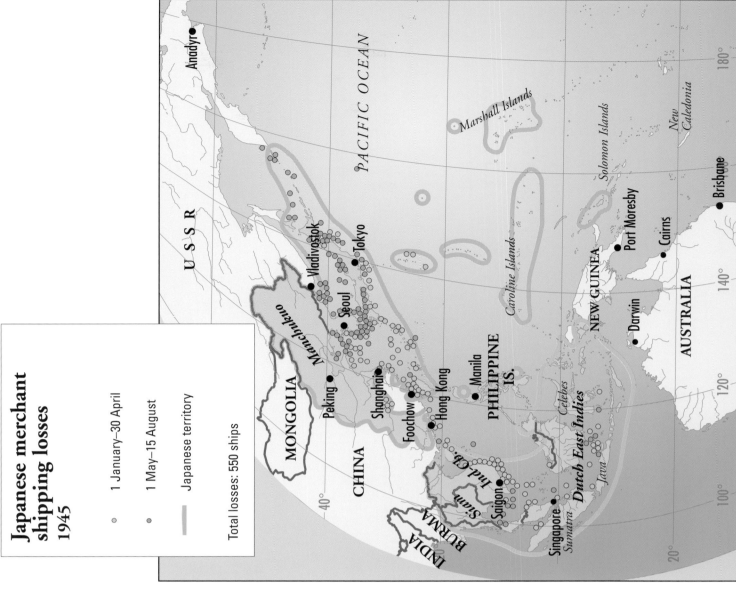

Japanese merchant shipping losses 1945

- ○ 1 January–30 April
- ◐ 1 May–15 August
- —— Japanese territory

Total losses: 550 ships

Japanese merchant shipping losses 1944

- ○ 1 January–30 April
- ◐ 1 May–31 August
- ● 1 September–31 December
- —— Japanese territory

Total losses: 385 ships

The Japanese Empire August 1945

Japan's Empire still covered a substantial area even as the Pacific War approached its end. Japanese troops still occupied Malaya, Indo-China, the Dutch East Indies and much of China.

H OWEVER, ALTHOUGH their conquests were still under Imperial control the overall position of the empire was hopeless. The American submarine blockade of Japan had created an iron noose around the heart of the empire. Supplies and raw materials could not get through to the home islands, and even if Japanese industry, battered into ruin by a devastating bombing campaign, had still been a functioning entity, it would not have been able to produce enough to keep the war going.

The same blockade also ensured that Japan could not send supplies or reinforcements to her far-flung garrisons. Most of Japan's colonies and conquests were isolated from the home islands and from each other. In effect, they had been left to 'wither on the vine', starved of food, ammunition, and hope.

The Japanese Empire
August 1945

— Japanese territory or area of Japanese occupation

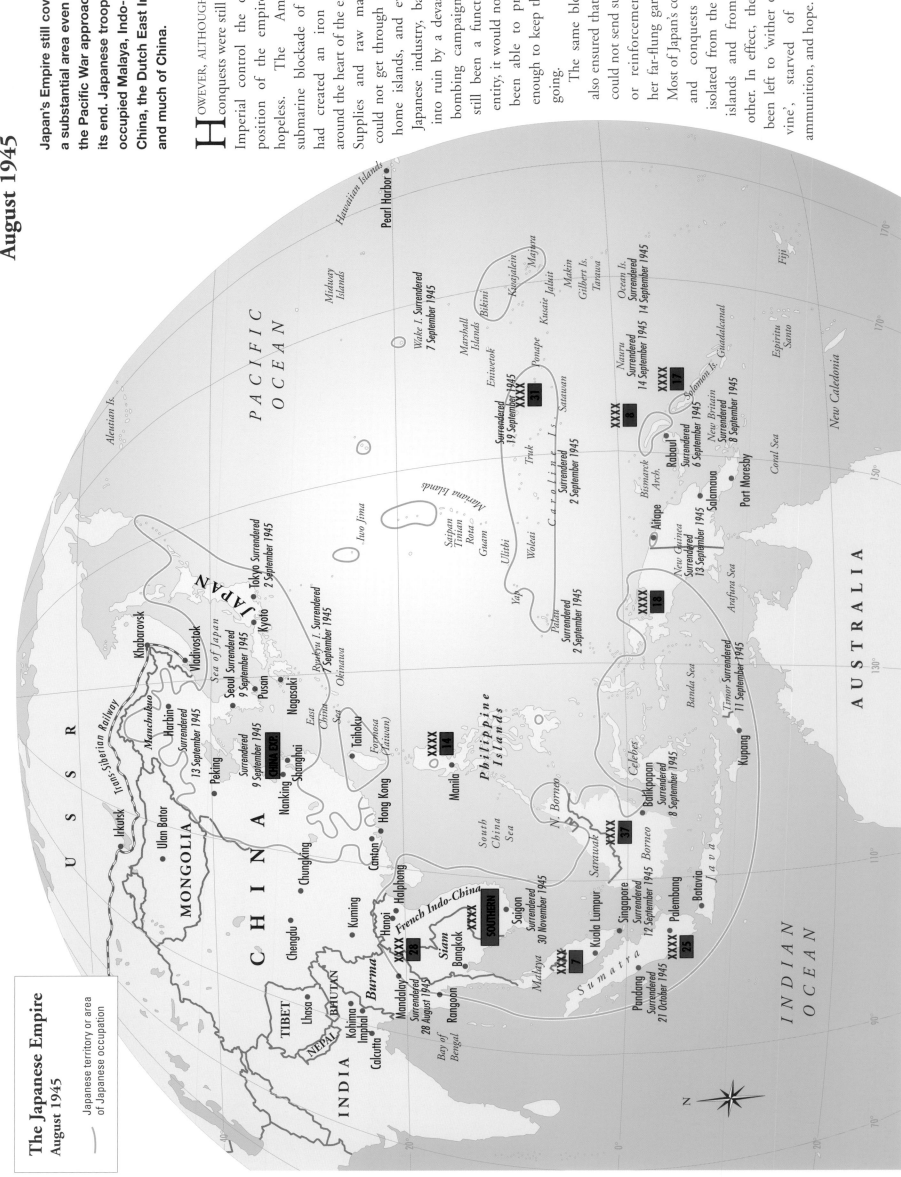

Allied Invasion Plan August 1945 version

Operation Downfall was the overall Allied plan for the invasion of Japan at the end of World War II. It was scheduled to occur in two parts: Operation Olympic, the invasion of Kyushu, set to begin in November 1945; and Operation Coronet, the invasion of Honshu, planned for the spring of 1946.

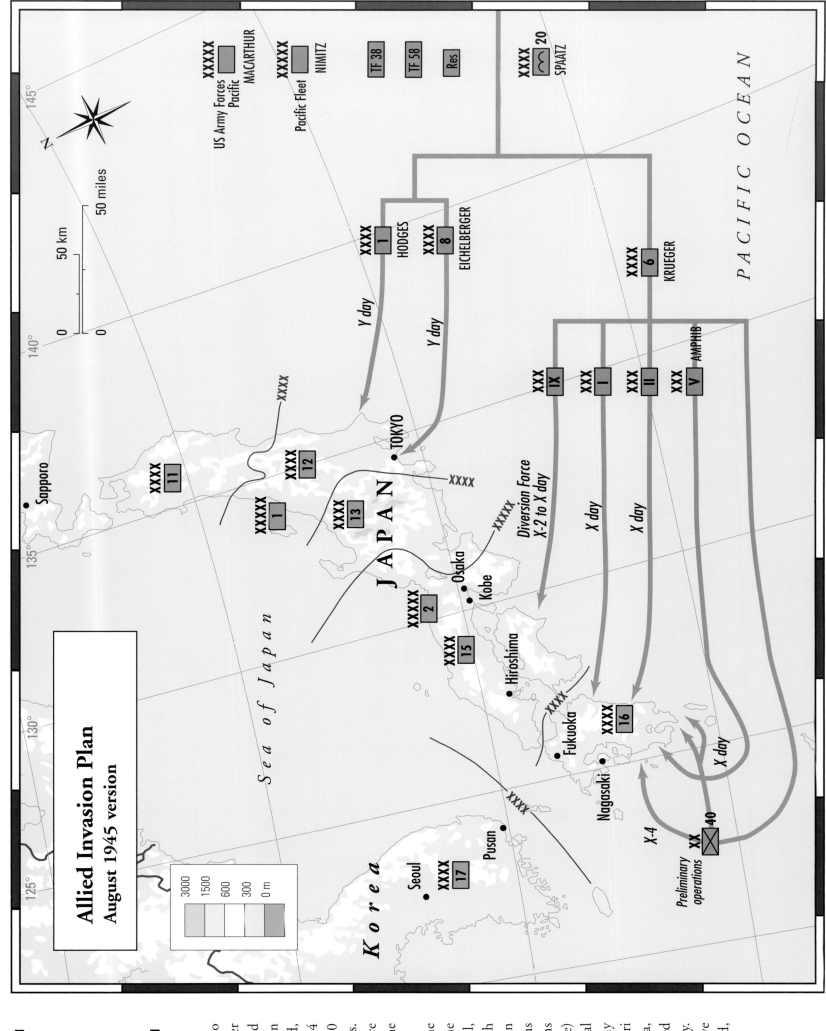

Allied Invasion Plan
August 1945 version

OPERATION OLYMPIC was to begin on 1 November 1945. The combined Allied naval armada would have been the largest ever assembled, including 42 aircraft carriers, 24 battleships and almost 400 destroyers and destroyer escorts. Fourteen US divisions were scheduled to take part in the initial landings.

Operation Coronet, the invasion of Honshu at the Tokyo Plain south of the capital, was set to begin on 1 March 1946. Coronet would have been the largest ever amphibious operation, with 25 divisions (including the floating reserve) earmarked for the initial operations. US First Army would have invaded at Kujukuri Beach, on the Boso Peninsula, while US Eighth Army invaded at Hiratsuka, on Sagami Bay. Both armies would then have driven north and inland, meeting at Tokyo.

Nagasaki
9 August 1945

The atomic bombs dropped on Hiroshima and Nagasaki on 6 and 9 August 1945 finally brought home to the Japanese the hopelessness of their situation. The 20-kiloton bomb dropped on Nagasaki killed fewer people than the earlier weapon, primarily because the city was more hilly and the terrain offered more protection. But losses were still horrendous, with some 35,000 people killed and over 50,000 injured.

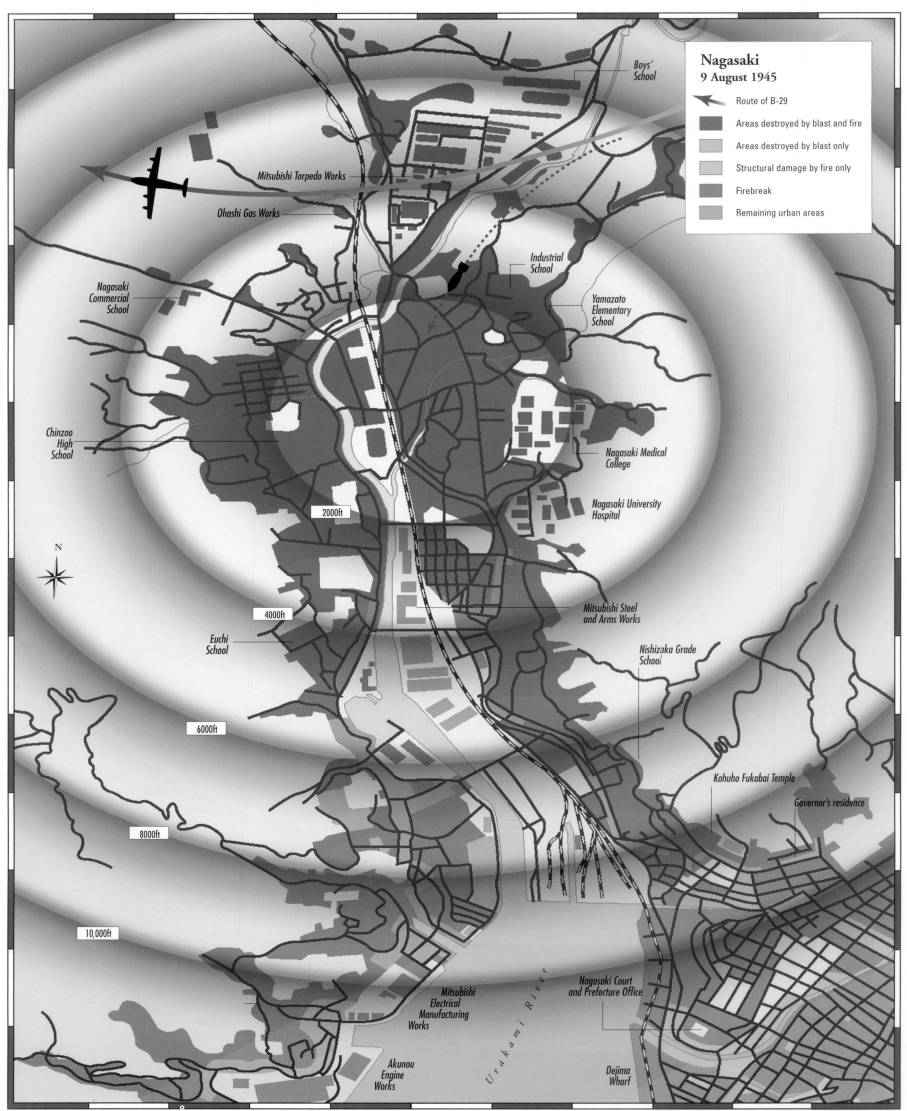

Nagasaki
9 August 1945

- Route of B-29
- Areas destroyed by blast and fire
- Areas destroyed by blast only
- Structural damage by fire only
- Firebreak
- Remaining urban areas

Boys' School

Mitsubishi Torpedo Works

Ohashi Gas Works

Industrial School

Nagasaki Commercial School

Yamazato Elementary School

Chinzoo High School

Nagasaki Medical College

Nagasaki University Hospital

2000ft

4000ft

Euchi School

Mitsubishi Steel and Arms Works

Nishizaka Grade School

6000ft

Kohuho Fukabai Temple

Governor's residence

8000ft

10,000ft

Mitsubishi Electrical Manufacturing Works

Nagasaki Court and Prefecture Office

Urakami River

Akunou Engine Works

Dejima Wharf

N

Soviet Invasion of Manchuria August–September 1945

The final act of the struggle against Japan came with the Soviet declaration of war. A million troops of the Trans-Baikal and Far Eastern Fronts invaded Manchuria on 9 August. Although the Japanese Manchurian Army had as many men, it was no match for a Red Army which had learned its lessons against the Germans on the Eastern Front. Vastly superior in equipment, tactics and experience, the Soviets smashed the Japanese in less than two weeks.

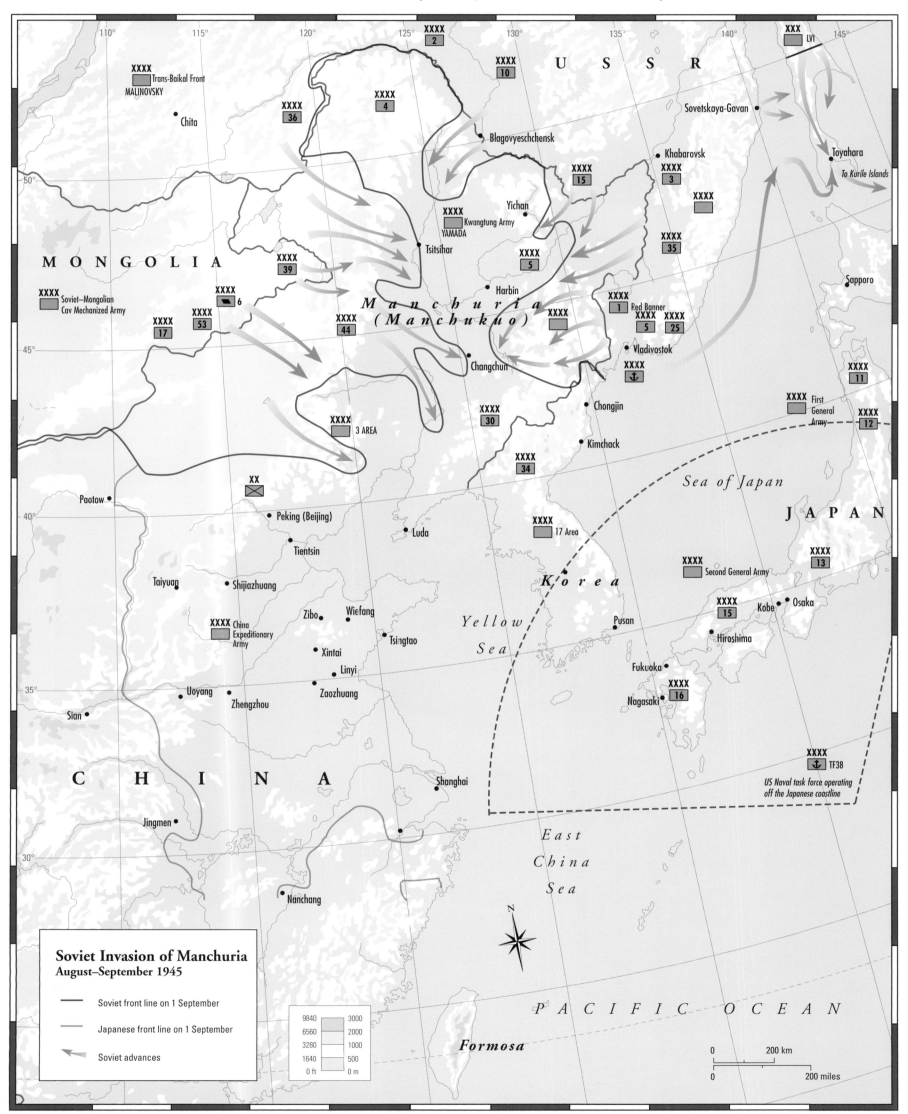

Soviet Invasion of Manchuria
August–September 1945

— Soviet front line on 1 September

— Japanese front line on 1 September

→ Soviet advances

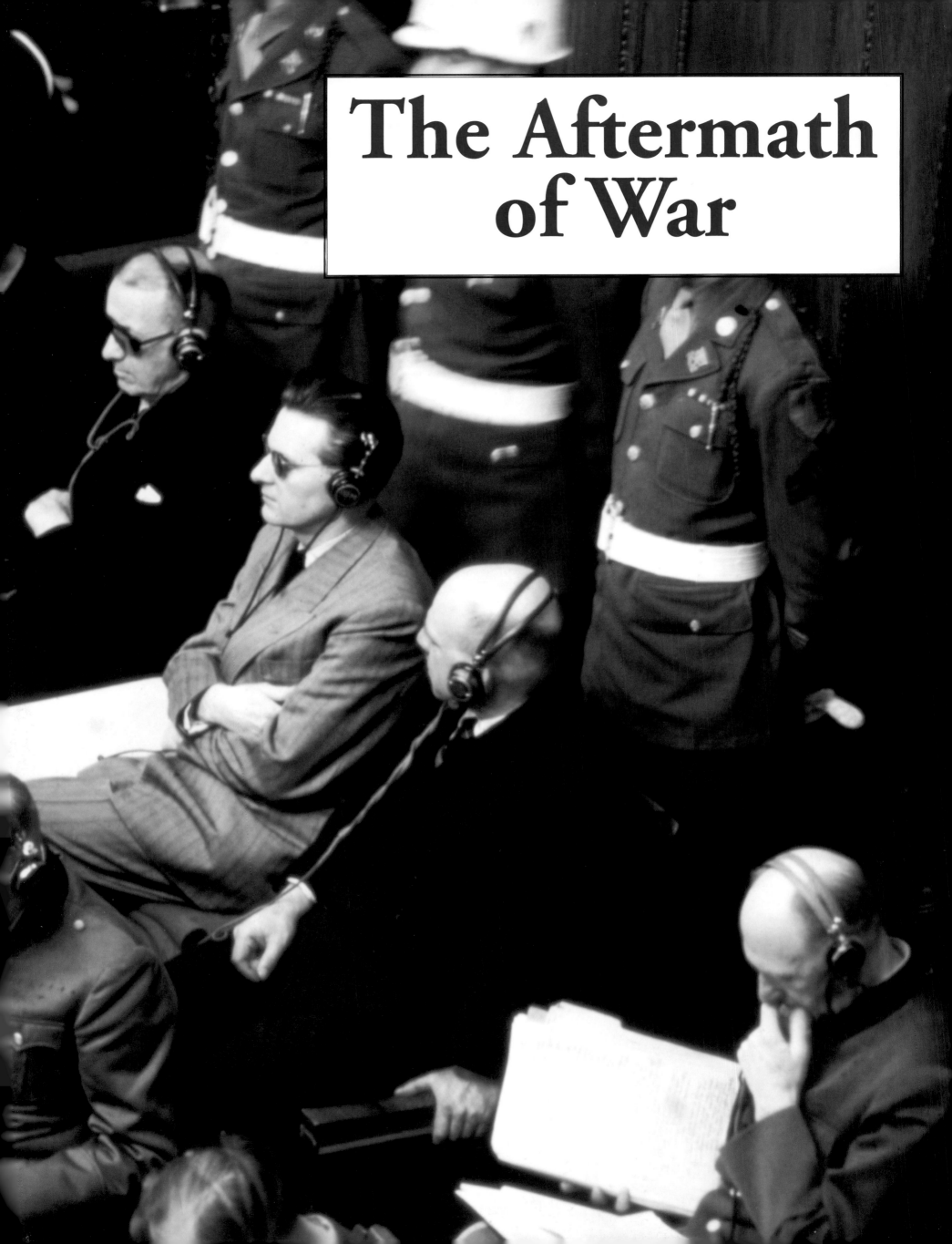

The Aftermath
of War

Mobilization for War 1939–45

World War II left its mark on nations around the globe in several different ways. Millions of men and women had served in their nations' armed forces, or had worked in the factories which kept the armies fighting. Millions more lost their lives, in combat, or through genocide, or in the aerial bombardments which for the first time had put civilian populations into the front line. The age of total war had arrived, and the costs were astronomical.

THE MOBILIZATION PROCESS FOR THE NATIONS involved in World War II began at different times, mostly in the 1930s. The Soviet Union had almost been on a war footing since the revolution in 1917, and its armaments industry continued to grow through the 1930s. Purges of generals in the late 1930s might have left the high command in tatters at the outbreak of war, but Soviet industry was always ready to provide the weaponry needed.

German rearmament was planned under the Weimar regime in the 1920s, and was set in motion with Hitler's seizure of power in 1933. Although the Wehrmacht seemed to be an unstoppable military machine in the early years of the war, the German economy was not really placed onto a war footing until several years into the war, by which time it was too late.

France's preparation for war was hampered by political rivalries in the 1930s. When war came in 1939, the French Army was large and fairly well equipped, but it lacked the political and military direction to be truly effective. British rearmament also got under way in the 1930s, primarily as a counter to Germany's rising power. The British were much quicker than the Germans to accept the necessities of total war, and the British economy was on a total war footing within months of the outbreak of hostilities.

Mobilization beyond Europe

In the Pacific, the military had gained control of Japan in the 1930s, and it was military ambition which inspired Japanese intervention in Manchuria and China. Increasing Japanese power brought the Empire into economic rivalry with the colonial powers in Asia, but although Japan prepared for war, it could never match the industrial might of its potential enemies. Greatest of these was the United States of America.

Emerging from the isolationism of the inter-war years, the United States increased its defence spending as the war in Europe broke out. US industry geared up to produce arms for Britain and France, but it was not until the USA was drawn into the war at the end of 1941 that its titanic industrial power was fully mobilized. the United States was able to field millions of men to fight in Europe and the Pacific, at the same time providing the bulk of the weaponry and equipment used by the Allies.

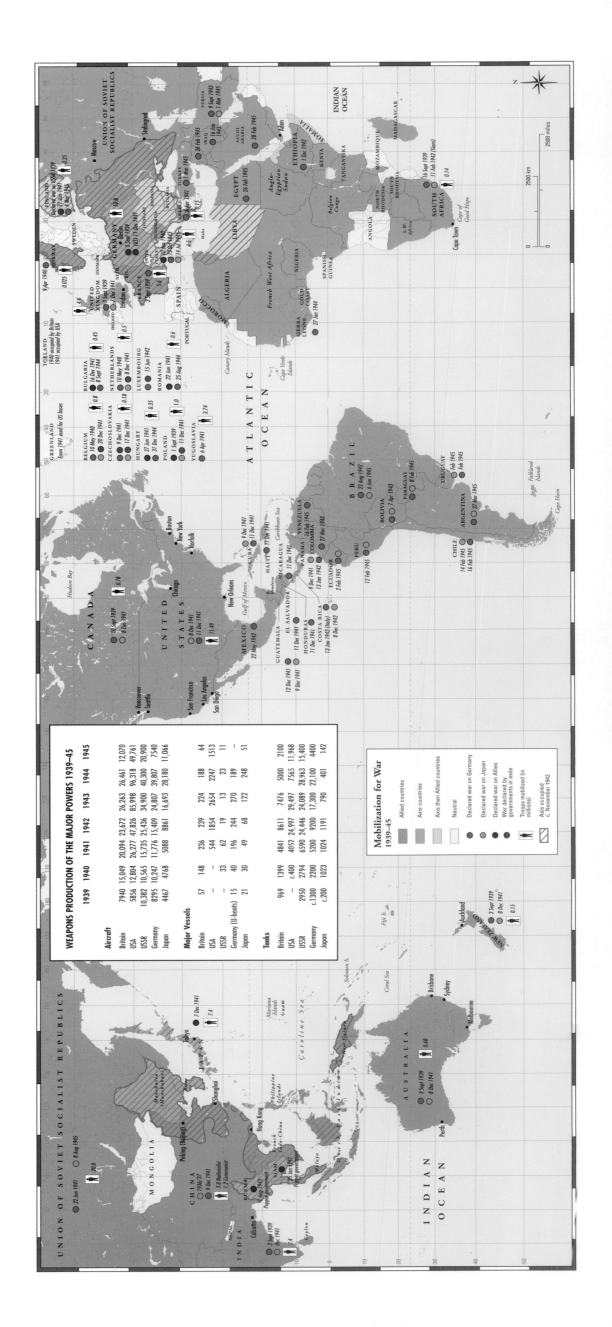

WEAPONS PRODUCTION OF THE MAJOR POWERS 1939–45							
	1939	1940	1941	1942	1943	1944	1945
Aircraft							
Britain	7940	15,049	20,094	23,672	26,263	26,461	12,070
USA	5856	12,804	26,277	47,826	85,998	96,318	49,761
USSR	10,382	10,565	15,735	25,436	34,900	40,300	20,900
Germany	8295	10,247	11,776	15,409	24,807	39,807	7540
Japan	4467	4768	5088	8861	16,693	28,180	11,066
Major Vessels							
Britain	57	148	236	239	224	188	64
USA	–	–	544	1854	2654	2247	1513
USSR	–	33	62	19	13	23	11
Germany (U-boats)	15	40	196	244	270	189	–
Japan	21	30	49	68	122	248	51
Tanks							
Britain	969	1399	4841	8611	7476	5000	2100
USA	–	c.400	4052	24,997	29,497	7565	11,968
USSR	2950	2794	6590	24,446	24,089	28,963	15,400
Germany	c.1300	2200	5200	9200	17,300	22,100	4400
Japan	c.200	1023	1024	1191	790	401	142

Mobilization for War 1939–45

Allied countries
Axis countries
Axis then Allied countries
Neutral
Declared war on Germany
Declared war on Japan
Declared war on Allies
War declared by governments in exile
Troops mobilized (in millions)
Axis occupied c. November 1942

Original Members of the United Nations 1945

At an Allied summit in Moscow on 30 October 1943, the USA, the USSR, the United Kingdom and China called for the early establishment of an international organization to maintain peace and security after the war. That goal was reaffirmed on 1 December 1943 at Teheran, when Stalin, Roosevelt and Churchill met to discuss the future direction of the war effort.

The first outline of what was to become the United Nations was drawn up between 21 September and 7 October 1944, at the Dumbarton Oaks conference in Washington DC. Diplomats from the four main Allied powers set out the aims, proposed structure and procedures for the new organization. The United Nations Charter was set up when representatives of 50 nations met in San Francisco just before the end of the Pacific War, and the charter was signed by all 50 countries on 26 June 1945. The United Nations officially came into existence on 24 October 1945.

Long before the outcome of the war was certain, Allied leaders had turned their attention to the state of the world after the end of the conflict. The failure of the pre-war League of Nations, largely because the United States had held itself aloof from the organization, dominated their considerations. This time, the Americans would be involved. The term 'United Nations' was coined by President Franklin Delano Roosevelt in 1942 to describe the 26 nations pledged to defeating the Axis dictatorships and to creating world peace.

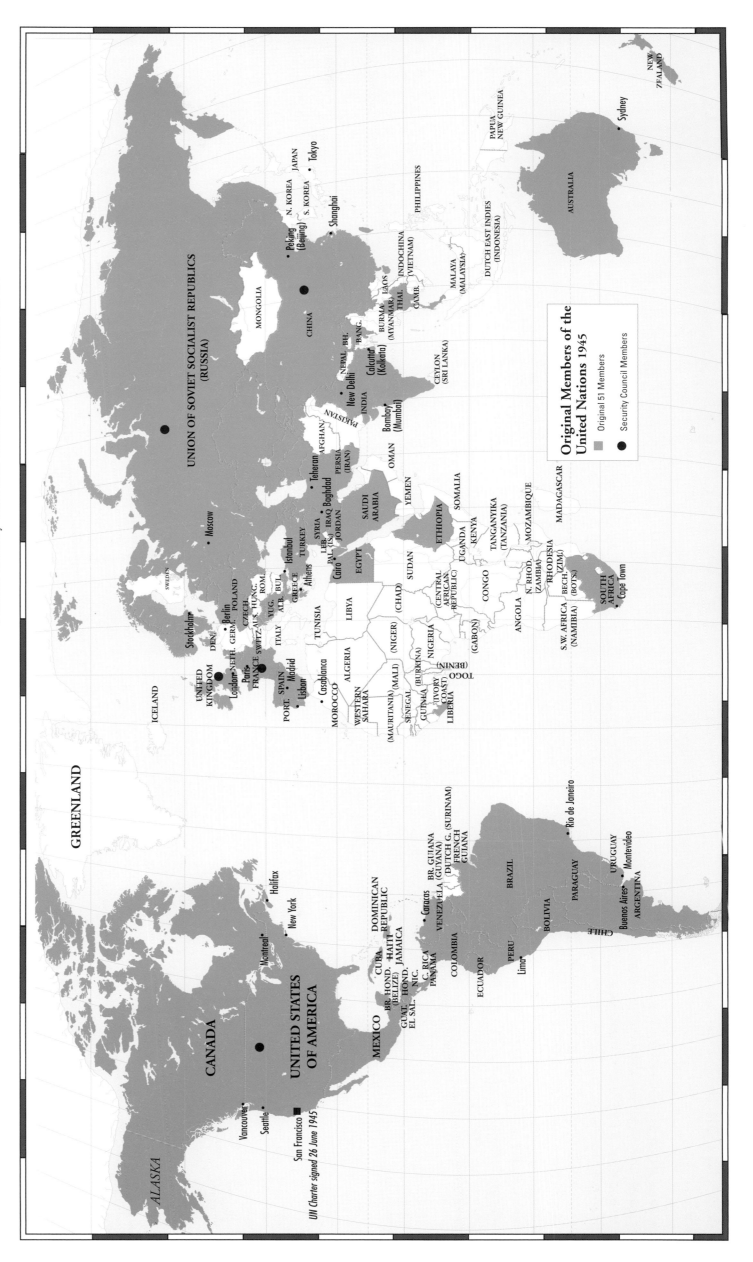

173

The Casualties of War 1939–45

In terms of human lives, World War II was the costliest conflict in history. Quantifying the exact number of casualties is an almost impossible task, estimates ranging from 40 million to 60 million lives being taken. By far the largest number of casualties occurred in the four years of fighting on the Eastern Front, with the Soviet Union bearing as much as 50 per cent of the entire war's casualties. China also suffered heavily, losing as many as ten million people between 1937 and 1945.

Combat casualties during World War II are generally regarded as being less intense than those incurred in the Great War, but this is something of a fallacy. For much of the war in the West, between the fall of France and the invasion of Normandy, none of the main combatants were actually engaged in major fighting except in peripheral areas. However, casualty rates in Northwest Europe in 1944 and 1945 were at least as high as they had been in 1914-18, and were sometimes even higher.

The Eastern Front was a different matter. From the beginning, the struggle between Germany and the USSR was a bitter war of attrition, with little mercy being shown by either side. Losses were incurred on an almost unbelievable scale in battle, and cruel treatment of prisoners meant that over four million out of the five million Soviet POWs taken by the Germans died.

In the Pacific, Japanese casualties were particularly high. This was primarily because of the ancient Samurai code of Bushido, which held that there was nothing more dishonourable than surrender. As a result, Japanese soldiers generally preferred to fight to the death, even in the face of hopeless odds. American losses were also high, though more US soldiers were killed by the efficiency of German armies than by the fanaticism of the Japanese.

Civilian casualties

Non-combatants have always suffered in war, but World War II was one of the few conflicts in history in which civilians were actually targeted by the fighting forces. For the first time, major population centres were the subjects of heavy air attack. Germany and Japan in particular suffered heavily under the bombers, but all of the main combatant nations with the exception of the USA saw civilians in the front line.

Civilians also suffered more directly. The Nazi Holocaust resulted in the slaughter of as many as six million Jews and other minority groups. The bitter partisan war in the East saw large numbers of civilians slaughtered in reprisal for guerrilla attacks. The largest losses occurred in the USSR where between 20 million and 30 million may have died by being caught up in conflict or from brutal repression. Similar behaviour by the Japanese may have killed as many as ten million in China.

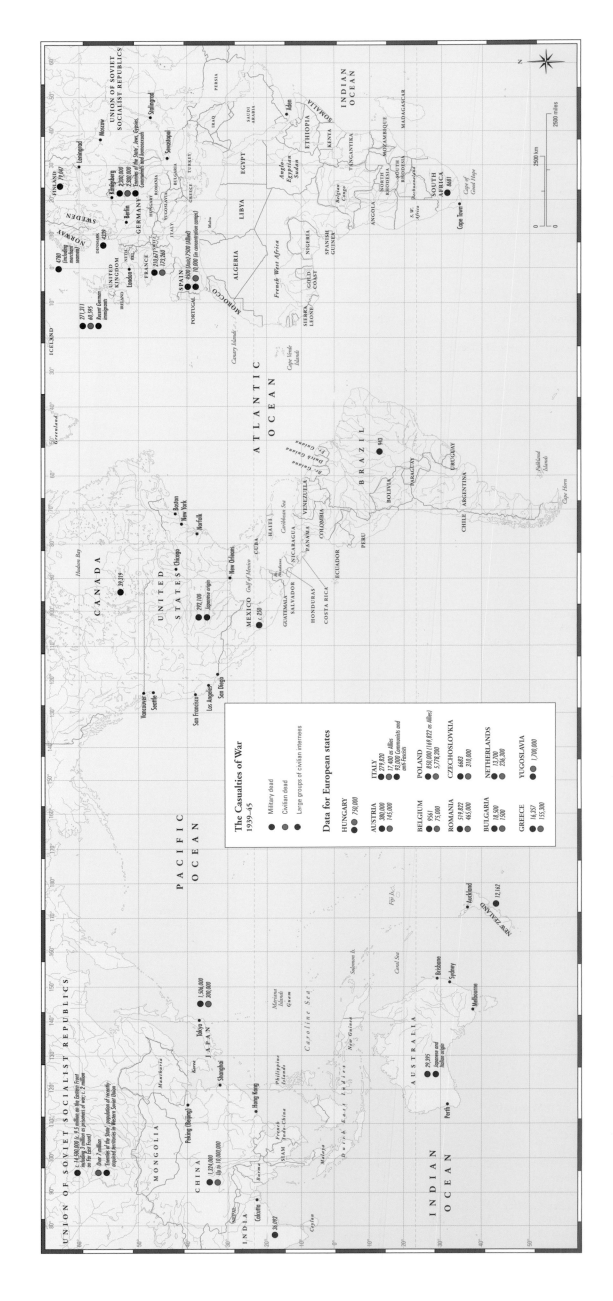

Index